Gay Latino Studies

Gay Latino Studies · A Critical Reader

Edited by Michael Hames-García and Ernesto Javier Martínez

Duke University Press · Durham & London · 2011

© 2011 Duke University Press

All rights reserved

Printed in the United States

of America on acid-free paper ∞

Designed by Amy Ruth Buchanan

Typeset in Quadraat by Tseng

Information Systems, Inc.

Library of Congress Cataloging-in-

Publication Data appear on the last

printed page of this book.

For our families

contents

acknowledgments

We have many people to thank as this collection goes to press. First, we deeply appreciate the patience and cooperation of our contributors. We also are grateful to the readers for Duke University Press and to our editor, Reynolds Smith, for their helpful feedback and support in ushering this project to its conclusion. Donella-Elizabeth Alston and Monica Guy in the Departments of Ethnic Studies and Women's and Gender Studies at the University of Oregon have also been invaluable through their administrative acumen and efficiency. Sharon Torian and Mark Mastromarino and others at Duke University Press contributed their support and assistance to this manuscript, and we are grateful for their efforts.

We would like to express our special thanks to Paula Moya and María Lugones for their sustained feedback on the manuscript and the project of gay Latino studies in general. Members of the Joto Caucus of the National Association of Chicana and Chicano Studies provided important emotional, social, and spiritual support, and this collection would be something entirely different without their inspiration. Finally we must thank Eric-Christopher García, whose friendship, conversations, and assistance were invaluable in originally getting this project off the ground.

Re-membering Gay Latino Studies

Michael Hames-García and Ernesto Javier Martínez

"QUE NO SE NOS OLVIDEN LOS HOMBRES"

In *Borderlands/La Frontera* the Chicana feminist Gloria Anzaldúa makes room in her theorization of "mestiza consciousness" for a brief but poignant consideration of *gay* Chicano men.[1] In doing so she not only expresses grief over the isolation imposed on *jotos* by a certain kind of lesbian separatist politics, but also associates the cultivation of such sharp and policed divisions with personal and political loss. She writes, "Asombra pensar que nos hemos quedado en ese pozo oscuro donde el mundo encierra a las lesbianas. Asombra pensar que hemos, como feministas y lesbianas, cerrado nuestros corazones a los hombres, a nuestros hermanos los jotos, desheredados y marginales como nosotros."[2] Understanding Anzaldúa's statement to be a courageous assertion of feminist solidarity, an assertion of mutual recognition and responsibility, we come closer to appreciating why a volume like *Gay Latino Studies*—dedicated as it is to cultivating a dialogic context for gay male Latino intellectual production—begins with its invocation, why perhaps it even finds comfort in it. As the editors of this volume we are not interested in imputing responsibility to feminists for any isolation that jotos and other gay Latinos have experienced. The history of that isolation—and of the divisions that have existed between gay Latinos and Latina lesbians (when they have existed)—is surely a long and complex one. In putting together this volume, however, we have been motivated less by histories of separation and isolation than by a commitment to the kind of deep solidarity modeled by Anzaldúa, a sense of remaining incomplete so long as the liberationist agenda that includes Chicanas and Latinas does not also include jotos, and vice versa. It is the unambiguous assertion of interdependence, coupled with the direct naming of jotos as "nuestros hermanos," that informs the creation of this volume.

"Not forgetting" gay Latino men, as Anzaldúa implores, is one way of framing the motivation behind the present volume. However, we are also keenly aware of the potential imprecision of that phrase and its resonance as patronizing benevolence in its self-assured commitment to what has been "left behind."

Ultimately it may even inaccurately suggest that gay Latinos, more than Latina lesbians, have been abandoned. Implying that gay Latinos are worse off than Latina lesbians is not only debatable, but as some of our contributors argue, politically and descriptively suspect inasmuch as such ranking of oppressions potentially underestimates profound moments of cross-mentorship and collaboration or mistakenly suggests that gay Latinos have been less active or more complacent than Latina lesbians. Antonio Viego's reprinted essay in this volume brings specificity to this issue by interrogating the relation of gay male Chicano literature to Chicana lesbian literature and criticism. Viego cautions against the assumption that gay Chicano cultural production should look like or even draw from queer Chicana cultural work. Such an assumption, he argues, forms the foundation on which gay Chicano cultural work is misrepresented as "lagging" behind the supposedly "plentiful" work of queer Chicanas. According to Viego, this misrepresentation, and the erroneous assumption on which it is based, makes it difficult to understand the emergence of gay Chicano cultural production—an emergence that may not share similar circumstances of political mobilization and hence might have different relationships to self-representation. In their joint response to Viego's essay the Chicana cultural critics Catriona Rueda Esquibel and Luz Calvo add clarification to his framing of the perceived tension and difference between Chicana lesbians and gay Chicano men, pointing to examples of relation, coalition, and cross-identification. For them queer as an analytic tool takes on complex meanings that allow for the elucidation of pasts that may not be otherwise visible in a discussion framed as gay or lesbian.

Questions as deceptively simple as "Where is the gay male version of This Bridge Called My Back?" or "What were gay men doing when Latina lesbians were fighting the publishing establishment?" resonate differently after engaging with the work of Viego, Esquivel, and Calvo. In fact questions that assume gay male apathy or deep rifts and irrevocable antipathies between gay men and lesbians fail to acknowledge the social movements that make certain forms of politics and documentation possible, not to mention the multiple ways that feminist volumes like This Bridge have spoken to gay men and represented our interests broadly speaking. As the editors of this volume we claim a lesbian feminist legacy of writing as ours in the sense that many gay Latino men have not only found political company in such a legacy, but have found it to be life-sustaining. As students, activists, and teachers we have taken care of those books and their insights, sharing them with our family and friends, quoting them and teaching them, learning to live their lessons, strategies, and leadership.[3] Still the question stands: What communal legacy has been left for future generations by gay Latino men? Is our labor traceable only in the way that the Panamanian American artist Patrick "Pato" Hebert cleverly explores in his art, by "tracing" the ephemeral dance steps of clubgoers?

Surely it is important to remember the recent explosion of texts by and about, in whole or in part, gay Latino men, as well as their numerous precursors. Early gay, bisexual, and queer Latino male writers include Miguel Algarín, Manuel Ramos Otero, John Rechy, and Miguel Piñero, who all began their careers before the 1980s, alongside artists like Gronk (Glugio Nicondra), Robert "Cyclona" Legorreta, and Rodrigo Reyes.[4] Joining them in the 1980s and early to mid-1990s were Valentín Aguirre, Francisco X. Alarcón, Luis Alfaro, Ricardo Bracho, Rafael Campo, Gil Cuadros, Arturo Islas, Jaime Manrique, Juanito "Xtravaganza" Rivera, Augie Robles, and the notorious Richard Rodriguez, whose neoconservative *Hunger of Memory* debuted in 1981 and became a bestseller.[5] Creative work by some of these and other Latino men found its way into print in literary collections such as Jaime Manrique's *Bésame Mucho* and Jaime Cortez's *Virgins, Guerrillas, and Locas* as well as in magazines such as *QV*, *Perra*, and *Corpus Magazine*.[6] More recently a host of up-and-coming gay male Latino writers and artists have come on the scene, including Aldo Álvarez, H. G. Carrillo, Rigoberto González, Erasmo Guerra, Dan Guerrero, Lorenzo Herrera y Lozano, Angel Lozada, Carlos Manuel, Manuel Muñoz, Yosimar Reyes, Héctor Silva, and Emanuel Xavier.[7] Academic work written both by and about gay Latino men picked up in the 1990s and the following decade as well, published at first in scattered venues. David William Foster's collection, *Chicano/Latino Homoerotic Identities*, is notable, as are earlier articles and book chapters by Tomás Almaguer, Juan Bruce-Novoa, Pedro Bustos-Aguilar, and Ramón Gutiérrez.[8] This body of work has been expanded through publications by Luis Aponte-Parés, Lionel Cantú, Ondine Chavoya, Daniel Contreras, Raúl Coronado, Arnaldo Cruz-Malavé, Rafael Díaz, Carlos Decena, Sergio de la Mora, Aureliano deSoto, Ramón García, Michael Hames-García, Larry La Fountain-Stokes, Ernesto Martínez, José Esteban Muñoz, Ricardo Ortiz, Daniel Enrique Pérez, José Quiroga, Ramón Rivera-Servera, Richard T. Rodríguez, David Román, Horacio Roque Ramírez, and Antonio Viego.[9]

Thus a more appropriate frame for the kind of work this volume intends to accomplish is one that, drawing on the work of the Caribbean feminist M. Jacqui Alexander, advocates less in support of "not forgetting" gay Latinos and more in support of actively "re-membering." As Alexander notes, re-membering does not entail obsessing over the past so much as "daring to recognize each other again and again in a context that seems bent on making strangers of us all."[10]

Alexander invokes re-membering within the context of the coalitional politics of women of color, but the concept can be useful for other antiracist feminist contexts as well. Re-membering asks us to bring together a coalitional body that has been dis-membered by a history of ideological violence. In actively resisting that history of violence we are able not only to remember a history of conflict and coalition but also to re-member possibilities for collaboration in the present. *Re-membering* gay Latinos, then, is not an act of nostalgic recovery. Instead it is a practice of piecing together and repopulating that which some would argue has never been ("gay Latino studies"), but which our presence now, in this volume, might work to confirm. We invoke gay Latino studies as an act of re-membering, as a gesture toward what has been and what might still be possible, even if it is only provisionally named.

Our purpose is not to recover a forgotten field of study or to inaugurate a future discipline, but to highlight relationships among ongoing intellectual projects that take the lives of gay, bisexual, and queer Latino men as a starting point. That such relationships require charting and emphasis testifies to the extent to which they have been, as yet, unnamed and dis-membered. Of course we understand the subject of gay Latino men as internally complex and coalitional, as related to, often overlapping with, and seeking coalition among other kinds of subjects (Latinas and women of color, Asian, Caribbean, and Native peoples, immigrants, transgender and transsexual people, antiracist and feminist whites, gay men, queers of color, etc.). However, as an intellectual center of gravity for discussions at the conjunction of class, gender, race, and sexuality in the United States, *Gay Latino Studies* provokes insights and perspectives that might remain opaque or even unattainable without focusing on or starting from the specificity of gay Latino men's lives, experience, and knowledge—even if they are also necessarily incomplete. Even those contributions to this volume that do not take gay Latino men as their principal conceptual category resonate differently within the context of a volume that does than they would in another context.

Despite rhetoric about absence and forgetting, gay Latino men are not without a history of political mobilization, artistic production, and intellectual engagement in the United States.[11] ACT-UP activists Ray Navarro of DIVA TV and Robert García of House of Color were artistically and politically active in the late 1980s, and Asco members Gronk, Willie Herrón III, Patssi Valdez, and Harry Gamboa Jr. brought the arts, politics, and style of punk and gay liberation to East Los Angeles in the mid-1970s, even if not all of the members were gay.[12] Thinking more broadly beyond a narrow understanding of gay Latino men, Sylvia Rivera spanned the decades from the 1960s to the 1990s, from her presence at the Stonewall riots of 1969 to her involvement as an out drag queen with the Puerto Rican Young Lords Party and her activism on behalf of transgender rights. These histories and other, more quotidian ones are increasingly coming to scholarly attention.[13] For the most part, though, scholars have not fully documented this history until recently. Richard T. Rodríguez's contribution to this volume, "Carnal Knowledge: Chicano Gay Men and the Dialectics of Being," unearths and theorizes overlooked connections between gay Chicano subjectivities and dominant expressions of Chicano consciousness, notably *carnalismo*. According to Rodríguez, ambiguous responses to Chicano gay male sexuality in early Chicano movement poetry and essays, as well as in the pages of lowrider magazines in the 1970s and early 1980s, reveal a rich archive of complex moments of acknowledgment and repression. Furthermore he believes that Chicano gay male engagements with these ambiguous responses (particularly in the lowrider magazines) suggest the importance of previously underacknowledged familial discourses in grounding Chicano gay male consciousness. Daniel Enrique Pérez's thoughtful engagement with these ideas in his response to Rodríguez urges scholars to continue to look for expressions of *queer* Chicano subjectivity in unlikely places, particularly where such expressions might not always be marked as explicitly gay. Certainly the history of Rivera's activist life and the sexual ambiguity of Asco are also suggestive of the richness lying just beyond the margins of lives that are intelligibly and definitively gay. While some contributors, like Calvo and Esquibel, use the term *queer* in order to highlight transgender and cross-gender identifications, Pérez's use is calculated to convey the fluidity and murkiness of sexual orientations and desires, many of which can seem unintelligible from within standard definitions of *gay* and *straight*.

The importance of locating and interrogating such barely intelligible expressions of queer Latino subjectivity in *unlikely* places is complemented by the work of the literary critic Ernesto Javier Martínez in this volume. In his essay "Shifting the Site of Queer Enunciation" Martínez turns to the work of the gay Chicano writer Manuel Muñoz and investigates the peculiar and provocative practice of narrating queer stories from nonqueer perspectives. In contrast to the liberatory tradition of first-person narratives, Martínez defines another tradition, one that astutely decenters queer narrators in order to more equitably distribute responsibility for queer experience and to enable a deeper understanding of the intersubjective and social contexts in which queer subjects come into being and become intelligible. The Chicana feminist critic Paula Moya offers a careful response to Martínez's essay by providing depth to the Chicano history that Muñoz is tapping. Drawing on the Chicano folktale of dancing with the devil Moya offers further support for Martínez's claim that narrating queer stories from nonqueer perspectives not only transfers some of the burden of queer representation, but also interrupts heteronormative logics that refuse marginalized subjects their place in the intermeshed cultural fabric and history of their communities.

By re-membering gay Latino studies in the ways initially suggested by the work of Rodríguez, Pérez, Martínez, and Moya, we seek to encourage more visibility and in-depth work in the histories and creative life strategies of gay Chicano and Latino men. We also want to signal the complexity with which we engage *gay Latino* as a rubric and frame of reference and the care with which we understand such an undertaking. As this discussion has already made clear, many of the terms we use in setting up this collection, including *visibility*, *gay*, and *queer*, remain contested ones throughout its pages, along with such as *identity*, *culture*, *representation*, and *politics*. Indeed debates about the meaning and use of these terms currently form some of the basic and most valuable discussions in gay Latino studies. What is most at stake in these debates often comes to the fore with unusual clarity in the critical responses following each chapter of this book.

For example, in "Entre Hombres/Between Men: Latino Masculinities and Homosexualities," the late sociologist Lionel Cantú uses interview data from two gay Latino men's service organizations to argue against cultural explanations for gay Latino sexual identities and behaviors. Even though culture plays an important role in the lives and identities of gay Latino men, Cantú contends, cultural arguments often obscure structural aspects of power in the lives of these marginalized men. Furthermore such cultural explanations for the lives of gay Latino men often result in a pathologization of culture in order to explain behavior considered deviant from Anglo-American norms. The positions he stakes out in this piece, originally published in 2000, put him in direct conflict with positions elaborated by the sociologist Tomás Almaguer, perhaps most notably in his important and highly influential essay, "Chicano Men: A Cartography of Homosexual Identity and Behavior," published in 1990. In his comment on Cantú's essay Almaguer takes the opportunity for the first time in print to clarify his own position, while noting the contributions of Cantú and others to furthering important and heterogeneous debates about the relationships among culture, ethnicity, and sexual identity.

A related exchange between the Salvadorian American scholar Horacio

Roque Ramírez and the Chicano historian Ramón Gutiérrez centers on sexual identity in relation to politics and visibility. In "Gay Latino Cultural Citizenship: Predicaments of Identity and Visibility in 1990s San Francisco," Roque Ramírez considers challenges posed for notions of queer Latina and Latino identity, visibility, and rights. He analyzes two case studies: a safer-sex ad campaign seeking to reduce HIV infections among married Latino "men who have sex with men" and their wives, and the advertising of the San Francisco Queer Pride Festival's "Latin Stage." According to Roque Ramírez, public acts of identity affirmation for queer Latinos (queer Latino cultural citizenship) can serve a valuable role for political and cultural organizing, but such acts are at high risk for co-optation by corporate interests, for "once reduced to prototypical sounds and symbols of culture, racial and queer group difference can easily become conduits for profit-driven consumption." His positions put him alongside his late mentor, Lionel Cantú, with regard to recent debates about identity in gay Latino studies. Gutiérrez's response (like Almaguer's) takes issue with some of the positions advocated by younger scholars like Roque Ramírez (and Cantú). Gutiérrez first offers a critique of group identity as an adequate basis for collectivity and then advocates a switch from identity to behavior as a descriptive basis for ethnography and for organizing. Gutiérrez sees political possibility in keeping a category such as queer open and unfixed, but from the perspective of activists like Ricardo Bracho, as described in Roque Ramírez's text, it is difficult to organize a politics based solely on behavior. Gutiérrez charges that identities are at risk of commodification and do not account for all possible configurations of sexual behavior and desire, while Roque Ramírez attends to the risks of commodification while also offering an argument for the importance of salient identities for political organizing and for understanding the relationships between identity and community. From the perspective of the editors, the behaviors Gutierrez lists at the end of his comment, while interesting ethnographically, risk being empty politically. It is difficult to imagine, in other words, an antipatriarchal politics like the one Roque Ramírez advocates emerging from "the sexual [illicit same-sex] practices of ostensibly married, heterosexual men," if only because identities are profound epistemic and social realities that structure how we see the world and live in it.[14] Such debates over the status of identity in general and the usefulness of specific identities, including gay and queer, reverberate throughout gay Latino studies, as in the fields of queer theory and gay and lesbian studies more broadly. To understand what terms are most useful scholars need to be clear on what they hope to achieve with them. Clearly gay is inadequate to capture the lived reality of many people's experiences and practices, yet it has produced profoundly meaningful and powerful ways of organizing knowledge, belief, and action for many others, in spite of its descriptive inadequacies.

José Esteban Muñoz is among the scholars in the humanities who has done much in recent years to rethink the basic questions that we should ask about identity, most notably in his book *Disidentifications*. There he argues that many gay, lesbian, bisexual, and queer performance artists and activists of color in the United States have sought to tack a course between identification with and counteridentification against dominant ideologies, rather than aligning themselves with mainstream assimilation or resistance. In an important and influential essay, reprinted here, Muñoz takes a slightly different turn by exploring two principal themes: the constitution of (pan-ethnic) Latina/o identity and the importance of affect for the constitution of communal belonging and identification. He thus proposes an original response to some of the questions raised in earlier chapters by Cantú and Roque Ramírez about how identity-based communities take shape, but he asks these questions from within the realm of aesthetics. Through an exploration of the language of *The Sweetest Hangover (and other STDs)*, a play by the gay Chicano playwright Ricardo Bracho produced in 1997, Muñoz argues that forms of ethnic difference and resistance can take shape through varieties of emotional response among different people rather than simply through claims to being the same. He contends that these emotional or affective bonds are essential to the establishment or performance of ethnic identity (in this case, a queer of color identity). His fellow Cuban American scholar Ricardo Ortiz draws from a rich theoretical archive in his comment in order to extend Muñoz's ideas. Ortiz notes, for example, the congruent (not equivalent) relation between brownness and queerness in Muñoz's essay. Ortiz suggests that in the creation of relational bonds affective responses can exceed the possibilities generated by claims to commonality or sameness.

Thus by taking the experiences and contributions of gay, bisexual, and queer Latino men as central to social inquiry, contributors to this volume not only offer much-needed insight into the lives and perspectives of these men, but also allow for a renewed attentiveness to the politics and theorization of intersectionality, multiplicity, coalition, and identity, including an overdue interrogation of racialized masculinities. Some of the internal debates, like those over the status of identity, sound like echoes of the debates within and between queer, gay and lesbian, and feminist studies. However, it would be a mistake to see differences between the positions of, for example, Pérez and Roque Ramírez as equivalent to differences between Judith Butler and Seyla Benhabib. Most obviously a shared concern with the racialization of sexual subjects defines the work of all of the contributors to this volume. That concern, along with others, means that even among those contributors who are most ambivalent toward *identity* as a stable or coherent category there is also a resistance to jettisoning the experience of class, gender, race, and sexuality as lived realities shaping people's lives. Similarly none of the contributors attempts to theorize experience at the level of abstract generality that one finds among many of the most cited feminist and queer scholars in the academy. All of the contributors to *Gay Latino Studies* share a commitment to attending to the rich complexity of concrete lived experience, even when they disagree on its implications. The work of *Gay Latino Studies* in re-membering gay and queer Latino subjects thus complements and overlaps with the groundbreaking work of lesbians of color and critical race theorists as well as queer theorists and gay and lesbian studies scholars, extending inquiry about race and sexuality in ways that are necessary for a fuller understanding of multiple oppressions and coalitional politics.[15]

"LO QUE NUNCA PASÓ POR SUS LABIOS"?

Through its thematic and structural organization, *Gay Latino Studies* attempts to cultivate conversations that facilitate future scholarship and new directions of inquiry. Still, as the preceding discussion notes, choosing *gay* and *Latino* as organizing rubrics raises important questions. We would therefore like to offer four qualifications to our title. First, in naming our collection *Gay Latino Studies* we seek to address a conjunction of intellectual and political questions rather than to delineate a discipline or field of study *separate from* existing rubrics of critical inquiry. Chicana/o and Latina/o studies, gay and lesbian and queer studies, comparative ethnic studies, and women's and gender studies—together and separately—form some of the rich networks, theories, communities, and relationships that make possible the conversations collected here. In other words, we understand gay Latino studies as emerging in conversation and continuing to overlap with these important forms of social inquiry and knowledge generation. We do not suggest that gay Latino studies should be a replacement of or an alternative to Latina feminism or Chicano studies or Latino and Latin American studies, to name just a few categories that might embrace multiple essays from this collection. Rather we hope to highlight a crucial location where many critical discourses, methodologies, and fields of study overlap. We also do not intend to champion *Latino* as a replacement for *Chicano* or *Puerto Rican* or *Central American* or *Caribbean*, but merely to offer a convenient way of grouping together related projects that might otherwise seem disparate.

Our second reason for framing a collection around gay Latino studies speaks to the sometimes fraught label *gay male* in relation to the equally fraught label *queer*. Current critical models, particularly in the humanities, often shift attention away from identity categories such as *gay* and *lesbian* to rubrics such as *queer*. This shift is sometimes motivated by legitimate concerns about the inadequacy of gay or lesbian labels to map individual behaviors, desires, politics, and identifications. At other times this shift simply demonstrates an effort at making gay, lesbian, bisexual, and transgender analysis inclusive and coalitional. Our second reason for choosing *gay Latino studies* therefore stems from the fact that this collection primarily focuses on *men*. While *gay* might mischaracterize some crucial aspects of Latino men's sexuality at a descriptive level, it seems to be far less misleading for the present collection than *queer* would be, given criticisms that the latter's use as an umbrella term has sometimes elided gender difference. It is an undeniable limitation of the current project that it does not explicitly address concerns of transgender Latinas and Latinos. The choice to use *gay* rather than *queer* in the title for this volume is thus in some ways an attempt at truth in advertising, an effort to avoid signaling an expectation on the part of potential readers that the fullness of transsexual and transgender experiences and identities (not to mention those of lesbian, bisexual, and queer women) will be addressed within it. Despite the focus of the collection as a whole, some of our contributors use labels other than gay (most often *queer*) to explicitly invoke larger coalitions or a broader range of sexual identifications (Esquibel and Calvo, Pérez, Martínez, and Roque Ramírez, among others).

In a related but different incarnation the term *queer*, particularly in its development within the body of thought known as *queer theory*, has formed part of a much broader skepticism toward identity categories per se and a generalized suspicion of normative claims. Reflecting on the heterogeneous projects included here, however, we believe that skepticism about identities, while sometimes justified, can often mistake political identities for attempts at transparent ethnographic description. Furthermore such deep-seated, a priori skepticism toward identity can also sometimes function as a cover for undertheorized racial politics. Our third reason, then, for choosing *gay* Latino studies is an awareness of the limits inherent in the radical anti-identitarian posturing of some versions of queer studies, although we by no means intend to imply that gay and lesbian studies have done much better at addressing race or that no queer theorists have successfully addressed its complexity. However, as several scholars, including Cathy Cohen, David Eng, Linda Garber, Sharon Holland, Patrick E. Johnson, and Hiram Pérez, have noted, queer politics can often mask not only an investment in whiteness, but also a Eurocentric insistence on whiteness as an unquestioned norm. In "You Can Have My Brown Body and Eat It, Too!" Hiram Pérez makes an observation along these lines:

> [A] great deal of queer theorizing has sought to displace identity politics with an alternative anti-identitarian model, often—and perhaps disingenuously—christened "the politics of difference." This model accommodates familiar habits of the university's ideal bourgeois subject, among them, his imperial gaze, his universalism, and his claims to a race-neutral objectivity. It is not surprising then to find buried underneath the boot of this establishmentarian anti-identity all sorts of dissident bodies.[16]

Part of the power of Pérez's charge against queer theory lies in its leveling against a purportedly liberatory theoretical practice an accusation of complicity with the most reviled aspects of traditional academic imperialism.

Pérez's criticism resonates with those of many other scholars of color. Sharon Holland, an African American critic, has written of her concerns about queer studies and its relationship to black feminist legacies:

> The academic market, at least its emerging "queer" constituency, seemed to be interpreting "identity politics" as the root of all evil—simply get rid of "race" (always a fiction?) and the category of "woman" (already a misnomer?) and we would have our rebirth on the other side of our problem(s).
>
> While "queer" studies began to define its origins from the complex remaking of identity politics, those of us already working in the field of black feminism found this "new" trajectory unsettling—scholars like Hazel Carby and Hortense Spillers had already unseated the idea of "woman" as a universal category; Gloria Hull, Barbara Smith, and others had already questioned the myopic identity politics of civil rights and women's activist networks. The question hardly seemed "new" to us at all, but rather more of the same: remaking discourse in the image of its rightful owners—whitewashing the product so that it could and would be more palatable to a growing constituency.[17]

Informed by scholars like Pérez and Holland our decisions in editing *Gay Latino Studies* have sought to work against the whitewashing tendencies of queer academic theorizing and against the deep suspicion of identity categories that too often serve as a crutch for white academic racism. We do so, however, by invoking *gay* complexly and resistantly and by including essays that debate the term's use.

Some of our contributors' work is closely in dialogue with the major currents of queer theory (for example, Muñoz and Ortiz), while others explicitly take issue with what they perceive to be shortcomings with this theoretical approach (for example, Hames-García and La Fountain-Stokes). Regardless of their perceived closeness to the queer theory mainstream, however, it is clear that all of the contributions to *Gay Latino Studies* have deep roots in the intellectual big bang caused by the late twentieth-century encounters among mainstream feminism, queer theory, women of color feminism (including Chicana and Latina feminisms), and critical race studies (including Chicano, Latino, Puerto Rican, and Latin American subaltern studies). The legacies of these encounters thus are themselves a subject of debate within gay Latino studies, and we open the volume with two chapters that seek to assess those legacies and to situate theories of race, sexuality, and Latinidad in relation to queer theory, the currently dominant approach to understanding sexuality in the humanities.

Like Pérez and Holland, Michael Hames-García has written critically elsewhere about the relationship between queer theory and critical race studies. In a revision of an earlier piece he revisits some of his concerns about the usefulness of queer theory as a political discourse for queer people of color. Queer theory has often justified its own existence and argued for its newness based on claims that it can link sexuality, power, and desire to considerations of race, gender, and society better than other, competing discourses. Paradoxically, as many scholars have observed, queer theory has simultaneously resisted the consequences of a truly substantive, thorough, and ongoing engagement with theories that are more centrally concerned with race and class. Hames-García responds to this contradiction by offering a countergenealogy for theorizing about race and sexuality, by demonstrating some limitations of queer theory's anti-identitarianism, and by exploring alternative models (such as the "modern colonial gender system"). María Lugones, a Latina feminist philosopher, responds by engaging the work of several women of color feminists to excavate some of the ontological and agential commitments of Hames-García's work, including a distinction between the logic of categories that are imposed through oppression and the enabling reality of identities that have their own historicity. She understands Hames-García as arguing that queer theory is mistaken in its deep assumptions about identity because it makes a conceptual move, "rather than a historical move performed by people at the point of oppression."

Also seeking to break with dominant queer studies paradigms and genealogies, the Puerto Rican cultural critic Lawrence La Fountain-Stokes raises challenges to recent queer work on the concept of shame. "Gay Shame, Latina- and Latino-Style: A Critique of White Queer Performativity" considers debates on the Puerto Rican drag artist Mario Móntez, the University of Michigan Gay Shame Conference of 2003, and the recent embrace by Latinas and Latinos of *sinvergüencería*, or shamelessness, as a productive site of politics and identity building. La Fountain-Stokes ultimately argues for a more ethically and racially nuanced account of gay shame that can take account of social and cultural difference. His ideas are picked up and extended in a comment by Ramón García, a Chicano visual culture scholar, who observes that La Fountain-Stokes "attempts to make sense of the disjunction between what shame means for people of color and the manner in which it has been recovered and rewritten by middle-class white gay men."

A fourth reason we use the category *gay Latino* is to respond to contemporary political contexts where the lives of gay men are in the balance. Within the HIV/AIDS-prevention industry, for example, there has been a move away from the use of categories such as *gay men* to broader categories such as *men who have sex with men*. The goal of this move is to address high-risk sexual behaviors without attributing identities to men who participate in those behaviors. While the logic here may in fact have pragmatic merits — insofar as it seeks to affect the lives of men who may not want to be stigmatized by the label or may not identify as gay — the case can also be made that much more ambitious and queer-positive prevention practices are necessary to connect with larger projects of social transformation and social justice. If it is easier in the context of HIV prevention — as it might very well be — to help modify people's high-risk sexual practices by circumventing their identities, what happens in the process to self-identified gay men or to potentially gay-identified men? In other words, what happens to those men who have not shunned identification as gay, joto, queer, or *de ambiente*? George Ayala, the director of education for AIDS Project Los Angeles, observes some of the issues implied by these questions, noting, for example, that, despite high rates of infection, "gay men see less and less salience in HIV-prevention campaigns as those campaigns become watered-down and fail to address the subjective experiences of gay men in visible and affirming ways."[18] He also notes that AIDS-prevention work has increasingly narrowed to the collection of epidemiological statistics (what he refers to as "obsessive fuck counting") rather than efforts to address the role of pleasure and desire in gay men's sexuality and the place of sexuality in the larger context of gay men's lives.[19] Perhaps most important, Ayala argues that male sexual behavior should not be addressed outside of an understanding of internalized homophobia, to which we would also add economic exploitation, sexism, racism, and patriarchy.

One hope we have in naming this collection is that calling attention to the specificity of gay Latino men can open up additional opportunities to ask questions of that category. What coherence might *gay Latino* have? What politics might be or might come to be associated with such a category? To what extent does the category foreclose or extend opportunities for collaboration and exploration that other configurations (for example, *queer*) might not? Perhaps most centrally, what limited, problematic, overlooked, misunderstood, or beautiful possibilities might we miss without sustained attention to the specific yet heterogeneous experiences and perspectives of gay Latino men?

One way to read this collection is therefore as a record of the emergence of several interrelated conversations among gay Latino scholars in the United States. Some of these conversations might be characterized as follows: (1) engagements with mainstream gay, lesbian, and queer academic discourses (especially in the chapters by Hames-García and La Fountain-Stokes, but also in several of the responses); (2) contestations over the significance of gay Latino scholarly and cultural production within Chicano and Latino studies more broadly, including their relationship to hegemonic masculinities and to Latina feminisms (especially in the chapters by Viego and Rodríguez, but also in those by Hames-García and Martínez); (3) renegotiations of traditional disciplinary practices, assumptions, and explanations, most notably within ethnography (especially in the chapters by Cantú and Roque Ramírez, but also in those by Martínez and Moya); (4) explorations of the possibilities and consequences of artistic representations of queer Latinidad, or queer "brownness" (especially in the chapters by Muñoz and Martínez, but also in those by La Fountain-Stokes, Viego, and Rodríguez); and (5) inquiries into the social and political contexts for queer performance and utopianism, most notably through theorizations of dance (especially in the chapters by Rivera-Servera and Román, but also in those by La Fountain-Stokes and Muñoz). These five themes correspond roughly to the organization of the book, although we do not intend these themes to foreclose other possible lines of connection.[20]

At this volume's end we have included two essays on dance because dance offers a paradigmatic illustration of the pas de deux between identity affirmation and world making that is so central to gay Latino studies in general. As gay Latino men, some of the most transformative moments in our own lives have centered on dance. With lovers and friends we have shared on the dance floors of our homes, clubs, and streets kinetic histories of intimacy and a need for public enunciations of emotion and desire through dance. There is of course the centrality of dance and dance clubs to the culture of coming out and gay life in the 1990s, a culture we found ourselves both attracted to and yet critical of. With lovers and friends we have shared histories of intimacy and desire through dance. We know the difference between a stance that says "I am waiting until midnight, because that is when the club gets good" and one that says "I am watching others dance because I am not really at the club to dance." We have also shared those moments in predominantly heterosexual spaces, where we have had to wonder whether or not to dance and at what risk. It is probably only because we have had such moments that the experience of dancing (and the interpretive and emotional labor that comes with it) gains importance.

Then there is the particularity of partner dancing, so common to Latina and Latino contexts yet absent from the gay club scene. As a gay couple, dancing to cumbia, salsa, merengue, or tango takes on entirely different meanings, in both queer and nonqueer contexts. This is in no small part due to the more highly gendered nature of partner dances: the male lead, the female follower. Our presence in Latin dance classes has led to the complete befuddlement of more than one dance instructor. However, we also recognize a political stake in claiming Latin dance as our own, in queering it. An early political intervention of the Joto Caucus and the Lesbian Caucus (now the Lesbian, BiMujeres, and Trans Caucus) of the National Association of Chicana and Chicano Studies was to claim space on the floor at the annual conference's Gran Baile. Over the years some same-sex couples became fixtures at the dance. These events eventually lost the early edge of riskiness. By the time the Association discontinued its tradition of the Gran Baile queer couples mostly felt fully accepted there, although we sometimes wondered what the local musicians were thinking and the occasional straight woman still wondered why so many men were dancing together when there were single women available as partners.

The essays on dance included here employ different methodological approaches, but both are ultimately concerned with the possibilities (and limits) of drawing connections between dance, on the one hand, and queer political and community-building projects, on the other. The Puerto Rican performance scholar Ramón Rivera-Servera's ethnographic essay, "Choreographies of Resistance: Latino Queer Dance and the Utopian Performative," explores the voices and choreographic approaches of multiple queer Latina and Latino clubgoers and argues for the potential of dance to produce feelings of community and agency. He is attentive to both the materiality of improvisational club dancing and its utopian promise. Despite the fact that social hierarchies inside and outside the club complicate utopian desires, Rivera-Servera suggests that the improvisations of the dancers can reveal possibilities for liberation from oppression and the constitution of community. Daniel Contreras's comment asks several questions of Rivera-Servera's project. These questions concern the nature of culture as an object of study, the politics of cultural meaning, and the essay's relation to other studies of dance.

In "Dance Liberation" David Román, a noted queer Cuban American cultural critic, explores the intertwining of dance and politics among queer communities, from gay liberation in the 1970s to AIDS activism in the 1990s. Through a combination of auto-ethnography and cultural criticism (considering the film *The Boys in the Band* and the musicals *Movin' Out* and *Radiant Baby*), Román argues for the importance of dance as a register and mediator of political feelings and commitments, not exclusive to but distinctive of queer life. The feminist scholar and filmmaker Frances Negrón-Muntaner takes Román's essay as an invitation to dance. Her comment improvises a response to his lead, offering up her own reflections on dance and queer and Latina/o politics in the 1980s and 1990s, drawing attention to the different geographic spaces that she has occupied, first as a young lesbian in Puerto Rico and later as a U.S. Latina lesbian in several major East Coast cities. The dialogue that emerges between these two scholars through their writing epitomizes the possibilities that we had hoped for when we envisioned this volume. It has an improvisatory feel and is an encounter, like much dance, that reminds us that no conversation (including those central to *Gay Latino Studies*) is ever complete. We therefore hope that this collection will invite many more responses, becoming an instrument to carry conversation forward as new partners join in movement and new tempos guide the steps.

NOTES

1. "Let us not forget the men" (Anzaldúa, *Borderlands/La Frontera*, 105).

2. "It is astonishing to think that we've stayed in that dark hole in which the world encloses lesbians. It is astonishing to think that we have, as feminists and lesbians, closed our hearts to the men, to our queer brothers, disinherited and marginal like us" (Anzaldúa, *Borderlands/La Frontera*, 106).

3. It is important to note that many collections by and about Latina lesbians emerged from the context of the feminist movement, a movement in which feminist presses and the anthology as a genre held a distinctive place. Thus one could argue that, rather than explaining the absence of gay Latino anthologies, one should instead explain the emergence of Latina lesbian anthologies, an emergence possibly attributable to the more general prominence of anthologies as a feminist genre in the 1970s and 1980s.

4. See Algarín and Piñero, *Nuyorican Poetry*; Algarín, *Love Is Hard Work*; Ramos Otero, *Página en blanco y staccato*; Piñero, *Short Eyes*; Rechy, *City of Night*, *The Miraculous Day of Amalia Gómez*, and *The Sexual Outlaw*. On Gronk, Cyclona, and Reyes, see Benavidez, *Gronk*; R. Hernández, *The Fire of Life*; and de la Garza and Roque Ramírez, "Queer Community History."

5. See Aguirre and Robles, *¡Viva 16!*; F. X. Alarcón, *De amor oscuro* and *From the Other Side of Night*; Alfaro, "Cuerpo Politizado," "Downtown," "Pico-Union," and "Straight as a Line"; Campo, *The Other Man Was Me*, *What the Body Told*, and *Diva*; Cuadros, *City of God*; Islas, *La Mollie and the King of Tears*, *Migrant Souls*, and *The Rain God*; Manrique, *Eminent Maricones*, *Latin Moon in Manhattan*, and *Twilight at the Equator*; Robles, *Cholo Joto*. On Juanito Xtravaganza, see Cruz-Malavé, *Queer Latino Testimonio*. Bracho has not published any of his plays to date; however, see Bracho, Cortiñas, and Muñoz, "Towards Translocalism."

6. See Cortez, *Virgins*; Manrique, *Bésame Mucho*.

7. See H. G. Carrillo, *Loosing My Espanish*; R. González, *Butterfly Boy*, *Crossing Vines*, *The Mariposa Club*, *Men without Bliss*, and *Other Fugitives*; Guerra, *Between Dances*; Lozada, *La patografía*; M. Muñoz, *The Faith Healer* and *Zigzagger*; Xavier, *Pier Queen*, *Christ-Like*, and *Americano*. Dan Guerrero's one-man show *¡Gaytino!* premiered at the Mark Taper Forum on 30 March 2005 and has been performed numerous times since. Carlos Manuel has performed a one-man show, *La Vida Loca*, as well as a number of shorter and longer plays. Yosimar Reyes is a slam poet based in California and Lorenzo Herrera y Lozano has edited and written several poetry collections. On Héctor Silva an artist from Los Angeles, see R. T. Rodríguez, "Queering the Homeboy Aesthetic."

8. See Foster, *Chicano/Latino Homoerotic Identities*; Almaguer, "Chicano Men"; Bruce-Novoa, "Homosexuality and the Chicano Novel"; Bustos-Aguilar, "Mister Don't Touch the Banana"; Cruz-Malavé, "Para virar al macho," "Toward an Art of Transvestism," and, "What a Tangled Web!"; R. Gutiérrez, "Community, Patriarchy, and Individualism" and "The Erotic Zone." See also Cruz-Malavé and Manalansan, *Queer Globalizations*.

9. See, for example, Aponte-Parés, "Outside/In"; Cantú, *The Sexuality of Migration*; Chavoya, "Internal Exiles" and "Pseudographic Cinema"; Contreras, *Unrequited Love*; Coronado, "Bringing It Back Home"; de la Mora, *Cinemachismo*; R. M. Díaz, *Latino Gay Men*; R. García, "Against *Rasquache*"; Hames-García, "Can Queer Theory Be Critical Theory?," *Identity Complex*, "What's at Stake," and "Who Are Our Own People?"; La Fountain-Stokes, "Cultures of the Puerto Rican Queer Diaspora"; La Fountain-Stokes, "Dancing La Vida Loca," "Entre boleros, travestismos y migraciones translocales," and *Queer Ricans*; Luibhéid and Cantú, *Queer Migrations*; Martínez, "On Butler"; J. E. Muñoz, *Disidentifications*; R. L. Ortiz, *Cultural Erotics*; D. E. Pérez, *Rethinking Chicana/o and Latina/o Popular Culture*; Quiroga, *Tropics of Desire*; Rivera-Servera, "Choreographies of Resistance"; R. T. Rodríguez, "Imagine a Brown Queer," *Next of Kin*, and "Queering the Homeboy Aesthetic"; Román, *Acts of Intervention*; Roque Ramírez, "Claiming Queer Cultural Citizenship," "That's My Place," and "¡Mira, Yo Soy Boricua y Estoy Aquí!"; Viego, "The Place of Gay Male Chicano Literature."

10. Alexander, "Remembering *This Bridge*," 96.

11. See, for example, Aponte-Parés, "Outside/In"; Aponte-Parés and Merced, "Páginas Omitidas"; La Fountain-Stokes, "1898"; Roque Ramírez, "Claiming Queer Cultural Citizenship."

12. On Asco, see Chavoya, "Pseudographic Cinema" and "Internal Exiles."

13. See, for example, Cruz-Malavé, *Queer Latino Testimonio*, and Montez, "Trade Marks," on the lives and forgotten influence of two young, gay Latino men: Juan Rivera (a.k.a. Juanito Xtravaganza) and Juanito Rivera Angel Ortiz (a.k.a. LA2), respectively.

14. This is similar to a realist theoretical approach to identity that we and others have argued for elsewhere. See, for example, Alcoff, *Visible Identities*; Alcoff et al., *Identity Politics Reconsidered*; Hames-García, *Fugitive Thought* and *Identity Complex*; Martínez, "Dying to Know" and "On Butler"; S. P. Mohanty, *Literary Theory*; Moya, *Learning from Experience*; Moya and Hames-García, *Reclaiming Identity*; Siebers, *Disability Theory*; Teuton, *Red Land*.

15. Recent edited volumes that broadly address race and sexuality and create a context for *Gay Latino Studies* include the following: Bergmann and Smith, *¿Entiendes?*; Eng and Hom, *Q & A*; Foster, *Chicano/Latino Homoerotic Identities*; Patton and Sánchez Eppler, *Queer Diasporas*; Hawley, *Postcolonial, Queer*; Cruz-Malavé and Manalansan, *Queer Globalizations*; Gaspar de Alba, *Velvet Barrios*; Torres and Pertusa, *Tortilleras*; Johnson and Henderson, *Black Queer Studies*; Luibhéid and Cantú, *Queer Migrations*. However, none of these collections offers an extended scholarly exploration of the specificities of gay Latino male politics, theory, and experience in the United States. Those volumes with a substantial partial focus on gay Latino men generally bring together essays from a single discipline (e.g., literary criticism) and do not focus specifically on Latino gay men in the United States.

The single-author volumes contributing to the broad field of "queer of color critique" include a number that address the intersections of gender, race, and sexuality. These are also an indispensable backdrop for the emergence of *Gay Latino Studies* and include, among others, the following: J. E. Muñoz, *Disidentifications*; Quiroga, *Tropics of Desire*; J. M. Rodríguez, *Queer Latinidad*; Lugones, *Pilgrimages/Peregrinajes*; Manalansan, *Global Divas*; Ferguson, *Aberrations in Black*; Esquibel, *With Her Machete in Her Hand*; R. L. Ortiz, *Cultural Erotics*.

16. H. Pérez, "You Can Have My Brown Body," 172.

17. Holland, "Foreword," ix.

18. Ayala, "Foreward," v.

19. Ayala, "Foreward," vi.

20. An unfortunate absence in this collection is any discussion of visual arts, including photography, painting, sculpture, and performance art. In these pursuits several gay Latino men have made outstanding contributions, and the work of José Esteban Muñoz, Ondine Chavoya, and others has germinated critical debate about the interventions visual artists have made in prompting others to rethink the relationships among gender, nation, race, and sexuality.

Queer Theory Revisited

Michael Hames-García

QUEER THEORY AND ITS DISCONTENTS

The critical work most often cited in discussions of queer theory entered the academy around the same time I did. Judith Butler's *Bodies That Matter* (1993), Michael Warner's collection *Fear of a Queer Planet* (1993), and *The Lesbian and Gay Studies Reader* (1993) were all published during my first year of graduate school. Most of what are now considered the foundational texts for queer theory appeared while I was an undergraduate: Eve Kosofsky Sedgwick's *Epistemology of the Closet* (1990), Butler's *Gender Trouble* (1990), the Diana Fuss anthology *Inside/Out* (1991), and "Queer Theory," a special issue of *differences* edited by Teresa de Lauretis (1991). Others came out while I was still in high school: the first issue of the journal *Out/Look* (1988), Leo Bersani's "Is the Rectum a Grave?" (1987), and Sedgwick's *Between Men* (1985). Gayle Rubin's oft-cited essay "Thinking Sex" (1984) was written in 1982. When I was in junior high and had my first serious homosexual fantasies, the so-called sex wars in feminism were already raging, as was the AIDS epidemic. I was just getting the hang of tying my shoes when the first volume of Michel Foucault's *History of Sexuality* was published in France as *La volonté de savoir* (1976), and I was born two years after the 1969 Stonewall Rebellion.

I begin this way to emphasize the context in which I first encountered queer theory. Rather than a corrective to my past experiences within the feminist and gay rights movements (since I had none), queer theory (along with ACT-UP and Queer Nation) comprised the milieu in(to) which I came out sexually, politically, and intellectually. *Queer* does not feel to me like a reclaimed term of derision, anymore than *gay* does. Having accepted my sexuality before I graduated from high school I found waiting for me in college and graduate school an exciting, sexy academic discourse for interpreting my sexual identity and desires and imagining their political significance. As a Chicano first-generation college graduate, however, I soon began to have questions about this new academic discourse, particularly in relation to race and class. Imagine my surprise when, as I began to voice these questions to professors and fellow graduate students, I met with exasperated responses: "We haven't read anything talking about race because you haven't brought us anything yet"; "I don't think racism is as big a problem in the gay community as some people say"; and "Well, I don't go through authors' footnotes to see the race of the people they cite." Furthermore while there was often praise for my contribution of a (colored, classed) queer experience, it was always accompanied by dismissal of my attempts to theorize that experience for myself, especially when my theorization challenged dominant presuppositions in queer theory. The message seemed clear: people of color were to provide raw experience for white academics to theorize. (In reaction I spent the next several years eliminating anything personal from my writing.)

What did I want from queer theory anyway? I had hoped that queer theory would be able to make sexuality and desire central rather than peripheral to radical politics and would be unrelentingly critical, in Herbert Marcuse's sense of simultaneously negating society as a given and imagining what more liberatory possibilities are being blocked by that given state of affairs.[1] For me this had to include critical understandings of race, class, gender, and capitalism. Despite the promises of many of queer theory's early proponents and its development over the past two decades, I still find myself at a loss to locate in it the tools for understanding such complex relations of meaning. None of the works listed in my opening paragraph tells me how to understand the connections between white homosexuality and white supremacy implied by my anecdotes, between the experience of class and that of race for a queer subject, or between the racialized misogyny faced (differently) by all straight women and the racialized homophobia faced (differently) by all gay men and lesbians. Nor do they engage the issue of how both gay white and straight white spaces serve class interests and how queer people of color might perceive the varying class inflections of those spaces. Certainly very little in queer theory has sought to answer such questions as effectively or with as much political conviction as some older works by feminists that queer theorists so often define themselves against. Given queer theory's promise to integrate race, sexuality, gender, and class, how have texts that do not fulfill that promise emerged as the field's classics? How do queer theory and lesbian and gay studies answer their discontents, those of us who signed on to their projects in the late 1980s and early 1990s, spending student budgets on Routledge books and GLQ only to find ourselves eventually (re)turning elsewhere for answers? And finally, what might an alternative to queer theory as it has come to be known in the U.S. academy look like?

In this essay I explore the construction of the dominant self-narratives of queer theory (queer genealogies) and some of their consequences. I then offer an alternative genealogy for critical thinking about sexuality in the United States, one that highlights the early emergence of intersectional thinking. This account is followed by an extended discussion of how some seminal texts in queer theory from the 1990s address (or fail to address) race, noting a consistent pattern of erasure, marginalization, and tokenization. I then explore a central claim to theoretical innovation within queer theory: the claim that the category of *queer* enables critique and transgression of boundaries, identities, and subject positions. Questioning some of the assumptions in this claim, I argue that it constitutes a form of ontological denial that enables queer theory to mask its own dependence on an unacknowledged white racial identity. The conclusion considers recent directions taken by activist-scholars who address the interrelations among race, gender, and sexuality. These include scholars who identify (often ambivalently) with queer theory and scholars who distance themselves from it. A closing look at recent work on the modern/colonial gender system points to some resources for thinking about sexuality outside the Eurocentric and colonial frameworks of queer theory.

Before continuing I want to separate my criticisms of broad tendencies (of which I see the texts and passages I discuss here as indicative) from a critique of individual theorists, their intentions, or the sum total of their ideas. For this reason I have chosen to engage with the projects of theorists whom I see as either especially prominent or generally sympathetic to my own positions. To see my position as one of rejection would be to participate in one of the things for which I criticize gay and lesbian studies and queer theory: the tendency to view criticism from people of color as external rather than internal to gay, lesbian, and queer debate. I hope that others will approach this essay as a productive engagement with queer theorists.[2]

QUEER GENEALOGIES

Genealogies of queer theory and gay and lesbian studies became something of a cottage industry in the 1990s. From these genealogies emerge two dominant narratives of the birth of queer theory, which I will call the *separatist* and *integrationist* accounts. Neither mutually exclusive nor solely identifiable with or identical to the positions of the authors with whom I associate them, these two accounts reflect differences in emphasis and strategy (for example, I see Sedgwick's *Epistemology of the Closet* as primarily separatist, but her later book, *Tendencies*, as primarily integrationist). Separatist and integrationist accounts differ most in their narration of the institutionalization of the academic study of sexuality in the United States and of its relation to feminism.

The proponents of separatist accounts for queer theory focus on the articulation of sexuality (sometimes, but not always, understood as only lesbian and gay sexuality) as distinct from gender, race, and class. These narratives depend for their coherence, however, on the erasure or rejection of several decades of persistent calls within feminism, antiracist movements, and lesbian and gay of color theory and activism to understand how different aspects of identity interconnect and mutually constitute each other so as to make separation futile at best and mystifying at worst. In offering a genealogy for queer theory proponents of the separatist account generally begin with Rubin's "Thinking Sex," one of the first articles to stake out a postfeminist space for theorizing sexuality. The essay is often characterized as a sex-positive response to feminism: feminism of the 1970s, lesbian feminism, Catherine McKinnon's feminism, or the feminism of Rubin's own *The Traffic in Women* (1975). Rubin argues that one should not reduce the politics of sexuality to the politics of gender and that it is therefore a mistake to assume that feminism (understood as the politics of gender) should occupy a privileged site for understanding all the workings of sexuality in our society. For her the politics of sexuality include the demands of prostitutes, "boy-lovers," and s/m practitioners, as well as gay men and lesbians. She therefore advocates the creation of "an accurate, humane, and genuinely liberatory body of thought about sexuality." She claims that feminism has (or rather had) not (yet) done this. Rubin is aware of the multiplicity of approaches to sexuality within feminism from its earliest days to the present. However, she advocates for a separate theorizing of sexuality, "challeng[ing] the assumption that feminism is or should be the privileged site of a theory of sexuality," reducing feminism to "the theory of gender oppression." She goes on to argue, "It is essential to separate gender and sexuality analytically to more accurately reflect their separate social existence. This goes against the grain of much contemporary feminist thought, which treats sexuality as a derivation of gender."[3] By collapsing *feminism* into *gender* and then pointing out the lack of congruence between sexuality and gender, Rubin argues for the study of sexuality outside of a feminist context.

In *Epistemology of the Closet* Eve Sedgwick takes her cue from Rubin. Defining *sexuality* more narrowly than Rubin does, Sedgwick provides a persuasive account of the uniqueness and importance of the binary division between homosexuality and heterosexuality in Western culture. Biddy Martin has carefully delineated Sedgwick's theoretical moves: the analytical separation of sexuality from gender and from race and the consequent argument for disarticulating gay theory from feminism and antiracist theory.[4] Paradoxically Sedgwick's argument for separating sexuality from gender relies on Rubin's claim that the polymorphous quality of sexuality is lost when its forms that focus on gender relations are privileged. Sedgwick continues, however, to privilege that classification of sexuality that is made according to gender of sexual object choice (homo-hetero) and to privilege especially male homosexuality, making her project gender-specific while simultaneously claiming to investigate sexuality without viewing it in relation to gender.

Writing in 1996 Lauren Berlant and Michael Warner further develop a separatist account of queer theory, charting the contours of what they loosely characterize as "queer commentary," something that "cannot be assimilated to a single discourse, let alone a propositional program." They do, however, have a sense of how queer commentary differs from lesbian and gay studies:

> Queer commentary has refused to draw boundaries around its constituency. And without forgetting the importance of the hetero-homo distinction of object choice in modern culture, queer work wants to address the full range of power-ridden normativities of sex. . . . Queer commentary in this sense is not necessarily superior to or more inclusive than conventional lesbian and gay studies; the two have overlapping but different aims and therefore potentially different publics.[5]

Queer commentary thus promises a broad and expansive study of sexuality. In keeping with both Rubin and Sedgwick, however, Berlant and Warner do not see queer commentary as necessarily promising a greater attentiveness to race or class. Rather it simply offers a different kind of attentiveness to sexuality, although one might wonder how different, given that queer commentary still seeks to separate sexuality from race—or at least to leave the whiteness of its object of study unmarked. Warner has elsewhere charted a genealogy for "queer social theory," which he situates within a lineage of radical thought that includes Georges Bataille and Herbert Marcuse as well as white gay liberationists and white feminists. He notes that queer theories of sexuality have been unable to answer fundamental questions about "whether or in what context queers have political interests, *as queers*, that connect them to broader demands for justice and freedom." The emphasis he gives to "as queers" perhaps indicates why, for example, he does not imagine a queer political genealogy beginning with (or at least including) James Baldwin, Bayard Rustin, or Audre Lorde. Indeed, citing Sedgwick, Warner is at pains to separate sexuality as a political issue from race and gender (which he associates with reproductive metaphors): "This very incommensurability between genetic and erotic logics suggests that queerness, race, and gender can never be brought into parallel alignment." Warner is aware of relations among these categories, but he argues that it is the unique task of queer social theory to "disarticulate" them as "styles of politics."[6]

Integrationist accounts of queer theory, on the other hand, attempt to respond to the challenges posed by the multiplicity of identity that separatist accounts avoid. While separatists attempt to distinguish or "disarticulate" sexuality from race and gender, integrationists advocate for queer theory as a way to address the multiple relations among race, gender, class, and sexuality better than how feminism or other progressive movements and theories have. Integrationists do so most often, however, by eschewing or bracketing identity questions and using the deliberately vague category queer to blur lines among different social locations. The most strident versions, drawing from postmodern critiques of the subject, see identity itself as oppressive and always or nearly always dangerous. They dismiss the concept of identity, writing instead of "discourses," "practices," "desires," and the "subjects" that they create. In her introduction to "Queer Theory," a special issue of differences, de Lauretis recounts the motivations behind a conference held in 1990, from which the special issue emerged:

> It was my hope that the conference would also problematize some of the discursive constructions and constructed silences in the emergent field of "gay and lesbian studies," and would further explore questions . . . such as the respective and/or common grounding of current discourses and practices of homo-sexualities in relation to gender and to race, with their attendant differences of class or ethnic culture, generational, geographical, and socio-political location.

As de Lauretis chronicles the emergence of lesbian and gay studies and theory she notes the separate trajectories of white gay studies and white feminism in the 1970s and 1980s. Next she introduces race, noting how little critical work has been produced by lesbians and gay men of color and suggesting that this may be due both to "restricted institutional access to publishing and higher education" and to "different choices, different work priorities, different constituencies and forms of address." She adds that the importance of race "urge[s] the reframing of the questions of queer theory from different perspectives, histories, experiences, and in different terms."[7] In her account gay liberationism and lesbian feminism appear to have been developed by whites without significant participation from people of color, with the consequence that their histories can be told without reference to works by people of color. The issue of how race relates to sexuality is asked at a chronologically later time, and will now be addressed by queer theory.

In his contribution to *Fear of a Queer Planet* Steven Seidman also separates lesbians and gay men of color from gay liberation and lesbian feminist discourses, portraying them instead as external critics of those discourses and of identity politics more generally. For example, Seidman discusses the sex wars in feminism separately from (and prior to) the critical writings of gays and lesbians of color. He associates these debates on sex "with publications such as *Pleasure and Danger*, *The Powers of Desire*, *Heresies*, *On Our Backs*, and . . . the writings of Pat Califia, Gayle Rubin, Dorothy Allison, Amber Hollibaugh, [and] Susie Bright." In two footnotes on the sex wars he cites several volumes and journals and fourteen individual articles; none of the articles is by a person of color.[8] This account of the sex wars erases the contributions of Cherríe Moraga, hattie gossett, Hortense Spillers, Rennie Simson, Felicita García, Jacquelyn Dowd Hall, Barbara Omolade, and Jayne Cortez, among others, to *Pleasure and Danger*, *The Powers of Desire*, and the sex issue of *Heresies*. How can that many women of color be invisible? Why this rewriting of history? Both de Lauretis and Seidman erase people of color from the center of debate in order to reintroduce them later at the margins of gay and lesbian theory.

The key issue separating integrationist from separatist accounts is most sharply honed in the work of Judith Butler, for whom the very existence of identity is at least part of the problem.[9] For Butler the individual subject comes into existence as subjugated by identity. Since there is "no outside" to the constituted frame of domination, resistance lies in dismantling identity through parody and reiteration. Like de Lauretis and Seidman, Butler enlists antiracist critiques to fortify her anti-identitarian position, making them external rather than internal to feminism. She argues that a new discourse is necessary to "remain self-critical with respect to the totalizing gestures of feminism."[10] This new discourse will serve more adequately, one presumes, the political needs of women of color, among others.

Queer theorists who favor the integrationist account tend to focus on the movement away from identity-based theorizing and politics toward analyses of power and desire as fundamental to the constitution of subjectivity. For the integrationist account queer theorizing will more adequately attend to nuances of race, class, geography, and other aspects of social location than identity-based theories of sexual oppression. These narratives often depend for their coherence, however, on ignoring earlier calls for understanding interconnections among forms of identity or on mischaracterizing such calls as external rather than internal critiques of the identity-based projects of feminism, gay liberation, lesbian feminism, and antiracist and anticolonial theory and activism. One could make any number of criticisms of both separatist and integrationist genealogies and what they imply about the nature of queer theory. Among other things they render "theorists of color" two-dimensional by assuming that we all make the same critique with the same theoretical tools. We seem to be rarely, if ever, useful to white queer theorists, except insofar as our words can be tucked into footnotes to support their claims.

I would like to counter these genealogies of queer theory with an alternative timeline. Though it is necessarily incomplete, I believe it to be illuminating nonetheless:

1962   James Baldwin publishes *Another Country*, a complex novel that focuses on the impact of multiple, shifting gender, racial, class, and sexual identities on interpersonal relationships. He later publishes *Just above My Head* (1979), which returns to many of the same themes.

1977   Barbara Smith argues for an inseparable understanding of race, gender, and sexuality in "Toward a Black Feminist Criticism."

1978   Audre Lorde articulates a strategy for integrating the power of eroticism into all aspects of life, including work and politics, in *Uses of the Erotic*. Pat Parker publishes *Movement in Black*.

1978   Foucault's *The History of Sexuality: An Introduction* is translated into English, bringing his account of the social construction and "implantation" of sexual identities to a U.S. readership.[11]

1979   The Combahee River Collective writes "A Black Feminist Statement," defending an identity politics based on the interrelations among race, class, gender, and sexuality.

1980   Adrienne Rich first publishes "Compulsory Heterosexuality and Lesbian Existence," arguing, among other things, that heterosexuality is enforced and reproduced through a complex series of erasures and injunctions and that it "needs to be recognized and studied as a *political institution*."[12]

1981   Cherríe Moraga and Amber Hollibaugh coauthor "What We're Rollin' Around in Bed With: Sexual Silences in Feminism." Published in the sex issue of *Heresies*, it articulates a complex understanding of the interplay between masculinity, femininity, eroticism, fantasy, race, and class in lesbian desire.

1981   Moraga and Gloria Anzaldúa co-edit *This Bridge Called My Back*, a collection of writings by women of color arguing for an identity-based politics (U.S. Third World feminism) that is attentive to multiplicity and the various contexts of economic exploitation.

1982   Gloria Hull, Patricia Bell Scott, and Barbara Smith publish *All the Women Are White, All the Blacks Are Men, But Some of Us Are Brave*, followed by Smith's *Home Girls* (1983), providing numerous arguments for interconnection and multiplicity.

1983   Moraga's *Loving in the War Years* expresses a keen understanding of the fundamental inseparability of race, class, gender, and sexuality.

1983   Marilyn Frye publishes *The Politics of Reality*, in which she argues for the need to understand sexual and gender identities as simultaneously racial and that gay men should embrace their marginality, demand citizenship "as women" instead of "as men," and invent new ways of enjoying the erotic possibilities of penises and male bodies.[13]

1983–84   The collections *Powers of Desire*, edited by Ann Snitow, Christine Stansell, and Sharon Thompson, and *Pleasure and Danger*, edited by Carole S. Vance, present challenges to restrictive notions of sexuality assumed by many in the feminist movement and strong statements about the mutual constitution of race and gender.

1984   Rubin argues in "Thinking Sex" that feminism has not and cannot articulate a radical theory of sexuality because it is only a theory of gender oppression.[14]

1986   Joseph Beam edits *In the Life: A Black Gay Anthology*, bringing a large number of out black gay male voices to the critical scene for the first time.

1987   Anzaldúa publishes *Borderlands/La Frontera*, relating the epistemological significance of being queer to being a woman of color and urging people to listen to their *jotería* (queer folk).[15]

1989   In *Essentially Speaking* Diana Fuss claims that black women theorists have shown a preference for essentialist modes of theorizing, rather than embracing poststructuralist critiques of identity.[16]

1990   Sedgwick's *Epistemology of the Closet* and Butler's *Gender Trouble* are published, the former arguing for an analytic separation of the "axis of sexuality" from other social axes of identity, the latter arguing for the need to subvert identity and to move away from identity-based politics.[17]

1991   Fuss edits *Inside/Out* and de Lauretis edits a special issue of *differences*, titled "Queer Theory: Lesbian and Gay Sexualities," in which she coins the term *queer theory* and laments the fact that queers of color have not produced much theory.[18]

Most accounts of the origins of queer theory do not introduce these texts in this order. More often they list the texts by white authors first, followed by those by people of color—presumably because most queer theorists first read the texts in that order. However, the repetition of a false chronology cements a genealogy for queer theory that obscures the presence of queer people of color and thereby misrepresents the shortcomings and errors of many of the texts by white theorists.

In light of the actual publication of critical work on race and sexuality by queers of color, I would like to propose that we have been there all along, and that arguments for an analysis of race, gender, class, and sexuality as inseparable are nothing particularly new, while arguments for their separation should be viewed with some suspicion as to their political motivations. Most queer genealogies chart a movement away from feminism to a study of sexuality and then a later addition of the question of race by people of color and queer theorists. However, critiques of mainstream feminism by straight women of color, white lesbians, and lesbians of color in the late 1970s and early 1980s were often accompanied (sometimes ambivalently) by calls for more complicated analyses of sexuality and desire *as they relate to and complicate analyses of gender, race, and class.* Later many queer theorists moved to separate sexuality from gender, race, and class as a unique concern, justifying this move in part with the claim that sexuality is not *reducible* to the terms of the other categories. The move to isolate sexuality as a field of inquiry, however, simultaneously marginalizes the legacy of intersectional analysis and centers critical work that takes the whiteness of its objects of study for granted. In other words, theorists with an implicit commitment to maintaining the centrality of whiteness can claim to be doing the basic work of sexuality to which "race scholars" will add.

Queer theory and lesbian and gay studies have never adequately addressed the fact that they are founded on the erasure of a substantial body of critical literature by people of color at the same time that these bodies of work are *included* in queer genealogies for strategic purposes.[19] Queer genealogies are written so that theorists of color are simultaneously marginal and new; white theorists provide insights into sexuality, and then theorists of color (and writings by working-class queers) show how sexuality varies in other contexts. I have argued elsewhere for an understanding of identity and oppression that is *always* attentive to the constant interrelations (rather than occasional "intersections") among race, gender, sexuality, and class, taking issue implicitly with what I have here called the "separatist" account.[20] I have also discussed elsewhere some of the problems with many attempts by gay liberation advocates and feminists in the 1970s to construct grand narratives.[21] These attempts frequently sought to locate the single historical foundation for all oppression and often resulted in gross reductions, like Shulamith Firestone's equation, "Racism is sexism extended."[22] Such reductionism was not the only way activist scholars in the 1970s attempted to understand the mutually constitutive nature of oppression. Others, predominantly women of color, sought to relate modes of oppression *without* simply reducing them to a single cause. Ironically many of these very calls against subsuming oppressions into one another were later cited as justification for separating them or for seeking to do away with the category of identity altogether.

QUEER DISCONTENT

Many insightful critiques exist of queer theory's engagement with race. Most of the canonical works of queer theory portray people of color as adding colorful, additional considerations to central questions about sexuality, without ever completely integrating an analysis of race into their primary frameworks. Biddy Martin, for example, has written about tendencies in some queer theory to cast "sexuality as that which exceeds, transgresses, or supersedes gender [and race.]" Gender and race, in turn, are then "construed as stagnant and ensnaring."[23] She has most notably directed her critiques at Sedgwick's axioms in *Epistemology of the Closet* and what Martin describes as an occasional overemphasis in Butler's work on "sexual differences and defiances of norms" that make invisible the "difference that it makes to be a women."[24] Evelynn Hammonds has further argued, "While it has been acknowledged that race is not simply additive to, or derivative of sexual difference, few white feminists have attempted to move beyond simply stating this point to describe the powerful effect that race has on the construction and representation of gender and sexuality." In her detailed reading of de Lauretis's introduction to "Queer Theory," a special issue of *differences*, Hammonds notes that de Lauretis includes in queer theory's goals the theorization of the complex interrelations of race, ethnicity, and class. Hammonds demonstrates that the special issue "fail[s] to theorize the very questions de Lauretis announces that the term 'queer' will address."[25] We can see how queer theory, following an integrationist account, has treated race by looking at three influential texts: *The Lesbian and Gay Studies Reader*, Sedgwick's *Tendencies*, and Butler's *Bodies That Matter*. (Rather than treating the ideas of all these works in their entirety, I hope to provide illustrations that can contribute to a picture of certain general directions in queer theory.)

Abelove, Barale, and Halperin's *The Lesbian and Gay Studies Reader* is racially diverse in subject matter and contributors, although many of the contributions to this and other queer collections that deal with race function according to a logic of tokenism, made to bear the burden of representing "difference." In *The Lesbian and Gay Studies Reader* contributions by theorists of color are not shunted off into a special section on race and ethnicity but integrated into "central" categories of analysis; however, in the anthology's "User's Guide," out of forty-two essays in the volume only two pieces by white theorists (Biddy Martin and Cindy Patton) are listed under "African American Studies" or "Ethnic Studies." One therefore wants to ask what function the essays by people of color serve in the context of the whole. Each category within the anthology seems to demarcate a particular field of inquiry within lesbian and gay studies, and most of the essays in that category offer theorization of and investigation into that topic. Contributions by people of color usually serve to provide a look into how that topic relates to race. Tomás Almaguer's "Chicano Men" is a useful example. The function of that essay in the collection is largely to present another, different construction of sexuality. This presentation throws Anglo gay male desire into relief, but simultaneously reaffirms it as the central construction of sexuality. A false sense of homogeneity within the group of Chicano gay men is implied, while Anglo gay male sexuality, treated diversely throughout the anthology, is allowed to float free of the fixed otherness to which Chicano gay sexuality has been tethered. Chicano gay sexuality is presented as a colorful addition to the anthology, while the category of Anglo gay sexuality is never named as a racial or ethnic identity and never questioned as such. Contributions to Fuss's *Inside/Out*, Warner's *Fear of a Queer Planet*, and Elizabeth Weed's and Naomi Schor's *Feminism Meets Queer Theory* that deal with race function similarly. In *Fear of a Queer Planet*, for example, the definitional centrality of white queerness is unquestioned (with the possible exception of Jonathan Goldberg's "Sodomy in the New World"). The two essays focusing on contemporary articulations of race fall largely into the pattern I have already noted. They analyze specific manifestations of homophobia in black communities, while the remaining essays in the volume do not present themselves as analyses of white communities, but as analyses of sexual politics, heteronormativity, and homophobia in general. Like salsa at a Thanksgiving dinner, contributions by queers of color remain zesty outsiders as long as the normative centrality assumed by white queer sexualities goes unquestioned.[26]

In *Tendencies* Sedgwick pushes further the theses of *Epistemology of the Closet*, although she pulls back from the separatist emphasis of the earlier book, embracing at times an integrationist queer theoretical approach with regard to race. In the first chapter of *Tendencies* she writes that one of the advantages of the term *queer* is its ability to refer to such a wide variety of things. However, for political reasons, she also wants to retain a connection between *queer* and gay and lesbian sexualities. She visualizes the relation of *queer* to gay and lesbian identities through a spatial metaphor of center and periphery: "To displace [same-sex sexual object choice] from the term's definitional center, would be to dematerialize any possibility of queerness itself." Thus Sedgwick, fearing the possibly apolitical nature of a queer theory without homosexuals, positions homosexuality as central to the project of queer theory and politics. "At the same time," she writes, "a lot of the most exciting recent work around 'queer' spins the term outward along dimensions that can't be subsumed under gender and sexuality at all." Once again "intellectuals and artists of color" are positioned chronologically later ("recent work") and spatially outside, on the margins ("outward along [nonsexual] dimensions"). While it is true that Sedgwick considers this work to be some of the "most exciting" and that she believes it deepens and shifts the meaning and the "center of gravity" of the term *queer*, one must consider what her positioning of work on sexuality and race, ethnicity, and postcolonial identity does.[27] Work like her own, which addresses white, Western homosexuality but does not necessarily frame itself as *particular*, can pose as both the center and the point of origin. Work by theorists of color is positioned as derivative, even if interesting, because it takes something already developed by white theorists and adds to it.

Butler's *Bodies That Matter* makes the promising claim that "the symbolic . . . is also and always a racial industry, indeed, the reiterated practice of *racializing* interpellations."[28] Given this claim, one might reasonably expect her discussions in "The Lesbian Phallus and the Morphological Imaginary" and "Critically Queer" to analyze the role of racial discourses in shaping the histories of psychoanalysis, radical democratic theory, and poststructuralism. One might expect to glean from her book an understanding of how dominant Western theoretical discourses are "also and always" inflected by race, perhaps especially when that inflection is unacknowledged and taken for granted, that is, *white*. One would be disappointed, however. In *Bodies That Matter* race surfaces on two pages of the book's introduction (where the claim is made that race needs to always be taken into account) and in the two chapters of the book dealing with black and Latina and Latino subjects. Race, in other words, as figured in *Bodies That Matter* is *only* and *always* present in the presence of nonwhite bodies.[29] Without the presence of a black author or a Latina drag queen bearing the bodily stigmata of race and dragging them into the theorist's field of vision, the "discursive limits of 'sex'" become falsely universalized into a deracinated whiteness. In the presence of such bodily stigmata race plays an interesting role. In the chapters on Nella Larsen's novel *Passing* and Jennie Livingston's film *Paris Is Burning* race becomes a limit, the limit to the mobility of bodies and desires. It is fixed and corporeal. In both chapters raced (black and Latina and Latino) subjects who attempt to exercise the fluid mobility promised by postmodern theories of identity find death (Clare Kendry and Venus Xtravaganza). Through what chain of events does race (supposedly always present) come to equal black or Latina and Latino, and then come to equal limit, limitation, and fixedness, and then further come to equal death? What is the relationship between this chain of signification and the fact that the other, sometimes more optimistic chapters are articulated around genders, sexualities, and desires apparently understood as *free* of race (that is, *white*)? Butler makes that relationship clear in her chapter on the documentary *Paris Is Burning*, where she deflects her discussion from race to a consideration of the mobility of the film's white director, whose desire and gender ultimately prove to be the transgressive center of the chapter. The white director and the white theorist prove to be capable of performing the subversion of identity that their black and Latina and Latino subjects could not. Given the structure of the chapter, however, this transgression is visible only against the backdrop of the failed "performances" of the black and Latina/o gay men and transsexuals depicted in the film. Within the terms of Butler's analysis their failure—and death—is a prerequisite for the intelligibility of Livingston's and Butler's successful transgressions.[30]

WHITENESS, QUEERNESS, AND ONTOLOGICAL DENIAL

Despite the failure of so many canonical works in queer theory to live up to their own promises to address race complexly and fully, queer theory clearly offers something useful to theorists, as it has continued to entrench itself in the academy. I suspect that the success of queer theory actually has much to do with that failure. Its disavowal of race (in the separatist guise) and its disavowal of identity (in either guise), in other words, offer theorists of sexuality a means whereby they might disavow whiteness. Among theorists who have championed queer theory in opposition to gay and lesbian studies there has been particular enthusiasm for the claim that the term *queer* "does not designate an ontological category or substantive entity."[31] Annamarie Jagose, for example, claims that "the delegitimation of liberal, liberationist, ethnic and even separatist notions of identity generated the cultural space necessary for the emergence of the term 'queer'; its non-specificity guarantees it against recent criticisms made of the exclusionist tendencies of 'lesbian' and 'gay' as identity categories." She elaborates this claim as follows:

> Queer may be thought of as activating an identity politics so attuned to the constraining effects of naming, of delineating a foundational category which precedes and underwrites political intervention, that it may better be understood as promoting a non-identity—or even anti-identity—politics. . . . The discursive proliferation of queer has been enabled in part by the knowledge that identities are fictitious—that is, produced by and productive of material effects but nevertheless arbitrary, contingent and ideologically motivated.[32]

Jagose thus summarizes the most strident argument for the uniqueness of queer theory.

According to theorists like Jagose, *queer* may be related to other identities, such as gay and lesbian, but it is not a normal kind of identity because its deliberately imprecise reference to any ontological substance, category, or state of being helps queer theorists to avoid the pitfalls of essentialism and exclusion. As the literary critic Colleen Lamos writes, a queer "subject does not possess an authentic, inner self waiting to be set free but is constructed by means of acts that, tentatively and provisionally, presuppose it. Thus, 'we' queers act as if 'we' are what 'we' will only have become by acting now as if 'we' already were queer. Because the *as if* is always a *not yet*, we do not know where we will end up."[33] It is possible that Lamos means only that queer identity is not an a priori, natural essence. It is difficult, however, to imagine how this claim differs significantly from the kinds of claims that most critical race theorists would today make about blackness or a Latina or Latino identity, or the way that most feminists and other scholars would view *woman*—or *gay* or *lesbian*, for that matter. Most scholars today agree that *no* identities are a priori, natural essences. Why should this revelation be particularly queer? To put the question differently, what is *queer* about queer theory? As Jagose suggests, many queer theorists are interested in something specific to *queerness* that makes queer identity (or anti-identity) more flexible and less ontologically bound than other identities. It is at this level that Lamos's claim makes sense as a claim about queer theory's uniqueness. Both Lamos and Jagose cite Butler's discussion of the term *queer* in *Bodies That Matter*. Butler, however, does not argue that queer is a nonidentity or that it is somehow different from other identities. Her concern is that the term's history of derogatory usage might prevent reinterpretation as a positive articulation of identity. She therefore *advocates for* a consistently self-critical and open use of the term (as well as such a use of *lesbian* and *gay*) rather than *describing* its use as in fact being consistently self-critical and open.

Butler's call, however, assumes a more general view of "the subject" that rejects the notion of a preexisting ontological substance as a referent for any identity whatsoever. Butler claims that one comes into existence as a given identity through performative speech acts (speech acts that bring something into being rather than describing something that already exists). A performative cannot succeed, however, without the authority lent it by a history of prior invocations: "If a performative provisionally succeeds . . . then it is not because an intention successfully governs the action of speech, but only because that action echoes prior actions, and *accumulates the force of authority through the repetition or citation of a prior, authoritative set of practices.*"[34] There is, then, never intention, but only repetition—no "doer behind the deed." Based on this model one can see why Lamos would describe the queer subject as posited in advance of its existence. The performative act of identity takes place in the present, constituting the subject, but that subject, which comes into being after the act, is assumed to exist first—before the performative act brings it into being—as the author or intention behind the act that will constitute it.[35] The philosophical core of queer theory's anti-identitarian argument in its most strident form thus runs as follows. There is no subject before its constitution by discourse because discursive acts create the subject along with the invocation of an identity. Identity therefore defines a person in a limited, arbitrary, and fictitious way, but also allows that person to exist as a subject with some kind of agency. Although identities are thus necessary (according to some) and enabling (in a limited way), one must subvert them in order to undo the exclusions performed by their limited and arbitrary nature. Queer anti-identitarianism furthermore *sometimes* contends that something specific to *queer* allows for this subversion. Through deliberate imprecision or lack of an ontological referent, *queer* is assumed to avoid the fixed exclusions of other identity labels.

However, enough evidence exists to find this ostensibly profound claim profoundly objectionable. In fact one might ask whether *queer* always subverts other identities, or whether it sometimes just hides them. For the history of the term's use is not the only history that one must take into account. In keeping with the idea that the queer subject does not preexist its performative invocation, Sedgwick suggests (albeit coyly and perhaps with tongue in cheek) that "what it takes—all it takes—to make the description 'queer' a true one is the impulse to use it in the first person." [36] Yet I wonder whether, to the contrary, one must already be recognized by others as in some way queer in order to use the term in the first person successfully. For example, if I call myself *queer*, my use of that term will be successful partly because a sufficient number of other people accept that my new identity makes sense (since identities are social). That success will have a lot to do with the already established fact of my identity as a gay man. By contrast, if my heterosexual friend begins to call herself *queer*, many people (not least of all her husband) will have many questions for her about what she means by that, questions that no one would ever ask about *my* queer identity. My point is not that my heterosexual friend cannot be or become queer, but that the possibilities for her success in being recognized as queer are different from my own. This has less to do with her practices and sense of self than with the facts of her social identity as they have taken shape over the course of her life. In other words, the kinds of identities that she and I already have determine differently the possibilities for our inhabiting a socially intelligible queer identity.

Furthermore queer, as an identity, is dependent upon *certain* other kinds of identities and histories—identities and histories that can be successfully (re) described as queer in an intersubjective way. Butler concedes that one cannot simply make *queer* mean whatever one wants it to mean; its use is constrained by the history of previous uses. According to Butler the term has a history, but the subject using the term does not. However, as my example shows, subjects always do have their own history, a history that includes an identity. Something about a queer subject's history and identity has moved it to take up the term *queer* and to use it in the first person. Since the subject is inseparable from its identity (although both might change over time), that identity and its historical construction are part of the context for using the term *queer*. In addition, since one's preexisting identity is social, a public sense of that identity is necessary for success in calling oneself queer. The questions posed to my heterosexual friend about her queerness are a case in point, seeking to establish intersubjectively a sense of whether and how her preexisting identity was or was not queer, and if it was not, then how it may or may not have become queer. (This process might include a renegotiation of the definition of *queer*.) The preexisting identity that motivates one to call oneself queer is thus *always* part of the context in which one can become queer at all. In other words, there would appear to be both always *and already* a potentially queer doer behind the queer deed.

More specifically—and this is crucial—identities such as gay and lesbian have a privileged position in relation to queer identification. While the possibilities for identifying as queer may be *relatively* open, some identities have a closer relationship to the term than others do, as Sedgwick reminds us. Furthermore those relationships and identities continue to function within queer identification rather than simply being replaced or subverted. Anti-identitarian uses of *queer* like those of Jagose and Lamos, however, perform an erasure of the queer subject after the fact. They imply that queer acts and identifications have taken place without a queer (or lesbian or gay) agent—a sleight of hand that renders the theorist (seemingly) invisible and irrelevant. This erasure allows queer theorists to suggest that *queer* enacts a subject posited in advance rather than simply renaming an already existing subject. The ontological denial that queer theory performs in order to erase the presence of the (surprisingly stable) identities behind *queer* can do more harm than good to the project of creating new possibilities for queer subjects. Too often the turn from *gay and lesbian* to the purportedly less identity-bound *queer* allows theorists to duck responsibility for thinking about how more traditional identities function in their work, that is, how *queer* can all too easily and without notice simply stand in for "white gay men and lesbians." It is as if once one makes the disclaimer ("I am talking about *queer*, not *gay* or *lesbian*—sex and desire, not identity"), one no longer needs to critically question the white identities hiding behind the queer curtain.[37] As Dorothy and company discovered in Oz, however, there is always a body behind the curtain, and it rarely appears as ethereal or impressive as the smoke and mirrors.

BEYOND QUEER THEORY? SEXUALITY, EUROCENTRISM, AND THE COLONIAL DIFFERENCE

The version of this essay that I published in 2001 concluded with some brief considerations of the then current state of queer theory, suggesting that some newer work on queerness, gender, race, and class was beginning to emerge.[38] I argued that it was vital to understand how sexuality and other aspects of identity are interrelated and how their apparent separateness is created by and facilitates domination and exploitation. I suggested that a "critical" queer theory might explore how expressions of homosexuality in Europe, North America, and Australia depend for their positive articulation on the imperially established position of power of the so-called West over the so-called non-West as well as how that very articulation of a gay or lesbian identity might enable some forms of resistance in Africa, the Americas, Asia, and the Pacific that may ultimately prove anticapitalist and anti-imperialist. One should not assume in advance that the point of origin of modern gay and lesbian identities will give them an essentially imperialist character, anymore than that their originally resistant character will remain unchanged across time and cultures. I argued that such an approach to sexuality would need to draw from activist scholars who have been theorizing at the intersections of race, gender, class, and sexuality for decades: from earlier theorists like Audre Lorde, Cherríe Moraga, Gloria Anzaldúa, Joan Nestle, Pat Parker, Barbara Smith, Bernice Johnson Reagon, and Marilyn Frye, to recent scholars like Jackie Goldsby, Deena González, Coco Fusco, Deborah McDowell, Essex Hemphill, Kobena Mercer, Paula Moya, Cindy Patton, Ramón Gutiérrez, Alan Bérubé, and Mab Segrest, to name but a few.

Since that time a virtual renaissance of what Roderick Ferguson calls "queer of color critique" has emerged. Any list would inevitably be incomplete but would likely include José Esteban Muñoz's *Disidentifications* (1999), José Quiroga's *Tropics of Desire* (2000), David Eng's *Racial Castration* (2001), Linda Garber's *Identity Poetics* (2001), Robert Reid-Pharr's *Black Gay Man* (2001), Ann Stoler's *Carnal Knowledge* (2002), María Lugones's *Pilgrimages/Peregrinajes* (2003), Martin Manalansan's *Global Divas* (2003), Juana María Rodríguez's *Queer Latinidad* (2003), Ferguson's *Aberrations in Black* (2004), M. Jacqui Alexander's *Pedagogies of Crossing* (2005), Gayatri Gopinath's *Impossible Desires* (2005), Dwight McBride's *Why I Hate Abercrombie and Fitch* (2005), Catriona Rueda Esquibel's *With Her Machete in Her Hand* (2006), and collections like David Eng's and Alice Hom's *Q & A: Queer in Asian America* (1998), Arnaldo Cruz-Malavé's and Martin Manalansan's *Queer Globalizations* (2002), and E. Patrick Johnson's and Mae G. Henderson's *Black Queer Studies* (2005).

While far from univocal, this scholarship has fundamentally transformed the landscape of gay, lesbian, and queer studies. Furthermore many, although not all, of these authors demonstrate ambivalence about the formal body of scholarship known as "queer theory." Ferguson, for example, grounds his book in citations to Karl Marx and to women of color feminists, eschewing the canonical texts of queer theory. Rather than explicitly marking a break, however, he scrupulously avoids any engagement, critical or otherwise, instead carving out an alternative scholarly tradition, not unlike the one I outlined above. Lugones's *Pilgrimages* similarly avoids direct engagement with most scholars identified with queer theory, instead drawing from lesbian feminists, women of color feminists, and radical philosophers. Alexander, while not naming queer theory specifically, delineates significant lines of political and epistemological incompatibility between white feminist theory, based in "hegemonic European thought," and "social thought emerging from communities and geographies of color."[39] While Garber often sees more compatibility than difference between queer theory and women of color and lesbian feminisms, she makes queer theorists' erasure of intersectional analyses of race, class, and gender the central thesis of her book.[40]

The tensions among scholars of race and sexuality over the legacy of queer theory emerges most pointedly in the special issue of *Social Text* published in 2005, titled "What's Queer about Queer Studies Now?" The introduction, by David Eng, with Judith Halberstam and José Muñoz, opens by repeating the more dominant genealogy that I examined earlier, dating the emergence of *queer* "around 1990," defining *queer* as "a political metaphor without a fixed referent," and calling for a "renewed queer studies" in the present moment. It may or may not be noteworthy that the editors prefer *queer studies* and *queer critique* to *queer theory*, but the introduction seems to ground its understanding of the term in the dominant theoretical assumptions of the field:

> That queerness remains open to a continuing critique of its exclusionary operations has always been one of the field's key theoretical and political promises. What might be called the "subjectless" critique of queer studies disallows any positing of a proper subject *of* or object *for* the field by insisting that queer has no fixed political referent. Such an understanding orients queer epistemology, despite the historical necessities of "strategic essentialism" . . . , as a continuous deconstruction of the tenets of positivism at the heart of identity politics. Attention to queer epistemology also insists that sexuality—the organizing rubric of lesbian and gay studies—must be rethought for its positivist assumption. A subjectless critique establishes, in Michael Warner's phrase, a focus on "a wide field of normalization" as the site of social violence.

While slyly and strategically using the rhetoric of queer ontological denial to move race to the center of queer theoretical debate (since sexuality cannot assume a privileged place as the subject of *queer*), the introduction risks an endorsement of some of queer theory's most problematic theoretical baggage. The editors acknowledge, however, that "queer studies" may not be the most important disciplinary framework or theoretical legacy for all of the contributors to the volume (alternatives include women of color and transnational feminisms, critical race theory, queer of color critique, or queer diaspora studies). They also note the limitations of much "mainstream queer studies," noting, "Much of queer theory nowadays sounds like a metanarrative about the domestic affairs of white homosexuals."[41]

Despite this criticism of mainstream queer studies and the acknowledgment that not all critical work on race and sexuality comes out of queer studies, the commitment to a form of queer ontological denial and the dating of queer studies at 1990 lies in tension with efforts by several contributors to distance themselves from dominant narratives of queer theory. Ferguson, for example, while characterizing his contribution to the special issue as an attempt to "intervene in queer studies," specifically distinguishes his work (and queer of color critique) from queer studies. Noting that "women of color feminism has the longest engagement with racialized sexuality," he argues that queer studies has understood itself as "the only and most significant" field of sexual inquiry by taking Foucault's *History of Sexuality* "as the principal engagement with the question of sexuality." He adds, "Doing so has meant occluding critical sexual formations that preceded queer studies and Foucault's wonderful intervention, formations such as women of color feminism."[42] Similarly Halberstam argues that "the future of queer studies . . . depends absolutely on moving away from white gay male identity politics and learning from the radical critiques offered by a younger generation of queer scholars who draw their intellectual inspiration from feminism and ethnic studies rather than white queer studies."[43] Most strongly in tension with the invocation of ontological denial is Hiram Pérez's contribution, which begins by noting, "Queer theorists who can invoke that transparent [white] subject, and choose to do so, reap the dividends of whiteness." He goes on to connect this transparent white subject to the subjectless queer of queer studies, in a way similar to what I have done above. He writes, "A great deal of queer theorizing has sought to displace identity politics with an alternative anti-identitarian model. . . . It is not surprising then to find buried underneath the boots of this establishmentarian anti-identity all sorts of dissident bodies."[44] I would ask the authors of the issue's introduction: If a "subjectless" queer critique continues to hide the significant differentiation still necessary between *queers of color* and *white queers, queer women, queer men,* and *trans queers, rich queers* and *poor queers, first-world queers* and *third-world queers,* then which "identity politics" precisely has "queer epistemology" successfully "deconstructed"?

Despite moments of convergence with queer theory, one might conceive a distinction between much of the new work on race and sexuality and mainstream queer studies along the lines of what Walter Mignolo calls "the colonial difference."[45] In other words, queer theorists tend to understand the history of sexuality from within a Eurocentric frame. "Modern sexuality" therefore emerges in the eighteenth or nineteenth century alongside the emergence of industrial capitalism, liberalism, and the nation-state. By contrast, for scholars studying race and sexuality modern sexuality emerges alongside the violence of European colonialism and indigenous resistance in the sixteenth century, the transatlantic slave trade in the seventeenth century, the imperialist wars and expansion of Europe and its former settler colonies in the Americas, southern Africa, and the Pacific in the nineteenth century, and the waves of postcolonial independence in the twentieth century. Sexuality looks dramatically different emerging from the first, Eurocentric narrative than from the second narrative. Furthermore these different points of origin for theorizing sexuality—these different loci of enunciation—have profound consequences for the relative identity attachments of queer theory and queer of color critique.

If class, gender, race, and sexuality are mutually constitutive, then they have given shape to one another over many centuries.[46] Following through with a similar claim, the philosopher María Lugones argues that the elaboration of racial hierarchies and Eurocentrism occurred coextensively with a reorganization of gender roles and the elaboration of two sides to what she dubs the "colonial/modern gender system." That is to say that its emergence resulted in two distinct ways of understanding gender. Both emerge interdependently and are thoroughly both modern and colonial insofar as the colonial relations constitutive of the modern era brought them together into being. This system made gender intelligible for Europeans by conceiving of white men and women as biologically dimorphic and adhering, respectively, to conceptions of activity and passivity, reason and emotion, publicity and privacy, and so on. By contrast the other side of the gender system imposed a different gendering on colonized peoples. For example, Europeans did not always think of colonized peoples as biologically dimorphic and did not necessarily even accord them genders, the violence of colonialism having constructed them as bestial and outside of modernity, civilization, and human gender:

> Females excluded from [the category of women] were . . . understood to be animals in a sense that went further than the identification of white women with nature, infants, and small animals. They were understood as animals in the deep sense of "without gender," sexually marked as female, but without the characteristics of femininity. Women racialized as inferior were turned

from animals into various modified versions of "women" as it fit the processes of global, Eurocentered capitalism. Thus heterosexual rape of Indian or African slave women coexisted with concubinage, as well as with the imposition of the heterosexual understanding of gender relations among the colonized—when and as it suited global, Eurocentered capitalism, and heterosexual domination of white women.[47]

In other words, the elaboration of a modern and colonial world system entailed violent processes that sought to devalue and disenfranchise colonized women. This necessitated the wholesale redrawing of traditional gender roles in many cultures across Africa, the Americas, Asia, and the Pacific through "slow, discontinuous, and heterogeneous processes that violently inferiorized colonized women." The dismantling of gender relations among colonized peoples and the imposition of new gender relations were central, according to Lugones and many other scholars, to "disintegrating" the relations, rituals, local economic structures, and forms of decision making that nourished resistance to European domination.[48]

Within the emerging colonial/modern gender system sexual difference from Europeans became simultaneously a justification for imperial subjection and an explanation for the economic and political inferiority brought on by colonialism. The processes of establishing military and economic dominance in a region and of elaborating beliefs about racial supremacy, in other words, entailed the European colonizers' construal of the colonized as sexually deviant. They subsequently required the newly colonized peoples to model European ideals of sex and gender relations, often encouraging conformity by force. However, this system remained highly flexible, so that Europeans could envision colonial others as possessors of violent and barbaric sexualities or as developers of mysterious and libertine erotic arts, as hypersexual beasts in a state of nature or as asexual prudes caught up in overly repressive moral traditions. It all depended on who had the power to elaborate or to contest the rhetoric of gender, race, and sexuality in play and what they deemed necessary in a given time and place. Teresia K. Teaiwa, for example, has studied how missionaries to the Pacific islands violently sought to convert the indigenous inhabitants, imposing "civilization" and modesty on people seen to be too naked and sexually libertine. However, the Pacific has more recently become a destination for Europeans, North Americans, and Australians seeking a savage state of relaxation, and "Islanders are increasingly exposed to sun-seeking and seminude 'First-Worlders.'"[49] This pattern took on different details in different parts of the world but retained remarkable similarities in each instance. In an irony of history the eventual success of many colonized people in conforming to Eurocentric ideals of gender and sexual morality would eventually become a justification for additional imperial interventions, this time in the name of liberating "their" women and defending freedom for sexual minorities.

Elsewhere modern gay and lesbian identities began to emerge in resistance to homophobia in the twentieth century in Europe and North America, but the sexual and gender relations of heterosexuality and homosexuality that gave birth to them arose as part of the colonial/modern gender system. The model of heterosexuality that crystallized in nineteenth-century Europe and North America was but one stage in the long development of one side of that system. It came into existence alongside other, sometimes violently coerced, sometimes resistant understandings of gender and sexuality. As part of the other side of gender in colonial modernity, these alternative understandings continue to shape both colonial representations and postcolonial self-understandings of Africans, Asians, and indigenous peoples of the Americas and the Pacific, giving rise to several questions: Are gay and lesbian identities simply complicit with the coloniality of power, or do they demonstrate a strategy of resistance to it, parallel to other strategies enacted by colonized and formerly colonized peoples? Is the question too complex for an either/or? And what are the possibilities for developing sexual identities that reject not only homophobia, but also the racism and Eurocentrism of the colonial/modern gender system?

I ended the earlier version of this essay with a call for a critical queer theory and practice in which the multiplicity of subjectivity and the interconnection of oppressions within a context of capitalist exploitation are not blind spots to be pointed out, but rather matters of common sense. While I see no reason not to reiterate that call here, I would like to add two qualifications based on the foregoing discussion. Most obviously scholar-activist work doing precisely this has emerged over the past decade. I do not think that one should necessarily expect the ongoing development of this work to see itself in relation to queer theory at all. Indeed transformative understandings of the relationships among race, capitalism, gender, and sexuality are probably stronger precisely when elaborated from outside of Eurocentric frameworks and intellectual genealogies, rather than from within them. To add race and colonialism to queer theory is to overlook the formation of queer theory as thoroughly grounded in the Eurocentric narratives of the coloniality of power. It is to take European thought as a starting point rather than to begin with practices of resistance to the sexual violence of colonialism.

This is not to say that I find nothing useful (say, for a gay Chicano) in queer theory. However, the most prominent queer theorists have too often justified their scholarship and argued for its originality based on claims that it could link sexuality, power, and desire to considerations of race, gender, and society better than other, competing approaches. This is not merely an act of theoretical overreaching, but a strategic (if not cynical and opportunistic) *justification* for political relevance and theoretical originality based on the legitimizing force of antiracist politics in the U.S. academy of the 1990s. At the same time most queer theorists have systematically sought to define the newness and uniqueness of their scholarship through a denial of past and ongoing efforts to integrate considerations of class, gender, race, and sexuality, the origins of which predate queer theory. In addition many queer theorists have consistently resisted the consequences of a truly substantive, thorough, and ongoing engagement with theories that are centrally concerned with race and class from the other side of a deep epistemological divide. When queer theorists have included considerations of race it has frequently been through gestures of marginalization, paternalism, or tokenism. Scholarship like that of Alexander, Ferguson, and Lugones shows us that complex, subtle, and expansive theories of queer sexuality and even liberation need not originate from within the terms of queer theory. Those of us who share their interest in radical social transformation would do well to look to convergences of women of color feminisms, transnational feminisms, and anticolonial theorists. There we might find new and better understandings of the interrelation of race, sexuality, gender, and capitalism and new ways to think outside of the historical frameworks and intellectual legacies of Eurocentrism.

NOTES

1. Marcuse, *An Essay on Liberation*, 3–4.
2. One reader has suggested that my own critique of queer theory is in fact enabled by queer theory, insofar as "queer theory . . . incites precisely the kind of intervention [I am] making," and that this intervention "would not have been possible if not for queer theory." On one level, of course, this is true; I would not be critiquing queer theory if it did not exist. On another level, however, I fear that this suggestion repeats one of the things for which I take queer theorists to task: namely a conflation of *complex* with *queer*, as if any attempt at complex, intersectional, or multivalent critique is necessarily queer theory (or necessarily postmodern or poststructuralist theory). This conflation overlooks (as queer theory tends to do) the fact that the origins of complex, intersectional thinking about sexuality (and race and gender and class) lie not in the work of

canonical queer theorists in the 1990s, but in the work of feminists, predominantly of women of color, in the 1970s and 1980s. I try to trace in this essay the ways queer theory has, in fact, simplified our understanding of sexuality rather than added complexity to it.

3. Rubin, "Thinking Sex," 274–75, 307, 308.

4. Martin, Femininity Played Straight, 75–79; Sedgwick, Epistemology of the Closet, 16, 27–39, 75–82.

5. Berlant and Warner, "What Does Queer Theory Teach Us about X?" 343, 345–46.

6. Warner, Fear of a Queer Planet, vii, xi, xviii, xix.

7. De Lauretis, "Queer Theory," iii–iv, viii, ix, x.

8. Seidman, "Identity and Politics," 124, 140–41 nn. 44–45.

9. Butler, Bodies That Matter, 16; Butler, Gender Trouble, 16–17.

10. Butler, Gender Trouble, 148, 3–4, 13.

11. Foucault, The History of Sexuality, 42–44, 47–48.

12. Rich, "Compulsory Heterosexuality," 232.

13. Frye, The Politics of Reality, 125, 132, 148.

14. Rubin, "Thinking Sex," 307–308.

15. Anzaldúa, Borderlands/La Frontera, 38–39, 85.

16. Fuss, Essentially Speaking, 94–95.

17. Sedgwick, Epistemology of the Closet, 33, 75; Butler, Gender Trouble, 13–16, 142–49.

18. De Lauretis, "Queer Theory," viii–ix.

19. A similar point is made by Linda Garber in Identity Poetics.

20. See Hames-García, "Who Are Our Own People?"

21. See, for example, my article on the history of European and North American theories of sexual liberation: Hames-Garcia, "Between Repression and Liberation."

22. Firestone, The Dialectic of Sex, 108.

23. Martin, Femininity Played Straight, 46.

24. I once made a similar observation to Martin (see Martin, Femininity Played Straight, 82). I would add to Martin's recapitulation of my observation that the difference that it makes to be nonwhite is equally occluded. In Butler's interpretation of the death of Venus Xtravaganza (a Latina, preoperative transsexual), she assumes her murder to be a result of her failure to completely pass as a woman (Butler, Bodies That Matter, 129–30). Martin writes that it is just as possible that she was murdered as a woman. I want to stress that she may also have been murdered for being Latina (most likely in combination with her gender, perceived gender, class, and occupation as a sex worker).

25. Hammonds, "Black (W)holes," 137, 140.

26. Two early exceptions to this pattern are the issue of diacritics edited by Biddy Martin and Judith Butler in 1994 and the issue of College Literature edited by Donald Hall, Jean Walton, and Garry Leonard in 1997.

27. Sedgwick, Tendencies, 8, 8–9, 9.

28. Butler, Bodies That Matter, 18.

29. Garber makes a similar observation in Identity Poetics, 195–97.

30. Butler, *Bodies That Matter*, 134–37.

31. Lamos, "The Ethics of Queer Theory," 144.

32. Jagose, *Queer Theory*, 76, 130.

33. Lamos, "The Ethics of Queer Theory," 146.

34. Butler, *Bodies That Matter*, 226–27.

35. Butler extends her critique of identity in later work, although the general argument remains unchanged. See, for example, *The Psychic Life of Power*, 92–105. For another articulation and my response to it, see Brown, *States of Injury*; Hames-García, "How Real Is Race?"

36. Sedgwick, *Tendencies*, 9.

37. Similarly *queer* is often used in relation to past and to non-European and non-Euro-American cultures in an attempt to not project a modern or Western identity where it does not belong. The very decision to carve out nonnormative sexualities and to analyze them in these contexts, however, frequently finds motivation in a concern for lesbian and gay identities in the present or the home culture. The best queer work, of course, makes this explicit and traces connections between immediate and more distant contexts. For an early example, see Goldberg, *Sodometries*.

38. These included Case, "Toward a Butch-Feminist Retro Future"; Gluckman and Reed, *Homo Economics*; D. Morton, "Birth of the Cyberqueer"; Ongiri, "We Are Family"; Povinelli, "Sexual Savages/Sexual Sovereignty."

39. Alexander, *Pedagogies of Crossing*, 172.

40. See especially Garber, *Identity Poetics*, 176–208.

41. Eng, Halberstam, and Muñoz, "Introduction," 1, 3, 12.

42. Ferguson, "Of Our Normative Strivings," 85.

43. Halberstam, "Shame and White Gay Masculinity," 220.

44. Pérez, "You Can Have My Brown Body," 171, 172.

45. Mignolo, *Local Histories/Global Designs*, 3.

46. The following three paragraphs, with some changes, are part of a much longer discussion of the colonial/modern gender system in my forthcoming book, *Identity Complex*.

47. Lugones, "Heterosexualism," 202–3. Omise'eke Natasha Tinsley observes a similar point in "Black Atlantic," 109.

48. Lugones, "Heterosexualism," 201, 202. See also Anzaldúa, *Borderlands/La Frontera*; Marcos, *Taken from the Lips*; Massad, *Desiring Arabs*; McClintock, *Imperial Leather*; C. T. Mohanty, Russo, and Torres, *Third World Women*; Najmabadi, *Women with Mustaches*; Sigal, *Infamous Desire*; Sigal and Chuchiak, *Sexual Encounters/Sexual Collisions*; A. Smith, *Conquest* and "Heteropatriarchy"; Trask, *From a Native Daughter*.

49. Teaiwa, "Bikinis." See also Aiavao, "Who's Playing Naked Now?"; Trask, *From a Native Daughter*.

It's All in Having a History: A Response to

Michael Hames-García's "Queer Theory Revisited"

María Lugones

When Gloria Anzaldúa inhabits her *tono*, the serpent, she acknowledges for the first time that she is body, *animal* body, and soul. She tells us that entering into the serpent constitutes that acknowledgment. Her connection with Guadalupe, the revered virgin of Mexicanos, Mexicanas, Chicanas, and Chicanos, is precisely through her inhabitation of the Mexica serpent. Guadalupe is a colonized being, animal body and soul torn from her. She is the colonial rendering and desexing of the double goddess Tonanzin (Coatlicue). Coatlicue (Coatlalopeuh), the serpent, sexuality, was excised, and Tonanzi, the provider, the germinator, was turned into the desexed mother. The serpent was taken out of her; she was forced to leave her animal body. Anzaldúa is not alone in connecting with the sexed goddess through her own inhabitation of the serpent. Thus Guadalupe, the one inscribed with the colonial *rajadura*, is both "the single most potent religious, political and cultural image of the Chicano/mexicano" and an old spirit deity who is worshipped under the guise of a Christian saint: "We have not all embraced the dichotomy [*virgen* or *puta*]." Indeed it is the undoing of dichotomies, the undoing of the Western and colonial imposition, deformation, muting of indigenous sexuality that is enacted through the writing on the ground, the slithering on the earth, the opening of the serpent's mouth. The serpent is "the symbol of the dark sexual drive, the chthonic, the feminine, the serpentine movement of sexuality, creativity, the basis of all energy and life." It is the knowing body *de su tono* that changes, that crosses: "Suddenly, I feel like I have another set of teeth in my mouth. A tremor goes through my body from my buttocks to the roof of my mouth. On my palate I feel a tingling ticklish sensation, then something seems to be falling on me, over me, a curtain of rain or light. Shock pulls my breath out of me. The sphincter muscle tugs itself up, up, and the heart in my cunt starts to beat."[1]

The creation of spaces in the U.S. academy for radical critiques of institution-alized, discipline-based knowledges wedded to what Boaventura de Souza Santos calls a "contracted present" has taken many years of devoted, unrelenting, costly participation by a smallish number of radical intellectuals.[2] The number is small when one considers the enormity of the task, its importance, and those who did not participate actively and enduringly in the nitty-gritty of creating programs, organizing with hundreds of students, writing requirements that underwent endless watering down and ended up being replaced by unacceptable alternatives that ended in protests, taking over of buildings, storing extraordinary frustration and undergoing extraordinary mistreatment, and, not unimportantly, writing fewer books than those colleagues who bathed in the hegemonic sunshine. The task involved not only radical critiques of knowledges, but also of knowledge production and of its consequences for the very hegemonic construction of that impoverished present. The most promising and sustaining part of the task, and the one most ferociously opposed by academic liberals and conservatives, involved the creation and centering of new frameworks and methodologies, new terms for understandings that defied all manner of reduction and exclusion and mapped liberatory turns. The positive task continues to enrich in spite of the constant lack of every manner of institution-alized support. Many of us who have carried out and continue to carry out these tasks have gained reputations for lack of collegiality, loud voices, ill humor, and overall lack of that precious calm, reflective countenance characteristic of the serious intellectual. How many hateful, contempt-full eyes does it take to disintegrate one's credibility as a knower? What does it take to endure in spite of such disintegration?

It is from within this history that I read Michael Hames-García's articulation of what he hoped from queer theory in "Queer Theory Revisited." As a young *joto* intellectual he had hoped that "queer theory would be able to make sexuality and desire central rather than peripheral to radical politics and would be unrelentingly *critical*, in Herbert Marcuse's sense of simultaneously negating society as a given and imagining what more liberatory possibilities are being blocked by that given state of affairs." He did not find in any of the works in what he calls "the construction of the dominant self-narratives of queer theory ('queer genealogies')" what that entailed for him: an understanding of "the connections between white homosexuality and white supremacy, . . . between the experience of class and that of race for a queer subject, or between the racialized misogyny faced (differently) by all straight women and the racialized homophobia faced (differently) by all gay men and lesbians . . . of how gay white and straight white spaces serve class interests and how queer people of color might perceive the varying class inflections of those spaces."

During the academic year 2006–7 I attended the discussions of a working group on queer theory that had as an immediate goal the creation of a queer studies program at the university where I teach. By this late date, late both in my life and in the life of the radical struggle for critique of institutionalized knowledges, I am not supporting any studies that begin by ignoring the hopes that Hames-García articulates in "Queer Theory Revisited." If he is right, and we are to begin the study of queer theory in academic institutions from within the self-narrative of queer theory that he articulates so starkly and tellingly, I am opposed to its institutionalization. But I am deeply interested in radically altering that narrative, precisely because the knowledges of the body, including the sexually colonized body in its germinating of its decolonial chrysalis, in "its making its own face," are as central to the radical critique as central gets. Thus the importance for me of Hames-García's alternative genealogy for critical thinking about sexuality in the United States, a genealogy that centers the early emergence of intersectional thinking and his focusing the recent directions that address the interrelations among race, gender, and sexuality, as well as efforts to think about sexuality outside the Eurocentric and colonial framework of queer theory.

When I critically and insistently proposed that we alter the order of knowledge in the queer studies working group and start, not from the queer theory canon, but from the critical alternatives, I felt immediately placed in the familiar "that's not the right kind of knowledge" situation: that's not philosophy, that's not theory, that's not this, that's not that. This time it was *that's not queer theory*. What I must want is something that has to go by some other name related to sexuality, but because this is queer theory what I want is not really on the mark. I began my comments here by focusing on Anzaldúa's knowledge, the knowledge of the *atravesados*, the knowledge of "those [who] cross over the confines of the normal," the embodied serpent knowing, because that is precisely what gets to be something other than queer theory.[3] Hames-García's argument convincingly leads me to understand the exclusion. In doing so he helps me regain my own sense of credibility as an embodied knower who gained her critical, radical, liberatory sense of "speaking cunt to cunt," as Gloria used to say when she introduced her public talks, in the knowing company of women like Audre Lorde, Emma Peréz, Chela Sandoval, Cherríe Moraga, Jacqui Alexander, Juanita Ramos, Barbara Smith, and Anzaldúa herself. Hames-García makes clear both why the self-narrative of queer theory begins in 1990 and why it excludes the intersectional work of Baldwin, Anzaldúa, Lorde, Smith, and other writers for whom race is central to their understanding of sexuality.

CATEGORIAL LOGIC AND ONTOLOGY

As a theorist of resistance to multiple oppressions I always try to make the weakest ontological commitments necessary to get the task accomplished. That is, I try both to make the weakest commitment and to be clear about why that is the necessary level of commitment. That is not just because I want to make the least assailable theoretical claim, but, more important, because I want to propose something politically feasible. I theorize from within a troubled social and a troubled real, where agency has to be reconceived because the full, heavy, modern sense of agency in modern moral and political theory is a fiction that is used against the resistant-oppressed. I reconceptualize agency, making room for a historicized oppressing⇔resisting sense of the peopled social, where the monologics of linear time are troubled and where the history of racialization and gendering constitute one timeline of colonial processes imprinted in bodies whose sexual urges and longings are tortured in the process of production in the plantations, the mita, the emptying of lands for the assemblage of the capitalist world order. But the complexities of sexual history and agency show other timelines crossing, challenging, meeting the torturing processes in a decolonial surge.

Hames-García's criticisms of queer theory significantly hinge on the question of ontological commitments. Though the strength of these commitments is not always clear to me, and though I am not clear as to why, politically speaking, the ontological commitments of queer theory are so weak, I understand what is at issue in his critique and what makes the critique compelling to me. Whatever the necessary ontological commitments, what needs to be made sense of is the idea that people have histories and that they have histories as complex, interrelated beings in multiple relations, including both relations of power and relations of resistance, of exuberant excess. It is because and to the extent that people have histories that the unhinging of sexuality from gender and race is problematic. And it is because that unhinging is problematic that the history of queer theory itself cannot be separated from reflections that theorize the imbrication. It is also because people have histories, because they are historical beings in a history that is neither linear, unilinear, nor unified, that they can be understood as resisting and exceeding a simultaneously reductive, limiting, erasing, and powerfully constructive past. If we look at Anzaldúa in her inhabitation of her *tono*, her making her face, her sense, her self makes sense only within and against a colonial history that places her in a state of intimate terror. It is from within the expanded and multiple sense of her past and present that she fashions, gathers, enacts a more exuberant possibility.

I understand this question of people having histories to be at the heart of Hames-García's critique of queer theory. For him the self-narratives of queer theory begin in the 1990s precisely because their focus is away from people as having histories. It is his own emphasis on people as having histories that explains his alternative genealogy. In both cases he understands that one's racialization and gendering are inseparable from each other and inseparable from the very formation of one's sexual desires.

So I will address two questions that seem to me to be at issue here that make the question of people having histories both important and difficult in relation to queer theory's own assumptions and politics. One is a question of ontology, the other a question of agency. These questions are not unrelated, but the question of agency is also a question about categorial thinking and whether to start the politics of sexuality from categories of oppression.

It seems to me that crucial to Hames-García's depiction of separatist accounts of queer theory is an underlying rejection in those accounts of taking up oppression as a good starting point for a politics of sexuality. They also seem to equate identity with particular forms of oppression. For Butler, Hames-García tells us, "race becomes a limit, the limit to the mobility of bodies and desires. It is fixed and corporeal. . . . Race (supposedly always present) comes[s] to equal black or Latina and Latino, and then come[s] to equal limit, limitation, and fixedness, and then further come[s] to equal death."

I myself begin from a framework that does not treat race, sexuality, gender, class, and other markers merely as *categories* of oppression. I understand the treatment of people in terms of categories to be itself part of oppression, because the logic of categories reduces and fragments, but it also conceals people as complex resistant beings that have lively histories. That is, categorial logic immobilizes and fragments, whereas people inhabit their expanded or contracted presents in a polilogical history. In that history they negotiate tensely what Aníbal Quijano calls the coloniality of power and what I call the coloniality of gender and decolonial possibilities. These are inextricable, constitutive aspects of their history, but they are not exhaustive. They also make vivid that the relations among class, race, sexuality, and gender are not cut-and-paste and categorial, but systemic. The systemic constructions of the social and the real render as complexly marked those individual human beings whose desires, movements, embodiments, and relations are lived from within a gendered or racialized matrix. But though this is one of the lines of thought that Hames-García contrasts with understandings of history embedded in queer theory's self-narrative, I will analyze why I do not focus on the logic of categories and why I think that it is a focus on the logic of categories that mars the debate. I make my own approach explicit because what is at stake in the argument requires that clarity. It is, significantly, a question of the *politics* of sexuality.

Categories of oppression are markers that constitute one aspect of the social given, and as such they have a powerful "degree of reality," as standpoint theorists put it. Categories of oppression are conceptualized hegemonically as independent from each other and often as natural rather than social *categories*. They are also conceptualized as inhering in people. I think it is important both to understand the logic of categories and not to be entrapped by it. Whether they are understood as socially constructed, historically variable, or natural and either unchangeable or historically variable, categories give themselves logically to addition and intersection, to homogeneous composition, definition, and classification. Because they can be defined or characterized well enough at particular times, their scope is pretty clear. The logic and systems of oppression use categories and categorial logic because doing so fits the classifying, warehousing, and fragmenting of people. To the extent that we want to understand oppression, reduction, and disintegration, the logic of categories needs to be understood and used critically.

When Kimberlé Crenshaw thinks about women of color at the point of the law and seeks to unveil the legal erasure of the violence perpetrated against them, she uses the logic of categories. But she makes clear that she is using them in the hegemonic sense precisely to unveil the erasure. She intersects two categories for the purposes of her argument, *women* and *black*, and after she explores the scope of each she uncovers that women of color are excluded from the scope of both. So at the intersection of these categories as constructed and used in the U.S. legal system there is an absence where women of color should be. That is, in understanding the oppressive given, the logic of categories is necessary and the oppression is logically categorial. But that is also to understand that there is a fictitious character to the categories as they are also real in their power to organize the social.[4] The absence of women of color at the intersection reveals both the fiction of *women* and *black* as categories of oppression at the point of the law and the power of the fiction in erasing women of color.

I am pointing this out because I am laying the ground for a thinking that is carefully attentive to the imbrication of what cannot be really expressed with the words *race, gender, sexuality, class*. Those words already betray a commitment to separation and reduction. Identity, that which can be broken in one ("In prison, they break you, they break your identity," an ex-prisoner said in a public discussion on prison abolition), starts at the *rejection of, opposition to* oppressive, reductive social constructions of human beings. That is, people do not identify with and through categories of oppression imposed through a history that crucially involves the coloniality of power. Reductive "identities" (read: categorial, fragmenting, forceful labelings and violent constructions of people) are imposed through structures of oppression. One bears reductive marks painfully, and one comes to a sense of oneself as a person in resistance to the imposition. The techniques, practices, and tactics, both collective and solitary, that resistance takes and the limits of that resistance are not the issue here. At issue are that people have histories; that those histories are themselves complex and multiple and given meaning within larger complex and multilinear histories; that those histories involve both oppression and resistance; and that identity arises at the point of resistance. We have come to very complex understandings of those identities or senses of self in relation. Important in the complex understandings have been the liberatory *poiesis* of making face in opposition to the inseparable productions of reduced beings in the imbrications of race, sexuality, gender, and class.

When Evelyn Hammonds thinks of those absented by the categories, she subverts the logic of categories without subverting the logic of identity using a logic of relation, of social effects on people from there being other people in their midst who are not in their position, who do not do or think or feel what they do. But they are also people to whom people relate, treat in particular ways, and have feelings and desires about. Thus she looks at the social in its complex interactions and interrelations. She thinks of black holes. She thinks of black holes as unseen stars that can be detected by their effects on other stars and by the effects of those stars on them. So she looks for black lesbian women with this device, and when she finds them she finds beings affected by and affecting others, so she does see the reductions and immobilizations, but she also sees beings that go beyond the limitations. She is thinking of sexuality relationally and historically. Her task is not divorced from the formation of identities.[5] But identities here are not fixed, oppressive constructions, nor are they complete unhingings from the social and the real. They are tight, fluid, changing, as they are negotiations in the historical and relational social. So the queer theorists' inclination to separate *queer* as having liberatory, resistant, or exuberant possibilities from categories of oppression seems to me in some sense necessary and misguided. It is necessary because categories do not capture anything at all about our possibilities. But the move is ultimately misguided because it is a conceptual rather than a historical move performed by people at the point of oppression.

HISTORY AND ONTOLOGY

According to Hames-García, queer theorists lean toward the claim that *queer* does not designate an ontological category or substantive identity. The positions on ontology differ. Some queer theorists, such as Jagose, argue that queer identity is an anti-identity. Butler, on the other hand, does not argue that queer is a nonidentity or different from other identities. So I looked at Hames-García's characterization of each position and his critique. I then related his position on ontology to the larger question of a person's having a history that I have presented as at the core of his argument. My argument focuses on Hames-García's own presentation of queer theory as I try to expose the crucial assumptions on both sides. I agree with his critique of queer theory so understood, but I make my own ontological presuppositions, my own understanding of categorial logic, and my own understanding of identity clear. A larger understanding of my position requires a look at what I call the modern/colonial gender system and at my own writing on categorial logics and resistance.[6]

Hames-García, unlike his presentation of anti-identitarian theorists and unlike Butler's understanding of identity as a limiting and enabling history of performative invocations of prior use, understands the queering of a subject (agent) as a process in time. He looks at the logic, the conceptual repositionings, and emphasizes the metamorphosis of the subject. That is, his emphasis is on persons as queer, existing as queer, coming to be queer, naming themselves queer. He describes the queer self-inhabitation as a living and a perceiving of sexuality by social beings who are not independent from their social environment. If one becomes queer, one's multiple history of inhabitation of the social can be hidden behind a less identity-bound term. Hames-García argues that this is precisely the move accomplished in queer theory in both of its guises. Contrast that hiding with the exhibiting of the resistant, syncretic inhabitation of sexual desire in candomblé, Santería, and Vaudou, as described by Roberto Strongman. He understands, for example, the practice of cross-gender possession as mastered by "the passive male homosexuals *filhos de santo*" and the polysexual, genderless, bisexual, androgynous, or multiply gendered identifications of the Orishas in Santería as syncretic practices that attest to slaves' embodied resistance to Christian religious conversion.[7]

In part the issue is how to understand identity, but crucial is the question of whether the liberatory and resistant turn is historical or conceptual. Emphasizing the history of the subject enables us to have a historicized understanding of identity as a liberatory and liberating poiesis. I want to end where I started, so I go back to Anzaldúa's making face as the writhing Mexica serpent seeking a renewed lesbian, jota, queer connection with Coatlicue (Tonantzin) and Guadalupe in the explosion of sexual desire. Hers is a historical poiesis that undermines the sense that we are bound to a monological linear understanding of history. It is also a poiesis that she lives from the inside as individual, but one that she enacts within a particular resistant social history. The interrelated sociality of making face is expressed by Martin Manalansan in invoking our liberatory immersion in the social poiesis of constituting a social erotics.[8] This poiesis is indeed a question of politics. Identity is framed by torture but fashioned with this resistant cloth.

NOTES

1. Anzaldúa, *Borderlands/La Frontera*, 48, 52, 53, 57, 73.

2. De Souza Santos, "A Critique of Lazy Reason."

3. Anzaldúa, *Borderlands/La Frontera*, 25.

4. Crenshaw writes, "In mapping the intersections of race and gender, the concept does engage dominant assumptions that race and gender are essentially separate categories" ("Mapping the Margins," 378 n7).

5. Hammonds, "Black (W)holes."

6. See Lugones, "Heterosexualism"; Lugones, *Pilgrimages*.

7. Stongman, "Syncretic Religion."

8. Manalansan, talk at Binghamton University, spring 2006.

Gay Shame, Latina- and Latino-Style:

A Critique of White Queer Performativity

Lawrence La Fountain-Stokes

People of color have always theorized—but in forms quite different
from the Western form of abstract logic. . . . How else have we managed to survive with such spiritedness the assault on our bodies,
social institutions, countries, our very humanity?
—Barbara Christian, "The Race for Theory"

THE ETHICS OF CRUELTY (OR HOW A *READ* QUEEN SNAPS! BACK)

A good number of years ago, on a slightly warm summer evening, I walked into
a West Village basketball court magically transformed into a festive meeting
place: it was the New York City Lesbian and Gay Community Services Center's
Annual Garden Party, a fundraiser that costs about fifty dollars per person to
attend.[1] It was 2000, and there weren't that many people of color present, perhaps because of the high price and the Center's mixed reputation (the Stonewall
veteran Sylvia Rivera was banned for many years, for example), but this did not
faze me at first. Alas, my bliss was not to last for long. Unfortunately I had forgotten that most (white, middle- and upper-class) gay men in New York didn't
wear loud colors to such events, favoring muted shades of brown, black, and
white (at least that year), and it seems my bright orange and yellow Hawaiian
shirt, bought in a San Francisco thrift store, shocked people's sensibilities to
such an extent that they found it hard to talk to me, almost needing to pull out
sunglasses in the early dusk just to shield their eyes.[2]

I'm so white most people (gay and straight) never guess I'm Puerto Rican,
but on the day in question something was different, or at least it felt different to
me. In fact I think I've never felt more Caribbean in my life, perhaps a modern-
day Jesús Colón or even a contemporary Bernardo Vega, arriving in the North in
August 1916, wearing his Sunday best only to learn months later that his clothes
offered little defense against the relentless cold.[3] It is strange that I think of
Vega at a moment like this. The light-skinned Puerto Rican tobacco worker and

labor leader is also well known for candidly describing in the opening of his memoirs how he threw his watch overboard even before he got here, as soon as his boat entered the New York harbor; someone had told him only effeminate men wore that kind of timepiece, and he didn't want to take a chance.

I am that forsaken watch, sinking to the bottom of the Hudson River estuary within sight of Lady Liberty, stuck somewhere in the muck among the other debris and the occasional fish; I am Vega's object of fear, except that my crime is to be "colorful" among pale-faced, Fire Island–tanned, North American gay white men (ah, the crass overgeneralization), whose greatest concern is not to be considered effeminate (unless they are in drag or camping it up) and whose main interest in Latino culture often seems to be to find a fuckable boy toy, a quality I do not seem to project. By synecdoche I become that colorful flowered shirt, an island shirt for a Caribbean island boy who shares a colonial past with other island boys from the Pacific, a shirt that for some reason seemed out of place in Manhattan, "that other island of Puerto Rico," as the writer Manuel Ramos Otero would say.[4]

I realize this anecdote and elucidation might seem a bit trivial: "Big deal, a bunch of faggots made fun of him because of his shirt. Who cares?" Yet for me it was a moment of being cruelly *read* and shamed by (what I remember as) gay white men for being Puerto Rican, for thinking that I could be trendy by wearing loud colors: an accusation of having bad *taste* (a category the French sociologist Pierre Bourdieu identified as central to reifying social differences) and thus not really fitting in; of being an outsider.[5] I say this fully aware that the judgment of taste can be at times a camp (and as such, queer) practice, and how historically many predominantly urban gay men have assumed this behavior (to be arbiters of taste) as a sign of identity formation and community definition (a trope capitalized upon in such dominant representations as *Queer Eye for the Straight Guy*).[6] Right now, however, I am more interested in the relevance of validating anecdote and lived experience (and anger) in the articulation (or *anecdotalizing*) of a more dynamic, alternative form of theory, and for the metaphorical SNAP!-*ing back* which I effect in this article, which is about counteracting the popularity of gay shame in current (white) academic queer theory circuits by counterposing it to Latina and Latino *sinvergüencería*, or shamelessness. I adopt Jane Gallop's critical methodology as articulated in her *Anecdotal Theory*, which is to say, a feminist, deconstructive, and psychoanalytically informed cultural criticism that privileges experience as a means to understand and theorize the world.[7] I particularly subscribe to her incorporation of Barbara Christian's insights from "The Race for Theory," where Christian argues (speaking of people of color), "Our theorizing (and I intentionally use the verb rather than the noun) is often in narrative forms, in the stories we create, in riddles and proverbs, in the play with language, because dynamic rather than fixed ideas seem more to our liking."[8] I also affirm my profound solidarity with Audre Lorde's feminist politicization of anger in her landmark "The Uses of Anger: Women Responding to Racism," where she clearly states, "My anger is a response to racist attitudes and to the actions and presumptions that arise out of those attitudes."[9] Like Gallop's and Lorde's essays, my essay is an occasional piece, originally written in the fall of 2003 and generated as the result of a series of unfortunate academic experiences. This essay, which has taken more than seven years to publish, is a SNAP! against racism in its many guises.

But back to my anecdotes. To quote the scholar Rubén Ríos Ávila: "Let me begin (or end?) with a modest confession: I am a Puerto Rican gay man."[10] I am led to ask, Can I only speak as a queer Puerto Rican? Then again, do all gay Puerto Ricans think alike? (Suddenly I start to think that I am some bizarre exception, a freak of Puerto Rican homosexuality: una loca loca, or a faggot gone mad!) Must I position myself in shame to understand shame and speak about shame? What if I don't believe in shame to begin with, or prefer to resist it as an ontological category? Is my shame (or anger) greater than or less than other shames, and does that matter? Is it the shame (read: anger) of failing the dictates of (white) homonormativity (as defined by Lisa Duggan), of becoming the object of shame of mostly gay white men?[11] Am I not shamed (or provoked to anger) in other spaces as well, by white women, for example, or by people of color?

Clearly stated, I do not buy into Michael Warner's suggestion in *The Trouble with Normal* that this "shaming" is a constitutive feature of gay life, a form of camaraderie and generosity that affirms gays as members of a community.[12] Quite the contrary: the bitchy queen attack I experienced — to describe the Garden Party event with different, unfortunately misogynistic, hurtful words — was a form of cultural self-centeredness, prejudice, and, dare I say, projected self-hate from that New York crowd. So I don't know how to take some *shade*, you say? Well, those weren't exactly some sisters putting me down, if you know what I mean. But then again, I don't exactly buy into *reading* or *throwing shade* either.[13] Such practices of disparaging one another through insults are (for the most part) hateful, mean, and cruel and do not necessarily empower anyone.[14]

To argue that *reading* (or verbal unmasking, particularly when it consists of the derisory act of pointing out someone's flaws or lack of taste) is a liberatory strategy, a form of subversion, is hard for me to accept, unless one believes that the constant breaking down of one's sense of identity and the resulting hardness or toughening of the character is necessary for survival in a hostile world, or that it is just simple fun, a deconstruction of bourgeois "civility" or manners—an Artaudian cruelty leading to change.[15] I do not believe the men at the Garden Party were doing me a favor by openly demeaning me as a person. Peer-oriented cruelty should not be a site of liberatory empowerment, even if people see it as a form of entertainment or survival.

READING QUEER THEORY AS A QUEER
(OR QUARE OR KUAER) PUERTO RICAN

Rubén Ríos Ávila offers several lucid and theoretically sophisticated answers, or perhaps I should say problematizations of my conundrum as it extends tò the field of queer academic research and to the constitution of coherent individual identity formations: the challenge of speaking from the I about queer theory when that field more often than not constitutes itself in an Anglo-Eurocentric vacuum, in negation of race and ethnicity as analytical categories; the challenge of speaking from a position of subjectivity when that leads to a questioning of one's critical acumen; the specificity of being torn by and reconciling sexual orientation and national or ethnic identity. He elaborates on these issues in the two final essays of La raza cómica: Del sujeto en Puerto Rico, a book in Spanish that curiously concludes with a switch to el difícil (the difficult one), that is to say, the English language.[16]

In the first essay, "Final Inqueery," the Puerto Rican scholar discusses the intersections of African American, poststructuralist, psychoanalytic, and queer theory, trying to reconcile divergent strands and ideas, while always insisting on his positionality as a gay Puerto Rican writing subject whose otherness permits these readings. In fact the final essay of the book, "Rambling," is precisely about the anecdotal constitution of his adult identity as a Puerto Rican gay man in New York City, stuck in Central Park between Grace Jones and the Gay Pride March on the one hand, and the salsa beats of post–Puerto Rican Day Parade celebrations on the other. He describes being led away by his nose from the gay sexual encounters of the Rambles to boiling cauldrons of lard and vegetable oil, the source of deep-fried Puerto Rican codfish and cornstarch fritters known as bacalaítos, the triumph of one hunger over another.[17]

But let us return to "Final Inqueery." I am struck by Ríos Ávila's insistence in the awkwardness of speaking from the I, in the admission of his shame or mixed feelings at focusing on his identity as a reference point for critical analysis:

Let me also admit a certain discomfort in seeming to "occupy" . . . the somewhat *improper* pronominal site of the first person, particularly when the role of the critic calls for the distant coolness, the supposedly neutral impersonality of the third. It is the kind of move that runs the risk of trading off all knowledge for feeling, authority for authenticity, the truth for evidence— and, of course, I am not so convinced it is such a good tradeoff. As with all confessions, there is always a modicum of embarrassment entailed, regardless of how open or closed, closeted or out of the closet, timely or untimely, publicly or privately the spectacle of confession is performed.[18]

Ríos Ávila's discomfort contrasts markedly with the assertive use of anecdote and personal history as theoretical and political tools in the work of scholars such as Jane Gallop, but also of queers of color artists and intellectuals such as Gloria Anzaldúa (*Borderlands/La frontera: The New Mestiza*), Cherríe Moraga (*Loving in the War Years: Lo que nunca pasó por sus labios*), and José Esteban Muñoz (*Disidentifications: Queers of Color and the Performance of Politics*). Their works (and others, such as Audre Lorde's *Zami: A New Spelling of My Name*) defend the legitimacy of self-referential writing as a source of knowledge and power. In fact Emma Pérez suggests that it is precisely these *sitios* (sites) and *lenguas* (discourses) that allow us to tell our stories, ones that are profoundly destabilizing and transformative.[19] #3 Authors such as Anzaldúa, Moraga, Muñoz, Lorde, and Pérez suggest that one should not feel shame (or *impropriety*) about engaging in self-testimonial narratives (what can be read as a very particular type of confession), particularly when these serve to validate, document, and even critique one's own and other people's experience (Puerto Rican gay experience, in my case, or even American queer culture, broadly speaking), even in the most serious and scholarly of environments. These authors empower me to "read" queer (or *quare*) theory (as in the African American gay vernacular, following E. Patrick Johnson), precisely privileging the self.[20]

Johnson's theorization on "quare," as his African American grandmother would say in her "thick, black, southern dialect" and as the Irish variant of *queer*, proposes a radical reconfiguration of the terms of analysis used in many contemporary critical debates on gender and sexuality.[21] While the theoretical stance of *queer* may aspire to be a radical, antitotalizing category that deconstructs all categories, it fails, quite particularly with regard to race and ethnicity (something that Judith Butler also points out in her essay "Critically Queer"). Johnson decries dominant queer studies' white-centrism and proposes a space of difference from what white queers called difference itself; he offers "quare" studies as "a vernacular rearticulation and deployment of queer theory to ac-commodate racialized sexual knowledge," a theoretical and methodological variation that I would like to fully embrace. Johnson's appeal to Anzaldúa and Moraga's concept of "theory in the flesh" as one that "emphasize[s] the diversity within and among gays, bisexuals, lesbians, and transgendered people of color while simultaneously accounting for how racism and classism affect how we experience and theorize the world" seems particularly relevant to my own theorization.[22] His provocative argumentation has led the Taiwanese scholar Wenshu Lee to extend his analysis; in her rather provocative essay "Kuaering Queer Theory: My Autocritography and a Race-Conscious, Womanist, Trans-national Turn," she proposes the neologism kuaer as a term that plays with as-sociations of Mandarin Chinese and English but resignifies them and adds a differently valenced feminist and global, diasporic, and migratory dimension. Lee's close attention to the multiple significations of words and the subtleties of language comes very close to my own interests.

Roderick A. Ferguson's questioning in Aberrations in Black: Toward a Queer of Color Critique is also an important complement to this project, even if the author him-self never comments on the shortcomings of dominant queer theory paradigms (specifically their lack of a critical race component). One of his contributions is a destabilization of the role of confession articulated in Foucault's model of sexuality. As Ferguson explains, it is not so much the confession per se, but who conducts it and to what end. Confession goes hand in hand with surveillance as part of the instrumentality of power (the technologies of race and sexuality) that serve to control minoritarian populations. Self-censorship (for example, Ralph Ellison's excision of the queer character Woodyear from the final version of In-visible Man) also shows the insidious, internalized workings of power.[23]

Ferguson's analysis is also valuable for its exploration of the relationship between hegemonic fields of knowledge and the cultural productions of sub-altern, minoritarian groups (African Americans, in his case). I build upon his analysis to show how the unexamined racial prejudices of a group of predomi-nantly white queer scholars have led to the rather unfortunate situation of one marginalized group (white queers) exploiting, appropriating, excluding, ignoring, and misusing queer of color cultural productions. I will address what Fredric Jameson has termed the "political unconscious" or unacknowledged ideological (racist) baggage of leading white queer theorists.[24] I strongly em-brace Ferguson's articulation of a queer of color critique as a corrective to domi-nant, white theory, activism, and practice. The process by which white queer theory has become a hegemonic knowledge formation will not be explored in depth in this essay; suffice it to say that this uneven, incomplete project of institutionalization is still very much a work in progress, and as such, one of the objectives of this essay is to make a timely critical intervention.[25]

IN SEARCH OF THE DISAPPEARING DIACRITIC:
LOOKING FOR AN INVISIBLE ACCENT ON MÓNTEZ

What happens at the intersections, crossroads, or contact points of queer Puerto Rican subjectivities, language, and "gay shame" (the queer political and theoretical movement to embrace shame)?[26] In what remains of this essay I examine several different moments or points of crisis and attempt to articulate a critique. This will entail engaging debates on the Puerto Rican drag queen Mario Móntez (particularly as framed at the University of Michigan Gay Shame Conference in 2003) and on the Latina and Latino embrace of *sinvergüencería*, or shamelessness, as a more productive site of politics and identity building. I will also engage Frances Negrón-Muntaner's work on what she claims is the constitutive shame of Puerto Rican colonial experience, paying close attention to her explorations of queer shame, and to José Esteban Muñoz's embrace of gay shame, and position myself in relation to these.

The discussion of gay shame became central to the development of (white) queer theory in the 1990s, perhaps most clearly articulated in 1993 in the essay "Queer Performativity: Henry James's *The Art of the Novel*" by the white scholar Eve Kosofsky Sedgwick. This discussion (also picked up by the queer and feminist philosopher Judith Butler) also had important activist and community dimensions, manifested in the global anti–Gay Pride celebration movement which started in New York in 1998 and then spread to San Francisco, Toronto, Sweden, and elsewhere. Activists argued that Gay Pride had been co-opted by apolitical (or conservative), normalizing, consumerist (pro-capitalist) interests; as Sara Jaffe stated, "Increasing numbers of queers feel disillusioned, alienated by and bored with Pride events," and as such defended the "celebration" or embrace of gay shame as a radical alternative.[27]

(Given that I share this critique, I believe that the real question is whether gay shame is really the best response to this phenomenon. Or does the embrace of gay shame take us down an equally undesirable [psychic] path? And how do we deal with the complex double valence of boredom as a genuine reaction or a jaded, elitist stance, something Jaffe also brings up? At the same time it is important to clarify that the use and meanings of *gay shame* vary among academics and even among different activists and has its own particularities. The actions of the direct action group Gay Shame San Francisco, as outlined by the group's originator, Mattilda (Matt Bernstein Sycamore), are of a profoundly radical and highly commendable nature.[28] Perhaps the biggest difference between my conception and that of those who embrace gay shame is that, for me, at the present moment, it is still appealing or possible to work within the framework of gay pride and attempt to push it to its limits; this seems to make more sense in the specific case of organizing or reaching nonacademic people of color. In other words, I have not given up on the possibility for radical democratization of gay pride, even when I fully sympathize and agree with Gay Shame San Francisco's and Mattilda's politics.)

In addition to Sedgwick and Butler, other academics have also discussed gay shame. The Cuban American performance critic José Esteban Muñoz, for example, claims coauthorship of the concept of a "gay shame day parade" in a chapter in Disidentifications (1999) in which he recounts an anecdote about his parodic celebration of it as an alternative to gay pride. He also discusses the concept of "antigay" as radical critique in relation to the "terroristic drag" of Vaginal Creme Davis. Muñoz sees these as useful strategies of resistance to capitalist commodification and conservative politics.[29] Yet his reference to gay shame in no way advocates a full embrace of this affect as a defining characteristic for queer of color liberation; to the contrary, his use of the term seems more like a playful, albeit perhaps slightly jaded tactic. The Puerto Rican scholar and filmmaker Frances Negrón-Muntaner, on the other hand, bases much of her analysis in her groundbreaking book Boricua Pop: Puerto Ricans and the Latinization of American Culture (2004) on what she sees as the intersections of ethnonational and sexual (queer) shame. She suggests that Puerto Ricans' situation as a colonized people (first by Spain, and since 1898 by the United States) creates a state of inferiority internalized as shame, particularly manifested in the diaspora; she argues that individuals constantly try to displace this shame by articulating discourses of pride. Puerto Ricans' racial and sexual identities become strongly enmeshed in this ambivalent performance of shame and pride, particularly among nonwhite and nonheterosexual subjects. These concerns lead the author to an examination of cultural phenomena such as West Side Story and the careers of performers such as Rita Moreno, Holly Woodlawn, Ricky Martin (whose oscillations between shame and pride have also been addressed by José Quiroga), and Jennifer López, in addition to scandals such as the ones that ensued after Madonna's use of the Puerto Rican flag in one of her performances and after the appearance of a Puerto Rican Barbie.[30] (As she stated in an interview with the Chicana filmmaker and scholar Rita González, Negrón-Muntaner does not advocate an embrace of shame, but rather a thinking through or a critical questioning of this affect.)[31]

The white queer scholar Douglas Crimp's intervention into this discussion appears in his essay "Mario Montez, for Shame," first published in a volume dedicated to Sedgwick in 2002. In this essay Crimp describes a particularly painful scene from Warhol's film *Screen Test #2* (one of the many Warhol films in which Móntez appeared in the 1960s, this one filmed in 1965), in which an off-camera voice (that of Ronald Tavel) viciously interrogates Móntez (whom Gary Comenas has referred to as "Andy's first drag queen superstar") and asks her to partake in embarrassing behavior, such as exposing her (male) genitalia and mouthing the word *diarrhea*, when in fact she believes she is auditioning for a glamorous Hollywood film role and perceives herself to be a woman (and not a drag queen).[32] Crimp is interested in exploring the feelings of shame he felt as a viewer of this pseudo-documentary, unscripted, improvised, reality-based art film, watching a person being visibly humiliated in front of a camera.

To read Crimp's essay about one of the most important Puerto Rican drag queens who worked with Warhol (a drag queen whose patronymic, following the rules of Spanish-language accentuation and orthography, should really be *Móntez*), constitutes a major disappointment, at least as far as advancing an understanding of Latina and Latino issues is concerned.[33] Crimp doesn't make much out of Móntez's Puerto Ricanness or of her ethnoracial difference or colonial status; in fact it is almost as if her Puerto Ricanness were irrelevant, except to mark her Catholic religiosity and origins in the culture of machismo. *De Móntez a Montez: ¿Qué le pasó al acento?* It is almost as though we were talking of two individuals, with two different names: one, Crimp's and Warhol's (orthographically) accentless version, that of a (flattened, racialized, colonial) Puerto Rican drag queen (Montez), the one who refers to the Hollywood career of the Dominican María Montez and whose Puerto Ricanness is taken as a sign of *absence* and abjection (but who maintains a strongly *accented* English, i.e., one marked *phonetically*, which reinforces her racial difference); another, a Spanish-language, orthographically correct variant, *Móntez* (that of normalized, rule-bound writing), the Móntez I am (metaphorically) interested in rescuing and reclaiming as my (or perhaps our) own.

But who is to say that the Spanish language and its rules of orthography are truly an *originating* site of empowerment for a Nuyorican drag queen? What was the role of Mario (née René Rivera, who also performed as Dolores Flores in Jack Smith's *Flaming Creatures*) in the disappearance of the accent mark from the name she borrowed from the B-movie diva María Montez (née María Africa

Gracia Vidal), who took her name from the Irish dancer Lola Montez (née Marie Dolores Eliza Rosanna Gilbert), both of whom seem also to have dispensed with it?[34] Let me make clear that I am *consciously* employing this diacritic as a *metaphor* or sign of difference (which is, after all, precisely what a diacritic is) and am not suggesting that the *Spanish language* is at the center of my argument. Then again, we should not forget that Mario's language (his Hispanic English) was inevitably haunted or marked by Spanish in the way that Julia Alvarez has suggested that Spanish (spiritually) underlies all Latino English in the United States, similarly perhaps to the way that all of Warhol's films are haunted or marked by Puerto Ricanness (and by Latinoness), because of Mario Móntez's and Holly Woodlawn's presence (and absence) in them.[35] It is here, of course, where the slippage between an accent mark as a diacritic and *accent* as a phonetic trait intersect or crash, for Americans routinely point to "foreigner's" accents in speech, while they simultaneously willfully ignore written diacritics, considering them irrelevant. In fact for a Latina or Latino to lose a diacritic from her or his name is seen as a successful measure of assimilation. Simultaneously Puerto Ricans' racial indeterminacy, as an Afro-diasporic mestizo people, comes into play; as Manolo Guzmán convincingly argues in *Gay Hegemony/Latino Homosexualities*, it is precisely this indeterminate status between black and white that made Puerto Rican gay men and drag queens particularly attractive to the New York gay world of the 1960s.

For a queer Latino scholar like myself, the experience of reading Crimp's essay is an act of once again becoming invisible, or more than invisible—a term that seems to buy into the whole ideological discourse of visibility: it is an act of violence, one that produces anger, fury, and rage. I am reminded of talking myself blue at certain lesbian and gay studies events in New York, having to explain over and over why race makes a difference to people who only want to talk about sexual orientation, as if it were possible to do that in a vacuum, people who in fact want to talk only about white people's sexual orientation, and assume that it is normative and universal.[36] I am also reminded of Ferguson's discussion in *Aberrations in Black* of the black transvestite prostitute from Marlon Riggs's film *Tongues Untied*, his contention that this figure represents the epitome of race, sex, and gender abjection and liberation, the nodal point for discussions of inclusion and exclusion, marginality and respectability. It is no coincidence that Ferguson's book has a sepia image of a glamorous black drag queen on its cover.[37] This symbolization is noteworthy and requires further elucidation. What does it mean for this one subject position to be raised to the status of an absolute embodiment of difference?

Crimp's essay on Mario Móntez was the subject of an entire panel at a conference on Queer Shame held at the University of Michigan in Ann Arbor in March 2003, a conference that turned out to be quite controversial for a number of reasons, one of which was the near absolute absence of scholars of color (only one out of thirty invited panelists, that being Hiram Pérez); in addition to Pérez, the only other person of color listed on the program was the African American Chicana performer Vaginal Davis, who was one of the featured entertainers. This conference produced several critical responses, including essays by Pérez ("You Can Have My Brown Body and Eat It, Too!") and Judith Halberstam (originally titled "The Real Shame: White Gay Men!" and later published as "Shame and White Gay Masculinity"), both of which appeared in a special issue of Social Text titled "What's Queer about Queer Studies Now?"; a critique by Mattilda, who along with some other activists renamed the conference "Gay Sham"; an open letter from me to Crimp, circulated via email before the conference and handed out during the event, which has been commented on in an interview of Frances Negrón-Muntaner conducted by Rita González and more recently reprinted in the Gay Shame anthology edited by David M. Halperin and Valerie Traub; a letter by Negrón-Muntaner herself; and an academic conference paper by Heather Love.[38] Arnaldo Cruz-Malavé has also elaborated on this issue of gay shame, particularly as it refers to Mario Móntez and to the Michigan Gay Shame conference; Rubén Ríos Ávila has also taken up the subject.[39] I should say that I was not initially invited, nor did I attend the conference, and an earlier draft of this same essay submitted for inclusion in the proceedings was vetoed by the conference organizers (David M. Halperin and Valerie Traub), who requested that my letter and all criticism of the event and of the work of white queer scholars such as Douglas Crimp and Michael Warner be eliminated from my text. I refused and withdrew my essay, understanding this to be an unwarranted act of censorship.[40]

This is the letter I wrote:

AN OPEN LETTER TO DOUGLAS CRIMP

March 22, 2003
Highland Park, New Jersey
Dear Douglas:

I have just finished reading your essay "Mario Móntez, For Shame."[41] On the one hand, I want to thank you for a thought-provoking piece which I believe will be very useful to me in furthering my understanding of shame and the terms "pato" [duck], "loca" [mad woman] and "maricón," used in Puerto

Rico and the Hispanic Caribbean as a synonyms for "queer," and in general in my work on queer Puerto Ricans and Latinos in the United States.[42] I am also thankful because you remind me and all of your readers that Mario Móntez was Latino, specifically Puerto Rican. I confess that I actually learned this first at a CLAGS conference on autobiography several years ago, from Ondine Chavoya and the Chicana filmmaker Rita González, after watching her wonderful *The Assumption of Lupe Vélez*, an homage to Móntez and to *Lupe*, the 1966 film by the experimental New York–based queer Puerto Rican filmmaker José Rodríguez Soltero.[43] In fact, your essay and Frances Negrón-Muntaner's recent work on Holly Woodlawn remind all of us of the profoundly Puerto Rican character of some of Warhol's film production and of his Factory world. Over all, I think that your understanding of queer shame is a valuable contribution.

And herein my question for you, perhaps my complaint, my own accusation of "For Shame!" Perhaps I have missed something, but as far as I can tell, race and ethnicity (as well as colonialism, for that matter) are all but invisible in your essay. Invisible, that is, in the sense that I could not perceive your analysis of them; for they are ever-present, an invisible normative whiteness and assertiveness of empire that blanket everything except the shamed (brown? powder-white?) body of Mario Móntez. And that is particularly true (again, please correct me if I am mistaken) as we read your theoretical elaboration, your long list of white queer scholars and intellectuals, white artists, whites, for shame: Eve Sedgwick (reading Henry James, of all people), Andy Warhol, Jack Smith, Ronald Tavel (the person I confess I know the least about), George Plimpton, Andrew Sullivan, Michael Warner, Douglas Crimp. So that for me the shame of Mario Móntez becomes that of Frantz Fanon, faced by a child who stares at him in horror, the shame of Gloria Anzaldúa and Cherríe Moraga and Audre Lorde, of those Puerto Ricans and other diasporic people of color shamed every day for being a subjugated and racialized people, and particularly, the shame of the Puerto Rican queer. My shame, perhaps.

Nowhere is this more evident than in the passage you quote (speaking about Ronald Tavel): "I enjoyed working with him," Warhol wrote, "because he understood instantly when I'd say things like, 'I want it simple and plastic and white.' Not everyone can think in an abstract way, but Ronnie could."[44] It is an association of whiteness and Warhol that makes me think, for example, of José Muñoz's insightful analysis in his book *Disidentifications* of the complex relationship between Warhol and Jean-Michel Basquiat.

I understand there is to be a discussion of your essay at the upcoming conference on Queer Shame at the University of Michigan, Ann Arbor, to be held March 27–29, 2003. I will unfortunately not be unable to attend, as it coincides with the Latin American Studies Association meeting in Dallas. I wish you and all of the participants fruitful sessions. The questions I leave for you are the following: How do you read the intersection of race and ethnicity in Mario Montez's shame? How does the colonial gaze fit into your scheme? What is there of Puerto Rican in his shame, other that the passing reference to a stereotypical Latin machismo and Catholic religiosity?

I hope my comments are of use to you and the conference participants.
Sincerely yours,
Lawrence M La Fountain-Stokes
Assistant Professor,
Department of Puerto Rican and Hispanic Caribbean Studies
Department of Women and Gender Studies
Rutgers University, New Brunswick[45]

Crimp's essay on Mario Móntez is similar to the other contributions in *Regarding Sedgwick* in that none of the other contributors mention race or take race into account, except for the volume's editors in their introduction, when they reference Sedgwick's work on African American gay men such as Marlon Riggs and Gary Fisher, and later on, obliquely, in their interview with Sedgwick, when she states, "At conferences where I've presented Gary's writing, there's been some very predictable stuff about 'You're a white woman,' for example."[46] Race, or at the very least the black and white dyad, seemed important to Sedgwick (even if she has been challenged for it), but somehow this critical concern got lost in the translation, to those (white?) critics who participate in the *Regarding Sedgwick* volume. This is quite bewildering, given that the names of the essays augur a Puerto Rican queer richness: Crimp's discussion of Mario Móntez and Melissa Solomon's analysis of the Puerto Rican bisexual novelist, cartoonist, and now performance artist Erika López.[47] No doubt the book is rich and provocative in many ways but certainly not with regard to being queer and of color. For the contributors of this volume, it seems, queer equals white.

Crimp's theoretical and methodological blind spot is shared by Melissa Solomon, at least as far as her essay in *Regarding Sedgwick* is concerned. Solomon's elaboration on Sedgwick's lesbian bardo (based on the Buddhist notion of in-between space, a transition) and its relation to Erika López's first novel, *Flaming Iguanas*, which focuses on the cross-country motorcycle narrative of a half-Quaker, half–Afro-Puerto Rican, bisexual art student, is enormously productive. Yet it boggles the mind to think that for Solomon the only ethnic difference that warrants sustained analysis in her essay is that of being Jewish.[48] How is it possible that López's radical approach to sexuality can be divorced from her ethnicity and from her profound and constant racial analysis? How can it be that the intricate relation of in-betweenness López explores in terms of race and class and ethnicity can disappear into a discussion of sexuality devoid of other considerations? What happened to Kimberlé W. Crenshaw's and Chela Sandoval's call for intersectionality as a critical practice?[49] Are readers of Sedgwick averse to Chicana lesbian or U.S. third-world feminism? Do you have to be a person of color to quote queer theorists of color? This, alas, seems to be precisely what is going on in a discursive and citational framework where theory is defined as white and (queer, Puerto Rican) people of color such as Mario Móntez and Erika López can, at best, be the objects of study or the illustration for white theory, but not radicalizing tools used by white people to deconstruct their own hegemony and power. Of course Audre Lorde had said it all along: "The master's tools will never dismantle the master's house." Perhaps it is foolish or naïve to expect white queer critics to generously give up their white privilege without a struggle (or to publish essays such as this one in their anthologies, for that matter).

Crimp's reading of Móntez makes one desire a critical engagement with the ideas of the Martinican intellectual Frantz Fanon, specifically with Fanon's horror in France, with his recognition of the pervasiveness of racism even in children, and how that moment of experience (racist interpellation) serves as a moment of revelation and knowledge production for the subaltern subject. Yet Fanon, much like Bernardo Vega, is a dangerous and slippery (queer) subject; the Fanon I wish to rescue is the Fanon queered by the black British filmmaker Isaac Julien, made queer by men caressing each other in films such as *Looking for Langston* and *Frantz Fanon: Black Skin, White Mask*. Fanon is like Bernardo Vega, a foundational figure, a leader and theorist of his collectivity, and a homophobe. I do not applaud or celebrate this, but I also manage to overcome this limitation and rescue what is of worth. Both Fanon and Vega are dead straight men of color from a different time and age, and while their myopia is not excusable there is little that can be done about it except offer a strong critique.[50] My fellow revelers at the Garden Party, the scholars who participated in the Queer Shame Conference, and the authors of *Regarding Sedgwick* seem quite alive, for the most part, and as such don't have the same excuse; their lack of engagement is deplorable.

When reading Crimp's essay one is struck at his insistence on the shared shame he experiences while viewing Mario Móntez's humiliations, reflected in the phrase "poor Mario," when in fact what I feel is not shame at all but rather anger, rage, and disgust. I would suggest that Crimp's shame is not an identification with or pity for Mario Móntez at all (something he suggests himself in the essay); it is not a placing of oneself in the shoes of the other (the victim). Rather it is precisely the shame of being complicit in that act of oppression: Crimp's conscious or unconscious identification with Ronald Tavel and Andy Warhol, his unacknowledged shame at the specter of racism, of his inability to transcend his gay white privilege.[51] I am struck at Warhol's and Tavel's "brilliance," if I might call it that, in being so unashamedly, transparently, or clearly racist: to be so upfront, so willing to enact a racist scenario in front of the camera and forgo the customary masks and sleights of hand that serve to cover up people's true intentions and beliefs. In his call for a validation of distinctiveness and heterogeneity Crimp fails to understand and acknowledge the role of race and ethnicity. What Warhol and Tavel fail to understand, or rather did not care to understand, is that sometimes cruel unmasking is not enough.

Crimp's essay is constructed as a response to or extension of Sedgwick's essay "Queer Performativity," which begins by discussing the Rutgers conference on gay and lesbian studies in 1991. She proposes an exploration of Butler's notion of performativity through the affect of shame. It is a strange essay. For most of her analysis the reader has the distinct impression that Sedgwick conceives shame as universal, when in fact what she offers is a theorization of a culturally specific Anglo-American affect (the meaning and connotations of *shame* in English, in dominant white U.S. communities); *vergüenza* (shame in Spanish) is a totally different thing, as we will discuss later on.

Anglo-American normativity frames and defines Sedgwick's argument, in much the same way that heterosexuality framed J. L. Austin's arguments on speech acts in *How to Do Things with Words*: for most of the essay race and ethnicity seem to be Sedgwick's blind spots. Then, toward the end, there is a striking observation:

It seems very likely that the structuring of associations and attachments around the affect shame is among the most telling differentials among cultures and times: not that the entire world can be divided between (supposedly primitive) "shame cultures" and (supposedly evolved) "guilt cultures," but rather that, as an affect, shame is a component (and *differently* a component) of all. Shame, like other affects, is not a discrete intrapsychic structure, but a kind of free radical that (in different people and in different cultures) attaches to and permanently intensifies or alters the meaning of—of almost anything: a zone of the body, a sensory system, a prohibited or indeed a permitted behavior, another affect such as anger or arousal, a named identity, a script for interpreting other people's behavior toward oneself.[52]

It is precisely this "*differently*" that remains unexplained in Sedgwick's essay, that Crimp seems to have so profoundly missed. I can only wonder how Sedgwick's theorization would have been different if she had earnestly engaged with her own proposal.

Sedgwick's essay appears in the inaugural issue of GLQ, a lesbian and gay studies journal edited at the time by Carolyn Dinshaw and David M. Halperin. Her essay is followed by a response from Judith Butler, "Critically Queer," which went on to become the last chapter of *Bodies That Matter*. Butler also calls for the recognition of cultural diversity as part of a critique of identity politics, and in fact questions dominant (U.S.) ideologies of outness, challenging them on cultural grounds. Her insistence on the "trouble" or problems with *queer* as a category of definition is a refreshing critical move; she herself, however, has been challenged by feminist scholars of color such as bell hooks and Coco Fusco for her own limitations regarding race, particularly in her analysis of the documentary *Paris Is Burning*.[53]

In the remainder of this essay I focus on Latina and Latino community activism, cultural production, and linguistic debates, and also return to the scene of the Gay Shame Conference. I propose that *gay shame* is a useful analytical category but hardly an unproblematic or universal one; in fact some Latinas and Latinos propose an "anti–gay shame" critique that is much richer and more interesting than Anglo-American deployments. Yet some queer Latina and Latino scholars' embrace of this term (such as Negrón-Muntaner's and Muñoz's) force me to acknowledge the multiplicity of views and divergences even within this much more narrowly defined Latina and Latino queer space.

QUEER LATINA AND LATINO SHAMELESSNESS

Gay shame, Latina- and Latino-style, can be seen as, among other things, the total and absolute lack of shame. Two events bring us back to Ann Arbor, to the source of this very reflection. The first is a conference organized by Tomás Almaguer, ¡Sin Vergüenza! (Shameless), held at the University of Michigan in

2000, where Muñoz presented "Latina Performance and Queer Worldmaking" and Negrón-Muntaner presented "Ricky's Hips" (later a chapter in Boricua Pop), where she discusses her understanding of how the closeted Puerto Rican pop star Ricky Martin negotiates the shame of his (at the time) undisclosed homosexuality and of what she calls his "ethno-nationality," and how he ironically becomes a spokesperson for Puerto Rican national pride. The second event is an unforeseen performance documented by Judith Halberstam at the Gay Shame Conference in 2003, when Michael Warner mouthed the word diarrhea in a parody or imitation of Mario Móntez.

One of the main arguments of the gay shame movement (particularly in its most radical incarnation as a direct-action activist group in New York and San Francisco) is precisely that the gay pride banner has been co-opted and commercialized beyond recognition, that it has lost all political significance and radical meaning. Gay shame is thus presented as a radical alternative, a view that seems common to activists and to those academics who champion its analysis. In his essay Crimp in fact calls for an "ethico-political" function of shame.[54] Yet this rejection of gay pride is curious if we consider the Latina and Latino embrace of the sinvergüenza label. To be shameless (or free of shame) is quite clearly not the same as to be proud; shamelessness is not the opposite of pride, but of shame itself. In Spanish "pride" is orgullo, and in fact there are now marchas and desfiles and paradas de orgullo gay across the Americas and in the Iberian peninsula, some more precarious and some more established. Pride, I dare say, has not quite won the battle, however, neither here nor in the rest of the world.

I am curious to know exactly how many queer people of color (besides Muñoz and Negrón-Muntaner) have embraced the call to gay shame. The unstable status of gay pride in the U.S. Latina and Latino environment is revealing; a comparison of the New York City Gay Pride Parade to that city's National Puerto Rican Day Parade, both held annually in June, will serve to illustrate this point (and remind us of Ríos Ávila's initial meditation on parades, public space, and identity formation). While Latina and Latino participation in the first might seem and in fact is significant, this participation is uneven. For example, in 2003 the Venezuelan, Peruvian, and Colombian contingents in the Gay Pride Parade were huge, but there was almost no organized participation of Puerto Ricans, who historically and numerically constitute the largest Latino ethnic group in the city. The participation of marchers with the longest standing pan-Latino queer activist and social groups, Las Buenas Amigas and Latino Gay Men of New York, was also noticeably limited. Yet Puerto Rican flags dotted the sidewalks and random contingents within the parade, and at least there was a marked space of tolerance. This is different from the experience of participating in the noticeably small queer contingent in the National Puerto Rican Day Parade, often the site of harassment by the spectators.[55] Queer Puerto Ricans are struggling to gain a space in their national ethnic imaginary, and an embrace of shame does not seem to be a productive move; in fact to ask a Latina or Latino to embrace shame is perhaps patently absurd (a point Negrón-Muntaner seems to agree with).[56]

What are the intrinsic differences between shamelessness and shame? Why would some queer Latina and Latino activists, artists, and scholars (myself included) be more inclined to the former? Shame, it has been argued, is a central constitutive behavior of Latina/o cultures, engaged as they are with Catholic religiosity, feelings of guilt, and remorse about improper behavior, be it religious (sins) or the failing of family or social obligations.[57] Shame is a structuring device that works especially in the maintenance of female subordination but also in the reification of (heterosexual) male masculinity. In his incisive analysis of Nicaraguan male homosexualities ("Subject Honor, Object Shame") the gay white American anthropologist Roger Lancaster has highlighted how stigma is attributed in Latin America to effeminate men precisely on the basis of their "passive" or receptive sexual role; the Chicano historian Tomás Almaguer has argued similarly for U.S Latino men.[58] As such, shame is a feeling Latinas and Latinos (especially queer ones) grapple with (and struggle against) on a daily basis.

To be a *sinvergüenza* is to have no shame: to disobey, break the law, disrespect authority (the family, the church, the state), and in a perverse and curious way to be proud of one's transgression, or at the very least lack a feeling of guilt. A comparison of dictionary definitions of *shame* and *vergüenza*, as well as of *shameless* and *sinvergüenza*, is quite useful in clarifying these cultural differences. It becomes immediately apparent that the terms are not exact cognates, that there are profound cultural differences in the linguistic shift. Shame is a central category in Latina/o cultures in a way that has no correspondence in dominant Anglo culture in the United States, even if Nathaniel Hawthorne's *The Scarlet Letter* would suggest otherwise.

According to the eminent Spanish lexicographer María Moliner, *sinvergüenza* has a quite explicit double meaning, including one "applied with benevolence" to those who are quick-witted, clever, and do not cause great harm: "(1) Se aplica a las personas que estafan, engañan o cometen actos ilegales o reprobables en provecho propio o cualquier clase de inmoralidades. A veces se aplica con benevolencia, como 'desvergonzado, granuja, perillán, pícaro, pillo' o 'tunante,' a la persona hábil para engañar, que engaña en cosas no graves, y hábil también para no dejarse engañar. (2) Descarado."[59] Compare that to the definition of *shameless* in *Webster's Third New International Dictionary*: "(1) devoid of shame: insensible to disgrace: unscrupulous; (2) showing lack of shame on the part of the agent." Webster's definition is followed by a large number of synonyms with quite detailed explanations. Of all the terms offered, the one which perhaps most approximates the meaning in Spanish I am alluding to is that for *impudent*: "now rare in this sense, implies bold and cocky defiance of modesty or decency <conduct so sordidly unladylike that even the most *impudent* woman would not dare do it openly—G. B. Shaw>."

The culturally specific Latina/o conception of shamelessness explains the variety of ways the term has been embraced, which includes the names of activist and social groups, artist's manifestoes, (unpublished) anthologies, and academic and student conferences. One example is a Latina lesbian group led by Emma Moreno in Seattle that has precisely adopted this as their name: Las sinvergüenzas (the Shameless Females).[60] Another is tatiana de la tierra's unpublished manuscript project, "Las Sinvergüenzas: Erotic Queer Latina Writings and Art," prefaced by her introductory essay "Las Sinvergüenzas," as well as her autobiographical text "Maybe I Should Be Ashamed but I'm Not: Autobiography of una Sinvergüenza."[61] Finally, as far as conferences go, we have Sin Vergüenza y Con Pasión (Shameless and with Passion), the third annual Queer Latino/a Youth Conference, held in Los Angeles on November 20, 1999, as well as "Sin Vergüenza (Shameless): Interdisciplinary Research on Latino/a Sexualities," a day-long roundtable held at the University of Michigan on April 15, 2000. The first conference, Sin Vergüenza y Con Pasión: The Unmasking of Queer Liberation and Culture, was sponsored by La Familia of UCLA and Stanford and Berkeley's ¿Y Qué? and attended by about 250 people.[62] At the second, visiting panelists, visual artists, and performers discussed the subtleties of Chicana and Chicano, Puerto Rican, and Cuban American identities and social and cultural formations, particularly those pertaining to gender and sexuality.[63]

It would seem that queer Latina/o usage of the term *sinvergüenza* (a noun which can also be written *sin vergüenza*, i.e., "without shame") signals a negotiation between the varied definitions that María Moliner offers: in part a resignification of the term, or perhaps an insistence on its "antisocial" meaning; in part an explicit allusion to the Hispanic tradition of tolerance of subversion, a culturally specific willingness to allow diversity or difference in particular spaces and times that is markedly different from Anglo-American practice.

In tatiana de la tierra's case, being a *sinvergüenza* is the result of a long process of self-liberation, of extended experimentation and coming together with diverse feminist groups and especially with queer Latin American and U.S. Latina women interested in channeling their energies into political and artistic projects. *Sinvergüenzas* are sex radicals who do not uphold dominant conceptions of propriety and are not afraid to tread on delicate ground, claiming pornography, erotica, s/m, and all types of physical expression as their own. As de la tierra explains, this radicalness has caused schisms within Latina lesbian circles, where more conservative women have opposed this provocative, iconoclastic stance. It is no surprise that de la tierra, born in Colombia and raised in Miami, who has self-published three books to date and was one of the key figures behind the Latina lesbian journals *esto no tiene nombre* and *conmoción*, has been unable to find a publisher for her *sinvergüenzas* anthology.[64]

MICHIGAN SHAME

What happened exactly in those almost three years that separated the two University of Michigan conferences? How did we go from Latina/o *sinvergüencería* to white, Anglo gay shame? I do not have an easy answer. I would like to conclude, however, by revisiting the scene described by Judith Halberstam of Michael Warner's lip sync at the Gay Shame Conference in 2003. As I mentioned earlier, I did not attend this conference; when I first wrote this essay (in 2003, as a recently arrived, untenured junior professor at the University of Michigan, Ann Arbor) my comments relied principally on Halberstam's written account (a draft) and on a substantial number of anecdotal and informal communications from people who were there. Halberstam has since sharpened her analysis (in the published version), and her vision is greatly complemented by Hiram Pérez's own account and theorization of what occurred, specifically in reaction to the display of images of a Puerto Rican porn star named Kiko by Ellis Hanson, a professor at Cornell University (whose name Halberstam misspells as Hansen), who spoke about Plato's *Symposium* and did not comment on the very particular images he chose to illustrate his talk.

According to Halberstam, Pérez, the sole Latino academic participant at the event (and at the time an assistant professor in New Jersey, who would be denied tenure in 2005), found himself in the position of having to articulate a defense of queers of color and a critique of the conference:

It was left to Hiram Pérez, one of the very few people of color presenting work at the conference, to address an angry and impassioned critique at Hansen [sic] when Pérez finally had his turn to speak on the last panel of the conference. Hansen [sic] responded defensively to Pérez, and shortly thereafter the conference disintegrated into the usual formulaic exchanges at the open mike about who was and who was not represented on the panels. The painful session only ended when Michael Warner grabbed the mike and mimicked Móntez saying "diarrhea."

The spectacular dissolution of communication at Gay Shame was predictable and in a way inevitable. The punctuation of the conference by the apparently humorous but actually deeply offensive image of a white gay man (Warner) mimicking a drag queen of color (Móntez) who is lip-synching to the voice of another white gay man (Tavel) captures perfectly the racial dynamics of the conference as a whole. Pérez found himself very much in the position of Móntez: he could speak but he would always be read as a queer of color performing as a person of color and leaving the space of articulation open to the *real* gay subjects: white gay men.[65]

I am entranced by the image of Warner "mimicking a drag queen of color (Móntez) who is lip-synching to the voice of another white gay man (Tavel)," as Halberstam so eloquently describes it, because of the uncanny (thematic) coincidence of this anecdote with my own experience reading one of my own short stories, "La mierda" (Shit), which I presented in public on several occasions in the late 1990s.[66] I am pleased that my verbal shit preceded Warner's, and that on both occasions of its public display it has been for Spanish-speaking Latina and Latino audiences in New York, for people who know what I mean when I say that cagarse encima es algo desagradable, pero total, así es la vida. Y uno qué va a hacer. Lo grande es que en el sexo y el amor, ocurren todo tipo de cosas misteriosas, divinas, horribles, maravillosas, apestosas, por qué no. Y por supuesto, a uno lo critican. ¿Y qué? Y con eso los dejo, queridos lectores y queridas lectoras. Con la memoria de una pobre travesti boricua diciendo la palabra "diarrea" para un hombre blanco que no la respeta, y con la imagen de éste, su servidor, cagándose en las injusticias del universo. Me rectifico: no digamos "pobre." Con la imagen de Mario Móntez, una travesti boricua extraordinaria que ha pasado a la historia del arte y de la cultura norteamericana y, por qué no, universal—perdonando la leve exageración—y de un pato que la venera y se complace en recordarla gloriosa, tal como ella se veía a sí misma; con la imagen de un maricón sinvergüenza (¡una loca enfurecida y rabiosa!) que está cansado de que en los Estados Unidos se ignore la cultura latina homosexual (y el idioma español) vez tras vez tras vez.

NOTES

My heartfelt appreciation to Michael Hames-García and Ernesto Martínez for all of their help with this essay, as well as to the anonymous peer reviewers of this book for their suggestions. Additional thanks to the numerous interlocutors who heard or read drafts of this paper at Bowling Green State University (2005), the American Studies Association annual convention in Philadelphia (2007), and the Tepoztlán Institute for Transnational History of the Americas (2008), and very particularly to Ben Sifuentes-Jáuregui, Yolanda Martínez-San Miguel, and Nicole Guidotti-Hernández.

1. The Center, which was established in 1983 at 208 West Thirteenth Street, has since changed its name and is now called the New York City Lesbian, Gay, Bisexual, and Transgender Community Center. The Garden Party event I describe occurred while I was living in New Jersey and teaching as an assistant professor at Rutgers University, New Brunswick.

2. For a history of the Hawaiian shirt, see Hope and Tozian, *The Aloha Shirt*; Steele, *The Hawaiian Shirt*.

3. Jesús Colón and Bernardo Vega are foundational figures of the Puerto Rican diasporic community in New York. See Colón, *A Puerto Rican*; Vega, *Memoirs*.

4. See Ramos Otero, "La otra isla de Puerto Rico."

5. Bourdieu, *Distinction*.

6. By *camp* I am referring to a series of processes of signification predominantly engaged in by gay men, in which objects and practices acquire particular meanings through humor and acerbic wit; it can also be seen as an aesthetics or style. See Sontag, "Notes on 'Camp'"; E. Newton, *Mother Camp*.

7. I should clarify that while I agree with Gallop's methodology, I do not always care for the anecdotes and interpretations she presents. For a pointed critique of Gallop (particularly of her earlier *Feminist Accused of Sexual Harassment*), see I. Reyes, "Conference Sex"; Jaschik, "Tricks of the Trade."

8. B. Christian, "The Race for Theory," 68.

9. Lorde, "The Uses of Anger," 124. My deepest appreciation to Nicole Guidotti-Hernández for seeing the profound methodological and thematic feminist links between my work and that of Lorde and encouraging me to reread "The Uses of Anger."

10. Ríos Ávila, *La raza cómica*, 301.

11. See Duggan, "The New Homonormativity," 175–94.

12. See Warner, *The Trouble with Normal*, 35–36. This passage is discussed by Douglas Crimp (see below).

13. The African American and Latino practices of *reading* and *throwing shade*, amply discussed in Jennie Livingston's *Paris Is Burning* (1990) and in E. Patrick Johnson's work,

consist of making others feel ashamed of who or what they are. These practices work by engaging the participants in a verbal or communicative competition in which opponents try to outdo each other by pointing out flaws or imperfections in appearance or character. *Reading* does not intrinsically have to be negative and can also be used as a form of flattery or praise. Johnson's definition of *throwing shade* differs somewhat from mine, as he argues that it is a nonverbal form of reading (thus not involving words). See Livingston, *Paris Is Burning*; Johnson, "SNAP! Culture."

14. Johnson makes fascinating observations in "SNAP! Culture" about the appropriateness and inappropriateness of reading and throwing shade in different contexts and among different people. In general he argues that more assimilated, "bourgeois" individuals within the African American community disparage this behavior, and that it is not appropriate for certain spaces, such as church.

15. See Johnson, "SNAP! Culture," where he argues that reading and throwing shade (and snapping) can in fact be positive or negative, aggressive or humorous, respectful or disrespectful, and harmless or offensive, depending on the context and the persons involved.

16. Ríos Ávila, *La raza cómica*.

17. Yolanda Martínez-San Miguel discusses Ríos Ávila's *bacalaíto* anecdote in her very lucid essay "Más allá de la homonormatividad."

18. Ríos Ávila, *La raza cómica*, 302, emphasis in the original.

19. See E. Pérez, "Irigaray's Female Symbolic."

20. Johnson, "'Quare' Studies."

21. Johnson, "'Quare' Studies," 2, 3.

22. Johnson, "'Quare' Studies," 1, 3. Johnson subsequently expanded his ideas in a performance piece, "Strange Fruit."

23. Ferguson, *Aberrations*, 54–81.

24. For a discussion of Jameson's concept of the "political unconscious" and its relevance to Latina and Latino studies, see Limón, *Dancing with the Devil*, 14–15.

25. For an overview of the development of (white) queer theory, see Jagose, *Queer Theory*.

26. In this section I am playing with the written accent mark on Móntez, but a more complete analysis would discuss issues of phonology and pronunciation in spoken English, especially as they are problematized (or pathologized) as signs of cultural difference and inferiority for immigrants and non-Anglo-Saxon, middle-class, white English speakers: language as the mark of stigma and, obviously, as the source of shame. See Zentella, *Growing Up Bilingual*. I thank Ben Sifuentes-Jáuregui and Yolanda Martínez-San Miguel for reminding me of the role of language and linguistic discrimination in the constitution of Latina/o shame. The issue of phonetic gender trouble for transgender individuals is also extremely complex and merits further discussion.

27. See Jaffe, "Gay Shame." Also see the web site for the direct-action group Gay Shame San Francisco, "Gay Shame: A Celebration of Resistance," as well as the resource

site "Gay Shame: A Virus in the System." For a history of gay shame activism, see Mattilda, "Gay Shame."

28. See Sycamore, *That's Revolting!*

29. In a section titled "Antigay?," Muñoz writes:

A close friend of mine and I have a joke we return to every June. On the occasion of gay pride celebrations of lesbian and gay visibility and empowerment held early in the summer in many major North American cities, we propose a *gay shame day parade*. This parade, unlike the sunny gay pride march, would be held in February. Participants would have to deal with certain restrictions if they were to properly engage the spirit of gay shame day: Loud colors would be discouraged; gay men and lesbians would instead be asked to wear drab browns and grays. (*Disidentifications*, 111)

Muñoz goes on to compare his scenario to that discussed by the contributors to Mark Simpson's anthology *Anti-Gay*.

30. See "Latino Dolls" in Quiroga, *Tropics of Desire*, 169–90.

31. Negrón-Muntaner and González, "Boricua Gazing."

32. Mario Móntez appeared in Jack Smith's *Flaming Creatures* (1963) and *Normal Love* (1963); Warhol's *Mario Banana* (1964), *Harlot* (1964), *Screen Test #2* (1965), *Camp* (1965), *The Life of Juanita Castro* (1965), *More Milk Yvette* (1965), *The Chelsea Girls* (1965), *Ari and Mario* (1966), and *Hedy* (1966); José Rodríguez Soltero's *Lupe* (1966); Jonas Mekas's *Walden: Diaries, Notes and Sketches* (1969; specifically in "Stephen Shore's party, Stephen Shore's home, New York City, 12 January 1966"); and Rosa Von Praunheim's *Underground and Emigrants* (1975). Also see Comenas, *Warholstars 2002*; Suárez, "The Puerto Rican Lower East Side."

33. The accent over the *o* in *Móntez* would correspond to the word's tonic stress on the penultimate syllable (*una palabra llana*), indicated by a written accent, as a word that ends in a consonant other than *n* or *s*. For a discussion of the formation of patronymics in Spanish with the addition of the suffix -*ez* (such as Benítez, Gómez, López, Márquez, Pérez, and Ramírez), see "Patronímicos." I must acknowledge, however, the possibility (indicated to me by the Puerto Rican linguist Gloria Prosper-Sánchez in a personal communication) that Montez is a name with the tonic stress on the last syllable (*una palabra aguda*), similar to other last names such as Cortés or Cortez or Marqués, suggesting a person from the mountains (*el monte*).

34. See V. Pérez and Peguero, "María Montez"; Seymour, *Lola Montez*; "Lola Montez."

35. See Álvarez, "Freeing La Musa."

36. Most distinctly I recall a very heated public argument with Ellis Hanson during a session at the CLAGS conference Futures of the Field: Building LGBT Studies into the 21st Century University at the Graduate Center of the City University of New York, 20–21 April 2001. Hanson moderated a lunch discussion group charged with identifying (or discussing) what would be key, foundational texts of lesbian and gay or queer studies; he was willing to recognize only texts written by white European authors.

37. Ferguson, *Aberrations*, 1.

38. La Fountain-Stokes's letter to Douglas Crimp, included in this essay; Negrón-Muntaner and González, "Boricua Gazing"; Love, "Gay Shame Redux." Mattilda accused the conference organizers of having appropriated the activist group's name and not giving it credit; yet as I have discussed, Sedgwick and Butler were discussing gay shame a good number of years before the activist group was formed. For a good discussion of confusions of origins and matters of appropriation, see Johnson, "SNAP! Culture."

39. See Cruz-Malavé, Queer Latino Testimonio, 95–119; Ríos Ávila, "The End of Gay Culture?"

40. An edited volume based on the conference appeared in 2009. See Halperin and Traub, Gay Shame. I should also indicate that my essay was subsequently submitted for publication in the special issue of Social Text titled "What's Queer about Queer Studies Now?," coedited by David Eng, José Esteban Muñoz, and Judith Halberstam, which includes Hiram Pérez's and Halberstam's essays on the conference; my essay was rejected.

41. The accent mark on Móntez was missing (or rather omitted) in my original email message, principally because of the inability of many U.S. email programs in 2003 to read "nonstandard" character sets which then became garbled into a strange, illegible machine language, especially disconcerting for people not accustomed to receiving such distorted texts.

42. Here I faced yet another quandary of email texts and of the incorporation of non-English words into a missive. The option of italics (with its complicated and problematic nature of signaling as different) was invalidated by plain text email programs' tendency to disregard such formatting; thus I relied on quotation marks, which also serve to denature (distinguish) the relationship of the words to the general flow of the text.

43. The conference I am referring to is Crossing Borders: Latino/a and Latin American Lesbian and Gay Testimony, Autobiography and Self-Figuration, held at the Center for Lesbian and Gay Studies, CUNY Graduate Center, New York, 11–13 March 1999. Ríos Ávila read "Final Inqueery" at this conference, in a panel in which Alberto Sandoval-Sánchez spoke about being a Puerto Rican gay man with AIDS. During the question-and-answer period Cherríe Moraga memorably insulted the audience by repeating, over and over, "You're stupid!," in reaction to audience members' apparent greater interest in the theoretical subtleties of Ríos Ávila's paper as opposed to the autobiographical ruminations on illness offered by Sandoval-Sánchez.

44. Crimp, "Mario Montez," 67.

45. Also appears in Halperin and Traub, Gay Shame, 26–27.

46. Barber and Clark, "Queer Moments," 10–13; Barber, Clark, and Sedgwick, "This Piercing Bouquet," 252. I am quite aware that there is also an extensive discussion of Buddhism in the book, but this analysis seems devoid of any connection to the actual lived experience of Asian Buddhists themselves; the religion is approached in the abstract.

47. Solomon, "Flaming Iguanas."

48. E. López, Flaming Iguanas.

49. Crenshaw, "Beyond Racism"; C. Sandoval, Methodology of the Oppressed.

50. For an unfortunately heterosexist critique of Vega, see Gil, *El orden del tiempo*, 55–80.

51. On this issue Negrón-Muntaner states (in her interview with Rita González), "Crimp's essay also has another quality that disturbs me—the repetition of 'poor Mario' as a chorus that underscores that the writer is looking at Mario from a white shaming gaze. The color blindness of so much queer theory is to a large degree what makes it thorny for my own work. And here I have to underscore a very different position than the one found in Crimp and other (white) theorists regarding shame" (Negrón-Muntaner and González, "Boricua Gazing," 1354).

52. Sedgwick, "Queer Performativity," 12, italics in the original.

53. See hooks, "Is Paris Burning?"; Fusco, "Who's Doing the Twist?," 198.

54. Crimp, "Mario Montez," 64.

55. See La Fountain-Stokes, "Culture, Representation," 136–91.

56. See Negrón-Muntaner and González, "Boricua Gazing," 1354.

57. See Díaz Barriga's extraordinary essay, "Vergüenza."

58. See Lancaster, *Life Is Hard*, 235–78; Almaguer, "Chicano Men."

59. Moliner, *Diccionario*.

60. "SUBJECT: Emma Moreno of Entre Hermanos and Hate Free Zone Campaign of Washington," City of Seattle news advisory, 27 November 2002.

61. Also see de la tierra, "Call for Queer Latina Creative Writing and Artwork: *Las Sinvergüenzas: Erotic Queer Latina Writings and Art*," "Buscando: Maricones y tortilleras latin@s for a Cool Literary Cause," and "Proposal for Las Sinvergüenzas Anthology" (electronic documents provided by tatiana de la tierra, 2004).

62. See Rattazzi, "Gay Latino/as Receive Support."

63. Sin Vergüenza! (Shameless): An Interdisciplinary Conference on Latino/a Sexuality was coordinated by Sylvia Orduño. I thank her for providing copies of the program, poster, and other forms of documentation of this event.

64. See de la tierra, *For the Hard Ones, Porcupine Love*, and *Píntame una mujer peligrosa*. Also see de la tierra, "Activist Latina Lesbian Publishing."

65. Halberstam, "Shame and White Gay Masculinity," 230–31. At the time Hiram Pérez was an assistant professor at Montclair State University in New Jersey; his research and scholarship did not focus on Latina/o issues but on African American ones. Pérez was subsequently denied tenure; see Gabel, "English Professor." He is currently an assistant professor of English at Vassar College. I have not had the opportunity to fully incorporate Pérez's important contributions, and as such invite readers to read his work.

66. La Fountain-Stokes, "La mierda." Readings at Diamela Eltit's Columbia University writing seminar (fall 1997) and at the third Puerto Rican Studies Association Conference, held at Brooklyn College, New York (October 1998).

Lawrence La Fountain-Stokes's

"Gay Shame, Latina- and Latino-Style:

A Critique of White Queer Performativity"

Ramón García

How is it that shame, which Frantz Fanon considered "an infernal circle," came to be regarded as an oppositional tactic by queer studies scholars?[1] La Fountain-Stokes's essay makes clear that the male queer reconfiguration of shame has been maneuvered by an all-too-familiar exclusion of race and social class that ends in an all-too-familiar triumph of all that is white, gay, and male—a "romanticization," as Judith Halberstam says, that "glosses over both the particularity of this formation and the damage of its myopic range."[2] It's as if the libidinal tendencies of queer studies had adapted neoliberal models, rapaciously claiming possession of the liberatory basis of queerness by disempowering all those whose intellectual labor has in fact given queer identity the wealth of its oppositional possibilities. And so we are left marginalized once again, in the third world of unequal exchanges, expected to pay our debt to the myth of gay politics originating in Stonewall.

We have to summon our resistance once again, which is both a necessity and an occasion to claim the legitimacy of our difference and the centrality of our experience. This seems to me the theme of La Fountain-Stokes's essay, which polemically dismantles the "shameful" manner in which queer shame has been conceptualized without consideration for those who have had shame directed at them from so many insidious quarters and whose courageous resistance to the destructive nature of shame has been the most radical and constructive. La Fountain-Stokes attempts to make sense of the disjunction between what shame means for people of color and the manner in which it has been recovered and rewritten by middle-class white gay men.

La Fountain-Stokes's discussion of Rios Ávila's shame or mixed feelings of speaking from the I articulates a significant problematic that many of us encounter as artists and intellectuals of working-class backgrounds. For even to speak shame, to name it, becomes a politically fraught decision. As La Fountain-Stokes indicates, some of the most significant literary and theoretical texts by Latino artists and scholars have used "anecdote and personal history." This, after all, is an American tradition. Walt Whitman built his universalist vision from the heart of a gay humanistic self, and the confessional poets of postwar North America (Robert Lowell, John Berryman, Sylvia Plath, Anne Sexton, and others) founded their school on the naming of shameful personal experiences. But unlike the confessional poets, the use of a testimonial or a confessional mode by Latinos (especially queer Latinos) has produced anxiety in the artists and a questioning of its intellectual legitimacy, so that the work of writers such as Cherríe Moraga and Gloria Anzaldúa is placed in a position of "defend[ing] the legitimacy of self-referential writing as a source of knowledge and power." But why should it have to be defended? As La Fountain-Stokes states, "Authors such as Anzaldúa, Moraga, Muñoz, Lorde, and Pérez suggest that one should not feel shame (or *impropriety*) about engaging in self-testimonial narratives (what can be read as a very particular type of confession), particularly when these serve to validate, document, and even critique one's own and other people's experience." This problematic, the anxiety of naming our experience, has less to do with artistry and intellectual rigor than with the unevenness of institutional power and racism. To speak of the shameful intricacies of the self becomes, for the white middle-class artist (Sharon Olds, for example), a claiming of power and a legitimate aesthetic stance with literary precedence in the confessional poetry of postwar America. However, when Latinos, and especially Latina queers, give voice to difficult experiences—experiences neither uplifting nor comforting—the intellectual validity of their confessional stance is questioned (sometimes by the artists themselves). What is the origin of this intellectual double standard? To represent *shame*, to narrate those things that have been coded with shame, often means countering the heteronormative narratives of Latino culture that silence the queer. And so we risk encountering resistance from our own community, as the controversies of the use of *joto* for a caucus at the NACCS conference demonstrated a decade ago.

But what does it mean to represent *shame*, to bear testimony to it? It means to honestly represent our lives, defying the internal and external censors. This, in and of itself, will be a political act, a text rooted in a historical and political reality. As in the Latin American *testimonio*, the confessions we voice will inevitably, unavoidably resist the structures of power currently in place. This is perhaps what causes the most opposition, and why shame is often questioned, disregarded, or invalidated. When Robert Lowell and Sharon Olds represent their most intimate experiences, their naming of what is supposed to be taboo is considered radical, is even accorded a sort of lurid glamour. Yet when Latino writers and theorists engage in a similar aesthetic enterprise, the validity of their artistic project is questioned, and they are accused of complaining, of portraying themselves as victims, of making the culture look bad. But it seems to me important and interesting to address the shame that permeates our experience of skin color, class, race, ethnicity, and sexuality, and I for one do not see how the coding of these human traits with humiliating shame can be transformed into power or resistance without first addressing the mechanisms which distorted them in the first place. La Fountain-Stokes addresses these mechanisms of distortion, and this is a real contribution to our understanding of shame.

One distortion is the elision of class and race. The occlusion of the specific cultural and class dimensions of shame is what is at stake in the consideration of work such as Warhol's *Screen Test #2*, which La Fountain-Stokes discusses in his essay. I watched this mean-spirited work at the Warhol Museum in Pittsburgh with the curator and filmmaker Rita Gonzalez when she was conducting research for her film *The Assumption of Lupe Vélez* (an homage to Mario Móntez and Lupe Vélez), and although I found Móntez's presence on the screen intriguing, the cinematic pleasure of witnessing her visual beauty was destroyed by the racist humiliation and sadism that she was made to endure. Obviously the dread I felt when viewing *Screen Test #2* was due to the fact that cultural identification with Móntez was inevitable. But the viewing of this film also revealed to me why it is important to represent ourselves, to tell our stories, to create our own images of who we are in order to end the voyeuristic and exploitive investments that often make claims on our lives.

One of the most important ideas in La Fountain-Stokes's analysis is a question: At what point does shame about sexuality intersect shame about skin color and social class? This question is so slippery and yet so obvious as it plays out in our lives, since the different shames cannot be separated, or dislodged or transformed separately. This crucible of distorted social and personal factors, operating together, is the metaphysics of shame that needs to be addressed when considering the difference between queers of color and the white, middle-class notions of shame that have defined a new queer politics that speaks exclusively to white, middle-class interests. I read La Fountain-Stokes's insistence on the specificity of shame as the critique running through the essay, especially nuanced in the first section, in his discussion of fashion as a marker of class, culture, and nationality. He describes an experience of shame whose root is class and culture (wearing the "wrong" shirt to a gay garden party), but the shame of social class cannot be separated from the fact that social class makes his queerness different from the queerness of the white males at the party.

The particularity of queer shame in a Latino context is further complicated if we consider that the queer shame I am describing operates in a parallel manner within the Latino community, for queer shame is different even among people of color, when, for example, the shame of skin color is absent in someone with light skin, because the residues of colonization survive in the pride accorded to whiteness. In other words, it is class and skin color that provide the variable and that disrupt any fixed or universalist notions of queer shame within the Latino community. This is the aporia or paradox that La Fountain-Stokes is addressing when he describes his experience of shame at the gay garden party: "I'm so white most people (gay and straight) never guess I'm Puerto Rican, but on the day in question something was different, or at least it felt different to me. In fact I think I've never felt more Caribbean in my life." It was no doubt his sensibility and taste in fashion (a marker of social class and culture) that starkly revealed how his queerness was different from the gayness of the white middle-class men at the New York City garden party.

La Fountain-Stokes is positioning class and culture as necessary factors in a consideration of shame and queerness. His critique of white middle-class queer studies scholars who have conceptualized a falsely radical notion of shame rests on his insistence on the centrality of class, nationality, ethnicity, and culture—on difference as a starting point for any real theorization of what shame is and has been. In exposing the obfuscation or disregard of fundamental differences, he makes a claim for a minoritarian and culturally specific understanding of shame, one that begins at the level of language itself. It is difficult to confront the Medusa face of shame. There is a poem by Alicia Partnoy that for me embodies the bold commitment to speak about the things that have shamed us, that have challenged our humanity and dignity, what Partnoy calls "a cadaver, turning / into seed":

There is the word,
the sweet and forgotten one,
fresh and with roots
or redolent of fear.
Iridescent thing
like the meat
of a cadaver, turning
into seed.[3]

In this fragment of a poem ironically titled "The Art of Poetry" the cadaver, an emblem of oppression and defeat, is paradoxically "turning / into seed." Shame is like that cadaver, a dead thing full of meaning and wounds, but also, paradoxically, something that can be turned into seed, something that has the possibility to heal and return the life that was denied.

NOTES

1. Fanon, *Black Skin/White Masks*, 116.
2. Judith Halberstam writes, "The future of queer studies . . . depends absolutely on moving away from white gay male identity politics and learning from the radical critiques offered by a younger generation of queer scholars who draw their intellectual inspiration from feminism and ethnic studies rather than white queer studies" ("Shame and White Gay Masculinity," 220).
3. Partnoy, "The Art of Poetry," 5.

The Place of Gay Male Chicano Literature in Queer Chicana/o Cultural Work

Antonio Viego

If one agrees to meet the challenge posed by *Tiro de dardos* (Dart Game, 1993), the self-portrait by the gay Mexican artist Nahum Zenil, what is one agreeing to? Those who possess a trenchant gaze whose aim is *true* will prove their acuity at great cost to the body in the painting, for the *bull's-eye* of this target is Zenil's heart. The point of agreeing or not agreeing to play along with the painting's morbid, sexual, and humorous demand may in fact be a moot issue since the *dart*, or any other missile for that matter, which might be thrust at the target is figured at the viewer's scrutinous gaze. To look at this painting is to acquiesce to its terms, to agree to the painting's passive seduction of the viewer, to penetrate the figure with an accurate gaze. A careful surveillance of the target is crucial for any success in Zenil's game. To *look*, then, means also to enter into a certain drama of surveillance of Zenil's body. I would like to suggest that the deployment of surveillance in this drama staged by Zenil indexes and then scrambles the codes by which a homophobic Western cultural imperative insists on the inherent textuality of the homosexual body in order to track it, locate it, read its surface as a target wherever it threatens to go unremarked upon by power-laden discourses and techniques.[1]

Positioned in front of an expansive target whose surface is keyed in the red and green colors of the Mexican flag, Zenil's naked body appears defiant in the face of danger. The painting's gambit suggests that something will be gained as a result of the initial sacrifice of the body. Its cruciform shape makes Zenil's body appear Christ-like, and indeed it would seem that his game draws its horrifying and magnetic erotics from the scene of crucifixion. Does it make a difference that the viewer thinks or knows that the body in the painting is the body of a gay man, that it is an image of Zenil's very own body? Those viewers who know Zenil's work in Mexico know that it is a gay male body because they *know* that Zenil is gay.

An ardent supporter of gay rights in Mexico, Zenil maintains an active role in the organization Círculo Cultural Gay, which since 1987 has presented an exhibition of erotic art by gay, lesbian, and heterosexual artists attended by "a large number of visitors from all sectors of the population, including many families and their children."[2] Many of the published critical accounts of his work, though recognizing some gay content, do not use Zenil's sexuality as an interpretive rubric for reading his work, do not, in short, see the ways Zenil's work may be informed by his deployment of sexuality in a particular way, as an effort to bring the gay male Mexican body into representation and thereby, on some level, address the terms and conditions on which this body's sustained visual intelligibility in Mexican culture is predicated. Zenil's compulsive use of self-portraiture is not read as an expressive practice of homosexual narcissism, but rather as a critical form of self-reflection, as an existential questioning, if you will, which serves as an indictment to all Mexicans to be more critical of themselves and the society in which they live:

> Within the world of Mexican visual arts, Nahum Zenil is an artist deeply re-
> spected and widely admired by the general public. Surely this has to do with
> the fact that his works show once again the importance of the human being's
> encounter with himself. Just as the Mexican School placed the nation before
> a mirror, Nahum has placed himself on the other side of the mirror, infusing
> reality and fantasy with his face, and giving those who see him the opportu-
> nity to reflect on their own existence.[3]

We would be hard-pressed to find a situation akin to this one in the United States, where a gay male artist's work (where the gay male body figures centrally and explicitly in the work) is perceived as interpreting in meaningful ways the experiences of the culture at large and not just speaking to the concerns of a homosexual community. I want to be careful not to overvalue the seemingly utopic dimension to the reception of Zenil's work in Mexico because the analyses which locate meanings of his work in terms of their speaking to a sexually undifferentiated Mexican community risk erasing the important ways his paintings might be remarking upon a specific gay Mexican experience. In other words, one might infer that the canonical status of Zenil's work in Mexican visual arts has been secured to the extent to which the threatening dimension of gay specificity in his work has been downplayed or erased entirely. Despite this possibility, though, Zenil's work continues to create and maintain a cultural intelligibility around the gay male body, where the gay male body contributes in meaningful ways to a culture's understanding of itself: "His ability to connect his interior world with what is essentially Mexican has reached the point where . . . no other artist is capable of reading Mexico and interpreting it as his is."[4]

My brief discussion of the reception and importance of Zenil's work in Mexican visual arts as well as the metaphoric significance of the gay male body as target and object of surveillance in his painting Tiro de dardos keys into a current discussion in Chicano studies concerning the location of gay male Chicano literary discourse. Latina, and Latino scholars find the paucity of gay male Chicano literary work to be somewhat inexplicable given the explosion of published Chicana lesbian literary work over the past ten years, work which is helping to redefine the field of Chicano studies as a literary, political, and critical endeavor. I am particularly interested in the way the observation that notes the paucity of gay male Chicano cultural work is routinely routed through a parallel observation that notes the plethora of Chicana lesbian work.

As a preliminary address to this routine critical observation I would like to first look at an image very similar to Zenil's Tiro de dardos: the photograph "Three Eagles Flying" by the Chicana lesbian artist Laura Aguilar. A signature piece in her portfolio, Aguilar's image, like Zenil's, is a nude self-portrait that juxtaposes the artist's body with the Mexican flag. Aguilar's photograph, however, also cites the U.S. flag, symbolizing her bicultural experience as a U.S. Chicana. Where Zenil's body appears more or less at home in relation to the Mexican flag, Aguilar's body, positioned in between the two flags, suggests "no home in either."[5] Aguilar's body is as confined and restrained as Zenil's is open and exposed. Where Zenil invites pursuit and capture, Aguilar has already been secured and bounded: the Mexican flag is wrapped tight around her head, the U.S. flag binds her lower body, and a rope is knotted around her neck. She is being held hostage in the image, seemingly awaiting execution. Both images pose the queer Mexican and Chicana body in relation to symbols of Mexican and U.S. nationalism, suggesting, among other things, the terms and conditions for queer intelligibility in Mexican and Chicana/o cultures.

During the week prior to my attending the Zenil exhibit held at the Grey Art Gallery in New York City (2 September to 1 November 1997), I was teaching Coco Fusco's English Is Broken Here in a Latina literature course I was offering at the University of Pennsylvania that fall. A reproduction of Aguilar's photograph appears in Fusco's book. One student was stunned at what appeared to be the image's ability to capture in an instant what we had attempted to investigate through the texts we had read up to that point, namely (and generally) the different deployments of the borderland metaphor in Latina literary work and cultural and political complexities that must be negotiated when living in the interstices between cultures. Having just finished reading Cherríe Moraga's play Giving Up the Ghost, this student astutely noted how Aguilar's image captured

Amalia's dilemma at the end of the play: if Amalia agrees to love Marisa according to Marisa's conditions, she will agree to a life of perpetual exile, since lesbianism for Amalia would represent a self-imposed exile from Mexico and thus an untenable divorce from her ethnic and racial community; at the same time she would not fit into the U.S. cultural framework either. Amalia would end up very much like the figure in "Three Eagles Flying," positioned between two cultures, able to claim no home in either. Indeed the entire class seemed to perversely enjoy the exhaustive critical account that Aguilar's image, like a bolt of lightning in our unremarkable classroom, seemed to index with respect to issues in Chicano studies around identity, sexuality, and nationalism. This is perhaps not surprising if we believe the claim of the Chicana literary scholar Yvonne Yarbro-Bejarano, that "in the field of Chicana/o Studies Aguilar's work interrogates certain cultural nationalist discourses of identity and community."[6]

The image of Zenil's queer, naked body positioned in front of a Mexican flag as target provided a powerful, instant visual analogue for what I was trying to think through and write about with regard to the place of gay male Chicano cultural work in Chicano studies, specifically the way the gay male Chicano body has become a target of sorts in different discussions attempting to locate his place in relation to Chicana lesbian literary and cultural work. Of course the image of Zenil's body is not, in any immediate sense, the historical or conceptual equivalent of the gay male Chicano body since Zenil's painting, quite simply, is speaking from within a specific Mexican context, not a Chicano context in the United States. However, given the largely shared ethnic and cultural backgrounds, one must anticipate some overlap with regard to representational practices between Mexican artists in Mexico and Chicano artists in the United States.

I would like to suggest that Zenil's and Aguilar's images serve as visual analogues to the discussion currently waged in Chicano and Latino studies concerning the demand for a more discernible, intelligible gay male Chicano body and discourse. It is my contention that it is somewhere between these two images of a gay male Mexican body and a Chicana lesbian body that we might begin to map out the cultural locations of a gay Chicano literary discourse, as well as determine the conditions by which this discourse is excluded from or provisionally included in the canons of Chicana and Chicano literary and cultural production. The gay male Mexican subject along with the Chicana lesbian subject constitute bookends of sorts, critical props, which keep upright the discussion attempting to discern the place of gay Chicano literary work and its contribution to the field of Chicano studies. For example, Tomás Almaguer's essay "Chicano Men: A Cartography of Homosexual Identity and Behavior" wants to account for the sexual behavior and sexual identity of gay Chicanos by turning first to what appears to be the gay Chicano subject's cultural Doppelgänger: the gay male Mexican subject. Failing to account for how gay Chicanos "negotiate their masculinity in light of their homosexuality" because of lack of research conducted in this area, and failing to discern how gay Chicanos negotiate the different European American and Mexican and Latin American sexual systems in their sexual behavior, Almaguer turns to the work of a Chicana lesbian writer, Cherríe Moraga's *Loving in the War Years: Lo que nunca pasó por sus labios*, in hopes that her autobiographical text might offer an interpretive model by which to account for the different silences around gay Chicano sexuality and identity.

> Unlike the rich literature on the Chicana/Latina lesbian experience, there is a paucity of writings on Chicano gay men. There does not exist any scholarly literature on this topic other than one unpublished study addressing this issue as a secondary concern (Carrillo and Maiorana). The extant literature consists primarily of semi-autobiographical, literary texts by authors such as John Rechy, Arturo Islas, and Richard Rodriguez. Unlike the writings on Chicana lesbianism, however, these works fail to discuss directly the cultural dissonance that Chicano homosexual men confront in reconciling their primary socialization into Chicano family life with the sexual norms of the dominant cultural. They offer little to our understanding of how these men negotiate the different ways these cultural systems stigmatize homosexuality and how they incorporate these messages into adult sexual practices.[7]

> Unlike the "queens" who have always been open about their sexuality, "passing" gay men have learned in a visceral way that being in "the closet" and preserving their "manly" image will not protect them, it will only make their dying more secret. I remember my friend Arturo Islas, the novelist. I think of how his writing begged to boldly announce his gayness, Instead, we learned it through vague references about "sinners" and tortured alcoholic characters who wanted nothing more than to "die dancing" beneath a lightning-charged sky just before a thunderstorm. Islas died of AIDS-related illness in 1990, having barely begun to examine the complexity of Chicano sexuality in his writing. I also think of essayist Richard Rodriguez, who, with so much death surrounding him, has recently begun to publicly address the subject of homosexuality; and yet, even ten years ago we all knew "Mr. Secrets" was gay from his assimilationist *Hunger of Memory*.[8]

It has become a fairly rote observation in Chicano and Latino studies that there is not enough gay Chicano and Latino literary work being produced. The critique draws the structuring logic of its inference from the scene of analogical thinking, which results in the impossibility in apparently nonhomophobic theoretical projects in Chicano and Latino studies of thinking about this paucity in gay Chicano and Latino literary work without indexing the supposed plentitude of published lesbian Chicana literary work. In fact the observation which cites the plentitude of lesbian Chicana literary work, routinely keyed by such rhetorical phrases as "in contrast to . . . ," becomes the very enabling point of entry for an analysis which attempts to contend with the reasons for the less discernible, intelligible canon of gay Chicano and Latino literary work. An accurate assessment of the situation might be this: In the face of so much lesbian Chicana and Latina literary work, why is there not more gay Chicano and Latino literary work? This forumulation of the question seems to be instantiated and supported by a certain common sense that blesses every scene of analogical thinking, where the variables in the equation are chosen for us in advance of the questions we pose, and which in this instance defends its inferences by assuming that if two things (lesbian Latina literary work and gay Latino literary work) are alike in some respect, they must be alike in other respects. In what ways are they assumed to be alike? Apparently both are seen to occupy a certain shared structural position in a European American social hierarchy based on the perception that they share similar (even identical) experiences of homosexuality and racialization. I challenge the extent to which this argument can continue to be framed in the manner that enjoys such repeated play. I want to ask a slightly different set of questions of the framing itself, to ask about the categories which come to be fixed between lesbian Latina and gay Latino identity and experience, which then results in the critical formalist demand that the story told from each perspective be structurally identical, where intelligibility is granted to the extent that the story told has deployed a certain narrativization of the relationship between Chicano and Latino cultural systems and homosexuality. Throughout this essay I would like to bring to bear on this analogical formulation a certain skepticism concerning the assumed relationship between the emergence of a gay Latino discourse and a lesbian Latina discourse. This skepticism challenges the assumption that the conditions of emergence would be the same for a gay Latino discourse as they would for a lesbian Latina discourse, not to mention challenging the assumption that these discourses will resemble each other in easily identifiable ways.

Currently the gay Latino subject serves as a melancholic incitement to critical discourse. He emerges as a point of discussion in Latina/o literary criticism as the occasion for a lamentation which bemoans his inability to *reproduce* himself as culturally intelligible through the different expressive practices of Latina/o literary and cultural work. Analyzing the representation of gay Chicano and Latino men in gay male pornography, Christopher Ortiz claims, "In comparison to the work of Chicana and Latina lesbians, Chicano and Latino gay men have been surprisingly silent in articulating the political and personal meaning of their cultural and sexual identities."[9] Ortiz develops a familiar critical account of how gay Chicano and Latino cultural and literary workers are perceived as failing to *reproduce* themselves in their work as a result of not narrativizing the complex join between the personal, political, cultural, and sexual registers of meaning. Is cultural intelligibility wedded to these registers alone? Ortiz's statement repeats the formula which measures the various failures (and few successes) of narrativity in gay Latino literary work (which is apparently the failure to narrativize experience in a very particular way) according to the expressive practices of narrativity in Latina literary work. What this amounts to is a formalist critical approach to narrativity which demands that the gay Latino subject emerge in cultural and literary work according to the same grid of experiential categories through which lesbian Latina cultural and literary work instantiates a lesbian Latina subject in narrativity. Is gay Latino cultural intelligibility wedded to an analysis of lesbian Latina cultural and literary work?

As an initial point of entry into this discussion, one needs to specify that Ortiz's lamentation is centrally concerned with the representation of a gay Latino subject who does not emerge though the various expressive practices of narrativity in the literary work of gay Latino subjects. Formulated as a question, the lamentation appears to ask, in earnest, Why are gay Latino cultural workers not reproducing gay Latino subjects in their work? One cannot help but take note of the restrictive and regulative notion at work here that seemingly demands a strict correspondence between the ethnoracial and sexual nomination of the cultural worker and the field of meanings available to him as he narrativizes his own style of occupying these ethnoracial nominations. Discursive intelligibility is granted to the extent that these subjects' expressive practices bespeak a dominant cultural understanding of ethnicity, race, and geographical place as the only explanatory models by which to exhaustively account for the ethnoracial subject's identity. One finds in both Almaguer's and Moraga's passages an interpretive practice which demands and enacts this very correspondence in order to determine, in a punitive tone in Moraga's case, the cultural intelligibility of certain gay Latino cultural work. The lamentation which mourns the fact of gay Latino invisibility at the same time also serves to discipline and punish those gay Latino writers, such as Rechy, Islas, and Rodriguez, who, provided with the opportunity to do otherwise, have failed in their work to inscribe the gay Latino subject. More to the point of the problem is the fact that these gay Latino writers have failed to effectively record (and one should read the verb *record* here in its most coercive sense, as a command that one *transcribe* experience faithfully, which in turn feeds the demand that one be legible, readable, trackable) the (assumed to be in advance) discordant relation between Latino cultural systems and lesbian and gay sexual practices. In contrast, the literary work produced by Chicana lesbians, according to Almaguer, translates and intervenes in the meanings for Chicano culture and homosexuality, effectively recording the "cultural dissonance" that Chicana and Chicano homosexuals "confront in reconciling their primary socialization into Chicano family life with the sexual norms of the dominant culture." It might be worth asking after the type of knowledge Almaguer's and Moraga's questions and concerns seek to index. What kind of knowledge is produced in the critique which notes these writers' failures? What is behind the lamentation and condemnation of gay Latino writers in the passages cited earlier?

The gay Latino subject construction in Moraga's passage emerges as a problem which she reads as ultimately weakening Chicana/o political effectivity in a U.S. neocolonial and Chicana/o crypto-nationalist context. Gay Latino men are often figured as the weak links in political movements for Latina/o ethnic and racial empowerment. We need to add to the problem of gay Latino cultural intelligibility in literary work raised in these lamentations a cluster of pertinent questions posed to the academy, questions which attempt to explore the conditions under which lesbian Latina subjectivity has emerged in dominant critical academic discourse and the conditions under which gay Latino subjectivity has failed to enter academic discourse. By *academic discourse* I mean the differently assembled departments and disciplines of American literature, and English literature, Chicano studies, ethnic studies, women's studies, Caribbean studies, Latino studies, American studies, and gay and lesbian studies in primarily North American academic institutional settings. The figure of the Chicana lesbian feminist subject enjoying, at least for the moment anyway, some form of representational employment has been used for various academic institutional needs, and the figure of the gay male Chicano has figured very little if at all. The exploration of the seeming paucity of gay Chicano literary work and the plethora of lesbian Chicana literary work must consider the issues raised earlier.

We know, in a different but related context, that ethnoracial groups in the United States have historically been racialized in unique and different ways, that different racialized populations have not necessarily shared the same structural position in relation to European Americans in the social hierarchy.[10] I think we can amplify the logic of this observation to establish the ways these shared structural positions are themselves traversed by other fracturing social determinants. For example, even though members of the same racialized population will appear to share the same structural position in relation to a dominant racial group, there will appear in the shared structural position other fault lines and fissures which reshape and help break apart the integrity of the spatiality of this structural position, which predominantly appears to cohere around the category of race. Homosexuality as a type of knowledge about social bodies of racialized subjects will constitute just this type of fault line or fissure. Gay and lesbian racialized subjects worry the determinations of a fixed limit or boundary in the spatialities of these structural positions in profound ways, since discourses of racialization will yield different visions of the social bodies of heterosexual and homosexual racialized subjects, not to mention, importantly, different visions of gay and lesbian subjects within the same racialized population. In any racialized population the bodies of lesbians will be subject to different racialization processes than will the bodies of gay men who belong to the same racialized population. I think Moraga's and Almaguer's analyses operate according to the assumption that the lesbian Latina subject and the gay Latino subject are racialized in the same way, that they occupy the same structural position. Understanding otherwise, however, will enable us to ask a different set of questions as to the uneven development of a gay Latino critical praxis in relation to a lesbian Latina critical praxis. Importantly, it will challenge the current critical assumption that the strategies of narrativity employed by Latino gay men in order to translate the experience of occupying identity through categories of race, class, and sexuality will unfold according to the same demands for the cultural intelligibility that determine the strategies of narrativity in Latina lesbian literary work.

Though the fact that the problem of gay Latino cultural intelligibility often emerges only as a point of discussion in relation to or from within the discussion that cites the plethora of Latina cultural work might seem to underscore the impossibility of thinking nonanalogically, we need to proceed against its logic, perversely, in order to detach these inquiries, which initially seem to be queer kin. We need to slow down right before the marker along the critical road which would entice us to assume an alliance between the two based in homosexuality. We seemingly anticipate (and assume) cultural alliances between gay Latino and Latina lesbian politics, and this cultural alliance indeed might be a problem. In a somewhat different but related context Homi Bhabha discusses the fact that the "enunciative position" of contemporary cultural studies attempts to group together a vast range of resistance discourses, for instance the critical discourses of "women, blacks, homosexuals, [and] Third Word migrants," where a generalized sense of "discrimination and misrepresentation" is shared. Bhabha posits that the grouping together of these different critical discourses constitutes a serious problem when one considers that the critical strategies in these resistant discourses are "elaborated around nonequivalent sites of representation": "However, the 'signs' that construct such histories and identities—gender, race, homophobia, postwar diaspora, refugees, the international division of labor, and so on—not only differ in content but often produce incompatible systems of signification and engage distinct forms of social subjectivity."[11] I want to suggest that the contemporary discussion concerning the problem of gay Latino cultural intelligibility expressed by Almaguer and Moraga, as it gets continually posed in relation to a discussion of Latina lesbian cultural intelligibility, constitutes the very problem Bhabha outlines. Moreover I would like to suggest that Latina lesbian and Latino gay cultural intelligibilities constitute potentially "incompatible systems of signification." The conditions of emergence for one discourse may occupy an ambivalent, perhaps even antagonistic relation to the possibility of the other's emergence. In other words, these discourses might not ever be visible (or present) to each other in ways that we recognize as empowering and supportive. Furthermore the values ascribed to the knowledge produced by Latina lesbian and Latino gay critical discourses will be quite different, which might help us understand why certain academic disciplines seem currently to be so fond of the Chicana lesbian feminist subject.

I would like to return to the passages from Almaguer and Moraga to pursue the curious links made between the paucity of gay Latino cultural and literary work, "passing" gay men, and ethnographic writing. On the surface of things Almaguer and Moraga seem to be responding to the same urgency concerning the absence of a recognizable canon of gay Latino literary work. Both passages zone in on the work of Richard Rodriguez and Arturo Islas, two gay Chicano writers, and subject them to different critical analytical treatments. Whereas Moraga questions the extent to which these authors have failed to articulate their homosexuality in their work, Almaguer faults them specifically for not sufficiently narrativizing the "cultural dissonance that Chicano homosexual men confront in reconciling their primary socialization into Chicano family life with the sexual norms of the dominant culture." In short, Moraga penalizes them for not *writing out* their homosexuality in their work, and Almaguer notes the authors' failure to write out what he assumes in advance to be the problematic join between their homosexuality and their ethnoracial cultural histories. Moraga questions the extent to which these authors transmit *any* knowledge of their homosexuality in their writing. Though Almaguer does read a certain transmission of knowledge about homosexuality taking place in the writing, he takes issue with the manner in which these narrativizations have failed to *write out* this knowledge in relation to the authors' Mexican and Chicano ethnoracial cultural histories.

Almaguer is quick to note that lesbian Chicana writers routinely index in their writing the manner in which different cultural systems stigmatize homosexuality.[12] His next move strikes me as odd. His formalist critical approach assumes that the emergence of a gay Latino discourse will be enabled by the identical conditions (conditions which apparently do not include the different histories of racialization experienced by gay Latino men and lesbian Latina women) that have enabled the emergence of a lesbian Chicana critical discourse, and moreover that these two discourses will have, as it turns out, the same story to tell *in the way* they tell it. Can we not think of the difference between the two discourses as the way they emerge according to their different critical address to cultural, racial, sexual, and class histories? A lesbian Chicana discourse has emerged in academic discourse to the extent that it has narrativized *experience* by engaging racial, sexual, cultural, and class histories in order to produce a recognizable, readable subject. In his essay Ortiz underscores the importance of consulting with Chicana lesbian texts for an understanding of Chicano male homosexuality: "The writings of Chicana lesbians . . . have openly discussed intimate aspects of their sexual behavior and reflected upon sexual identity issues. How they have framed these complex sexual issues has major import for our understanding of Chicano male homosexuality."[13] There are going to be some obvious benefits from consulting with Chicana lesbian texts to see "how they have framed these complex sexual issues" and how a particular residing in a racialized, homosexual identity is textually constructed. At the same time I believe that gay Chicano texts might frame these issues differently. One might say that a gay Latino discourse has not emerged according to the same discursive code, or indeed will not emerge by way of narratives that elaborate the knot (or the braiding) of sexuality and race. What may be distinctive about the narrativization of a gay Latino subject concerns the different ways this expressive practice apprehends categories such as race and sexuality in an effort to textually inscribe a coherent, readable "self." Some critics may demand, in restrictive ways, that the emergence of a gay Latino subject can be culturally intelligible only to the extent that he unfolds through an address to Latino culture in discernable ways and that he "teach" us about "cultural dissonance."

The specific aim in Almaguer's essay is to explore the behavior of gay Chicano men in the context of a dominant "European-American sexual system." The following passages outline some of the more pressing questions his study wants to raise:

> How do Chicano homosexuals structure their sexual conduct, especially the sexual roles and relationships into which they enter? Are they structured along lines of power/dominance firmly rooted in a patriarchal Mexican culture that privileges men over women and the masculine over the feminine? Or do they reflect the ostensibly more egalitarian sexual norms and practices of the European-American sexual system?

> Why does only a segment of homosexually active Chicano men identify as "gay"? Do these men primarily consider themselves Chicano gay men (who retain primary emphasis on their sexual preference)?[14]

I find the critical methodology of Almaguer's project both compelling and troubling because it taxonomizes, weighs, graphs, plots, and evaluates every sexual practice in which gay Chicano men engage. Even the title sounds a bit suspect, betraying the timbre and cadence of a sexological study from the turn of the century. The essay reads both as an aggressive, invasive intervention into the sexual spaces of Chicano gay men and as an insightful, careful study conducted in the service of collecting important Latino gay community life-sustaining knowledge. Of course the knowledge this study wants to gain is also already the problematic knowledge of homophobia, since it can make of this kind of analytical focus a treatise on the development of finer surveillance techniques to read and track homosexuals.

Almaguer's essay is a sociological study and to this extent he has gleaned his knowledge of gay Chicano men's sexual practices from the real-life sexual experiences of gay Chicano men. He concludes that there is not enough information on the sexual behavior of some gay Chicano men to answer the questions he initially poses. I should specify that it is three particular groups of gay Chicano men who resist Almaguer's knowledge-gathering analysis:

> They include . . . Latino men who openly consider themselves gay and participate in the emergent Latino subculture in the Mission district; . . . Latino

men who consider themselves gay but do not participate in the Latino gay subculture, preferring to maintain a primary identity as Latino and only secondarily a gay one; finally, . . . Latino men who are fully assimilated into the white San Francisco gay male community in the Castro District and retain only a marginal Latino identity.[15]

He notes, "We know very little, however, about the actual sexual conduct of these individuals." At this moment in the essay the analysis reaches an impasse, where the failure to gather any further sexual knowledge in the field forces the social scientist to look elsewhere, *elsewhere* denoting a place other than the place of the sexually practicing gay male Chicano: "In the absence of such knowledge, we may seek clues about the social world of Chicano gay men in the perceptive writings of Chicana lesbians." I will not pause long at the word *clues*, which transports us into the vernacular of the detective and modern policing systems. Instead I will concentrate on Almaguer's reasons for turning to the literary work of Chicana lesbians to gather knowledge on "the social world of Chicano gay men." Why turn to these fictional texts? "Being the first to shatter the silence on the homosexual experience of the Chicano population, they have candidly documented the perplexing issues Chicanos confront in negotiating the conflicting gender and sexual messages imparted by the coexisting Chicano and European-American cultures."[16] In the remainder of his essay Almaguer focuses on the work of Cherríe Moraga, primarily her *Loving in the War Years: Lo que nunca pasó por sus labios*. One might ask about the seemingly illogical move from a sociological essay rooted for the most part in the truth of real-life sexual experience among gay Chicano men to a work of fiction by a lesbian Chicana. As I stated earlier regarding Christopher Ortiz's claim that we turn to Chicana lesbian texts to see how a Chicana lesbian discourse gets staged in writing, I think of this turn as a critical stop along the way and not the final critical destination. Almaguer's and Ortiz's critical gesturing to Chicana lesbian texts as repositories of cultural and sexual truths is problematic based simply on the fact that Moraga's writing, even in its claims to autobiographical truth, can never be an untroubled, transparent, exhaustive account of gay Chicano and Chicana lesbian subjects.

For our purposes here we should retain two crucial points from Almaguer's essay. The first point concerns the critical trajectory he effects in his study, from a studied approach to the sexual lives of gay Chicanos *through* the fictional work of Chicana lesbians in order to construct a knowledge about the sexual lives of gay Chicano men. The second point has to do with the politics informing a study that wants to gather knowledge on Chicano gay male sexual practices that seeks to textualize these practices, and perhaps more important, that insists on the readability of gay male Chicano bodies. As for the critical trajectory sketched in Almaguer's essay, most scholars working on gay Latino literary and other cultural work will find it is a critical trajectory that seems to anticipate an approach to this work in the first place, given the diminished presence of a gay Latino critical praxis. I have been trying to suggest that we need to rethink the ways we conceive of the paucity of gay Latino cultural and literary work. Almaguer creates a curious tension when he states the general scope of his essay as the study of the ways Chicano and Mexican men negotiate a "'gay' identity (based on the European-American sexual system)" within a Latino culture that may not "recognize such a construction" for sexuality. The tension arises because Almaguer seems to read the Chicano gay male body according to the scopic logic of a "European-American sexual system." In short, Almaguer may fail to see and catalogue a body that refuses to "recognize such a construction."

If Almaguer's essay seems to insist on the readability of gay male Chicano bodies in order to bring his analysis to some sort of theoretical closure, Moraga repeats this insistence with the proviso that this readability is crucial for any sustained, empowered queer politics. To make her point Moraga draws out the binary pair "queens" and "'passing' gay men": "Unlike the 'queens' who have always been open about their sexuality, 'passing' gay men have learned in a visceral way that being in 'the closet' and preserving their 'manly' image will not protect them, it will only make their dying more secret."[17] What is at stake here is the readable body of "queens" as gay and the scrambled text of the "passing" gay man; in short, the queen is an easy read, but the passing gay man is a difficult text. It is never quite clear in what context *queen* is being used. On one level she seems to want to denote effeminacy, and on another level she gestures to the body of the drag queen. Drag may have less to do with sexuality or gayness than Moraga lets on. Simply put, drag and passing as bodily performances do not occupy the same discursive plane, since drag's self-conscious performativity is about spectacle, while passing is often about survival. We should note, and I think this is an important distinction to make, that Moraga reflexively associates the readability of gayness on Chicano bodies with "outness" and therefore, at the very least, with the possibility of a radical queer politics, and the failure to read gayness on Chicano bodies as closeted and always already politically regressive. Moraga's perspective here indexes another familiar account in gay and lesbian politics in the United States, which distinguishes and assigns different values to the political gay activist who is already out and the gay subject, not out, who retreats from an active political engagement. At no point in her argument does it matter what the particular intent of these bodies might be. For example, one might then assume that a gay man who cannot be read as gay in Moraga's scopic logic therefore cannot contribute to an empowering queer politics. His body must register within the dominant culture's image repertoire as gay. Passing, which in Moraga's vernacular does not entail a decision to pass but is rather always a morphological, indeed bodily passing, is even related to dying, specifically a secret kind of dying.

Interestingly Moraga does indeed problematize any assumed alliance between gay Chicanos and Chicana lesbians based on homosexuality as a common nodal point about which to rally. Ultimately "Queer Aztlán" aims to effect a kind of alliance between gay Chicanos and Chicana lesbians, but not before Moraga makes the gay male contingency own up to some of its politically conservative behavior. Her problematization of this alliance proceeds according to a critique of the ways gay men have not confronted their own homophobia and sexism, instilled in them by their Mexican and Chicano cultures: "By openly confronting Chicano sexuality and sexism, gay men can do their own part to unravel how both men and women have been formed and deformed by racist Amerika and our misogynist/catholic/colonized mechicanidad; and we can come that much closer to healing those fissures that have divided us as a people."[18] Now let us think through Moraga's critical move here. To the extent that her essay does exactly what Almaguer says is crucial for a better understanding of sexuality as it relates to dominant and minority cultural understandings of sexual categories, to the extent that it does exactly what Almaguer believes gay Chicano work is not doing, one cannot help but notice that it is done, at least partially, at the expense of a gay male Chicano discourse. The discursive conditions for the emergence and sustenance of a Chicana lesbian discourse in Moraga's essay depends upon the sacrifice of a gay male Chicano discourse. Moraga's essay works not simply because it successfully annihilates passing gay Chicano men. Rather it succeeds only to the extent that she can prove that gay Chicano men are simply not talking, not writing, not being open enough about their sexuality, and the proof for these facts may involve no more rigorous a task than the simple statement of these facts. This truth begins to underscore the terms of our earlier discussion concerning the possibility that the emergence of one discourse may occupy a seemingly antagonistic relation to the emergence of the other discourse. Ironically this antagonism relies on the assumption that there is no antagonism, that there is always a potential alliance between the two on the critical horizon. I do not mean to imply that there is a nefarious and natural antagonism between Latina lesbian and gay Latino critical discourses; at the same time I do not want to eliminate that possibility. The different set of questions I claimed should be asked of the current framing of the discussion addressing the paucity of gay Latino literary work through the discussion that cites the plethora of published lesbian Latina literary work would borrow certain critically energizing suspicions from Bhabha's following question: "How do strategies of representation or empowerment come to be formulated in the competing claims of communities where, despite shared histories of deprivation and discrimination, the exchange of values, meanings and priorities may not always be collaborative and dialogical, but may be profoundly antagonistic, conflictual and even incommensurable?"[19] To claim that these two discourses proceed according to some discursive antagonism is to underscore the productive aspects of antagonism, that it produces and amplifies text, and not to assign a qualitative judgment.

Both Moraga and Almaguer create an urgency around the imperative to produce knowledge about Latino male homosexuality, to make it the object of critical scrutiny. In this regard their imperatives centrally inform any political project committed to bringing into visibility obscured, ignored, unremarked-upon histories of homosexualities. I do not mean, however, to imply that Moraga's and Almaguer's attempts to bring the gay Latino subject into theoretical view does not entail traversing some very tricky terrain. Lee Edelman reminds us that bringing the homosexual into view as part of a "liberationist project can easily echo, though in a different key, the homophobic insistence upon the social importance of codifying and registering sexual identities." He discusses the importance that Western culture has historically placed on the need to locate the homosexual though figures of "nomination" and "inscription": "Homosexuals, in other words, were not only conceptualized in terms of a radically potent, if negatively charged, relation to signifying practices, but also subject to a cultural imperative that viewed them as inherently textual—as bodies that might well bear a 'hallmark' that could, and must, be read."[20] As a critical addendum to Edelman's claim, one must consider the fact that racialized homosexual subjects are imbued with an even more excessive textuality than he describes for the seemingly racially unmarked homosexual subject he deploys in this passage. The cultural imperative which views the homosexual as inherently textual, as a social body that can be read, makes a similar case for the racialized subject's body as an inherently textual body and its racialized texts as necessarily readable. Almaguer and Moraga seem to view the possibility of a gay male Chicano discourse and politics as inherently tied to the conditions of the male homosexual figure's relation to writing and textuality, specifically that this figure must emerge through writing (that is, readable writing) so that the figure can be identified as such. Almaguer's and Moraga's insistence on the readability of the gay male Chicano subject in an effort to locate him seems to mimic the dominant culture's homophobic insistence on taxonomizing deviant sexual identities. However, in defense of Moraga's and Almaguer's urgent claims for gay male Chicano readability and intelligibility one might cite the difficulty dominant cultural institutions in the United States have had historically in recognizing or accommodating the literary work of gay men of color. The demand that this cultural and literary work be made intelligible through dominant cultural reading practices participates in the belief that creating visibility and intelligibility where there was none promotes life-sustaining, community-building, and politically crucial acts in the realm of concrete social struggles. What amounts to a particularly vexed moment in Almaguer's and Moraga's essays concerns the fact that they cannot insist that the literary work of gay Latino men be more culturally intelligible according to the narrative conditions they place on the emergence of this work without also insisting on an explicit, visual mapping of the gay Latino body in a dominant cultural space. The latter insistence, though in the service of discerning what appears to have always been a potential gay Latino literary canon, highlighted by Moraga's list of the crypto-gay Chicano authors Rodriguez, Islas, and Rechy, echoes too clearly the homophobic insistence that homosexual bodies be tracked and located wherever they threaten to circulate unremarked upon by policing mechanisms.

In closing I would like to think through what Almaguer and Moraga have to say about certain gay Chicano and Mexican authors. Moraga's indictment of Rodriguez and Islas has to do with these authors' inability to narrativize their homosexuality. I should add that Moraga discusses these authors specifically in reference to AIDS and the silences around it in the Mexican community and their failure to address this issue: "Islas died of AIDS-related illness in 1990, having barely begun to examine the complexity of Chicano sexuality in his writing. I also think of essayist Richard Rodriguez, who, with so much death surrounding him, has recently begun to address the subject of homosexuality." One cannot help but note that Islas's failure to narrativize openly gay characters does not mean that the complexity of Chicano sexuality remained unaddressed in his work. It *was* addressed, albeit by way of oblique, obtuse points of entry. Islas failed in Moraga's assessment because his characterizations did not correspond to her fairly rigid and simplistic schema for gay male Chicano subjectivities, either the queen or the passing gay man. Almaguer's critique of Islas and Rodriguez, as I noted above, involves the extent to which these authors have only partially narrativized the intersection between Chicano cultural socialization and the dominant Anglo culture's categorization of "deviant" sexualities. Moraga insists on a more readable, intelligible gay male Chicano body in narrativity, and Almaguer insists on a gay male Chicano narrativity that yields the fact of "cultural dissonance" Chicano gay men experience in reconciling Chicano cultural-symbolic pressures and "sexual deviancy." Both of these accounts tell more or less the same story of failure with regard to the literary practices of gay Chicano writers, where failure is marked by the writers' narrative reticence, a certain incommunicativeness, a reserve expressed in the gay male Chicano writer's refusal to transcribe his own homosexuality (whatever *own* means in this context) in his writing; each text is seen as the mandatory site for the writer's inscription of his homosexual self. It is shocking that a quite simple fact has occurred to so few of us with regard to this argument: the refusal to be exhaustively forthcoming with regard to these matters is often the very enabling condition for survival and defiance.

NOTES

1. My point concerning the Western cultural imperative which insists on the inherent textuality of homosexual bodies in order to more definitively taxonomize and track their cultural locations is inspired and informed by Lee Edelman's compelling argument in "Homographesis," the introductory piece to his collection of essays, *Homographesis: Essays in Gay Literary and Cultural Theory*. Edelman explains, "Homosexuals . . . were not only conceptualized in terms of [a] radically potent, if negatively charged, relation to signifying practices, but also subjected to a cultural imperative that viewed them as inherently textual—as bodies that might well bear a 'hallmark' that could, and must, be read" (6).

2. Sullivan, Arteaga, and Pacheco, *Nahum Zenil*, 15.

3. Ibid., 22–23.

4. Ibid.

5. Yarbro-Bejarano, "Laying It Bare," 277.

6. Ibid.

7. Almaguer, "Chicano Men," 265, 256.

8. Moraga, "Queer Aztlán," 163.

9. C. Ortiz, "Hot and Spicy," 83.

10. Almaguer, *Racial Fault Lines*, 6–7.

11. Bhabha, *The Location of Culture*, 176.

12. Barely disguised in the praises often bestowed on Chicana lesbian literary work is the dangerous assumption that works by canonized writers like Gloria Anzaldúa and Cherríe Moraga represent complete, total, and exhaustive accounts for what it means to

be a Chicana lesbian subject in the United States. We would be better served critically if we stressed the necessarily incomplete and partial narrativizations of these issues in lesbian Chicana writing such as Anzaldúa's and Moraga's (indeed in all Chicana and Chicano writing). Otherwise we participate in the belief that ethnic and racialized subjects emerge as the determinate meaning of language and that they are somehow equipped to tell the whole truth when they write and speak.

13. C. Ortiz, "Hot and Spicy," 40.

14. Almaguer, "Chicano Men," 256, 255.

15. Ibid., 265.

16. Ibid.

17. Moraga, "Queer Aztlán," 163.

18. Ibid., 162.

19. Bhabha, The Location of Culture, 2.

20. Edelman, Homographesis, 3–4, 6.

Our Queer Kin

Luz Calvo and Catriona Rueda Esquibel

In theorizing "the place of gay Chicano literature" Antonio Viego provocatively begins his argument between the nude self-portraits of Nahum Zenil and Laura Aguilar, between the gay Mexican and the Chicana lesbian, between the dart game and the subject in bondage. "It is somewhere between these two images," asserts Viego, ". . . that we might begin to map out the cultural locations of a gay Chicano literary discourse." While he opens his essay with a contrast between the bodies of a Chicana lesbian and a Mexican gay male, the major thrust of his argument concerns another binary. On the one side is "the" Chicana lesbian who, he argues, has for many critics come to represent plenitude and has been viewed as intelligible, readable, straightforward, visible, and (a bit too self-righteously) political. On the flip side is the gay Chicano subject, whom Viego associates with paucity; he is illegible, unreadable, complex, invisible, and (somewhat intriguingly) apolitical.[1] In our response to his essay we wish to call attention to a concern that we share with Viego, a concern with the dangers of reinscribing such a binary structure in relation to gay and lesbian cultural production in Latino and Latina contexts. Rather than resurrecting the rigid identities of *gay* and *lesbian* in these contexts we hope to incite—through our scholarship, friendships, reading practices, and political work—new formations of queer kinship, ones that might cross the multiple and shifting terrains of gender, sexual, and racial difference in Latino and Latina queer communities.

We hope to ensure that others do not use Viego's argument to reinscribe the binary of paucity/plentitude in relation to gay Chicanos and Chicana lesbians. While we appreciate his desire to unhinge gay Latino identity from an automatic reference to Cherríe Moraga or Gloria Anzaldúa, we would like to add a broader acknowledgment of the multiple and complex ways that Chicano and Chicana subjects represent and enact queer desire. Viego writes, "Latina and Latino scholars find the paucity of gay male Chicano literary work to be somewhat inexplicable given the explosion of published Chicana lesbian literary work in the late twentieth century, work which is helping to redefine the field of Chicano studies as a literary, political, and critical endeavor." What is not made clear in this passage is whether Viego believes there was an actual paucity of gay male Chicano literary work, or if he is *solely* concerned with narratives of paucity in academic discourse. While we presume that his focus is the latter, we are ultimately concerned that such statements may leave the uninitiated reader with the false impression that Chicana lesbian authors are powerful and widely published. We are reminded of this scene from *Alice's Adventures in Wonderland*:

> "Take some more tea," the March Hare said to Alice, very earnestly.
>
> "I've had nothing yet," Alice replied in an offended tone, "so I can't take more."
>
> "You mean you can't take less," said the Hatter: "it's very easy to take more than nothing."

The language of paucity and plenitude observed by Viego implies that Chicana lesbians receive more than their fair share of academic attention, when they might, like Alice, argue that they have received nothing at all. Viego's reference to the "plethora of Chicana lesbian work" is perhaps ironic; clearly, for some *any* Chicana lesbian work is too much, and thus it may seem to be always everywhere.[2] Moreover a focus on quantity doesn't begin to account for the material conditions that influence who gets published and where, nor what kind of readership writers might expect and how their work might circulate. For example, in the years Viego references (1989–99) Richard Rodriguez was arguably the most read Chicano in the nation. *Hunger of Memory* (1982) was required reading on high school and college campuses, especially in first-year writing classes. The chapter "Aria" from *Hunger* was widely anthologized. Rodriguez could publish in major newspapers and magazines at will and was a frequent guest expert on PBS. While we acknowledge that Rodriquez is indeed a "complex" figure whose contested identity as a gay Chicano has produced ambivalent identifications, we reference him to contextualize (in more concrete and material terms) the conditions under which Chicana lesbian writers at the time struggled. Moreover we don't believe that Rodriguez is somehow more complex than Chicana lesbian authors writing in this period (see especially Sandra K. Soto's reading of Cherríe Moraga).[3]

Viego's assertion that "certain academic disciplines seem currently to be so fond of the Chicana lesbian feminist subject" seems deliberately overstated as a factual description, although it may indeed get at the perception of those who are either resentful or critical of any attention paid to Chicana lesbian work. According to such perceptions, Chicana lesbian feminists are feasting in the restaurant while slender, melancholic gay Chicanos gaze with dark dewy eyes through the glass window from the cold, cold street. This is a charming fantasy, but it has little basis in the power structures of the academy. The late Gloria Anzaldúa is a case in point. Yes, *Borderlands/La Frontera* has been taught and cited by feminists in women's studies departments across the world. However, Anzaldúa herself was never offered an academic position, and she supported herself primarily through speaking engagements. As with Anzaldúa's works, much of Chicana lesbian literature in the 1980s and 1990s was published by small feminist or alternative presses, many of which have since gone out of business. Many of these books are now out of print (even such classics as *This Bridge Called My Back*). Reader take note: the Chicana lesbian library is not to be found in an ivory tower in heavy bookcases of cherry wood and glass, filled with cordovan-bound volumes with gilded pages. We're talking about paperback books and obscure journals disintegrating in cardboard boxes. At the same time we recognize that our response to Viego's essay is shifting us right back to the he/she binary that we would like to disrupt with the notion of "queer kin."

More important to us is a recognition that Chicana lesbian writing does not always represent Chicana lesbians as "culturally intelligible" subjects, and moreover these writings should not be read as transparent nor as representing experience. This last assertion is particularly dangerous, given the way that feminist writings so often propose their own binary: white women write "theory," while women of color write (mere) "experience."[4] In *With Her Machete in Her Hand* Esquibel argues against the idea that "Chicana lesbian fiction" produces a single, unitary subject. Rather Chicana lesbian fictions are produced by a community of writers, and their works produce some fundamental disagreements about what constitutes Chicana lesbian identity. Conflicts occur regularly on such topics as ways of talking about queer women in history: Do Chicana lesbians "claim" Catalina de Erauso as a Chicana lesbian, or is she FTM? Does her disparagement of women of African descent and her killing of indigenous people move her out of the *Women of Color* column into the *Colonizer* column? Are *curanderas* backward, superstitious women keeping our people in ignorance, or are they purveyors of indigenous traditions and women's ways of knowing? Is Sor Juana a lesbian separatist or just another member of the Spanish ruling class? What of women who question their gender identity or refuse the label *lesbian*? These are some of the ongoing questions in queer Chicana fictions. In light of these and other questions, we call for *more* critical attention to be paid to the multiple, ambivalent, and conflicting ways that Chicana lesbian identities have been formed through identification (or, in Muñoz's terms, "disidentification") with both heterosexual and gay Chicanos, and visa versa.[5]

On that note we turn our attention to Tomás Almaguer's "Chicano Men: A Cartography of Homosexual Identity and Behavior," which features prominently in Viego's essay. Particularly troubled by Almaguer's turn to Moraga, Viego reads him as initiating the binary of Chicana lesbian plenitude and Chicano gay paucity. However, Almaguer too is one of a community of writers. He's mapping discussions about identity and sexuality occurring among gay Chicanos. Another way to read Almaguer is to see that, in the course of his essay, he takes a queer turn: he expands his imagined community to include Chicana lesbians, in particular Cherríe Moraga. It's important to situate the publication of Almaguer's essay in 1991 in *differences*, the very first publication devoted to the then emerging field of queer theory. His essay stands alongside a series of essays, each of which, according to the journal's introduction, aims to "recast or reinvent the terms of our sexualities, to construct another discursive horizon, another way of thinking the sexual." [6]

While we appreciate Almaguer's move to cross the gender divide, we feel the need to reiterate that Moraga does not speak for Chicana lesbians in an unproblematic way. In "Queer Aztlán" she deploys Chicano nationalism for a queer and feminist cause at the same time that she critiques those whom she describes as closeted gay Chicanos. Like Viego, we find the following passage particularly problematic:

> I remember my friend Arturo Islas. . . . I think of how his writing begged to boldly announce his gayness. Instead, we learned it through vague references about "sinners" and tortured alcoholic characters. . . . Islas died of AIDS-related illness in 1990, having barely begun to examine the complexity of Chicano sexuality in his writing. I also think of essayist Richard Rodriguez, who, with so much death surrounding him, has recently begun to publicly address the subject of homosexuality; and yet, even ten years ago, we all knew "Mr. Secrets" was gay from his assimilationist *Hunger of Memory*. [7]

Moraga's implied emphasis—that it is only now (in the midst of the AIDS epidemic) that gay Chicano academics and cultural critics are willing to be out or political—adds insult to injury. To some extent she's arguing that feminism has provided for Chicana lesbians a space in which to politicize their sexuality, while gay Chicanos are seen as being dragged unwillingly from their institutionally secure closets in order to attend their own funerals or those of their friends. She invokes Audre Lorde's saying "Your silence will not protect you," more as an "I told you so" than as a call for action. She references the epidemic of breast cancer among lesbians, not to show that lesbian communities face similar challenges or to bring to breast cancer the kind of challenges that demanded the passive AIDS victim become the activist PWA,[8] but instead to argue that gay men remain too narrowly (selfishly) focused on AIDS issues and are not helping their lesbian sisters. Moraga's essay takes the tone of chiding our gay brothers, "What have you done for me lately?" In this regard "Queer Aztlán" is not queer at all but rather stubbornly stuck to gender difference as a seemingly unbridgeable gulf between Chicana lesbians and Chicano gay men.[9]

In his reading of this passage Viego takes issue with Moraga's condemnation of Rodriguez and Islas for the way they write their sexuality. Questioning the value of "cultural intelligibility,"[10] Viego tries to carve out a space for a gay Latino sensibility that is not constrained by the strictures to be out or, in his terms, "culturally intelligible." He argues that gay Chicanos are racialized differently from Chicana lesbians, so Moraga cannot hope to understand the decisions made by Islas and Rodriguez. This fascinating claim is worthy of further elucidation: if race, gender, and sexuality are co-constitutive, then of course Moraga is socially constituted in ways that are different from Islas and Rodriguez. However, collapsing all of this into racialization and the subsequent inference that such different racializations translate into an inability to understand the position of the other puts us right back into the "he said, she said, gay Chicanos are from Mars, Chicana lesbians are from Venus" binaries. Further Viego's logic here leaves us unable to account for the closeted Chicana lesbian (of whom there are many) and the out gay Chicanos (more each day!).

What seem to be lost in both Moraga's "Queer Aztlán" and the binary that Viego's essay draws our attention to are the radical critiques of normativity that emerged in the period in question, 1989–99. This was an era of radical AIDS activism, of claiming and reframing the despised epithets in publications such as *Diseased Pariah News* and *Infected Faggot Perspectives*.[11] During the 1990s Queer Nation railed against the previous era of assimilationist gay and lesbian politics but also refused the politics of lesbian feminism of the 1980s, with its essentialism and false belief that "lesbians aren't promiscuous like gay men—that lesbians are more like straight women who value intimacy and relationships."[12]

The queer 1990s had a profound impact on Chicana and Chicano identity formation, and not just because there were Chicanos and Chicanas in the queer movement and being trained in queer theory. Rather the very terms of identity formation shifted in profound ways for a great many people. We might even say, to use a term from Viego's lexicon, that subject positions were "scrambled" during that period. Previously "legible" Chicana feminist lesbians became scrambled texts, emerging as transgendered subjects, bi-mujeres, or pansexual radicals. Queer identification creates and imagines a "we" that includes men, women, and gender queers. Critically, queers demand an acknowledgment of transgender and gender queer to account for those who refuse or reoccupy the categories of male and female. And bisexuals at long last are imagined as part of "us" and not as part of some other disparaged category. Yet as the dust settles from the trauma of AIDS and the reorganization of identities that occurred at the end of the twentieth century we are left to think about a postqueer future.

At this point not all of us wish to accept the division between "us" Chicana lesbians and "you" gay Chicanos. Indeed a few of us no longer feel comfortable with the identity *Chicana lesbian* precisely because of the closed system it has come to represent. Recently the lesbian caucus of the National Association of Chicana and Chicano Studies renamed itself the Lesbian, BiMujeres, and Trans Caucus, a move that begins to account for the range of desires and identifications (those that were always already present as well as those more recently developed) that motivate our politics and affiliations. As an example of the way that we, the authors of this essay, imagine new identities—with identification and desire running back and forth between us and our queer kin—we offer our own narrative pleasure derived from gay Chicano fiction:

> In summer 1996, the two of us were in grad school. Luz was living in a cabin in Bonnie Doone, above the UC Santa Cruz campus, and Catriona was still driving down from San Francisco. The cabin trapped the day's heat, and pushed us out in the evening in search of some cooling ice cream. Luz had the Alyson (gay press) editions of Michael Nava's mysteries—*Golden Boy*, *The Little Death*, *The Hidden Law*, and a mass market paperback of *How Town*. We sweated through those novels, shaking our heads when Henry Rios would make a bad decision, nudging each other when there was a sex scene coming on. Three and a half years later, we were in a small town in New Mexico, bundled up against the cold (it was probably thirty-five degrees). We had gotten our hands on *The Burning Plain* and were taking turns reading it. It was really hard to stop at the end of the chapter and hand the book over and wait till your next turn. We must have read the last few chapters aloud, because we couldn't wait any longer and neither wanted to be the second one to finish it. Through them all, we talked: about how uptight Henry was, his alcoholism, his depiction of the Silver Lake scene, our excitement at Josh's growing radicalization with the AIDS ACT-UP crew, our frustration with Henry, the way

the novels dealt with childhood sexual abuse, which CSUN Chicano Studies professor was being satirized.

As Tomás Almaguer looks to Cherríe Moraga to puzzle out gay Chicano identity, we turn to gay Latino literature and scholarship, to our queer kin, to decode the past, to influence the future.

NOTES

1. This emphasis on binaries brings to mind Aguilar's *Clothed/Unclothed* series (1990–94) in which she depicts the significance of clothing in self-presentation of race, gender, power, and sexuality. This series of diptychs implies a binary until you get to the final image, of Luis Alfaro: Alfaro's nude is part of a triptych in which the two clothed images depict him as masculine, in male garb, and feminine, in women's clothing.

2. Those of us who teach general education courses or the one required "people of color" course for the major are quite familiar with this phenomenon. Our instructor evaluations frequently decry "Too queer" or "Too much emphasis on race," not because, as the students really believe, there is a large amount or percentage of these voices, but because in this case "any" is too much when the expectation is "none at all."

3. Soto, "Cherríe Moraga's Going Brown."

4. See, for example, B. Smith, "Toward a Black Feminist Criticism"; Scott, "The Evidence of Experience"; V. Smith "Black Feminist Theory"; Chay "Rereading Barbara Smith."

5. Muñoz, *Disidentifications*.

6. De Lauretis, "Queer Theory," iv.

7. Rodriguez, *Hunger of Memory*, 165.

8. Person with AIDS.

9. Moraga's works themselves are often in conversation with one another and can take different critical perspectives. According to Esquibel's definition of Chicana lesbian literature as "expressing desire between women," neither *Shadow of a Man* nor *Heroes and Saints* is a "lesbian" text, though each is queer in its own way. If the reader or audience member challenges Moraga's portrayal of gay Chicanos in either of these texts we hope she or he will bring the same challenge to Moraga's lesbian characters (Esquibel, *With Her Machete in Her Hand*). For differing views on Moraga, see Soto, "Cherríe Moraga's Going Brown."

10. The implication that Chicana lesbian fictions are transparent and "culturally intelligible" is another sweeping statement that fails to account for the incredible diversity of the writings under discussion.

11. Daniel Brouwer contextualizes and analyzes the interventions of these two publications in his essay "Counterpublicity." Cory Roberts-Auli, one of the creators of *Infected Faggot Perspective*, was Puerto Rican, a fact often overlooked in representations of queer

activists of this period as exclusively white. Although Brouwer doesn't discuss Roberts-Auli as Latino, he draws attention to the way the magazine raised issues of medical access for Latinos and Latinas. See Shearer et al., *Diseased Pariah News*; Karr and Roberts-Auli, *Infected Faggot Perspective*.

12. We'd like to direct the reader to *Out/Look* magazine (1988–92), whose letters to the editor were evenly divided between those who were thrilled that "at last" there was intelligent discussion of racial identities, bisexuality, s/m, and queer activism, and those who angrily canceled their subscriptions, offended by the magazine's "perversity," its radical agenda, and its refusal to focus on normal gay and lesbian lifestyles.

Carnal Knowledge: Chicano Gay Men and the Dialectics of Being

Richard T. Rodríguez

to the world
we are nothing
but here together
          you & I
are the world
—Francisco X. Alarcón, "Dialectics of Love"

In their introduction to *Chicano Renaissance: Contemporary Cultural Trends* the editors David R. Maciel, Isidro D. Ortiz, and Maria Herrera-Sobek list the sociopolitical struggles which, as they would have it, "contributed in no small part to inspire Chicana/o artists" during the Chicano movement of the 1960s and 1970s: "the drive by César Chávez and Dolores Huerta to unionize the farm workers; the land struggle of Reies López-Tijerina; the formation of the La Raza Unida party; the Crusade for Justice; the sit-ins, love-ins, and marches against the Vietnam War; the feminist movement; and the gay and lesbian liberation movement." Although Maciel, Ortiz, and Herrera-Sobek do not specify how the feminist movement and the gay and lesbian liberation movement inspired Chicano and Chicana artists, their inclusion of these struggles suggests an affirmative influence at this particular historical juncture. While mentioning the lesbian writers Cherríe Moraga, Gloria Anzaldúa, and Alicia Gaspar de Alba, who, we're told, "battle against what *they perceive* to be a homophobic and antilesbian society," the editors nevertheless return us all to a politics of solidarity.[1] Such movements indeed contributed to the growing influence of feminist, gay, and lesbian politics for Chicano and Chicana social and cultural projects, but they also influenced others to express a curious ambiguity—if not at times outright resistance—toward those movements' members who might perhaps be part of the Chicano movement as well but nonetheless troubled the conventional family narratives it promoted. Indeed gay, lesbian, and feminist struggles were often seen as antithetical to Chicano liberation.[2] Feminism and gay and lesbian rights, after all, presented a challenge to prescriptive kinship formations, the normativity of heterocoupling, conventional gender roles, and heterosexual male privileges and desires. By invoking these movements Maciel, Ortiz, and Herrera-Sobek raise the stakes of a revisionist solidarity which potentially forecloses discussion on the contradictory reception of feminist, gay, and lesbian issues in movement-influenced cultural production and leaves us with what might itself be called a curiously ambiguous response to queer politics.

In this essay I simultaneously take aim at curiously ambiguous responses to Chicano gay male sexuality in particular and focus on how Chicano gay men implicitly counter these responses through various modes of self-representation which in turn form an archive too often said not to exist. Curiously, ambiguous responses are formed by acknowledgment and repression; they straddle the border that divides admittance and disavowal in the struggle and negotiation to determine solidarity against and through kinship discourse. Many times curious ambiguity hinges upon the assumption of a "reproductive futurism" for Chicano politics that finds homosexuality's adoption difficult, if not impossible, given heteronormative prerogatives of la familia in its cultural and historical deployments as an organizing principle.[3] Yet as I take up such an engagement I show that it is virtually impossible to suggest that kinship discourse and practice—and their ability to generate a collective consciousness—are of no use to queers of color. Understanding Chicano gay male articulations of identity, desire, and experience in relation to this discourse sheds light on the impulses behind the simultaneous embracing and resignifying of family narratives, such as carnalismo, that contribute to the constitution of Chicano gay male consciousness, that is, the recognition of oneself in relation to a community, a brotherhood, of men who sexually desire men, the generation of a "dialectic of love," as Francisco X. Alarcón puts it, that functions as a "world-making" endeavor disproving invisibility and silence.[4]

In "The Place of Gay Male Chicano Literature in Queer Chicano Cultural Work" Antonio Viego maintains that it "has become a fairly common observation in Chicano and Latino studies that there is not enough gay male Latino literary work being produced," in contrast to "the plenitude of lesbian Chicana literary work." Viego suggests that it behooves us to not compare Chicana lesbian cultural production to Chicano gay male cultural production (or the lack of it) given the different social and historical trajectories from which they evolve. He insists that to stake a comparison "demands that the gay Latino subject emerge in cultural and literary work according to the same grid of experiential categories through which lesbian Latina cultural and literary work instantiates a lesbian Latina subject in narrativity." He then asks, "Is gay Latino cultural intelligibility wedded to an analysis of lesbian Latina cultural and literary work?" Historically the answer has been a resounding yes, reflected in how two influential queer commentators, Tomás Almaguer and Cherríe Moraga, lament Chicano gay male consciousness in contrast to that tangibly, or rather textually forged by Chicana lesbians. Yet one of the dangers implicit in this comparison, Viego persuasively argues, is how "gay Latino men are often figured as the weak links in political movements for Latina/o ethnic and racial empowerment." While it is true that Moraga's and Almaguer's lamentations can indeed function as an alarm call for Chicano gay men to speak up, the ways that gay men are rendered "weak links" through their purported silence do not assist in challenging the tendencies to cast gay men as nonproductive and, ultimately, passive.

The most troubling aspect of Moraga's and Almaguer's presentations of Chicano gay men is how certain modes of presentation are assumed to inaugurate the means by which they, in the first place, must speak. Chicana lesbian discourse, Viego declares, is a "discourse [that] has emerged in academic discourse to the extent that it has narrativized *experience* by engaging racial, sexual, cultural, and class histories in order to produce a recognizable, readable subject." Claims such as "[Chicana lesbians were] the first to shatter the silence on the homosexual experience of the Chicano population" (Almaguer) and "In the last few years, Chicano gay men have also begun to openly examine Chicano sexuality" (Moraga) assist in scripting Chicana lesbians as the original queer speaking subjects while resolutely discounting the historical moments in which homosexuality could be broached outside the realm of assumed, charted contexts. To be sure, such published statements as "Gay Chicano men are simply not talking, not writing, not being open enough about their sexuality, and the proof for these facts may involve no more rigorous a task than the simple statement of these facts" wield an authority determining suitable forms of being.

The issue of literary representation, however, is crucial as far as who gets to count in the conjugation of queer and Chicano or Chicana. Along with the recognizable body of Chicana lesbian literature, a handful of works written by both Chicano heterosexual and gay men have served as the springboards for discussing queer sexuality. While the presence and circulation of Chicana lesbian texts are credited as single-handedly promoting Chicana lesbian visibility, Chicano gay men have not been exempt from consideration within Chicano literature and literary history and criticism. Juan Bruce-Novoa's "Homosexuality and the Chicano Novel" initiated a critical conversation about gay male sexuality in Chicano literature, specifically in the work of José Antonio Villarreal, John Rechy, Floyd Salas, Oscar "Zeta" Acosta, and Arturo Islas. More recently Ricardo L. Ortiz, Carl Gutiérrez-Jones, and John Cunningham have investigated, to varying degrees, homophobia and homosexuality in the writings of recognizable gay and straight Chicano authors.[5]

Despite the ability of these authors to broach the subject of Chicano gay men, such work, in the final analysis, is insufficient for Moraga and Almaguer, who insist "on a gay male Chicano narrativity that yields the fact of 'cultural dissonance' Chicano gay men experience in reconciling Chicana/o cultural-symbolic pressures and 'sexual deviancy.'"[6] That is, most of these literary texts do not match the work of Chicana lesbians because they fail to adopt an explicit Chicano agenda that grapples with the "cultural-symbolic pressures" that not only govern the everyday life practices of Chicano/a populations, but that also root the interlocking discourses of family, nationalism, and community that have come to define Chicano and Chicana cultural politics.

Viego is keenly aware of the cultural politics which have come to frame much of Chicano studies when he writes, "Almaguer faults [Richard Rodriguez and Arturo Islas] specifically for not sufficiently narrativizing the 'cultural dissonance that Chicano homosexual men confront in reconciling their primary socialization into Chicano family life with the sexual norms of the dominant culture.'" Viego's point is well taken when he disputes Almaguer's demand for gay men to speak like Chicana lesbians (based on the assumption of "queer kin," as Viego puts it), but I also agree with Almaguer given the crucial significance of the family institution—within both public and domestic spheres—for Chicano and Chicana sexual politics, and how Chicano men must "lift the lid on their homosexual experiences and leave the closeted space they have been relegated to in Chicano culture."[7] Yet Almaguer's claims short-circuit when we consider cultural forms that have not been accounted for to begin "interpreting and redefining what it means to be both Chicano and gay in a cultural setting that has viewed these categories as a contradiction in terms."[8] Recognizing that "the gay Latino community is characterized by an absence of traditional texts," Manuel Guzmán maintains that, "consequently, for this community, inhabited spaces should become the location par excellence for the objectification of its generative schemes—the principles on which the production of thought, perception, and action are based."[9] Indeed as Almaguer points out, ethnographic research can help locate these "inhabited spaces," such as the Latino bar La Escuelita, where Guzmán conducts research. But I read "inhabited spaces" more loosely, and insist that Chicano gay men inhabit spaces that haven't been easily detected, spaces that exceed readily accessible literary texts but are nonetheless spaces where "family life" has necessarily been addressed. Chicano gay male articulations of experience, identity, and desire to forge a Chicano gay male consciousness do indeed exist and have existed, yet they have taken form in mostly nontextualized, noncanonical arenas. Furthermore while gay men were being written out of the Chicano family narrative by poets and essayists who were writing from movement trajectories, they were also scripted in curiously ambiguous ways as antifamily and rendered as such because of their inability to procreate. In other words the value of gay men to Chicano cultural politics was curious at best since gay men always fail to produce or reproduce the family.

While his critique of the incessant comparison of work by Chicano gay men and Chicana lesbians yields imperative insight, Viego's refusal of "analogical thinking" ultimately prevents any consideration of how the cultural productions and practices of both Chicana and Chicano queers comprise not only a field called Chicano studies, but, most significant here, occasionally strives for a sense of collective consciousness. Moreover, one needs to recognize that the cultural production of Chicano gay men is both in the emergent stage as well as contingent upon recovery work. To establish a similarly solid body of work, projects must be pursued which would (1) recover and compile materials which are out of print, unpublished, or published in obscure journals and periodicals; (2) conduct and amass oral histories of Chicano gay men (perhaps even, with the help of family and friends, writing the histories of those lost to AIDS); (3) promote and distribute recent writing, visual art, and films and videos (perhaps through curatorial efforts, festival acquisition, and the publication of literary anthologies); and (4) critically examine the representations of Chicano gay men in various social and cultural contexts (such as in literature and film) to unveil their positionings therein.[10] The aim of this essay is twofold: part recovery project, part critical analysis, a genealogical effort which stakes claims for Chicano gay male recognition within Chicano/a cultural history.

HISTORIOGRAPHIES OF DIFFERENCE

Ramón Gutiérrez's essay "Community, Patriarchy and Individualism: The Politics of Chicano History and the Dream of Equality" incisively offers two important historical flashpoints. First, Gutiérrez writes that Chicanismo in the 1960s and 1970s was directly linked to "the cultural assertion of masculinity by young radical men. . . . Chicanismo meant identifying with la raza (the race or people), and collectively promoting the interests of *carnales* (or brothers) with whom they

shared a common language, culture, religion, and Aztec heritage."[11] Brotherhood in movement discourse was regularly synonymous with la familia. More
often than not brotherhood was an allegiance between heterosexual men, excluding women and gay men who threatened the potency of the homosocial—
not homosexual—bond. Yet brotherhood, like la familia, is not always predicated on exclusion, as Gutiérrez would have it. Could it not function as a bond
between gay men—brother to brother, carnal a carnal—who would seemingly
exist outside the word's realm of signification? What does it mean to promote a
brotherhood that does not rely strictly on a gay or straight bond but rather aims
to bridge the interests of Chicano men despite sexual identification?

The other important critical strand in Gutiérrez's essay is his mapping of the
emergence of Chicana resistance to Chicano patriarchy by highlighting a feminist counternarrative of the Chicano movement that utilizes poetry as an alternative historiography. In the spirit of Gutiérrez's work, I suggest that poetry
and other literary forms of this era, including that which awaits recovery from
newspapers and limited-edition, out-of-print anthologies, must be considered
important historical documents which offer vital information about the complexities of Chicano movement history and the cultural discourse it evokes. As I
hope this essay makes clear, noncanonical poetry and unconventional documents must be read and analyzed for the purpose of unraveling the politics
of gender and sexuality, especially pertaining to Chicano gay men, which are
subjects too frequently taken for granted as "presentist," here signifying either
materialization in the recent present or after the fact of Chicana lesbian literary
production. Texts which may have originally circulated in limited quantities and
were published in venues that made their canonization virtually impossible are
still key documents that can reflect the sentiments of their authors but which
also speak to the not so imagined communities fashioned by and through such
publications.

One such poem that has gone unnoticed and that expresses a curious ambiguity toward gay male sexuality is Joe Olvera's "Gay Ghetto District." Read at a
flor y canto festival either in 1977 or 1978, the poem was subsequently published
in Flor y Canto IV & V: An Anthology of Chicano Literature.[12] Since the beginning of the
Chicano movement flor y canto festivals were important components of cultural
and political events; they also constituted a tradition on their own as "oral literary symposia" in which "a national character, chicanismo," was conveyed.[13] "Literally translated as 'flower and song,'" writes Cordelia Candelaria, "the phrase
flor y canto has become synonymous with Chicano poetry itself." Fittingly, in her
discussion of the meanings of flor y canto Candelaria writes, "Every familia is a

collection of different individuals, habits, and interests which—despite the differences and even contradictions—are nevertheless bound together as one unit sharing aspects of a common identity. So, too, is Chicano poetry in its multiplicity and concomitant unity."[14] This claim may hold true, that is, until homosexuality enters the scene. Indeed Olvera's poem precisely shows how gay men are virtually impossible to assimilate into the plural singularity (read: familial framework) of Chicano poetry's "common identity" that Candelaria assumes.

The curious ambiguity of the speaker in "Gay Ghetto District," Joe, is immediately evident. His introduction of a gay couple, Ricardo and Michael, paves the way for a critique of the Gold Rush fervor of 1848, the scramble for land and railroads in northern California in the 1880s, and a well-known antigay activist that at first glance seems to adopt a gay-affirmative stance but ultimately collapses into problematic verse.

> Hand to hand—'neath peaceful blue 'Frisco skies—Trees swaying gently
> to ocean breeze—Ricardo y Michael's hideaway is beautiful tree-lined
> home at top of hill—Eureka! "Thar's gold in them thar hills"—or some
> such nonsense of old greed—gold's the answer to Livermore—

> Also Gay men walk streets and arms around one t'other—
> so that Rosa sees and says, "How cute."
> Er you kidding, Rosa? Because one thing these
> here folks don't need is more put-downs.
> Anita Bryant is Elmer Gantry look-alike wants
> to save the folk from their own proclivities—sexual
> or sensual—or otherwise—dig?

> Who is this Anita Bryant by the way? Has she
> evuh felt the prick on shrunken vagina? Is
> homosexual love her loss or Plato's gain?[15]

The first stanza of the poem provides a critical historical context in which racial and sexual politics could either be compared or conjoined. With the line "Thar's gold in them thar hills" the speaker adopts the accent of the American opportunist who, fueled by "old greed," is lured to the "Golden State" (California) by the discovery of gold in 1848 and the "availability" of property thereafter. At this moment in history Mexicans are robbed of their land (which of course was originally Indian land). As a reversal, the gold in the hills in the contemporary scenario is the San Francisco "hideaway" of two gay lovers. The analogy painted here is difficult to read as affirmative, however, since the association of San Francisco as gay Mecca for Ricardo and Michael and San Francisco as Mecca for greedy white settlers is curious at best. And yet Joe goes on to cast Anita Bryant—the entertainer turned born-again Christian who in 1977 spearheaded the widely supported campaign called, appropriately enough, Save Our Children—as a modern-day opportunist desiring to take away Ricardo's and Michael's "golden moment." Likening her to Elmer Gantry, the greedy salesman turned preacher of the eponymous Sinclair Lewis novel, Joe desexualizes Bryant, "shrunken" from the realm of both heterosexual and homosexual desire, and counters her antigay platform with ancient Greece via Plato, a (mythologized) historical moment in which homosexual relations epitomized true love.

In the final two stanzas of the poem, however, the speaker clearly reveals his discomfort with male homosexuality, particularly when the line of demarcation between gay identity and his heterosexual proclivities is blurred.

> Anyway—Ballyhoo—Ricardo and Michael—arms around
> each other smile and ask of me: "What makes you think we're
> gay, Joe?"

> Why it's so obvious that even liberal as I is—must move
> on—cannot truly dig alternative life-style. Oh yes—can dig it
> for them—but not fer me is fat arse arisen to air in full fucking
> position—oh blasted sex—why the blight?[16]

The question "What makes you think we're gay, Joe?" functions as a pivotal moment. If Joe does not (and cannot) possess the knowledge to determine who is gay and who is straight, how does he know he's not gay? To sharply distinguish between himself and Ricardo and Michael, Joe turns the gay men into caricatures (they are ballyhoos with arms around each other, smiling) and conjures up "a fat arse arisen to air in full / fucking position," the readily penetrable anus, the commonly phobic-postulated site of gay male sexual pleasure recognized as "the vanishing point of allowable male behavior and of representation."[17] Despite admitting his "liberal" perspective (he supposedly "can dig it for them"), Joe insists he "must move on," he "cannot truly dig alternative life-style." This alternative lifestyle, in other words, runs counter to permissible, normative sexual practices and the naturalized technique for procreation, the basis of the family (even though, by beginning with a vision of their home, he potentially sets up Ricardo and Michael as a family). Joe sees gay identity—an "alternative life-style" to be sure—as a wavering of male potential to rule and reproduce, especially since it is premised on receptive anal sex. Moreover in the poem the act of getting fucked falls in line with the cultural and historical consequences attached to this practice.[18]

In his work on ancient and medieval homosexual practices John Boswell has argued that for all the emphasis on homosexual eroticism associated with these particular historical eras, passive anal sex was nonetheless considered an abomination. In the case of medieval Islam "the position of the 'insertee' is regarded as bizarre or even pathological," whereas in ancient Rome "the distinction between roles approved for male citizens and others appears to center on the giving of seed (as opposed to the receiving of it) rather than on the more familiar modern active-passive division" in which to be the recipient of seed was an "indecorous role for male citizens."[19] Paraphrasing the work of the anthropologist Roger Lancaster, Tomás Almaguer notes that in the contemporary Latin American context, the "penetrator" in homosexual acts embodies "a superior masculine power and male status over the other [the 'penetrated'], who is feminized and indeed objectified."[20] While *giving* seed always places a man in a preordained position sanctioned as male, a man who *receives* seed renders himself female. A penetrated man, however, is always a failed woman because a man who receives seed cannot procreate. As a nonfertile recipient he signals the end of reproduction. And by refusing to claim his right to patriarchal authority he cuts all ties to the naturalized family. Since, according to Guy Hocquenghem, "homosexual desire challenges anality-sublimation because it restores the desiring use of the anus," it follows that "homosexual desire is the ungenerating-ungenerated terror of the family, because it produces itself without reproducing."[21] The homosexual, in other words, is rendered a "blight," an impairment, for those who propagate the family genealogy. In Olvera's poem it is not simply gay "blasted sex" which repels Joe; it is his association of "passive" gay male sex, anal penetration, as, to paraphrase Leo Bersani, an abdication of power. Thus to "move on" for Olvera means to resist passive subjugation for the sake of generating Chicano progeny *and poetry* (or any form of literature for that matter).

Within the terms of Chicanismo contoured by machismo, the integration of gay and lesbian sexual politics complicates nationalist projects that are family-based. The terms of these complications correspond with prevailing ideas of what counts as family given these projects' demands for nuclear, patriarchal, and heteronormative networks. In his essay "Machismo," published in 1975, José Armas attempts to rescue the macho and his or her "machismo traits" from those whose slogan is "Smash Macho!" Armas claims that women's and gay liberation movements are adversary struggles that chastise the values of a machismo which "equipped people to face the challenge of exploitation, discrimination, racism, sexism, classism with self confidence, determination and dignity." He argues, "In contemporary times, the White women's liberation and the gay liberation movements condemn the macho as a cold chauvinistic person incapable of humanistic exchanges."[22] But while Armas describes these movements as Anglo phenomena and irrelevant to Chicano struggles (not to mention that he conflates women's liberation with gay liberation), the point is not merely that whites are imposing their belief systems on Chicanos. In fact certain white men, such as Ernest Hemmingway, are said to embody a brand of machismo very similar to that of Chicanos.[23]

The notorious fear that feminism and homosexuality strive to undermine the heteronormative prerogatives of familia (seen as absolutely necessary for political action) is perhaps the more salient point articulated in Armas's desire for machismo. Gay liberation and feminism are, as he sees it, antimacho and as a result antifamily: "The failure of the white women's liberation movement to attract a mass following from the Chicana woman indicates something important. This is apart from the fact that the family is the basis for all social development in the Chicano community and the woman plays the key role in that development. The white women's liberation has little regard for the family as an institution. At least in the Chicano sense."[24] If "in the Chicano sense" means the way family is articulated in Armas's La Familia de La Raza — that is, an extension of private domestic family relations to public communal kinship politics — one must argue otherwise when considering the complexities of the women's movement. However, I believe Armas is suggesting that the women's liberation movement and the gay liberation movement hold little regard for the family as an institution because of their outright rejection of machismo as a sign of male heterosexual superiority.[25] In his defense of machismo Armas denies that it is "a negative, violent and destructive trait . . . a sexist trait and . . . a definition that is used as a distinction between men and women." And yet, in a move that signals a curiously ambiguous impulse behind staking claims for machos, that is, recognizing the importance of resisting patriarchy only to chastise feminism's growing significance for galvanizing women, Armas concedes that sexism is a subjugating force with which Chicanas must contend, admitting to the "chauvinistic and sexist attitudes that arise and do exist in the Chicano culture."[26] The white women's liberation movement, however, is incapable of attending to the needs of Chicanas, thus Chicanas should look to la raza in order to solve the problem. To remain faithful to a Chicano nationalist ideology, the problems of the community must be kept entre familia, solvable within the community.

In "Machismo" Armas fittingly reveals that he was raised solely by his mother, a "macho" woman. "Sometimes we had a stepfather," he writes, "but mostly she raised us alone." Despite the lack of a father figure, Armas insists, he was raised to be macho, as were his three brothers: "A family of machos raised by a woman alone. A woman, a mother who raised machos!" Yet the macho woman must always be a mother, a woman never lacking femininity. Armas maintains, "My mother, who was extremely feminine when she dressed up, taught the girls to dance and the nonverbal language of feminine communication." Contrary to white culture's perceptions of machismo, his two sisters, "who are today as feminine as [his] mother, also have machismo." In short, machismo is an essentialist trait embodied by all Chicanos despite sexual differences. However, circumscribed by what Armas calls "a total nature which makes the whole (i.e., the Chicano nature)," machismo is ultimately disseminated through reproductive futurism and rests upon the hubris of traditional gender roles. He implicitly suggests that sexism can be addressed through the macho and familia framework, but what about gay liberation and its tense relationship with machismo that Armas mentions at the start of his essay? Although he notes that "it is not uncommon to see Raza men greet with a hug and walk with arms around each other," dealing a blow to the myth of the macho superman, given the heterosexualized contours of masculinity and family established within his work it would be impossible (not to mention culturally sacrilegious) for him to identify these Raza men as gay. After all, figuratively echoing Olvera's poem, Armas insists that "passivity is not permitted." [27]

CRUISING (THROUGH) CHICANISMO

Thus far I have examined texts charged with the political currents of the Chicano movement. But unlike many scholars who use the 1960s and 1970s as bookends to bracket Chicano movement discourse, I want to insist that such periodization does not always account for the rhetorical force of Chicanismo that bleeds into the 1980s—and into the present for that matter—as evident in popular culture. In "Ondas y Rollos (Wavelengths and Raps): The Ideology of Contemporary Chicano Rhetoric" José Angel Gutiérrez argues that the movement figures César Chávez, Reies López Tijerina, Rodolfo "Corky" Gonzales, and he

> embarked on a course to legitimate Chicanismo, an operational working definition of Chicano culture. In their speeches, these men utilized new words to give life to the social protest movements of the 1970s. These words—Chicano,

Aztlán, La Raza, La Causa, Huelga, Carnalismo, for example—broke with assimilationist thought because they set up an ideological framework of action against the Anglo system. The Chicano slogans called for goals that would result in independently created Chicano social institutions. The words and slogans became self-identifiers that represented pride, cultural identity, political militancy, and concerted, collective action. The young, the women, and the poor saw themselves as the authors of their own advocacy and destiny.[28]

Such words and slogans—part and parcel of Chicano movement discourse—persisted throughout the 1980s and 1990s in poetry, music, the media, and other cultural forms. New Chicano left movements also adopt (often with a difference) the lexicon of Chicanismo typically deemed a phenomenon of the 1960s and 1970s. A particular example of Chicanismo's impact within a more recent popular frame is the culture of car customization, or, as the subtitle of Rick Tejada-Flores's documentary film Low 'n' Slow (1983) announces, "the art of lowriding."[29]

In 1981 the lowriding magazine Firme, based in the Los Angeles suburb of San Gabriel, initiated a discussion on homosexuality among a predominantly working-class Chicano readership by publishing an interview with "a gay Chicano" named Victor.[30] "A Gay Life Style (Only If La Familia Approves)" not only sought to inform its presumably heterosexual readership about gay male identity and sexual practices, but it juxtaposed two seemingly disparate identificatory terms at that time: Chicano and gay.[31] Moreover this rather obscure article from the Chicano queer studies archive is but one example of how debates about gay identity were taking place within working-class Chicano communities, and it serves as evidence of how heteronormative impulses underscored familial and nationalist politics.

Produced by the Mexican-American Ventures Corporate Operations, Inc., Firme's first issue was released in early 1981. The magazine published six issues in 1981, two in 1982, and disappeared until almost a decade later, when in 1993 it reappeared as a double-feature publication with (Firme Magazine Presents:) Chicano Arte. In 1994 the magazine became Q-vo (although the title Firme still appears in various locations throughout the magazine), the publication which Firme absorbed back in 1982. Over the years and despite its numerous changes, Benjamin Francisco Hernández remained the publisher. At first glance Firme is comparable to the format and general content of the widely recognized Lowrider Magazine (whose premiere issue appeared in January 1977), mainly because both appeal to a young Chicano male readership and highlight car culture (either customizing or cruising). Evident by the simple fact that both magazines emphasized the term *Chicano*, *Lowrider* and *Firme* stressed Chicano cultural pride informed by *el movimiento*.[32] A closer inspection, however, reveals that while *Lowrider* stressed the art of car customization first and foremost, *Firme* featured a wide range of Chicano artistic forms and practices.

Unlike *Lowrider*, *Firme* did not succeed on a national or international level. Yet in the early 1980s, while *Lowrider* was receiving complaints from readers for selling out the community in the name of business expansion (as a concerned incarcerated reader put it in a penetrating letter to the magazine, "I hate to think you vatos are going capitalist on your own Raza"), *Firme* remained loyal to the Chicano communities of Aztlán.[33] Although *Lowrider* too spoke the language of Chicanismo, it was never clear, as Luis F. B. Plascencia points out, who owned and operated the magazine and what the magazine's goals were.[34] Thus Hernández made sure to inform his readers that *Firme* was "media owned and operated by Chicanos for Chicanos." Moreover Hernández firmly stated, "We must take what belongs to us. The most valuable commodity around is ourselves. We can build a better mas firme barrio society, truly a la brava. The success of this magazine stands on this." *Firme* too published business advertisements, but it is evident that the magazine was less concerned with selling cars and car parts to Chicanos than with the multifarious dimensions of, as the magazine's subtitle declares, "Chicano life": politics, art, music, film, and community happenings. Additionally a regular section titled "Barrio Chicanada" displayed photographs in a format which reminds one of a family photo album. Indeed "Barrio Chicanada," which depicts *Firme* readers and members of the Chicano community in general, almost always included the standard family images of father, mother, and children.[35] In short, the *arte* in *Firme* was more than cars; art was also the practices of everyday life. As Hernández states in his "Note from the Publisher" column in the second issue:

> We all know the creative Chicano mente. "Cars as art." A lot of jale goes into a firme ride, and most of the work is done by the owner himself. We like to give credit where credit is due. As for you vatos who disagree, Bueno hay tienen los magazines de los gavas, tu sabes, "Street Chatter," "Hot Chatter," y "Road y Traques," etc. A puro bore! Con nada de estillo! Inside the pages of this issue you will find "puro arte Chicano." Check it out, ese y esa![36]

Firme stood apart from car magazines published by *los gavas*, or white people, as it remained indebted to la causa and the goals of the movement. And since accusations were flying at the time that *Lowrider* was possibly white-owned (mainly because it was unclear who was behind the magazine's operation) or selling out, Hernández's critique is most likely directed at *Lowrider*, their rival publication, not the fabricated titles he lists. Early editions of the magazine contain a subscription ad with a cartoon of a frenzied Chicano wanting to purchase a (sold-out) copy of *Firme* at a newsstand. Appropriately enough, in the background we see a magazine called "Blowrider," adopting the trademark *Lowrider* symbol of a man in a porkpie hat and dark shades and wearing a thin mustache, which together create the silhouette of a pachuco. On the cover of "Blowrider," however, the pachuco's mustache is gone; in its place is a set of feminine lips. The title "Blowrider" and the image beneath it are quite suggestive. Certainly *Firme* is implying that *Lowrider* sucks. Figuratively, this insinuates that *Lowrider* is inferior to *Firme*. Literally, for *Lowrider* to suck it must be placed in the passive role of a woman, hence the replacement of a man's mustache with a woman's lips. This gesture underscores the need to render *Firme* "on top" and *Lowrider* "on the bottom."

One aspect which ultimately links both publications, making them virtually indistinguishable, is their display of *firme rucas*, the scantily clothed women within and on its covers. The common perception among Chicanos and Chicanas that the communities who subscribe to these magazines are sexist and homophobic makes sense given how the provocatively dressed women—which are part and parcel of *Firme*'s "Barrio Chicanada" section—unabashedly cater to male heterosexual desires. A letter to the editor from Macho Man "De Hollywood" in the second issue of *Firme* suggests, "You should . . . show more girls showing off their beautiful bronze bodies, make them wear G-strings with their flesh exposed to the camera, make them pose in erotic positions that will make every Chicano proud." Even if this letter is fictional (as some of the letters seem to be), both *Firme* and *Lowrider* took Macho Man's suggestions seriously. After all, the success of these magazines hinges not only on their display of souped-up car bodies but also on displaying the "beautiful bronze bodies" of Chicanas.

Chicanas, however, did not remain silent about the exploitation of women in these magazines. Beginning in the late 1970s published letters chart the discomfort—and fury—at the way women are portrayed in both *Lowrider* and *Firme*.[37] Despite the published objections to the sexist practices of these publications, no attempt was made to eliminate the images of provocatively dressed women because the reader was always assumed to be a heterosexual man whose gaze and libidinal desires were being courted.[38] Like other well-documented moments in the movement, women's objections were nevertheless occasions for men of la raza to brand outspoken Chicanas as belligerent feminists and man-hating lesbians. This was the case in an issue of Firme in 1993, crystallized in "Dear Tommy Tapado," a column of fictional letters answered by "Tommy," an abrasive *vato loco* who doesn't hold back. Although intended as comic relief, one letter highlights the serious homophobic impulse of the magazine: "Dear Firme: Although I know you probably won't print this letter, I have to tell you that your magazine stinks! I bet the publisher is a pompous male chauvinistic pig, who doesn't know the difference between a hole in the wall and the hole in his head and probably has an I.Q. of 3." The letter is signed "Debbie Dyke" from "Hollyweird, Ca." Although the letter may be based on those Firme received throughout the years, it also functions as a warning for those who may be tempted to complain about the magazine's sexism: objecting women will be written off as dykes.

ONLY IF LA FAMILIA APPROVES?

Firme's heterosexist tendencies were firmly established back in 1981, also within the Tommy Tapado letter section. In issue 4 "Lupe La Loca" writes, "Dear Tommy: Why is it that you guys at Firme always show girls that are always half naked and not guys?" Tommy answers: "Dear Vieja Bomba: We show girls half naked because that's the way we like them and we don't show guys that way because we're no fags!" The very next issue features an interview conducted by Special Projects Editor Carlos Hernández with a Chicano gay man named Victor.

In his "Note" to this issue Benjamin Hernández writes, "Our interview with Victor shares some alarming and confusing attitudes on sexual identity. On the other hand, Firme's finest of the month is Frank Abundis, a second generation Chicano businessman, who aspires for success and life's pleasurable endeavors."[39] Here Victor is juxtaposed with "Firme's Finest," a presumably heterosexual "page-three" male model who appears in each issue of Firme (and very similar to the "Page Three Fella" in the British tabloid The Mirror).[40] Whereas Frank must be lauded for his accomplishments (not to mention his unabashed manliness, as evident in his photo, in which he appears shirtless and displays his muscular physique), Victor as a gay man can offer only "alarming and confusing" perspectives on a contorted sexual identity.

Unlike Benjamin Hernández, who dismisses Victor as sexually confused, Victor's interviewer, Carlos Hernández, seems more sympathetic and willing to take seriously what Victor has to say. In fact Carlos Hernández begins his piece not with the sensationalized introduction we would have expected to read after Benjamin Hernández's jeering comment. The interview begins as follows:

> As Chicanos are a minority in America, homosexuals are a minority within la gente. And, like anyone who is different from the majority, gays sometimes find they are misunderstood and disliked. However, according to Victor, a gay Chicano, attitudes are slowly improving toward gays.

> Firme is publishing an interview with Victor to give insight into the gay life style and beliefs. Nevertheless, it's important to remember that Victor is just an individual and not necessarily reminiscent of all gay Chicanos.[41]

Contrary to José Armas, who believes Chicanos and homosexuals are disparate subjects and thus refuses to recognize the existence of Chicano homosexuals, Hernández acknowledges the presence of Chicano gays as a "minority within la gente." He also aligns homosexuals with other disenfranchised groups, "like anyone who is different from the majority," and not as the enemy of Chicanos (as is typically the case). If we can agree that the interview is conducted in good faith (that is, operating from an antihomophobic platform), then it is possible to see Hernández as part of a contingent whose "attitudes are slowly improving toward gays."

The questions Hernández asks Victor are wide-ranging, extending from the essential to the dubious (and perhaps I'm being overly critical of someone who wants to know if a gay man would court a "transsexual who, because of a sex operation, turned himself into a beautiful woman"). Yet for those who want to learn about "the gay life style and beliefs," Hernández's questions, such as "Are you one of those people who feels you were born a homosexual?" and "How does your family feel about your being homosexual?," are crucial. To his credit Hernández also provides important, critical background information after some of his questions and Victor's answers. For example, Hernández asks Victor, "When you first started 'coming out,' as they say, was there anyone who told you that being a homosexual was wrong?" Victor answers, "Well, I went to Catholic school all my life, and of course they teach you from the Bible what things are wrong. But, in answer to your question, I would say it was one of my school teachers that I first heard say it was wrong." As an aside Hernández offers the following insights:

> Gay Christians admit that the Bible condemns sexual relations between two people of the same sex, calling it an abomination. But because the Bible also calls camels and eagles abominable things (Leviticus 11) and condemns

to death stubborn children as well as any man who picks up sticks on the Sabbath (Deuteronomy 21; Numbers 15), gay Christians say the Old Testament prohibitions cannot be rashly quoted or easily understood outside their historical and cultural contexts. Furthermore, gay Christians state that nowhere in the New Testament does Christ condemn homosexuality, and that St. Paul warned against idolatrous sexual worship practiced by pagans but was not referring to true, Christ-believing homosexuals.[42]

Hernández's gloss on the Bible, and the contradictory interpretations of it, illuminates that dismissals of homosexuality as a "sin against God" do not hold when considered within a more comprehensive and judicious historical frame. He seems to be diligently carving out a space for Victor within Chicano religious and popular cultural contexts traditionally unaccustomed to housing queers.[43]

The recuperative aspects of the interview, however, exist in tension with the larger, ideological premises of heteronormativity, highlighted in the formalistic presentation of accompanying imagés, title, and of course Benjamin Hernández's casual dismissal of Victor's perspectives as "confusing" and "alarming." Printed alongside the text are two uncredited drawings. The first is of a man wearing heavy makeup, large hoop earrings, and string (a necklace? a dog collar? a whip?) around his neck, a corset, black panties, and stockings supported by a garter belt. (One gets the sense he is into s/m given the style of clothing and the absence of his hands; they are presumably tied behind his back, thus accentuating his "passivity.") In spite of his having a penis—of which the outline through his underwear and corset is curiously accentuated by the artist—and a muscular, clearly male chest, he is portrayed as effeminate. That he looks white evokes the idea that only whites can be gay or that gayness is a "white thing." The second image is in the same vein as the first, although here, along with what looks like a carbon copy of the transvestite, we are also presented with what appears to be a transsexual. Her facial features are similar to her counterpart's; the distinction lies in the fact that she has large breasts (sustained and covered by suspenders). Are these figures supposed to provide us with an idea of what Victor looks like? Or are they merely exaggerated representations sketched by a phobic imagination?

Although Victor admits to "doing drag," he insists that he is gay and not a transvestite. (Hernández asks Victor if he would consider himself a transvestite, to which Victor answers, "No, not really. I'd rather be considered gay.") This point, however, is subsequently buried by the signifying force of these salaciously deviant images, which crudely collapse transvestites, transsexuals, and gay men. In short, these images conjure up well-worn perceptions of gay men as effeminate and, ultimately, wanting to be women. (One thinks of the exaggerated lowrider aesthetics in which women's femininity and sexuality are juxtaposed against the hardness of "real" men.)

The title, "A Gay Life Style (Only If La Familia Approves)," is provocative. But to which familia does it refer? When asked how his family feels about his being gay, Victor answers, "Well, it was about a year ago that I first told my parents that I was gay. My dad said, 'Oh, I kind of figured that a long time ago.' But my mother was in shock and wanted me to see a doctor because she thought I wasn't normal."[44] Although his parents' responses are far from congratulatory, they do not appear to be preventing him from asserting his gayness. In other words, his family's consent (or lack thereof) does not necessarily deter Victor's leading "a gay life style," as the title of the interview suggests it would. What is meant by "la familia's approval," then, is that which is conceived and wielded by Firme. La familia de la raza would most likely object to Victor's lifestyle since it conflicts with the principles to which this particular family adheres. The accompanying drawings of hyperfeminine transvestites and transsexuals assist in the prohibition of Victor—whose words presumably breathe life into these drawings—from the "Barrio Chicanada" section, with the male-female couples and nuclear families, given la familia's obligatory disapproval of his gay lifestyle. Moreover despite the detectable good intentions of Victor's interviewer, the capacity to include Victor as part of the Firme scene—a scene which is undeniably familial—is undermined by the normative tenets of Benjamin Hernández's, and Firme's, Chicano cultural politics.

The final question posed to Victor, "Do you ever plan to marry?," is not asking whether Victor ever plans to marry a man. Instead it returns to a previous question, "Have you ever thought of going straight?," thus foreclosing any possibility in shifting the terms of not only conjugality but, more imperative, familial constitution. When Victor answers, "No, I haven't [thought of going straight]. But I've thought of having children," a perplexed Hernández asks, "Having children? How?" Victor responds, "Yeah, you know. Maybe in the future I can adopt or acquire one through artificial insemination (a surrogate mother). Any which way really, as long as I wouldn't have to get down with a woman."[45] Unfortunately it seems that both Carlos and Benjamin Hernández do not know, nor do they desire to reconsider the sanctioned terms of family organization. No matter how many times Victor declares that he is not sexually attracted to women, Carlos Hernández is unable to disentangle conventional and alternative conceptions of gender roles and the family. The institution of marriage and its attendant accessories (spouse and children) are tangible only within the heterosexual matrix.[46] Those like Victor who challenge or refuse to adhere to the matrix are, in the final analysis, written off as confused (and not only by magazine editors). Clearly he could never qualify for inclusion in the magazine among the "real" barrio chicanada who are eligible for partaking in "a memorable Firme wedding."

Victor's candid comments about his sexual identity and practices cannot help but establish an undercurrent of heterosexual anxiety. This anxiety is not unlike the sentiment conveyed in Joe Olvera's "Gay Ghetto District." In both texts Chicano gay men function as a fetish for straight men, which is apparent in their interest in and curiosity about what gay men do and how they do it. But like any fetish, this harbored interest and curiosity must always result in disavowal, here the disavowal of (homosexual) desire.[47] As I have shown, any affirmative constitution of gay male identity with the potential to short-circuit the nationalist ambitions that rest upon heterosexual presumption and reproduction must be taken into custody. Thus in order to sustain the primacy of fixed notions of manhood, nation, and family, gay men must be seen as failed men, literally and figuratively converted into failed women, subjected to a nonreproductive, sexually submissive (that is, anally receptive) role, simultaneously branded as confused men who require a sex change to become women. In either case they thwart the generation of la familia and its heteronormative codification.

YA VAS, CARNAL

Despite, or because of, the ambiguous aura surrounding the Firme interview, I want to read "Victor" as a precursor to Chicano gay male historical consciousness articulated not only by writers, but also by painters, photographers, filmmakers, and video artists. His self-assured stance reverberates well beyond the curious ambiguity containing and disciplining his unabashedly queer desires. But what does one make of his willing inclusion on the pages of Firme? I understand Victor to be engaging his brothers—his familia, as it were—about himself as not only a gay man but a Chicano gay man within and beyond the boundaries of a preconceived community. To be sure, this is merely one hypothesis about why he grants the interview. Victor knows his inclusion within "Barrio Chicanada," so to speak, will always be thwarted by those "brothers" who do not embrace him. Yet as the Chicano gay writer Eric-Steven Gutiérrez writes, "Our families may reject us but we belong to them nonetheless. . . . We must not abandon them. They are ours. Even if it is impossible to stay, they remain ours for as long as we claim them; for as long as we attempt to reconcile our queer and Latino communities and identities."[48] To my mind Victor is, to paraphrase Gutiérrez, a Chicano gay man claiming la raza. He is like the activist Rodrigo Reyes, founder of the historic Gay Latino Alliance in San Francisco, whose essay "Latino Gays: Coming Out and Coming Home" appeared the same year as the *Firme* interview in the Latino magazine *Nuestro* (Us), who insisted on working "side-by-side with [our] heterosexual *vecinos*, serving the community in which [we] feel [we] rightly belong."[49] These are not simple bids for inclusion into heteronormative family arrangements but desires to recast the terms that define who has traditionally counted as la familia.

Chicano gay men have concurrently initiated families of their own, families of choice.[50] Moreover there remains a need to hold onto kinship discourse in the formation of Chicano gay subjectivity and community. Nearly twenty years later, car culture and the magazines that promote lowriding exist within Chicano gay male cultural production as iconography which is not simply contested but also reconfigured in the name of challenging old and creating new collectivities. Augie Robles's documentary video *Cholo Joto* (1993) employs shots of *Lowrider* and family photographs (many of which could be included in *Firme*'s "Barrio Chicanada") after a young gay man, Valentín Aguirre, waxes critically on the narrow nationalism of Chicano movement ideologues in his native San Diego neighborhood of Logan Heights. Aguirre calls out the sexist and homophobic nationalists, telling them, "You might as well be in the sixties, still listening to 'Angel Baby' and thinking you're on the cover of *Lowrider*." In his reading of this scene (which emphasizes Aguirre's commentary on a mural of Che Guevara), José Esteban Muñoz rightly argues that Aguirre's "performance does not simply undermine nationalism but instead hopes to rearticulate such discourses within terms that are politically progressive."[51] Fittingly, Aguirre confesses, "I love *Lowrider*, but, I mean, I'm not on the cover!" Although men generally don't appear on the cover of *Lowrider*, Aguirre is stressing his absence from the magazine's cover as a gay man. I read his commentary—after Gutiérrez, Reyes, and Muñoz—as Aguirre's declaration of love for la raza, and yet a desire for inclusion into a community whose embrace is nonetheless always without guarantee.

Al Lujan's video s & m in the Hood (1998) takes Aguirre's exclusion seriously and addresses it with a touch of queer humor. In an opening shot that flashes what may as well be the "Blowrider" symbol but with an added beautifying facial mole à la Marilyn Monroe, the logo, also used by the gay comedy troupe

Latin Hustle (to which Lujan belongs), recasts the heteronormativity of low-rider culture in a Chicano-specific context of queer world making. The presence of the image, I would argue, sets the stage for a provocative depiction of eroticism, cultural identity, and humor within the contours of a gay-affirmative Chicanismo. The way the tape scrambles traditional cultural discourses—gay male s/m, lowrider iconography, and a Chicano or Mexicano piñata-breaking contest (we must remember that piñatas are most often found at family gatherings such as birthdays)—mirrors the strategies undertaken by Chicano gay men like Victor, Gutiérrez, and Aguirre, who strive to create and define complex yet historically specific identities and communities.

I end this chapter with a poem by the activist Rodrigo Reyes, who founded the Latino queer organization GALA in San Francisco. Allow me, however, to say a few things about Reyes which I believe give his poem and my reading of it a suitable historical context. According to Horacio N. Roque Ramírez, Reyes was deeply involved in the Chicano movement during the 1970s, reporting extensively on it for KPFK, the Bay Area's Pacifica Radio station.[52] His LGBT community ties were ultimately woven into his ties to the Latino community, thus giving way to GALA's formation. A prolific and highly influential activist during his lifetime, on 19 January 1992, Reyes passed away from complications due to AIDS. In her "Tribute" Cherríe Moraga writes, "Last night at the service, I kept thinking . . . Rodrigo loved his own kind, his own brown and male kind. Listening to the tributes made to him, it was clear that the hearts he touched the most deeply were his carnalitos. And each one, as lovely as the one preceding him, spoke about Rodrigo, 'mi 'mano, mi papito, mi carnal, ese cabrón . . .' con un cariño wholly felt." Although Moraga confesses to not always feeling recognized as a sister by Reyes and questions his dedication to his sisters (attributing this to "all the wounds of family betrayals and abandonments"), she nonetheless identifies him as a brother and, more to the point here, acknowledges his impact on his Latino gay male *carnales*, so much so that she ends her tribute with the following verse:

He did make space for them, his brothers
he did plant seeds,
he did lay ground.
And this is where the young ones pick up . . .
¡Adelante 'manitos![53]

Reyes was one of many Chicano gay men no longer with us who inscribed his experiences as a Chicano gay man not only in the public sphere, where he made his presence known as an activist, but also in his writing, which is in need of redistribution and recirculation. In his writing it becomes clear that his 'manitos were the objects of his desire, a desire charged with a crucial sexual current as well as a bond that extends beyond heteronormative kinship.

Appearing in 1985 with Humanizarte Publications in San Francisco and now out of print, a collection of Chicano gay male poetry titled *Ya Vas, Carnal*—which I translate from the Chicano Spanish as "You go, brother!"—featured the work of three gay Chicano poets: Francisco X. Alarcón, Juan Pablo Gutiérrez, and Rodrigo Reyes. (This is also where Alarcón's poem, which serves as this chapter's epigraph, appears.) "Carnal Knowledge," Reyes's poem that opens the collection is, as I understand it, about Chicano gay consciousness, desire, and brotherhood, the stuff about which this chapter has been concerned.

> Carnal,
> ése,
> sabes qué,
> don't I know you?
>
> Didn't we meet
> eyes, una vez,
> didn't I kiss
> your heart
> once? Calmado.
>
> I am sure
> I know you
> Oye carnal,
> didn't you
> use to live
> next to me,
> a un ladito?
>
> I remember
> that if I
> reached out
> I could touch
> you.
>
> It was a long time ago
> Then you split.

Querías conocer mundo.
Te acuerdas?

Simón, I'm sure
it was you.
Do you know
me,
carnal?[54]

Who is this carnal, this brother? Not simply his *hermano* ("proper" Spanish for *brother*, usually connoting a biological kinship brother), this *carnal* (Chicano Spanish for an extended kin-like brother), is the speaker's lover. Perhaps an MSM with whom he has made love, or perhaps an openly gay man who has turned his back on him, the carnal in question is being asked to acknowledge the speaker, with whom he not only shares the experience of bodily contact—carnal knowledge—but also the knowledge of brotherhood, a knowingness exchanged between carnales. In this poem Rodrigo Reyes helps flesh out a history of gay consciousness between Chicano men in which to love a "brother" fuels the ability to enact "brotherhood" in queer political projects informed by desire. This stance, I believe, is akin to the group of African American gay men whose influential writings appear in the foundational collection *Brother to Brother*, influenced by the well-known declaration "Black men loving black men is the revolutionary act" from Marlon Riggs's documentary *Tongues Untied*. So the question at the end of Reyes poem—"Do you know me, carnal?"—is not merely a one-way, interpellative inquiry; rather its provocation stimulates a generative request for mutual recognition: As I call you, my brother, acknowledge me as yours.

NOTES

For their generous feedback and comments on this essay, I wish to thank Talia Bettcher, Dionne Espinoza, John Ramírez, Pete Sigal, Luz Calvo, and Catriona Rueda Esquibel. I am particularly indebted to Ernesto Martínez, Michael Hames-García, and the IPRH Queer Studies Reading Group at the University of Illinois, Urbana-Champaign, especially Siobhan Somerville and Martin Manalansan, for help in tightening the loose screws of my arguments.

1. Maciel, Ortiz, and Herrera-Sobek, *Chicano Renaissance*, xvi, xix, emphasis added.

2. The groundbreaking work of Chicana feminists has certainly made this clear. See, e.g., Moraga, *Loving in the War Years*; E. Pérez, "Sexuality and Discourse"; D. González, "Malinche as Lesbian"; A. M. García, *Chicana Feminist Thought*; Espinoza, *Revolutionary Sisters*. In a personal communication the artist Barbara Carrasco pointed out to me that

members of the United Farm Workers, at the request of César Chávez, often marched in gay pride parades as a show of support for a community historically in solidarity with farm workers' struggles. Yet participation, according to Carrasco, often rendered marchers suspect by some UFW members as well as by blood relatives.

3. My use of *reproductive futurism* is influenced by Lee Edelman's important work on futurity and heteronormativity, *No Future*.

4. Here I take the lead from José Esteban Muñoz's critical engagement with "world-making" queer cultural productions to tease out oppositional modes of "being in the world." See *Disidentifications* and "Feeling Brown."

5. R. L. Ortiz, "Sexuality Degree Zero"; Gutiérrez-Jones, *Rethinking the Borderlands*, especially 129–51; Cunningham, "'Hey, Mr. Liberace.'"

6. Viego, "The Place of Gay Male Chicano Literature."

7. Almaguer, "Chicano Men," 97.

8. Almaguer, "Chicano Men," 97.

9. Manuel Guzmán, "'Pa' La Escuelita," 215.

10. Recovery projects to unearth Chicano gay male narratives would not be unlike the Recovering the U.S. Hispanic Literary Heritage project based at the University of Houston, an attempt at restoring the narrative voices in literature and personal memoirs by Latinos in the United States from the nineteenth century to the 1950s. Recently a significant number of publications focused on Latino gay men have appeared. See, for example, Gil Cuadros's compilation of essays and poems, *City of God*; Bernardo García's qualitative study, *The Development of a Latino Gay Identity*; Jaime Cortez's literary anthology, *Virgins, Guerrillas, and Locas*; Frankie Barrera's collection of poems and diary entries, *The Diary of Baby Chulo*; Manuel Muñoz's compelling book of short stories, *Zigzagger*; and Daniel T. Contreras's cultural studies investigation, *Unrequited Love and Gay Latino Culture*.

11. R. Gutiérrez, "Community, Patriarchy and Individualism," 45, 46.

12. Olvera, "Gay Ghetto District," 111. Olvera's essays and poems appeared in numerous Chicano journals, including *Grito del Sol* and *Caracal*, during the 1970s.

13. Armas and Zamora, *Flor y Canto IV and V*, 10.

14. Candelaria, *Chicano Poetry*, 34. Often used is the word *floricanto*, the term in which the words *flor* and *canto* are condensed. Flor y canto, or floricanto, symbolizes a neo-indigenous aesthetics grounded in Aztec or Nahuatl cultural expression and represented by the writers Alurista and Luis Valdez. See, for example, Alurista, *Floricanto en Aztlán*. For more on the Aztec significance of flor y canto, see León-Portilla, *Aztec Thought and Culture*.

15. Olvera, "Gay Ghetto District," 111.

16. Ibid.

17. Leo, "The Familialism of 'Man,'" 34. In contemporary popular culture evidence of gay men's being reduced—both literally and figuratively—to "assholes" is exemplified by the white rapper Eminem, also known as "Slim Shady," in his response to his use of the word *faggot* ("'Faggot' to me doesn't necessarily mean gay people. 'Faggot' to me just means . . . taking away your manhood. You're a sissy. You're a coward. This does not necessarily mean you're being a gay person. It means you're being a fag. You're being an

asshole.") and in his song lyrics ("Slim Anus? / You're damn right, slim anus / I don't get fucked in mine / Like you two little flaming faggots"). See DeCurtis, "Eminem's Hate Rhymes," 18.

18. For a related discussion, see Ramírez, "The Chicano Homosocial Film." Ramírez insightfully reads the family "as a fundamental social technology for the construction and management of gender and sexuality" in the rocky relationship between Chicanos and Hollywood (262).

19. Cited in Bersani, "Is the Rectum a Grave?," 212.

20. Almaguer, "Chicano Men," 78. However, see also Cantú, "Entre Hombres/Between Men," which rightly problematizes Almaguer's reification of culture, which in turn allows him to make sweeping claims about Latino and Latin American male sexual practices. Even in contemporary Western gay culture, for example, these roles continue to be played out as men may identify or are identified as "tops" or "bottoms."

21. Hocquenghem, *Homosexual Desire*, 98, 107. On these issues I have also benefited from Edelman, *Homographesis*.

22. Armas, "Machismo," 64, 52.

23. Chicano machismo's codes of behavior are said to be "not unlike [those] which Hemingway tried to live by. Much of Hemingway's fondness for the Raza, for Latino values, is closely tied to the values and attitudes toward life and death that he found in these communities and that he shared" (ibid., 54). Hemingway's devotion to the bullfight is also said to closely link him to Chicanos. Armas argues in "Machismo," as well as in *La Familia de la Raza*, that the bullfight is an exemplary metaphor for how to exercise one's machismo not because it is a "manly" act, but because it "is a ceremony and a ritual in which an individual is pitted with the dark forces of the world" (ibid.). In *La Familia de la Raza*, however, the bullfight scene is *very* manly in Armas's description of the male torero doing battle with the forces of evil symbolized by the bull (24–25). In 1971 Américo Paredes, a noted folklore scholar and, to some, one of Chicano studies' founding fathers, published "The United States, Mexico, and *Machismo*," in which Hemingway is figured as "the most hallowed interpreter of the macho" (Paredes, *Folklore and Culture*, 226). According to Paredes:

> The popularity of Hemingway's works in the period between the two world wars—as much among the critics as with the general public—shows the attraction the *macho* still had for the North American, although in real life the man of the United States made less and less of a show over his masculinity. Hemingway himself understood this, and almost all his novels and short stories develop the theme of *machismo* in Spain, Mexico, or Cuba. Today Hemingway is scorned by the critics. This is not surprising, since the protagonist of the novels now acclaimed by the critics no longer is the macho but the homosexual—the other extreme, or perhaps the same thing seen from another point of view. (226)

Although John Cunningham reads Paredes as offering "a radical challenge to an understanding of male homosexuality as antithetical to masculinity," I am not convinced that situating homosexuals and heterosexuals on opposite sides of a continuum—thus making them "the same thing" depending on the point of view—is all that radical (Cunningham, "'Hey, Mr. Liberace,'" 69).

24. Armas, "Machismo," 62–63.

25. Even in the early 1970s homophobia in radical movements could be confronted by heterosexual men. For example, Armas's position stands in stark contrast to Huey Newton's essay "The Women's Liberation and Gay Liberation Movements" (1970), which argues that the Black Panther Party would be wise to "form a working coalition with the gay liberation and women's liberation groups." Confessing his own "hang-ups" with (male) homosexuality, Newton insists that homophobia is ultimately the result of one's own sexual insecurities: "We want to hit a homosexual in the mouth because we are afraid we might be homosexual." Although there is a question about whether the homosexuals he is talking about are exclusively white (Can there be black gay men in the Black Panthers?), it is exhilarating to read Newton declaring, "There is nothing to say that a homosexual cannot also be a revolutionary. And maybe I'm now injecting some of my prejudice by saying that 'even a homosexual can be a revolutionary.' Quite the contrary, maybe a homosexual could be the most revolutionary" (153).

26. Armas, "Machismo," 53, 62.

27. Ibid., 64, 63–65, 61, 58, 59. This statement coincides with an articulation of nationalism when Armas writes, "Machismo is [an] element which shields the individual from outside forces. . . . There is, then, the aggressivity of Machismo that says that one cannot be static within the world in which the individual lives. That aggressivity demands that positive interaction must take place if one is to live successfully. The individual must interact, passivity is not permitted" (ibid., 59).

28. J. A. Gutiérrez, "Ondas y Rollos," 147–48. See also Powers, "Chicano Rhetoric."

29. For the history and cultural politics of lowriding, see, e.g., Trillin and Koren, "Low and Slow"; King, "Low Riders"; Plascencia, "Low Riding"; Stone, "'Bajito y Suavecito'"; Vigil, "Car Charros"; Bright, "Mexican American Low Riders" and "Remappings"; recent issues of Lowrider, which have published excerpts from Paige R. Renland's forthcoming Lowrider History Book (also available on the magazine's web site).

30. The term firme is Chicano Spanish for "fine" or "cool."

31. The interview in Firme forces us to rethink the historical genealogy of queer Chicano discourse that has traditionally been said to begin with Chicana lesbians, who then enabled Chicano gay men to speak. It should also compel us to examine how such discourses have been authorized within institutional settings and ignore or overlook how Chicana lesbian and Chicano gay communities and identities were being established well before the published works of creative writers or academics. In an interview with Dorothy Allison, Tomás Almaguer, and Jackie Goldsby for Out/Look: National Lesbian and Gay Quarterly, Cherríe Moraga acknowledges, "In 1983, when Loving in the War Years came out, I left the country because I was very frightened of bringing up the issue of being lesbian and Chicana together within the covers of a book" (Moraga et al., "Writing Is the Measure," 54). Although the Firme interview lacks the Chicana feminist agendas of

writers like Moraga, it is important to note that two years earlier the issue of being gay and Chicano together was raised in a popular magazine (and not a book to which mostly middle-class readers, particularly academics, had access). The article also contradicts the argument Moraga has made about the historical silence of Chicano gay men as compared to the audibility of Chicana lesbian voices: "In the last few years, Chicano gay men have also begun to openly examine Chicano sexuality" (Moraga, *The Last Generation*, 160). Both Moraga and *Firme* are from San Gabriel, California.

32. *Lowrider*'s founders were involved in Chicano movement activities. See D. M. Sandoval, "Cruising," 185.

33. Letter cited in Plascencia, "Low Riding," 165.

34. Plascencia, "Low Riding," 165.

35. *Lowrider* also requested photos of their readers' families, especially families from the 1940s who adopted "pachuco" aesthetics, which they would in turn publish in the pages of the magazine.

36. B. F. Hernández, "Note," 1, no. 2 (1981), 7.

37. For a short yet insightful history and commentary about representations of women in lowriding magazines, see Chappell, "'Take a Little Trip,'" esp. 112–14. D. M. Sandoval offers an interesting interpretation of the significance of such letters in *Lowrider* in "Cruising through Low Rider Culture," especially 188–94.

38. Over the years provocative representations of women in *Lowrider* have increased, and they are certainly more risqué today than they were in the late 1970s. Furthermore while many women were protesting these images, they were also noting the disparity of male models, thus crystallizing the magazine's general heterosexual inclination. Again I would like to emphasize the importance of perusing the letters sections of these magazines; they are excellent sources for tracking the sentiments of readers, both male and female, about gender issues impacting working-class Latino communities in which these magazines circulated.

39. B. F. Hernández, "Note," 1, no. 5 (1981), 55.

40. These "images of men aimed at women," as Richard Dyer has described the "male pin-up" in *The Mirror*, are nevertheless images informed by *Firme*'s chauvinistic assumptions of knowing what women want and the presumption that these men are indeed straight (Dyer, *Only Entertainment*, 104). Ironically in *Firme*'s fourth issue, "Firme's Finest," David Valdez, a business major at UCLA who is know to frequent Club Juárez and the Red Onion," also "occasionally goes to . . . Circus Disco." It is well-known that Circus Disco in Los Angeles was a *gay* disco throughout the 1970s and 1980s. See Luis Alfaro's poem "Heroes and Saints" from his spoken-word CD *Down Town*, about Chicano gay men, the rise of AIDS, and "the great Latino watering hole, Circus Disco." Indeed it seems the editors of *Firme* were aware of this, given the ellipsis before mentioning Circus Disco. One might assume that David is in fact Victor in the next issue, but the magazine cannot reveal this information because of the heterosexual tendencies of the magazine and the heterosexual female gaze for which "Firme's Finest" was created.

41. C. Hernández, "A Gay Life Style," 18–19.

42. Ibid., 18.

43. See Barbosa's and Lenoir's documentary video *De Colores* (2001), which carries out a similar project.

44. C. Hernández, "A Gay Life Style," 18.

45. Ibid., 19.

46. For an elaboration on the constitution of the heterosexual matrix, see Butler, *Gender Trouble*, esp. 45–100.

47. And yet not all straight men disavow homosexual desire and practices. This is evident when Victor reveals that he has "picked up on" not only gay but also straight men. One must bear in mind, though, that although these men may not be straight in terms of sexual practices, they are with regard to self-identification. In fact even when naming those Latino married or straight men MSMS, or "men who have sex with men," it is still important to point to the homophobia pervasive in the community, sometimes perpetuated by these men. For a compelling ethnographic analysis of MSMS, particularly Mexican immigrant men, in relation to the family, see Cantú, "A Place Called Home."

48. E.-S. Gutiérrez, "Latino Issues," 350.

49. R. Reyes, "Latino Gays," 44.

50. Weston, *Families We Choose*.

51. J. E. Muñoz, *Disidentifications*, 15. Rosemary Hennessy critiques Muñoz on the grounds that he fails to foreground Aguirre's transformation of self-shame into a "love for his community," opting instead for what she understands as a queer reading of Che Guevara that comprehends "El Che" as nothing more than an eroticized figure (Hennessy, *Profit and Pleasure*, 206). This would be a valid critique had Muñoz not written the sentence I have quoted. Overall Hennessy neglects the crucial politics of nationalism of which Muñoz is cognizant.

52. Roque Ramírez, "Rodrigo Reyes."

53. Moraga, *The Last Generation*, 175–78.

54. R. Reyes, "Carnal Knowledge," 8–9.

Entre Machos y Maricones: (Re)Covering
Chicano Gay Male (Hi)Stories

Daniel Enrique Pérez

I didn't have to get whipped too many times before I realized that
being a sissy boy had no place in our home. And yet I could not stop
myself. I had no control over my girlish behavior. It came so naturally.
—Rigoberto González, *Butterfly Boy: Memories of a Chicano Mariposa*

Despite the fact that the lives of Latino gay men have historically been a taboo subject and a topic that truly encapsulates the essence of the familiar saying *De eso no se habla*, Richard T. Rodríguez's essay suggests that Chicano gay men have a long history of participating in such a discourse. According to Rodríguez, the participation of Chicano gay men in various cultural spaces and in multiple forms of cultural production has often been underestimated, overlooked, and undervalued. Even though the process by which their participation has taken shape has been at times unconventional and somewhat limited due to social, cultural, and historical factors, Rodríguez makes the excellent and convincing argument that a number of such texts exist and need to be recovered, analyzed, and included in a discourse on Chicano gay male sexuality. As Chicanos we know and understand that although we encourage a politics of solidarity with other marginalized groups we cannot allow anyone else to write our (hi)stories or regulate our cultural production. Therefore the task at hand is, as Rodríguez suggests, to support emerging artists and recover those who exist in nontraditional or noncanonical texts. Rodríguez makes it clear that this is a task *entre hombres*.

By choosing to analyze the lowrider magazine *Firme* and its interview with an out Chicano gay male named Victor, Rodríguez focuses on a site where Chicano men engage in a rich dialogue on queer sexuality in an archetypal Chicano landscape. This analysis unequivocally allows multiple elements of Chicano identity politics to be considered in a discourse that has historically been accused of being mired in some form of cultural dissonance.

One critical issue that Rodríguez's analysis raises is the way Chicano men have often been placed in diametrically opposing categories: *machos* or *maricones*. As has been the case for Latinas contending with the problematic *virgen/puta* dichotomy, Latino men have often been measured and judged according to standards associated with either of these two categories for men. The juxtaposition of these seemingly disparate identities in a heteronormative — or, in the case of *Firme*, hypermasculine — cultural landscape proves to be a productive site for conducting an analysis of what Rodríguez refers to as a "curiously ambiguous response to queer politics."

Considering the dynamics of homosocial spaces, one can examine the relationship between the quintessential *macho* and *maricón* male figures as they have been portrayed in Latino cultural production. Certainly the stereotypical representations of these two figures are not representative of the wide range of complex identities and experiences that actually exist among Latino men. Nevertheless these two figures, often caricatured, have consistently been present in Chicano cultural production, and when they occupy the same space their interaction can become a fertile location for examining a multiplicity of Chicano identities and sexualities. Rodríguez's essay serves as an excellent model for such an examination. His use of the concept of *carnalismo* to demonstrate the ties that bind all Chicano men underscores the role that *familia* and *raza* play in facilitating male bonds, regardless of sexual identity. Besides allowing a stereotypical macho to engage in a discourse on queer sexuality with a stereotypical maricón, the concept of carnalismo becomes a site where Chicano men share a common language and develop intimate bonds. Furthermore their interaction becomes an exchange of ideas that inevitably influences all individuals involved and forces them to reconsider or resignify their values. Because the two must develop a medium by which they can communicate, the thick lines that tend to be drawn to maintain them in separate locations are ultimately obfuscated. Therefore an open dialogue on homoerotic desire, irrespective of who is actually participating in it, creates an inclusive queer space that in some way queers all of its participants because the act of engaging in a queer conversation is in and of itself queer.

Rodríguez's essay raises a number of important questions. One relates to the works that could be included in a recovery project of this nature. In addition to searching for the participation of Chicano gay men in the alternative mediums Rodríguez proposes, I suggest that we also consider those sites where queer identities that are not overtly marked as gay may be present. Here I think it is important to distinguish between the use of the terms *gay* and *queer*. I employ the terms as defined by David William Foster, who proposes that *queer* be used to "signify the critique of the heterosexist paradigm," whereas *gay* refers "to a set of sexual identities that refer to a preference for same-sex erotic relations and to whatever overall subjectivity and lifestyle is necessary to ensure the legitimation and realization of homoerotic acts."[1] By including queer subject positions the discourse on Chicano sexuality can be amplified exponentially, and more important, this process can destabilize the straight/gay or macho/maricón binary, thereby allowing for the possibility of a Chicano sexual continuum. Central to this discussion is the recognition of a wide range of nonheteronormative sexual identities that reflect the diversity and complexity of lived experiences.

As Ilán Stavans contends in his well-known essay "The Latin Phallus," the "Hispanic macho goes out of his way to keep up appearances, to exalt his virility, but he often fails. Sooner or later, his glorious masculinity will be shared in bed with another man."[2] Certainly Stavans is highlighting the difference between public and private identities. Nevertheless, by repositioning the macho in a queer subject position, he demonstrates how subjective and temporal identities can be. Although it may be considered blasphemous to correlate *machismo* with *mariconismo*, it is a natural component of the more widely accepted notion that all Chicanos embody some elements of machismo irrespective of their sexual identity. A direct correlative would be that all Chicanos also embody some elements of mariconismo.

The maricón paradigm can be reframed in a similar fashion. Typically being a maricón is associated with an effeminate role that demoralizes men. As Jaime Manrique contends in *Eminent Maricones: Arenas, Lorca, Puig, and Me*, the term is used "as a way to dismiss gay men as an incomplete and worthless kind of person." He engages in the process of resignifying the term by recognizing and accepting that he is a maricón: "This is another memory I have of those years: one of my younger uncles masturbated in front of me in an attic of the house and asked me to give him a blow job. Revolted and horrified, I wondered: Is it obvious I am a *maricón*?" Furthermore he converts the term to a badge of courage by including the eminent Hispanic queer figures Arenas, Lorca, and Puig, claiming that they "spoke for the oppression of the marginal" and "had the *cojones* that many heterosexual writers lacked." "And thus," he asserts, "I arrived at the true meaning of *Eminent Maricones* — locas, patos, jotos — who achieved true eminence by the courageous audacity of their examples."[3]

Similarly in his essay "Nationalizing Sissies" José Piedra reverses the traditional roles assigned to maricones by claiming that "sissy behavior" can be seen as a "nation-building trick: an active mediation in the exchanges between colonizers and colonized, a role or type ready to qualify, modify, taint, neutralize, and even trap—at least into an illusion of domination—whomever and whatever attempts to occupy him/her or his/her territory." In this way a maricón becomes what Piedra refers to as a "model anticolonialist or postcolonial being" and "a rebellious agent in the colonial exchange."[4] This process by which the resignification of the terms *macho* and *maricón* can take place—queering the macho and masculinizing the maricón—demonstrates that they intersect and can at times be considered one: ultimately, queer multipositionalities. Macho men can be queer just as queer men can be macho. I call such figures *queer machos*: men who possess the courage to be who they are without bowing to the heteronormative or ethnocentric precepts of the dominant culture.

In my own research I have been fascinated by the number of silences that exist in many of our texts with respect to a character's sexual identity. I base my research largely on the work of the queer theorist Alexander Doty, who contends that all texts can be read as queer and that we must prevent ourselves from falling into the "heterocentrist trap," the tendency to read characters and situations that are not marked as queer as heterosexual or heteronormative.[5] He suggests that the silences that exist in texts regarding a character's sexuality are prime locations for conducting queer analyses. For example, there is absolutely no reason why the unnamed protagonist in Tomás Rivera's *. . . y no se lo tragó la tierra* must be read as heterosexual. As a bildüngsroman the novel includes the youth's sexual awakening, but there is never any clear indication that he is heteronormative. In fact I argue that there are more clues that he will reject heteronormativity. In the same way that he rejects religion and separates himself from the structure of the family through his solitude, the protagonist appears to be disaffected by heterosexual acts. The source of his disaffection is unclear, but this is precisely the point that I am trying to make. When the protagonist discovers what "sins of the flesh" are, he believes he has committed one merely by accidentally witnessing a man and a woman engaging in sexual intercourse on the floor of the local cleaners. The image stalks him and serves as the impetus for him to imagine other adults engaging in the same act:

> When I saw my Dad and my Mother, I imagined them on the floor. I started seeing all of the grown-ups naked and their faces even looked distorted, and I could even hear them laughing and moaning, even though they weren't even laughing. Then I started imagining the priest and the nun on the floor. I couldn't hardly eat any of the sweet bread or drink the chocolate. As soon as I finished, I recall running out of the house. It felt like I couldn't breathe.[6]

What I find compelling about this scene is that none of the acts the protagonist witnesses or imagines is heteronormative. Despite the existence of heterosexual coupling, the acts themselves are queer: an extramarital affair, a priest and nun engaged in a sexual act, and couples having sex on the floor instead of on a bed. Moreover, the boy's reaction can be read in multiple ways. He could be distressed by his role as a voyeur, by imagining people he knows engaging in intercourse, by the thought of placing himself in one of the sexual positions, or by something else. Regardless, what is imperative is that we recognize that the protagonist does not have to be read in any particular way. We have absolutely no way of knowing exactly how to classify his response to his sexual encounter or what shape his sexual development will take. The few markings we have that are related to sexuality render his sexual identity and erotic interests as inconclusive. Nevertheless the ambiguity that the lack of such markings presents can certainly contribute to a discussion on queer Chicano sexuality. In the same way that no two people truly read the same text because reading is influenced by individual experiences and distinctive personal identities, no characters have to be read in the same way. I believe this is one reason why many Chicano gay men can identify in some way with Rivera's protagonist. Claiming such characters as queer is not only legitimate but also one way to expand the breadth of our representation in cultural texts.

Another question that surfaces from Rodríguez's essay is, What are some of the factors that have limited the participation of Chicano gay men in certain spaces? Without a doubt the contributions Chicano gay men have made through their participation in various forms of cultural production, wherever and whatever they may be, need to be examined through a unique gender, sexual, and racial lens. As Rodríguez makes clear, instead of questioning the amount of cultural production that is published as or incorporated into the Chicano canon, we need to (re)examine texts that already exist, including those that might be found in alternative or obscure forms of cultural production. One reason this is so essential is because of the way the presence and articulation of Chicano queer sexualities have been problematized by the homophobia that has persisted in varying degrees throughout the history of Chicano cultural production. Chicano gay men have always experienced and responded to homophobia in unique ways and homophobia has always limited the visibility and cultural production of gay men and lesbians to some degree.

In any patriarchal society and every one of its concomitant institutions women *and* queers are often the target of ridicule, humiliation, acts of violence, and all the other acts that stem from misogyny and homophobia. But unlike women, gay men must also contend with being placed into the "failed men" or "not 'real men'" (e.g., "sissies," "faggots," "jotos," and "maricones") categories. Additionally, as Rodríguez points out, they have historically been converted to "failed women" due to their inability to procreate and their perceived location in sexually submissive roles. Elizabeth Badinter suggests that "homophobia is the hatred of feminine qualities in men whereas misogyny is the hatred of feminine qualities in women."[7] Of course homophobia can also be the hatred of masculine qualities in women and misogyny can include the hatred of feminine qualities in men. Nevertheless Badinter is attempting to delineate the differences between homophobia and misogyny. At the same time she is underscoring the privileging of masculinity, irrespective of gender.

Even though gay men and lesbians may both experience homophobia, the way they experience it may be entirely unique. Moreover the experiences of gay men who exhibit masculine traits may be very different from those who exhibit traits deemed effeminate. One might consider how someone who is out and proud experiences homophobia compared to someone who is in the closet, or how someone who has stereotypical gay or lesbian attributes regardless of his or her sexual identity might experience homophobia compared to someone who manages to remain undetected by the infamous gaydar. These are some of the things I believe need to be considered when examining the experiences of Chicano gay men. We must recognize that there is no singular Chicano gay male experience and that Chicano gay men have been relegated to marginal spaces in ways that are unique to their experiences. They have been invisible and visible, silent and loud, maricones and machos, and, naturally, everything in between. While engaging in a recovery project of the nature that Rodríguez is proposing it would behoove us to consider all of these possible locations.

NOTES

1. Foster, El Ambiente Nuestro, 7.
2. Stavans, "The Latin Phallus," 156.
3. Manrique, Eminent Maricones, 112, 18, 113.
4. Piedra, "Nationalizing Sissies," 375.
5. Doty, Flaming Classics, 2.
6. Rivera, . . . y no se lo tragó la tierra, 116.
7. Badinter, XY, 115.

Entre Hombres/Between Men:

Latino Masculinities and Homosexualities

Lionel Cantú

On a cool May evening in the city of Santa Ana, California, approximately fifty Latino men boarded a bus for a weekend-long retreat in the southern California mountain resort of Big Bear Lake.[1] The congregation of men may have attracted the attention of casual onlookers, but the men themselves probably seemed nondescript in this predominantly Latino city. Yet this was not a usual gathering: These Latino men were meeting to confront and discuss the challenges in their lives as "gay Latino men."

This chapter utilizes data collected during two retreats, or *encuentros* (encounters), organized by the Entre Hombres (Between Men) program of Santa Ana's Delhi Center (a Latino community service organization). The weekend retreats at which my research was conducted were held at a campground in the immediate area of the town of Big Bear, California, in November 1997 and May 1998. These retreats were the third and fourth such events, which began in November 1996 for the purpose of exploring how issues of masculinity, sexuality, HIV, and culture impact participants' lives as "gay Latino men."[2]

The challenges that these men face as "gay Latino men" are multiple and complex. Although these challenges include such dimensions as homophobia, racism, and poverty, these men are differentially constrained and have different means by which to resist these constraints depending on their specific social locations and histories. To attempt to understand the lives and struggles of these men as "gay Latino men" is thus in many ways a constraint itself. I use the term "gay Latino men" in quotation marks because the phrase implies a given unity or homogeneity that must be questioned.

Although I believe that *culture* plays an important role in the lives and identities of "gay Latino men," in this chapter I argue that cultural arguments often obfuscate the structural power dimensions that shape the lives of men in marginalized social locations. It is not my intention to enter the ongoing anthropological debates over the problem of defining culture; neither is it my intent to reify culture, but rather to critique the manner in which culture as a focal argument not only obscures other structural dimensions that shape Latino men's lives but also pathologizes our culture. To borrow from Lila Abu-Lughod's conceptualization of this theme, in a phrase, I am "writing against culture."[3]

PROBLEMATIZING "GAY LATINO MEN"

In his treatise on sexuality Michel Foucault argues that theories of sexuality that focus on the policing functions of the state through laws and censorship (which he calls the "juridico-discursive" theory of power) are misled.[4] He asserts that sexualities and identities can only be understood through discursive strategies and an "analytics" of power that examines the multiple sites where normalization occurs through discourse and knowledge production. In her articulation of feminist standpoint theory Dorothy Smith has helped to elaborate how discursive practices operate in "relations of ruling," which she defines as "a complex of organized practices, including government, law, business and financial management, professional organization, and institutional institutions as well as the discourses in texts that interpenetrate the multiple sites of power. A mode of ruling has become dominant that involves a continual transcription of the local and particular actualities of our lives into abstracted and generalized forms."[5] To examine the lives of "gay Latino men" as an "abstracted and generalized" group is to reproduce some of the very social relations that we wish to challenge.

Similarly, contemporary scholarship in queer theory examines how these normative discursive practices operate in binary oppositions (e.g., natural/unnatural, normal/abnormal, heterosexual/homosexual) at sites of production such as medical texts, film and television, and literature. Informed by these conceptualizations of normative discourse, knowledge production, and the "relations of ruling," I review the literature on gender and sexuality as it relates to gay Latino men and examine its discursive role in a normative project of sexuality, race and ethnicity, and gender.

This literature exemplifies how a focus on culture limits our understanding of Latino masculinities and sexualities through a discourse of two cultures—the normative and the exotic. I am not arguing that this literature is without merit; on the contrary, such scholarship has shed light on a topic that few were willing to investigate, however, by giving primacy to culture to explain difference this literature in effect creates difference. Through such discourse the dominant culture is made nearly invisible, while Latino cultural differences are placed in a critical spotlight. I am not arguing against non-Latino scholarship;

such an argument would be too simplistic. What I am arguing is that as re-searchers and scholars (producers of knowledge) we are all directly implicated in "relations of ruling" even as we challenge them through our research on sexuality and gender.

One of the aims of recent scholarship in men's studies is to examine how some men have power over others in what Carrigan, Connell, and Lee refer to as "non-hegemonic masculinities."[6] Nonhegemonic masculinities are types of masculinities (e.g., gay men and men of color)[7] that are subordinated by the ruling, or hegemonic, masculinity of Western white, heterosexual, middle-class men. By examining nonhegemonic masculinities we are better able to under-stand not only gendered relations between men and women (as patriarchy) but also the multiple and intersecting axes between men themselves, such as race and ethnicity, class, and sexuality.[8]

Cultural studies scholars such as Said, Clifford, and Gilroy, to name but a few, have argued that culture is a means by which the specificities of non-Western Others are homogenized and the power of the center is masked.[9] In addition third-world feminists argue that through discursive practices in the production of knowledge such scholarship reproduces the colonial project.[10] Yet such critiques have largely been ignored by those doing research on Latino men. "Latino masculinity" continues to be represented as a cultural singularity that as a nonhegemonic masculinity pluralizes the hegemonic—providing an exotic Other relational to the normative *one*. "Culture" thus serves to reify dif-ference in a sort of "one size fits all" representation of the Other. We must then ask to what extent such cultural arguments serve a cultural hegemony rather than counter it. By this I mean to say that "culture" has been used uncritically in at least three ways in much of the literature on Latino men, particularly with respect to gender and sexuality.

The first analytical problem is rooted in the homogenization of Latino cul-ture.[11] Latinos are commonly represented as a homogeneous entity without cultural differences. Even using the most simple cultural characteristics, such as language, religion, music, and food, there are innumerable cultural differ-ences within the Latino cultural category. Which is not to argue that similari-ties are nonexistent. Ignoring differences between Latinos, however, shadows the extent to which Latinos are drawn together by the material conditions in which they share a sociopolitical space rather than a shared essentialized cul-ture. By ignoring differences within, essentialist cultural arguments reproduce, through knowledge production, the distance between hegemonic and non-hegemonic men (as well as women). As Mohanty argues, "The idea of abstracting particular places, people, and events into generalized categories, laws, and policies is fundamental to any form of ruling."[12]

The second problem is that Latino culture is commonly represented as if it were fixed or static. Contemporary scholarship on U.S. Latinos often refers to past anthropological scholarship on Latin American cultures, implying that culture does not change with time, context, or global influences. Cultural arguments, (ab)used in this manner, suggest that "what is different about [marginal peoples] remains tied to traditional pasts, inherited structures that either resist or yield to the new but cannot produce it."[13]

One example lies in scholarship of Latino gender roles that perpetuate stereotypes of male and female roles according to the *machismo/marianismo* sex-role model.[14] Mainstream scholarship's perspective on this model marks Latino cultures with "traditional" views of gender: woman are supposedly submissive, maternal, and virginal; men are characterized by verbal and bodily aggression, frequent drunkenness, and sexual dominance.[15] Some scholars have argued that *macho* performances of masculinity are a response to feelings of inferiority, but such arguments are deterministic and maintain a static concept of Latino culture.[16]

More recently Gutmann has critiqued this static view and argued that the traditional macho stereotype is inappropriate for describing the multiple and changing meanings of contemporary Mexican masculinities.[17] He asserts that gender identities must be understood as historical constructs (in a Marxist sense) that are shaped by changing political, social, cultural, and economic conditions. Thus the static and monolithic definition of the Mexican "macho" is problematic both in its failure to capture the diverse social locations of Mexican men and in its assumption that Mexican gender identities transcend time. Furthermore Hondagneu-Sotelo and Messner argue that varying displays of masculinity are shaped by both the power relationships of men over women and the power relationships of some men over other men, so that "marginalized and subordinated men tend to overtly display exaggerated embodiments and verbalizations of masculinity that can be read as a desire to express power over others within a context of relative powerlessness" and in which men in powerful positions may project more "egalitarian" images of masculinity.[18]

Finally, I refer to the "culture as Other" to describe a third problematic, a more general characteristic of the literature that examines subordinated racial or ethnic groups. Culture in this (mis)application becomes a defining characteristic of the Other to explain exotic behavior and position-dominant social forms as normative, that is, Western civilization. As Abu-Lughod states, "Culture is the essential tool for making other."[19] Although culture is important analytically, its importance is not necessarily greater for nonhegemonic groups. When "culture" is used as a factor of analysis only of U.S. minorities or non-Western peoples, there is a tendency to either directly or indirectly imply that their culture, that is, a "backward" culture, is to blame for what are represented as pathological traits or what may be called "cultural pathologization."[20]

Although scholarship on Latino sexuality is relatively sparse, the sociological and anthropological literature suggests that Latino men's sexual identity is determined not by the biological sex of the sexual partner but rather by the culturally defined roles of *activo* and *pasivo* (i.e., dominant and submissive) assumed by the actors.[21] For instance, Almaguer argues:

> Unlike the European-American system, the Mexican/Latin-American system is based on a configuration of gender/sex/power that is articulated along the active/passive axis and organized through the scripted sexual role one plays. It highlights sexual aim — the act one wants to perform with the person toward whom sexual activity is directed — and only gives secondary importance to the person's gender or biological sex.[22]

Almaguer further argues that this system genders and devalues the passive as feminine. Thus, according to this framework, as long as Latino men maintain an activo or dominant sexual script, their masculinity, as culturally defined, remains intact. Although the active/passive typology seems to fit a culturally defined typology of Latin American and U.S. differences toward homosexuality, other research suggests that this dichotomy is too simplistic.

In his study of male homosexuality in Mexico, Joseph Carrier asserts that the traditional dominant/submissive dichotomy of Mexican sexual identity is being transformed by migration to the United States, changes in traditional gender roles, and the development of a third category of homosexual identity characterized by a more versatile definition of sex roles referred to as *internacionales* (internationals).[23] Annick Prieur's work on *travesti* (transvestites) in Mexico City demonstrates as well that social class plays an important dimension in shaping the gender identities of men who have sex with men.[24] Such findings point to the importance of examining structural influences such as class, globalization, and migration on constructions of masculinity and sexuality.

The problems of cultural arguments become more evident when juxtaposed to studies of what might be called mainstream homosexuality in the United

States. Scholars such as Kinsey, Pomeroy, and Martin, Reiss, Humphreys, Chauncey, Kleinberg, and Pronger demonstrate that both in the past and the present European American males' meanings of homosexuality are multiple and shifting depending on context.[25] Kinsey's early survey research showed that not all American men who experienced sexual relations with other men defined themselves as homosexual. Humphreys demonstrated as well (albeit in a highly controversial manner) that married professional men who identified as heterosexual participated in sexual encounters with other men in public bathrooms. Furthermore, in his study of adolescent homosexual prostitutes in Tennessee, Albert Reiss argued that a homosexual identity was very much influenced by power relations nearly identical to the "gendered/sex/power" system of Almaguer's discussion. Likewise, Chauncey argues that European immigrants in New York in the early part of the twentieth century had a meaning system similar to that which Almaguer describes as a Latin American one. In a more contemporary light Kleinberg and Pronger both argue that today's gay man displays a hypermasculinity with straight behavior coupled with an overt gay identity. These examples suggest that the Latin American "gender/sex/power" system described by Almaguer and previously discussed may be organized by intersecting dimensions of class, race, gender, and sexuality. Almaguer's formulation of the gender/sex/power system remains a powerful analytical concept, but culture (i.e., Latino culture) may be less of an axis of organization than posited.

Yet culture remains central to most analyses of gay Latino masculinity, creating a language of difference that has material consequences in the everyday lives of gay Latino men. The focus that the literature on gay Latino men has given to culture has served to "other," by suggesting that deficiencies in Latino culture are responsible for nonnormative forms of sexuality, race or ethnicity, and gender. In "Chicano Men and Masculinity" Maxine Baca Zinn challenges these cultural deficit models of Latino masculinity and argues for research on Latino masculine roles and identities that examines sociocultural factors that shape these identities rather than cultural differences between Latinos and non-Latinos.[26]

Informed by such a framework I utilize ethnographic data collected from two retreats as case studies to examine how Latino men in the sociopolitical *borderlands* of southern California negotiate and contest unequal power differentials of gender, sexuality, and race or ethnicity in their everyday lives. Integral to understanding these Latino men's lives as men is examining how their masculinity is shaped by structural dimensions.

The data for this chapter were collected at two weekend retreats sponsored by the Delhi Center. Eighty-four men participated in the two weekend retreats: thirty-one at the November retreat and fifty-three at the May event. Participants were between twenty and forty-eight years old (median age 29.8) and were predominantly Spanish-speaking immigrants. Thus, although some English is spoken at the retreats, they are for the most part held in Spanish. Ethnographic methods such as field notes, participant-observation, and focus groups were used during the two events. I conducted in-depth personal interviews with ten of the participants and additional interviews with retreat organizers (mostly in Spanish), at other times and locations, lasting between forty-five minutes and three hours. In addition an evaluation survey given before and after the May event was also analyzed for descriptive type variables (rather than evaluation, which is not the focus of this chapter).

The data derived from these retreats are not meant to be representative of gay Latinos or even gay Latino immigrants. The men who participate in the program are to varying degrees open to a weekend retreat with men to talk about HIV and sexuality issues. They vary as well in terms of "closetedness." Some are what might be considered very out, but the majority are coming to terms with their same-sex attraction. The men therefore have a variety of labels that they use to define their sexuality. My use of terms such as *gay*, *queer*, and *homosexual* are imposed unless noted otherwise. For that matter, even the label *Latino* is imposed, as many men identify themselves by their nationalities.

In addition, two methodological components need further explanation. The first is my use of the term *focus groups*. The retreat program included exercises in which the men gathered either in small groups or in a single group to discuss such issues as personal and community challenges, what they had in common, and HIV. The groups were facilitated by Dr. Damian Goldvarg, a psychologist and retreat coordinator, or by one of five cofacilitators who assisted with the event. My role was mostly as observer, although I did facilitate several exercises. Through each of these group discussions, which I refer to as focus groups, I took notes and recorded the discussions on a standard cassette recorder. Another exercise that was helpful in gathering data about the men was one in which participants decorated a sheet of butcher paper (approximately 14 inches by 24 inches) with markers and Polaroid photos of themselves and answered the following questions: name, age, place of birth, occupation, if they consider themselves in or out of the closet, the label they used for their sexual identity, if they were in a relationship, and the names of three people whom they admire. Each of these methodological components served to gain insight into the issues that influence their lives as *hombres gay*.

For several reasons the retreats served as an ideal ethnographic site at which to conduct this research. As I elaborate later in this chapter, gay Latino men, particularly in the Orange County area, have limited social spaces and resources that allow them to interact as gay Latino men. The retreats provide an alternative, albeit temporary, site at which gay Latino men can be themselves and freely discuss issues that concern them. Methodologically the rationale for the site also resonates with Coltrane's suggestion that "researchers attempt to integrate men's standpoints into gender studies in at least three ways: (a) by focusing on men's emotions, (b) by studying men in groups, and (c) by placing men's experiences in structural context."[27]

The Entre Hombres retreats allow for the exploration of such an approach in that they provide a site where men gather to discuss the emotional, psychological, and structural dimensions that are part of their everyday lives. The site alone is insufficient to realize Coltrane's methodological suggestions, however, for as Coltrane and Hondagneu-Sotelo and Messner assert, analyses must be informed by a structural-feminist approach (rather than a cultural one) to understand the intersecting axes that cross the social locations of "gay Latino men."[28] In this chapter, I attempt to examine these intersecting dimensions in the lives of men and as they relate to masculinity. Discussions of class, race, sexuality, and cultural issues should therefore be understood as being intimately linked to masculinity and not separate from it.

ENTRE HOMBRES

The stated mission of the Encuentro Entre Hombres (EEH) program is to "improve the quality of life of the gay, bisexual, and transgendered Latino community. Creating spaces for self-understanding, integration, and social well-being, starting from our human values."[29] The mission statement is reflective of the way in which the Delhi Center, a Latino-staffed organization, envisions its role in the larger Latino community. As the program coordinator, Luis Lopez states, "The agency [Delhi Center] really looks at developing the leadership capabilities of the individuals it serves so they can provide their own opportunities and advocate for their own issues and really be involved in their communities. So, we're not concerned so much with provision of services as we are with persons—person skills, volunteerism, and leadership development." This ideology seems particularly useful in dealing with a community that is in many ways difficult to define. Although gay communities or enclaves exist in most, if not all, major urban areas, they are shaped by a mainstream culture that is predominantly a gay, white, male, middle-class culture. There are no gay Latino enclaves.[30] In the words of Luis Lopez, the gay Latino community is

> not a geographically defined area. . . . There are social networks in place, people know people, there hasn't been a whole lot in terms of formal organized efforts. It's starting. In the last couple of years since the onset of prevention work, in the county, it's started but it's never been there before. What's been in place has been informal social networks of people that just know who's gay and where you meet and those type of informal networks. Which are in my mind not any less valid, but for whatever reasons they haven't addressed issues like HIV in an organized way, or issues of social isolation, that a community needs to address for its collective well-being.

Whether the roots of queer Latino communities in the United States trace back to a time prior to the HIV/AIDS epidemic is debatable, but it is clear that HIV/AIDS has had a tremendous influence over queer Latino social space. As an "imagined community" that lacks geographic specificity and is marginal to the mainstream gay community, queer Latino communities have in many ways been constructed out of the necessity to confront the threat of HIV/AIDS.[31] Participants are recruited by utilizing social networks and outreach programs at local bars that cater to gay Latino men and other sites where Latino men who have sex with men congregate. These sites and networks are not confined to geopolitical boundaries. Thus, although the program targets "gay Latino men" in the Orange County area, in this fourth retreat approximately 28 percent of participants came from other areas in southern California, including Los Angeles, Riverside, and San Bernardino Counties.[32]

Events sponsored by the Entre Hombres program, such as the weekend retreats, are aimed at HIV education and prevention among this high-risk group, but such programming must juggle the understood needs of the population that Delhi serves with the expectations and constraints placed on the center by funding agencies. Luis Lopez explains:

> I firmly believe you can't address some of these issues, prevention of HIV, without addressing all of the cofactors, all the other issues involved with gay Latino men. I think with Latino gay men you really have to address some of the self-esteem issues, some of the mental health issues, some of the discon-

nectedness, the marginalization, the alienation that some of these individuals feel. . . . Funders have a hard time with that, they want to see that we're preventing HIV period, and for them, it's difficult to conceive of it as something that's going to include coming out to my family, cause that's not HIV prevention, of belonging to a strong healthy gay community, cause that's not HIV prevention, that's a political agenda, all these other issues are very real and very impacting.

As Lopez eloquently illustrates, "disconnectedness" is more than a client problem. Funding agencies, such as the county and state, which regulate the Entre Hombres program, regulate such programs through an institutional discourse that is based in part on academic studies of "gay Latino men." Such discourse reproduces "relations of ruling" by either ignoring the social locations of Latinos altogether or masking them in the terminology of culture. The end result is that programs such as Entre Hombres must either coach their administrators in the language of regulatory and funding agencies ("learn the language") or take the risk of alternative programming on their own.

The Entre Hombres program walks a fine line trying to negotiate the requirements of regulatory agencies with its own understanding of its clients' needs. Events therefore combine the two demands in an attempt to find a balance, however precarious. Programs like the retreat commonly mix HIV-prevention techniques with leadership training. Furthermore, the organization's events are attended by both HIV-negative and HIV-positive individuals in order to deconstruct the sexual myths at an interpersonal level. The events also include cultural components that seem to help the clients feel that they are in a supportive environment. The inclusion of a spiritual dimension in the programs is one such cultural component. It is not unusual for events to open and close with a candle-lighting ceremony in which the men form a circle and reaffirm through prayer the gift of life as well as gay existence. Culture in this instance is utilized in a somewhat subversive way to open up supportive spaces for queer Latino men.

Although cultural affinities are partly responsible for bringing these men together, the social isolation that Lopez describes cannot be attributed to cultural differences between mainstream and Latino communities alone, that is, cultural isolation in mainstream Anglo culture. Although many HIV-prevention programs that target gay populations are based on the generalized research of gay white men, a few programs attempt to address the special needs of minority communities such as gay Latino men. One such program that attempts to address HIV prevention in alternative terms is the Hermanos de Luna y Sol program in San Francisco's Mission Health Center. The program is designed in part after research conducted by Rafael Díaz of the Center for AIDS Prevention Studies (CAPS) at the University of California, San Francisco, and is described in his book *Latino Gay Men and HIV: Culture, Sexuality, and Risk Behavior*. Although Díaz's scholarship is much needed and to be commended, his sociocultural paradigm falls into the same cultural analysis discourse trap that much of the literature on Latino men falls into. Discussing the problem of gay Latino men's "limited ability to self-regulate sexual activity," Díaz argues:

> Limitations in the ability to self-regulate sexuality, however, should not be understood as the result of a personal deficit, but rather as the natural outcome of socialization within a culture that promotes sexual silence about homosexual activity from the interpersonal, affective, and rational lives of gay men at the same time that it undermines perceptions of sexual control; and breeds fatalism. The causes for the sexual self-regulatory problems observed in Latino gay men can be found within the context of our socialization into homophobic-machista culture, coupled with harsh experiences of poverty and racism as members of an ethnic minority group in the U.S.[33]

By giving primacy to a "homophobic-machista culture" and subordinating "the experiences of poverty and racism" to it, Díaz's argument cloaks the structural dimensions of homophobia and sexism. Lest we forget, gay Latino men's experiences of homophobia and sexism are not bound to their Latino communities. I do not mean to imply that homophobia and sexism do not exist in Latino communities; they obviously do, but in which communities do they not exist? If we understand the homophobia and sexism that Latino gay men face as a "cultural problem," are we not then caught in a discourse that "others" Latino gay men and minimizes how homophobia, sexism, and racism are linked and tied to a dominant culture?

When directly asked what they felt were the personal challenges in their lives, the men listed the following: (a) coming out of the closet, (b) preparing to be in a relationship, (c) maintaining a relationship, (d) being more assertive, and (e) dealing with loneliness and depression. These challenges point less to the homophobia of Latino culture specifically than they do to a sense of isolation and a need for intimacy. Culture is obviously a component of these challenges, but the homophobia, sexism, racism, and poverty that many of these men face are shaped by structural dimensions beyond Latino culture.

Despite the fact that these men came together as "gay Latino men," retreat organizers knew from their experience with previous retreats that differences among the men would be one of the first obstacles to overcome. Therefore an early exercise of the May retreat called on participants to list what they actually had in common. The exercise proved to be somewhat difficult even though the men had broken into six smaller groups. Participants in each of the groups would call out a topic until they found a characteristic that they all shared. Common responses were centered around hobbies or entertainment such as music, dancing, and sports, but they also included what can be best described as a shared need for intimacy, for example, looking for a relationship, love, romance. The men responded in a variety of ways, such as grunts, laughter, and sighs of frustration, when an assumed similarity failed to be shared. One such characteristic that proved to be a problem was sexual identity.

Although the literature on gay Latino male homosexuality asserts, as discussed above, that sexual identity is dependent on the active or passive role of the actors, only one of the participants of the November and May retreats referred to himself as activo, and none identified as pasivo. To the question, "How do you classify your sexual identity?" only one of the participants identified as straight.[34] Sixty-four percent of the November group and 26 percent of the May group identified as either gay or gay Latino; 4 percent of the November group and 56 percent of the May group used the term homosexual; and 28 percent of the November group and 13 percent of the May group had an ambiguous answer, such as "excellent" or "normal." Although one could interpret such ambiguous answers as a cultural resistance to identifying as gay, one could also interpret such responses as individual resistance to use any label or, quite simply, as a result of the question not being understood.

During my interviews with some of the participants I asked them about their sexual identities and why they had chosen particular labels. The majority of respondents explained that homosexual and gay were interchangeable terms for them, and one of the respondents who had given an ambiguous answer explained that he was not quite sure which label to use since he had sex with both men and women. When asked directly about the labels of activo and pasivo, most of the men I spoke with either in interviews or informally explained that the terms were somewhat archaic, especially as identity labels, and that one might ask a prospective sexual partner what "he liked" but that they expected a partner in a committed relationship to be more versatile in his sexual repertoire.

Sexual identity and its relationship to structural dimensions arose in my interviews as well. In this respect Tomás Almaguer's assertions of gay Chicano identity seem most relevant. Almaguer argues that because Chicano gay men are located in a subordinate racial position they are more dependent on familial relationships for their survival than Anglo gay men—a gay identity is therefore constrained from development. The argument is conceptually linked to John D'Emilio's assertions, which link sexual identity to capitalist development; the lessened dependence of family; and migration of homosexuals to urban gay communities in San Francisco, Los Angeles, Chicago, and New York after the Second World War.[35] Thus economic dependence on family members may constrain the development of a gay identity, but the reverse may happen as well.

Rafael is a twenty-nine-year-old Mexican immigrant, born in Mexico City but raised in the state of Michoacan. He moved to the United States in 1991 to join family members and help his infirm mother financially. Eventually he brought his mother, who is separated but not divorced from his father, to the United States to live with him. At the time of my interview with him Rafael was working two jobs as well as doing volunteer work with an AIDS services organization. Despite the fact that Rafael has two paid jobs, his annual income was only about $26,000. Rafael describes his family situation the following way:

> My siblings think of me as their father because for a very long time I've given them the confidence to speak to me about anything. They all care for me a great deal, my mother cares for me a lot too. She knows that I'm gay, she doesn't completely like it, but she accepts it. She's very Catholic and at times we have our little problems because she thinks that God doesn't permit my lifestyle. She won't talk to me openly about the issues but loves me for my support of the family. My sisters all know about me and I can speak openly with them but not my mother. I think that with time, you know, I'm her son and she loves me. Then with time, if God permits, she will accept me. I don't blame her.

Rafael's story exemplifies the complexity of sexual identity among "gay Latinos." Although he uses the term *Latino gay* for self-identification, the coming-out process has been constrained at a certain level by his family obligations. Yet Rafael is out to his family and tries to maintain a balance between his individual needs and a sense of respect for the family. Although these identity issues may seem at a superficial level to be cultural constructs, they are also influenced by social and economic dimensions. Rafael's economic situation seems to parallel those of *travesti* in Mexico City reported by Prieur, where family members became dependent on the income of a queer family member and thus to some extent were forced to accept the family member's queerness.[36] Yet Rafael is an undocumented immigrant, which places social as well as economic constraints on his lifestyle as a gay man. Rafael explains:

This is where I really opened up to the experience of being gay, to my dreams of finding someone who cares for me and understands me and I him. I think I've changed a lot, over there I didn't express who I was, in Mexico it wasn't so easy, people wouldn't accept me. Even more so because I lived with my sisters and I was worried about scandals that arise when people talk. . . . I've learned to live differently, that life isn't necessarily tragic.

Rafael's words suggest that although he did not explicitly move to the United States because of his sexual orientation, his sexual identity and perspective as a gay man have been transformed by the move. This is due in part to greater economic opportunities, which have transformed his relationship with his family and his ability to assert his right to live his life as a gay man and to meet others like him.

Despite a common perception of a homogeneous Latino community, Latinos in the southern California area are a diverse group. This diversity can contribute to a sense of isolation when differences in language, class, culture, and legal status outweigh commonalities. Thus U.S.-born gay Latinos may differ markedly from gay Latino immigrants; in many cases they are literally unable to communicate. But differences exist even among gay Latino immigrants such as most of the *encuentro* participants. Although the participants are predominantly from Mexico, which has numerous regional differences alone, they also come from Colombia, Guatemala, Honduras, Nicaragua, Peru, and Venezuela. As immigrants from Latin America they must deal not only with communication issues (i.e., English fluency) but also with the constraints of their different legal statuses as immigrants and being in a new cultural environment.

Some of the encuentro participants shared with the group that they had in fact migrated to the United States to find a place where they could more openly express their sexuality. Armando, for instance, is a thirty-two-year-old Mexican national, born in the state of Jalisco, where he spent eight years in a seminary studying to be a priest. Three years earlier, after much inner turmoil and reflection over his suppressed homosexuality, he spoke to his religious mentor about his feelings. His mentor, a Catholic Mexican priest, advised him to accept himself as God had created him and not hide in the shadows of the church but leave it to discover himself. He accepted the advice and decided to move to the United States. Armando's knowledge of gay life in the United States was based on a combination of conversations with gay friends who lived in the United States and his frequent visits here as a missionary. He explains, "I decided to come out of the closet, to accept my homosexuality and whatever comes with it. . . . [I came to the United States] because I feel as if the environment here, with respect to the services, the way that it is more open to homosexuals, there are more roads open to us, more forms of help." Armando's coming-out story reveals the contradictions in the narrative that the literature constructs of a "pervasively homophobic and sexist" culture. Although Armando migrated to the United States because he felt that the environment was a better place than Mexico to be gay in, it was a Mexican priest who advised him to do so. This illustrates one of many contradictions of gay life in Mexico. As in other countries, including the United States, there are contested spaces of queer resistance and visibility in the streets, in politics, and in the media even as antigay forces of the right try to repress them. I am not trying to suggest with this narrative that Armando's story is representative of the Latino experience. On the contrary, what I am trying to suggest is that the "Latino experience" is far more complex than a universalizing notion can capture.

Like Armando, Eduardo is also an immigrant from the state of Jalisco. But Eduardo's story is a different one. Eduardo is forty-two years old and from the city of Guadalajara, commonly referred to as the San Francisco of Mexico due to its large gay and lesbian population. In expressing his observations at the May retreat, Eduardo says:

> I noticed many people expressed frustration and discrimination in child-hood and there's a lot of self-policing because of social norms. I found that many people felt the frustration of trying to be their true selves. Some try to leave, to escape. In my case, I don't think it has affected me as much. I am who I am and I like being who I am. I've had people in my life to support me. If I had the choice to be a man, woman, or a gay man, I'd choose to be gay. We have to be who we are.

The "choice" to be gay may be easier for Eduardo to make than for others, however. Eduardo's background is a middle-class one. In Mexico he worked as an accountant and as a performer. He currently has a job in the United States as an accountant but is thinking of returning to Guadalajara, where he can perhaps be himself to a greater degree than he can here. In Eduardo's case, his social class allows him more freedom in Mexico than some of his queer contemporaries; these freedoms are in many ways constrained in the United States, due not so much to homophobia (although that too is part of it) as to the effects of racism and a different class.

The stereotypes of Latino culture, discursively produced in academic texts, scientific research, and HIV/AIDS policies and programs, are both accepted and challenged at the ground level. Although gay Latino participants may accept the stance that machismo is a barrier for Latinos, they also resist totalizing applications. For instance, in one exercise the retreat director, Damian Goldvarg, raised the issue of the social norms for Latino men around crying. When he said, "We are all taught that it's not appropriate for men to cry, aren't we?," the dissenting voices of several participants rang out across the meeting room. A few minutes later, discussing the issue of homophobia in Latino culture, one participant announced, "In my case, my uncle, my father's only brother, is gay. My parents raised us using him as an example, not to copy him or be like him, but to teach us that we have to be ourselves." The sentiment was reinforced by another participant: "I also had a positive gay role model, my uncle on my mother's side—the only male. He went to college in Argentina and we all knew he was gay. Above all, he was a role model of a positive human being who was gay." Such responses, which in reality should not come as a surprise, contradict the stereotypes that arise from the one-dimensionality of cultural arguments in the literature on Latino masculinity. Again the point here is not to argue that these examples are the rule, but rather that Latino masculinity and sexuality issues are far more complex and contradictory than the dominant construction or rules allow for. Most of the men, for instance, also discussed the personal contradictions they felt for being attracted to men and not believing (nor wanting to believe) that they themselves fit the feminine homosexual stereotype.

Beside the men who had role models who were different from dominant stereotypes, there were also several men who were in fact more stereotypically gay. These individuals made the social regulation or self-policing of gender dynamics more evident. Throughout the events it was obvious that many of the men were consciously trying to behave and dress in accordance with a masculine gender performance. Yet, two exercises in particular challenged these concepts. The first was during one of the spiritual sessions, when the facilitator spoke of the need to get in touch with one's feminine side, to accept it and embrace it as part of one's uniqueness. Subsequently I overheard several of the men discussing the fear they had of "letting their feathers show" (i.e., letting down their guard and allowing their feminine side to show).

The second was an event held on the Saturday night of each weekend retreat. At this event a drag show is held, and some of the more masculine men are selected from the group (as well as volunteers) and then made up in complete female drag. A Miss Big Bear is then selected from the performers, who compete for the award through events that include lip-synching and answering a question provided by a panel of judges (who are also retreat participants). Sunday morning, many of the participants commented on a sense of liberation they felt at either directly participating in the drag show or witnessing it. This is not to suggest that the participants suddenly come in touch with an essentialized feminine side. It does, however, point to the restrictions that these men feel in terms of normative definitions of gender performance—a gender performance that is driven not just by cultural factors but also by socioeconomic ones. Most of the men work in jobs that are physically demanding or pay minimum-level wages. This means that their everyday displays of gender are shaped by class and labor dimensions and that maintaining these jobs depends on a traditional gender performance.

BETWEEN MEN: BARRIERS AND BRIDGES

In their article titled "Theorizing Unities and Differences between Men and between Masculinities," Hearn and Collinson argue against a uniform notion of masculinity. Instead, they argue for an acknowledgment of diversity, whereby scholars "not only consider diversity but also interrelationships and contradictions."[37] In the preceding sections I have attempted to demonstrate not only how cultural arguments in the literature on gay Latino men serve to create a discourse of difference but also that such explanations mask the structural dimensions that shape gay Latino men's lives.

The othering that the cultural discourse produces is made more visible in a review included on the cover of Díaz's book *Latino Gay Men and HIV: Culture, Sexuality, and Risk Behavior* by the editor of the *Journal of Homosexuality*, who states that safer-sex guidelines for gay Latino men "must be embodied in an understanding of subjective meanings of their sexual unions within a culture that is pervasively homophobic and sexist." The discursive implication is that Latino culture is deviant or deficient relative to the unspoken hegemonic norm and that interventions—*cultural interventions*—are necessary to correct the problem. Is an Americanization program the solution? To what extent is the dominant American culture not "pervasively homophobic and sexist" or, for that matter, racist?

Alternatively, by examining homophobia and sexism as structural issues, as is done with poverty and racism, can we better understand how the social locations of gay Latino men relate to social inequalities, including their higher risk of HIV infection? By examining issues of poverty and racism Díaz has made some important inroads in this regard, as have other scholars who also examine structural issues. For instance, scholars argue that the combination of increased migration between Mexico and the United States in conjunction with resistance to discussing homosexuality in an informed manner has contributed to the prevalence of AIDS among gay Mexican men.[38] Although homophobia and sexism are probably linked to resistance to discussing homosexuality, such resistance may also be linked to social class, education, and the availability of HIV literature in Spanish. Furthermore the social locations of Mexican men in a global economy that induces migration should not be downplayed.

From the standpoints of the men of Entre Hombres, experiences of sexism, racism, and homophobia as "gay Latino men" resist flat cultural explanations. These men face many challenges in which they try to find a balance between the demands placed on them as men and the factors that constrain their development. The challenges that many of these men must face as "gay Latino men" are exacerbated by a sense of isolation. The social isolation, or disconnectedness, that they experience is influenced by multiple and intersecting dimensions, such as racism from mainstream and gay communities, homophobia outside and within the larger Latino community, limited accessibility (due to physical and social distance as well as financial constraints) to gay community resources, and different legal migration statuses.

By representing Latino culture as static, monolithic, and exotic (if not primitive) cultural arguments fail to give an accurate analysis even on a purely cultural level. The lack of scholarship on Latino sexuality and the tendency of scholars to attribute differences to cultural influences call for new research that investigates Latina/o sexuality in a political economy framework that examines the multiple and intersecting dimensions of gender, race and ethnicity, culture, class, and migration. What is needed is a move toward a "political economy of identity" that examines the multiple sites of power with historic specificity at the same time as it unveils commonalities across intersecting dimensions of power. By examining the interrelatedness of power differentials across groups we can achieve a better understanding of the margins and bring the margins to the center of men's studies.[39] Incorporating these multiple and intersecting dimensions is by no means an easy task, but when the complexities of "gay Latino men's" lives are attenuated to cultural reductionist arguments we are not only misdiagnosing the problem through cultural pathologization but also reproducing the very inequalities that we strive to address.

This study is part of a larger dissertation research project examining how sexuality influences migratory processes and how sexual identity is constructed in a migratory context. Funding for the research was provided by the Social Science Research Council's Sexuality Dissertation Fellowship and the Ford Foundation. The author is indebted to the Delhi Center and the Entre Hombres program as well as the comments of numerous readers, including Peter Nardi, an anonymous reader, Nancy Naples, Pierrette Hondagneu-Sotelo, Raul Fernández, David Valentine, and the illustrious members of the DLA.

1. Santa Ana is the county seat of Orange County, California, a 782-square-mile area located in southern California between Los Angeles, Riverside, and San Diego counties. With 2,410,556 inhabitants counted in 1990, Orange County is the fifth-largest county in the nation and the fifth fastest growing county in the state. Although Orange County's population remains less diverse than that of other metropolitan areas in California, such as Los Angeles and San Francisco, the ethnic composition has changed dramatically since 1980, most notably in the proportion of those in the Asian/Pacific Islander and Hispanic categories. In 1990 approximately 23 percent of Orange County identified as Hispanic (Cantú, "Latino Poverty and Immigration in California and Orange County").

2. Retreats have been held during the months of May and November each year since the inception of the program.

3. Abu-Lughod, "Writing against Culture."

4. Foucault, *The History of Sexuality.*

5. D. E. Smith, *The Everyday World, as Problematic,* 3.

6. Carrigan, Connell, and Lee, "Toward a New Sociology of Masculinity."

7. These categories are often treated as mutually exclusive.

8. Coltrane, *Theorizing Masculinities in Contemporary Social Science*; Hondagneu-Sotelo and Messner, "Gender Displays and Men's Power."

9. Said, *Orientalism*; Clifford, *The Predicament of Culture*; Gilroy, "Cultural Studies and Ethnic Absolution."

10. C. T. Mohanty, Russo, and Torres, *Third World Women and the Politics of Feminism.*

11. Some scholars erroneously include Brazil in the "Latino" category.

12. C. T. Mohanty, "Introduction," 16.

13. Clifford, *The Predicament of Culture,* 5.

14. The terms *macho* and *machismo* are often abused in the literature by racist discourse.

15. Social science scholars have argued that Latino machismo is a symptom of a traditional culture and "an inferiority complex based on the mentality of a conquered people [i.e., Spain's conquest of Mexico]" (Baca Zinn, "Chicano Men and Masculinity," 200).

16. Peña, "Class, Gender, and Machismo"; Mirandé, *Hombres y Machos*.

17. Gutmann, *The Meanings of Macho*.

18. Hondagneu-Sotelo and Messner, "Gender Displays and Men's Power," 214.

19. Abu-Lughod, "Writing against Culture," 143.

20. Oscar Lewis's "culture of poverty" thesis, which blamed Latino culture for Latino poverty, serves as a prime example of such a cultural analysis. In a similar vein, *machismo* is a racialized marker of gender oppression, a "culture of masculinity," that is read as a pathological cultural trait. The structural dimensions of sexism thus are displaced under the racist subterfuge of machismo. See Lewis, *Five Families*.

21. Almaguer, "Chicano Men"; Carrier, *De los Otros*; Lancaster, *Life Is Hard*; Murray, *Latin American Male Homosexualities*.

22. Almaguer, "Chicano Men," 257.

23. Carrier, *De Los Otros*.

24. Prieur, *Mema's House, Mexico City*.

25. Kinsey, Pomeroy, and Martin, *Sexual Behavior in the Human Male*; Reiss, "The Social Integration of Queers and Peers"; Humphreys, *Tearoom Trade*; Chauncey, *Gay New York*; Kleinberg, "The New Masculinity of Gay Men, and Beyond"; Pronger, "Gay Jocks."

26. Baca Zinn, "Chicano Men and Masculinity."

27. Coltrane, *Theorizing Masculinities in Contemporary Social Science*, 55.

28. Ibid.; Hondagneu-Sotelo and Messner, "Gender Displays and Men's Power."

29. Delhi Center, *Encuentro Entre Hombres IV*. Unless otherwise noted, all Spanish-to-English translations are mine.

30. In this respect it is important to note that gay enclaves in many urban areas have historical roots that arise from marginal areas, which have been either African American or Latino neighborhoods. Thus many contemporary gay enclaves not only border Latino neighborhoods, but due to gentrification force Latinos out of these spaces. The social relations that arise from such dynamics as well as how queer Latinos are positioned within them is a subject that to my knowledge has yet to be studied.

31. Although Anderson uses the concept *imagined community* in terms of the nation, the concept may also apply to those who form communities within and marginal to the nation, such as Chavez's application of the concept among undocumented Latino immigrants (Anderson, *Imagined Communities*; Chavez, "The Power of the Imagined Community").

32. To what extent educational information from the retreat reaches beyond even those boundaries is unclear, but given the transnational social networks that many of the men maintain it seems almost certain that some information is transmitted via these networks.

33. R. M. Díaz, *Latino Gay Men and HIV*, 150.

34. ¿Cómo calificas tu identidad sexual?

35. D'Emilio, "Capitalism and Gay Identity." In a similar vein Gayle Rubin in "Thinking Sex" argues that gay identity is a result of the rural-to-urban migration of "homo-

sexually inclined" men and women, whereby communities and economic niches (which Rubin calls a "gay economy") were formed based on a shared identity as an "erotic minority."

36. Prieur, *Mema's House, Mexico City*.

37. Hearn and Collinson, "Theorizing Unities and Differences between Men and between Masculinities," 110.

38. Alonso and Koreck, "Silences"; Wilson, *Hidden in the Blood*.

39. G. González and Fernández, "Chicano History."

The Material and Cultural Worlds of Latino Gay Men

Tomás Almaguer

We remain deeply indebted to the late Lionel Cantú for his important theoretical and ethnographic contributions to social scientific research on the lives of Latino gay men. One of his early essays, "Entre Hombres/Between Men: Latino Masculinities and Homosexualities," offers a particularly valuable intervention into how we might best explore the study of their intimate social worlds. Cantú challenges us to move beyond the shortcomings of earlier works on Latino gay men that "not only obscures other structural dimensions that shape Latino men's lives but also pathologizes our culture." He maintained that by "giving primacy to culture to explain difference this literature in effect creates difference. Through such discourse the dominant culture is made nearly invisible, while Latino cultural differences are placed in a critical spotlight. . . . 'Culture' thus serves to reify difference in a sort of 'one size fits all' representation of the Other."

More specifically Cantú confidently asserts that any analysis of Latino homosexualities and masculinities "must be informed by a structural-feminist approach (rather than a cultural one) to understanding the intersecting axes that cross the social locations of 'gay Latino men.'" This is crucial because in

> representing Latino culture as static, monolithic, and exotic (if not primitive) cultural arguments fail to give an accurate analysis even on the purely cultural level. The lack of scholarship on Latino sexuality and the tendency of scholars to attribute differences to cultural influences call for new research that investigates Latina/o sexuality in a political economy framework that examines the multiple and intersecting dimensions of gender, race and ethnicity, culture, class, and migration. What is needed is a move toward a 'political economy of identity' that examines the multiple sites of power with historic specificity at the same time as it unveils commonalities across *intersecting* dimensions of power.

He concludes, "Incorporating these multiple and intersecting dimensions is by no means an easy task, but when the complexities of 'gay Latino men's' lives

are attenuated to cultural reductionist arguments we are not only misdiagnosing the problem through cultural pathologization but also reproducing the very
inequalities that we strive to address."

These are harsh admonitions and a strongly advanced point of view. There
is no denying that Cantú's points are well taken, because no one wants to un-
wittingly pathologize or render a one-sided view of the complex lives of Latino
gay men. As one of the guilty parties identified in his polemical critique of this
early literature, I welcome the opportunity to comment on his various challenges here. In so doing I have no interest in disrespecting him or disparaging
his intellectual position. We all mourn his sudden passing and lament the fact
that he can no longer push us on these important matters or respond to those
that may take issue with his perspective.

That said, I believe that what is fundamentally at stake here is the relative
importance of material and cultural factors in shaping or structuring the social
worlds of Latino gay men. This is a very old academic debate, but we must be
grateful to Cantú for raising it in the context of studies of Latino gay men. He
is correct in noting that some of the literature written in the 1990s invoked the
activo/pasivo model as a way of mapping and understanding the nature of homosexual behavior and identity among Latino gay men. Sociologists and anthro-
pologists were at the time seeking a way to appreciate how these social identities were given cultural meaning among Latinos and how they differed from the
homosexual identity formation being constructed among middle-class, white
gay men in the United States.[1] According to Cantú, "Although scholarship on
Latino sexuality is relatively sparse, the sociological and anthropological literature suggests that Latino men's sexual identity is determined not by the biological sex of the sexual partner but rather by the culturally defined roles of activo
and pasivo (i.e., dominant and submissive) assumed by the actors."

I was particularly singled out by Cantú for my role in arguing that "this
system genders and devalues the passive as feminine. Thus, according to this
framework, as long as Latino men maintain an activo or dominant sexual script,
their masculinity, as culturally defined, remains intact. Although the active/
passive typology seems to fit a culturally defined typology of Latin American
and U.S. differences toward homosexuality, other research suggests that this
dichotomy is too simplistic."

No one would disagree with this point since no one actually believed that this
model was anything more than an ideal type construction in the first place. It
merely attempted to identify the normative ideals or metanarrative that shaped
the way gender and sexuality were giving meaning through the honor and

shame system structuring different pan-Latino cultures. This cultural argument invoked this cultural template in order to discern how particular constructions of manhood and womanhood and erotic role preferences among ethnic Mexicans were given specific cultural meaning. While male honor and female shame are not timeless and unchanging social constructions, neither are they merely "pathologizing" or "simplistic" ways of marking off what is distinctive and unique about the way Latinos/as give meaning to these intimate aspects of our social identities. I still believe that these normative ideals continue to provide deep cultural meaning for the way Mexican men and women socially organize and structure intimate aspects of their gender and sexual identities, roles, and relationships. We enter into them with a cultural worldview that provides the dominant script or narrative storyline that we use to give specific meaning to our interpersonal relationships with others. These cultural and interpersonal scripts also have deep embedded intrapsychic dimensions anchored in our childhood socialization that we still have not yet fully appreciated.

Contrary to Cantú's rather polemical position, there was never any lack of appreciation of the complex way that these aspects of our identities were individually experienced or negotiated in the real world. Invoking the activo/pasivo framework simply offered an alternative way of mapping out differences in how homosexual identity and behavior were being constructed among Latino gay men. In so doing it offered a way of challenging a more linear, one-sided, materialist point of view suggesting that Latinos were on the road to modernizing their sexual identities in ways that paralleled that of middle-class, white gay men. John D'Emilio's essay "Capitalism and Gay Identity" is perhaps the best example of the point of view being implicitly challenged in these early works. It is one that Cantú was quite sympathetic to as it too offers the type of "queer materialist" point of view at the heart of his later writings.

My point is that the world operates in more complex and interrelated ways than Cantú was willing to concede in his essay. Our embodied lives are given specific meaning by the intersections of both material and cultural factors that jointly structure, organize, and give cohesion to our intimate sexual lives. No one would deny that the particular social location of Latino gay men is an important aspect of how we come to terms with sexual identity and behavior issues. The very notion of the closet that one presumably comes out of is itself a concept layered with class-inflected meaning. As many others have noted, being in the closet presumes a space and place wherein men have privacy and refuge from the entangling world of our families and the expectations of manhood that we are socialized into. Clearly working-class men from large Latino families are not in the same structural location as the middle-class, white gay men who come out of the closet and openly declare their sexual identity.

My initial point was merely to make note of this difference and the way that the absence of any meaningful ethnic identity among white men probably played an important role in the emergence of their alternative sexual identity. Sociologists have long appreciated that ethnic identity is essentially an "option" for most third- and fourth-generation European American immigrants and that their racial identity as white has fundamentally eclipsed the potency of ethnic identity in ways not possible for Latinos. In this regard being Mexican or Puerto Rican is simply not an ethnic option in the same way that being Irish, Italian, or English is for the white men that embraced the gay identity in the early twentieth century that the historian George Chauncey has so insightfully chronicled in *Gay New York*.

Cantú's contribution to this debate was to remind us to never lose sight of the fact that class, capitalism, and other forms of structural inequality impact powerfully on our individual lives. The central issue being contested is the relative importance of cultural and material forces in the construction and constitution of sexual subjectivity. In other aspects of my academic work I have resolved this long-standing dilemma by staking out a middle ground. It makes more sense to argue that it is the "elective affinities" between the material and cultural domains that are mutually constitutive of the identity-formation process. Rather than merely flip the coin on one side, it seems more prudent to spin it on its axis and allow it to more fully refract or illuminate the scholarly dilemma at the heart of this academic debate.

While I do believe that homosexual identity is certainly shaped and impacted by globalization, transnationalism, and other historical processes, we should not lose sight of the fact that these identities are fundamentally social categories or constructs that are ultimately given meaning and potency discursively. In other words, while capitalism and changing material conditions do undeniably shape aspects of our everyday lives and individual identities, this is not the only place to look for answers to the conundrums of sexual identity constructions among Latino gay men.

It is short-sighted to look at only one part of the larger story and thereby miss aspects of our homosexual realities that political economy—no matter how nuanced or queerly inflected—will never fully explain. Where, for instance, does our deeply felt and often intensely driven and frenetically experienced sexual desire for other men come from? What is the determinant role that political economy plays in the construction of Latino gay men's erotic desires and personal investments in certain form of sexual role-playing?

A simple answer to these questions would be that these aspects of our homosexuality are given meaning through the circulation of images and desires that consumer capitalism ignites in contemporary white gay culture. In other words, it is structural factors that provide the material base that shapes and propels our most intimate sexual desires and practices. Yet this particular construction of sexual desire and identity seems woefully incomplete and one-sided. Surely there is also an intrapsychic process at work here, one that involves our embeddedness in Oedipal dramas within our families and identifications with our mothers and fathers. Who would deny that our initial objects of identification and affection would in some important ways play a role in how we eventually construct in adulthood our objects of affection and intimate sexual desires?

In this regard we need to take more seriously Cherríe Moraga's acknowledgments that core aspects of her sexual desire and connectedness to other women had deep cultural and psychological moorings in her love for her mother.[2] Similarly I believe that aspects of male homosexual desire, and the relentless pursuit of other men, are deeply implicated in our desire for bonding and connectedness with our fathers. "Looking for Papi" has always been a part of this homosexual desire, no matter how much we choose to deny or close our eyes to this reality. In other words, we need to look (if I can borrow a phrase from Luis Alfaro, Beto Araiza, and Monica Palacios) "deep into the crotch" of the Latino gay psyche in order to fully appreciate the nature of our homosexuality and irrepressible desire for other men that takes into account the world of our particular ethnic cultures and our initial socialization in Latino families.[3]

In this regard I would suggest that the pioneering work of John Gagnon and William Simon on "sexual scripts" may provide the nuanced assessment that we should be looking for.[4] They argue that aspects of our sexual identities and behavior are fundamentally shaped and produced at three discrete levels: through "cultural scenarios" (instructions in collective meaning), "interpersonal scripts" (the deployment of specific cultural scenarios by and between individuals), and "intra-psychic scripts" (the psychological management of desires experienced by the individual). Gagnon and Simon argue that these three discrete domains powerfully shape and "script" aspects of our most intimate sexual behavior.

Following their lead I believe that the most intimate aspects of our sexuality are shaped and organized by "sexual scripts" that are culturally conferred, integrated into our interpersonal sexual relationships with others, and deeply ingrained in our individual psyches. These are aspects of Mexican men's homosexuality realities that a queer materialist paradigm does not take seriously or adequately explain.

Consequently it seems more prudent and fruitful to acknowledge that sexual identities are largely social categories embedded in and deeply internalized through direct socialization in the cultural worlds that socially confer meaning to all aspects of our embodied lives. One does not have to be a strict constructionist on these matters to fully appreciate that our individual sense of self is socially conferred and that time, place, and context are important considerations in this process. It is here, at the intersection of history, social structure, and personal biography, that we need to more fruitfully explore our interrogations of the lives of Latino gay men.

It is in fact precisely here where the complexity of the lives of the Latino gay men that Cantú interviewed comes most clearly into view. One of the most telling ethnographic examples that he uses to support his perspectives is the life experiences of Rafael, "a twenty-nine-year-old Mexican immigrant, born in Mexico City but raised in the state of Michoacan." According to Cantú, "He moved to the United States in 1991 to join family members and help his infirm mother financially. . . . At the time of my interview with him Rafael was working two jobs as well as doing volunteer work with an AIDS services organization. Despite the fact that Rafael has two paid jobs, his annual income was only about $26,000. Rafael describes his family situation" as follows:

> My siblings think of me as their father because for a very long time I've given them the confidence to speak to me about anything. They all care for me a great deal, my mother cares for me a lot too. She knows that I'm gay, she doesn't completely like it, but she accepts it. She's very Catholic and at times we have our little problems because she thinks that God doesn't permit my lifestyle. She won't talk to me openly about the issues but loves me for my support of the family. My sisters all know about me and I can speak openly with them but not my mother. I think that with time, you know, I'm her son and she loves me. Then with time, if God permits, she will accept me. I don't blame her.

While these experiences, Cantú maintains, "may seem at a superficial level to be cultural constructs, they are also influenced by social and economic dimensions." Through his financial support, Rafael's family in Mexico was "forced to accept [his] . . . queerness. Rafael is an undocumented immigrant, which places social as well as economic constraints on his lifestyle as a gay man."

It is true that Rafael's immigrant status, economic obligations, class background, and social location in the United States all require that he "maintain a balance between his individual needs and a sense of respect for the family." But to argue that his entire social world and identity as a Mexican gay man is essentially the product and function of a "political economy of identity" seems incomplete. While there may be important structural constraints that impinge on Rafael's life as a Mexican gay man in the United States, his situation seems to reflect the importance of the "cultural constructs" that impact on his life.

It is after all the entire Mexican Catholic world that he was raised in, and that his family continues to fervently embrace, that appears to be at the crux of the issues he continues to negotiate with his family, his mother in particular. It is this religious worldview that accounts for the silences between them about his homosexuality and the dreaded damnation that his family believes will result from his new sexual identity and lifestyle. Both Rafael and his family ultimately believe that if God permits, all will be well. This divine approval would enable him to live without blame and the ultimate shame that befalls someone not comporting himself according to traditional constructions of Mexican manhood. It is his devoutly Catholic mother who communicates to Rafael that "God doesn't permit [his] lifestyle," not the structural dislocations of advanced capitalism in all its globalizing permutations.

The main point I want to make is rather straightforward. We need to listen very closely to the men we interview in order to learn more about the complex social worlds in which they live. Social theory is indeed useful in this regard, but not when it distorts our informant's voices and we lose sight of the complex way that both material and cultural worlds structure the intimate lives of Latino gay men.

NOTES

1. Almaguer, "Chicano Men"; Carrier, De los Otros; Lancaster, Life Is Hard; Murray, Latin American Male Homosexualities.
2. Moraga, Loving in the War Years.
3. Alfaro, Araiza, and Palacios, "Deep in the Crotch of My Latino Psyche."
4. Gagnon and Simon, Sexual Conduct.

Gay Latino Cultural Citizenship:
Predicaments of Identity and Visibility
in San Francisco in the 1990s

Horacio N. Roque Ramírez

It's about freedom!
—Official jingle of San Francisco Gay Pride 2000

The sweetest things are always Latin!
—Jingle for ¡Azucar!, a gay dance club with a Latino theme,
summer 2000

In her exploration of queer Latino activism, the law, and cyberspace, Juana María Rodríguez makes an important conceptual shift in relation to identity. Rather than ask, "What is identity?," she looks at three particular case studies that turn this question into "What is identity *for*?"[1] With this move Rodríguez is able to explode essentialist characters of this key term for understanding political and cultural visibilities for LGBT and queer Latinas and Latinos, permitting a critical appreciation of the multiple possible uses of identity for generating more grounded visions of health, freedom from repression, and desire. Unlike the vague San Francisco Gay Pride slogan on behalf of freedom, or the exoticizing, consumerist queer jingles widely used to sell things Latin, Rodríguez's "What is identity for?" compels us to interrogate how and why questions of identity circulate for queer women and men of color. Her work asks us to consider political and historical moments when narratives of identity are profoundly a necessity, and others when the exact same terms may become overused, reductionist, and essentialist representations of complex social life.

Queer multiracial cultural and political formations have been the reality in the San Francisco Bay Area since at least the 1950s.[2] Third-world movements, women's movements, civil rights and nationalist struggles, and gay and lesbian liberations—these and other social movements in the Bay Area have compelled people of color to claim identity, visibility, space, and rights. And yet in San Francisco, that queerest of world Meccas, the representation of a "universal citizen" remains white and male. Whether in the romantic, pastoral writings of Herb Caen in decades past, or the cultural representations of queerness since the 1990s in the likes of Armistead Maupin, whiteness remains discursively central in the imagining of the city.[3] There have always been "others" in this geography, including queer ones, but even then, the hegemonic gay subject remains the same: seemingly wealthy, white, and male. The queer differences among white subjects in this imagination exist largely on the horizontally conceived realm of sexual difference (as opposed to a vertical plane of stratification and inequality); the white male subject, though queer, still lives, eats, works out, dances, drinks, gets high, and eroticizes in the city. Gas prices may rise, home costs may increase, and demographics may shift, but there will still be enough resources and opportunities for pleasure for his (queer) class, or at least the semblance of such abundance.

In such contexts of cultural exclusion, to rise to the podium of cultural identity (individually and collectively) can have profound results. Latina and Latino scholars have found theoretical and political use in the concept of cultural citizenship. This concept, Renato Rosaldo first proposed, addresses notions of belonging and equal representation in a democratic society without losing respect for individual and group differences. "The term cultural citizenship is a deliberate oxymoron," Rosaldo explains,

> a pair of words that do not go together comfortably. Cultural citizenship refers to the right to be different and to belong in a participatory democratic sense. It claims that, in a democracy, social justice calls for equity among all citizens, even when such differences as race, religion, class, gender, or sexual orientation potentially could be used to make certain people less equal or inferior to others. The notion of belonging means full membership in a group and the ability to influence one's destiny by having a significant voice in basic decisions.[4]

To claim identity, space, and rights based on lived differences—to struggle for cultural citizenship actively in a society structured through cultural domination, inequality, and marginalization—holds particular queer racial promise: to activate these differences in order to situate ourselves as entitled, legitimate members of the body politic where heteronormativity and whiteness rule. In the era of AIDS, when queer identities and subjectivities are central in our prospects for health and life, the right to be different honestly, legitimately, and publicly matters. As Rosaldo suggests, group-based, structural oppression in turn requires that we consider how organizing as groups based on sharing these group differences can serve as a creative antidote to structural forms of exclusion.

But identities and other forms of visibility based on difference can be slippery epistemic paradigms, which not only the disenfranchised can use. As tactical terms that can neutralize if not co-opt oppositions to structures of marginalization, identity may work against social groups' goals in the hands of power elites invoking the exact same terms for inclusion, but for quite different objectives (to garner the Latino vote, for example, or using Latino images of the family). In consumer capitalism identity can also be used for the goal of economic profit (e.g., to sell authentic frozen Mexican food). In both of these cases, identity and visibility through claims of shared group experiences become residual, secondary dimensions. The politician gets elected, multinational corporations reap profits, and the communities whose essentialized collective identities make it possible remain (at best) structurally unchanged in a position of subordination.

My discussion of gay Latino cultural citizenship in San Francisco in the 1990s speaks to both the necessity of cultural identities and what can be considered the capitalist commodification of gay Latino identitarian logic.[5] I discuss a safer-sex ad campaign from the mid-1990s targeting married Latino "men who have sex with men," designed to reduce HIV infections among them and their wives. Bypassing gay and bisexual identities while acknowledging Latino men who engage in (unsafe) sex with other men, the ad was not well received by local health workers (though not all) trying to make sexual minority Latino subjectivity explicit in the context of HIV prevention. It was precisely the gay Latino invisibility that the ad structured publicly that was in contention for many HIV health educators. In concealing, disguising, or obscuring a gay Latino historical subject through the use of a public figure who did not self-identify as sexually gay, the ad disappeared a segment of the community that actively fought against its erasure. I also discuss the relationship between queer Latino visibility and commodity culture, specifically through the advertising of the Latin Stage during San Francisco's Queer Pride Festival in 2000. In this case I analyze how the literal and figurative selling and advertising of many things Latin during Gay Pride festivities depend on an extreme, essentializing project of cultural appropriation. Through these two projects for (dis)claiming gay Latino identity and visibility I investigate the challenges in using notions of identity, visibility, and rights under the rubric of cultural citizenship for queer Latinos in San Francisco. While gay and queer cultural citizenship can indeed function as a position for group entitlement, belonging, and social membership to help negotiate desire, safety, and risk, once reduced to prototypical sounds and symbols of culture, racial and queer group differences can easily become conduits for profit-driven consumption.

RISKY IDENTITIES: GAY AND BISEXUAL (IN)VISIBILITY IN AIDS

Questions over gay identity became quite contentious in the 1980s with the emergence of AIDS and the increasingly unavoidable debates over which segments of the Latino community were most at risk and thus required more focused attention. The early naming of the syndrome as GRID (Gay-related Immunodeficiency Disease) literally offered an identity-based social category of membership that conveniently distanced many men (including Latinos) from considering themselves at risk; not identifying as gay, they believed the new disease had little to do with them and their (homo)sexuality. For Latinos who did identify as gay or bisexual, the representations of the disease (either as GRID or as the less identity-based AIDS) primarily as a white gay men's disease offered yet another level of convenient denial of the stigma associated with the disease and these men.[6] But once the discourses of AIDS and HIV prevention shifted to include both identities and behaviors, including the more generic and ambiguous "men who have sex with men" (MSM), Latino men engaging in sex with other men, whether they identified as gay or bisexual or not, could not as easily distance themselves either from the possibility of risk or from health workers and HIV agencies targeting them.[7] Indeed the existence of the former funded the existence of the latter.

This matrix of identity, sexuality, and invisibility presented several challenges for HIV health programming for reaching men having sex with other men without consistently using condoms. In the historically Latino Mission District of San Francisco, HIV health agencies and community projects such as Proyecto ContraSIDA Por Vida (or simply Proyecto), Gente Latina de Ambiente, Instituto Familiar de la Raza, AGUILAS' El Ambiente, and the Mission Neighborhood Health Center devised advertising and outreach efforts to make these men more conscious about their sexual practices. These community efforts engaged the large numbers of Latino men who forthrightly claimed public queer identities, as gays, as maricones, as homosexuals, as culeros, as jotos, as queers, and, less so though not uncommon, as bisexuals.[8] Yet a significant amount of their educational campaigns also targeted Latino MSMs, who made up a large proportion of new cases of HIV infection in the 1990s. Accordingly the images used in the prevention campaigns did not acknowledge same-sex desire among men with a social identity or name; in fact the point has been precisely to avoid them. This deliberate non-naming strategy is what is at stake through the images and text: to suggest as much as possible same-sex desire or practice among men without offending or scaring away a potential viewer or consumer of the ad by overly inferring an identity with which he is not comfortable or that he may entirely reject.

In targeting this prototypical Latino man, however, who engages in homosex without adopting a nonheteronormative social label, an image and narrative of the MSM has made impossible a closer engagement with this population. At the same time gay and bisexual Latino men who indeed have felt part of a community openly *as gay or bisexual Latinos* have been left out of the picture—literally—in these advertising campaigns. Part of the justification for not publicly naming these men within a social category of membership has involved the belief that a great number of MSMs continuously engage in sex with men while married or involved in primarily heterosexual couplings. To encourage MSMs to practice safer sex and reduce the risk of infecting their women partners, the argument goes, images and text need to suggest the sexual behavior, but not a social identity other than the implied heterosexual one. Yet one of the consequences of such as a strategy is to make Latino men who *do* identify as gay less visible. In addition, in the process of having to choose or negotiate the rigid oppositional binary between gay and MSM, men adhering to a bisexual identity find less support and less visibility.

One popular example of health advertising campaigns aimed at MSMs took place in 1995 inside San Francisco's public buses. Highly visible in the ever-crowded bus lines 14 and 49 that run along Van Ness and Market streets, respectively, and jointly along Mission Street, the longest street in the city, this ad was one of the most noticeable advocating condom use and targeting Latino men having sex with other men. Immediately below the black-and-white photograph of a handsome Latino, smiling provocatively while firmly holding an unused wrapped condom in his hand, text in Spanish declared, "En mi familia nadie sabe que yo tengo sexo con hombres. Por eso los protejo." (In my family no one knows that I have sex with men. That's why I protect them.) Suggesting no distinct emotion but a decisive stance, the masculine figure and the accompanying narrative communicated an assured, calculated decision, a man capable of considering his heteronormative responsibilities in relation to his (covert) sexual practices. In this presumably rational paradigm for negotiating risk, safety, family, and responsibility one possible analytical equation might be translated as follows: "Given condition A (silence), I practice B (condom use)." The first part of the equation, the description of fatherly silence around his homosexuality (or bisexuality), was presented simply as that: a quick description or acknowledgment of a condition that simply is, unalterable and natural. Given this situation that simply "is," the second part of the equation is presented as a corrective for a silence that has the potential for negative consequences: having unprotected (anal? oral?) sex with men in cultural silence and (also in silence) bringing the disease of AIDS to the home. The dynamics invoked by the ad are not questions of pride (in behaving safely, for example) or of cultural shame (for having sex with men or for maintaining silence), but of manly responsibility, perhaps cultural propriety.

Community health workers I interviewed for my queer community history project and who commented on the usefulness of this ad campaign had a range of interpretations. Several found it problematic on three distinct levels: its assumptions about men's ability to be honest with themselves and act accordingly in terms of making choices during sexual play; the ideological complicity of the message for leaving intact a heteronormative, patriarchal family organization, with the man being the responsible member of the family to protect it from outside disease; and the simplistic or uncomplicated way the ad's narrative suggests that the decision to use a condom is rather easy and logical. The ad was particularly troubling, if not useless, for health workers invested in de-stigmatizing queer sexualities and practices in the Latino community. The staff and volunteers at Proyecto, for example, working under a model of "sex-positive" notions of open queer sexualities, sought to acknowledge and celebrate queer sex for Latinas and Latinos. For these front-line AIDS educators and the sex-positive goals of the agency, weakly suggesting same-sex behaviors was counterproductive to a more open community dialogue around queer sexualities, identities, and AIDS.

One Proyecto staff member critical of the ad was Diane Felix. A well-known butch Chicana activist who had socialized among straight, gay, and bisexual men since her teens and who for years had also socialized on a bar strip where queer and straight Latinos gathered, Felix was skeptical of men's ability to act as the ad claimed. When asked about the ad's efficacy for reducing HIV and AIDS in the Latino community, she was sarcastic and unconvinced. Her comments were not simply quick, uncritical responses to the ad. Living in San Francisco since the mid-1970s she had been part of the historical growth of cultural and political gay Latino organizations, such as the Gay Latino Alliance (from 1976 to 1983), her own women's dance club, COLORS (since 1986), and the first grassroots community response to the AIDS crisis (as part of Comunidad Unida en Respuesta al AIDS/SIDA, Community United in Response to AIDS/SIDA, since the mid-1980s until its collapse around 1992). At the forefront of building cultural citizenship for gay and lesbian Latinos and Latinas since the 1970s Felix had also been part of the cadre of caretakers and friends burying dozens of community members dying from AIDS. In relation to an ad purposefully working for hidden homo- and bisexual practices, she expressed mistrust in MSMs' ability to change not only their sexual behavior but also the conscious decisions these men made in relation to their wives and children:

> I think it's a dream [laughter]. I don't think that it's real. . . . I don't think the majority of Latino men think like that. Because when I hung out at [the gay Latino bars] La India Bonita and Los Portales, I would see those men there at night, carrying on all night. And then I would go to Twenty-fourth Street in the morning to buy my *fruta* [fruit], and I would see them with their wife, with their children. And they'd look at me and they knew that I knew who they were. And they would just like turn their head and try to get out of there as soon as possible. And then when I would see them again at the bar I would say, "*Oye* [Hey], I saw you. I didn't know you were married. What are you doing to protect her?" "Oh, no, no. Yeah, you see me here, but I'm not having sex with them [men]. I'm not having sex with these guys, I know you've seen me, but I'm not . . . that's my wife, you know."[9]

Felix's frustration often grew to the point of confronting Latinos, getting involved in their personal life in public, and reminding them that as careful as they thought they were in trying to hide their sexual play with men, she suspected otherwise. That non-gay-identified men had sexual relations with male-to-female transgender women and gay, bisexual, and heterosexual men was a very likely scenario given the multigender character of the first gay Latino bar strip in the Mission District since 1979, Sixteenth Street or simply "16" or "la dieciséis." Since its beginning la dieciséis became the central hub for queer Latino men, especially Spanish-speaking immigrants seeking same-sex social and sexual space. The gay Latino immigrant strip remained a local and regional Latino destination in the 1980s and 1990s.[10]

Felix's critique suggests a level of hypocrisy among men asked to "protect" their wives and their families through condom use while not addressing the overall social patterns heterosexual male privilege affords them. If these men could easily party, drink, and be with either queens or other men on the gay Latino strip or elsewhere in the Mission, what could their incentive or motivation be, she argued, to think of their wives' and their kids' health during such intense moments of unrestrained pleasure?

> I wished men thought like that. "How do I protect her?" Well, you wouldn't be in a cantina [bar] with a bunch of *hombres* [men] if you were really that in love with her, or cared about her, right? I mean, would you? It makes me laugh how when I go down Twenty-fourth Street or even that bar across the street from Proyecto on the corner, Capp and Sixteenth—they're all straight men and you walk in and you look and they got each other's ass in their hand, they're hugging each other, they kiss, they're drunk kissing, they're fighting. These are all straight men, and they're just all over each other. They can't even go home to their wife and kids; they'd rather be there with them. How straight is that? [laughter]. But, if you really *cared* about your woman, and you really *cared* about your children, I don't think that you would be there.

As an advocate for sex-positive education and a staff member of Proyecto, Felix was adamant about the need to be more explicit in discussing sex and sexuality. She believed the behaviors putting these men at risk for contracting HIV needed to be spelled out more honestly to reflect the place of desire and satisfaction in their practices. While recognizing that the men and behaviors such ads target exist (even across the street from Proyecto's offices), Felix challenged an educational approach that assumes men's ability to change their behavior largely on the premise of presumed care for the heterosexual family unit.

Related to Felix's doubts about the ad's ability to impact men's sexual decision making based on the cultural ideal of protecting the heterosexual family unit, Ricardo A. Bracho argued that the ad strengthened patriarchal ideology. As the coordinator of one of Proyecto's health education components, Colegio ContraSIDA, and one of the founding members of the agency, Bracho further critiqued the ad's evasion of, or rather complicit relation to homophobic cultural practices. By focusing only on closeted sex acts and tacitly validating the dimension of denial or hiding ("My family doesn't know"), the ad, Bracho believed, continued a series of problems in AIDS education generally:

> That whole thing about "My family doesn't know I do, but I try to keep them safe." What it does is [point to] this patriarchal protection of the family. It's like, "Oh, yet I still provide and I am *not* infecting them." . . . So let that *man* decide if he really wants to *be* in that . . . in a position of *privilege*, because that's what he has. Let's talk about homophobia and masculinity. I *hate* this whole, like, "men who sleep with men" shit. And that's really big

in the AIDS economy, like men who are not gay-identified. Well, make them gay-identified. That's a *problem*. They should become gay-identified. They do *not* need to stay in their lives, fucking men, and not talking about it, and not being able to be happy with it.[11]

In his analysis the discourse and politics of homophobia allow for the possibility and acknowledgment of same-sex behavior but stop short of recognizing a gay or queer subjectivity. The investment the ad makes in maintaining heteromasculinity through the central visual image of the decisive (male) Latino figure continues a pattern of homophobia prevalent in many advertising campaigns targeting MSMs. By popularizing such images of male masculinity the ads not only bypass but actually make *invisible* gay-identified Latinos of various genders, many of them still identifying as men but who also forthrightly take on gay or queer subjectivity. In disagreement with a long-held argument that Chicano and Latino men are unable to take on a gay sexual identity openly, Bracho argues that ads like these make dialogue about this assumed inability more difficult.[12] The ads not only play on this nonidentification, but also preempt an analysis of why many men indeed play sexually with other men without interrogating their place in heterosexual privilege. Neither Felix's nor Bracho's critique suggests replacing the MSM position with another fixed, essentialist subject position or, as Rodríguez argues about Proyecto's subtle strategies, "mak[ing] representation and identity equivalent."[13] What they do argue, however, is that the definite textual and visual markers in the ad foreclose queer possibilities for these men practicing homosexuality.

Not all narrators addressing the ad found it ineffective. The late Gustavo Martín Cravioto (1965–2006), for example, working with both gay- and straight-identified Latino men's populations on la dieciséis and elsewhere in the city, supported the ad's rather direct, uncomplicated approach to raise awareness of condom use. Working for the Latino AIDS Project at the Instituto Familiar de la Raza in the capacity of street outreach worker, Cravioto argued that, as a health worker, his primary interest was not so much with men's identification as with their use of condoms:

> For us as health educators or as people who work with the problem of AIDS, we do not take [gay identification] into consideration so much; it does not matter to us. It does not matter to us that people remain inside their closet or remain inside their denial. Or that they do not accept themselves as bisexual or as gay. What matters to us is that they protect themselves. In other words, the most important thing about this is that people learn to protect

themselves, be that they are openly gay or openly bisexual or openly whatever you want. . . . We have to consider that there is an incredible amount of different ways of knowing, of being, of thinking.[14]

In Cravioto's analysis the ad's lack of discussion of identity reflects the different types of thinking and being of men who have sex with other men who never connect their pleasure with a socially constructed category. Working for a Latino agency that did not place as great a priority in the visibility afforded to gay or queer Latino men (when compared to Proyecto) as in promoting safer sex among Latinos generally, Cravioto took a position emphasizing behavioral change. As an immigrant himself working mostly with immigrant Latinos, he took into account the many "ways of thinking" and "ways of being" represented in several generations and countries of immigrant Latinos in San Francisco. In San Francisco's demographic profile of Latinos there are widely varying groups of men artificially grouped through their sharing of the city's borders: Salvadoran men who recently migrated from rural sectors with little access to a sexual literacy beyond heterosexuality, gay Mexican immigrants from urban centers like Mexico City and Guadalajara with long histories of gay liberation, and second-generation Nicaraguan men born in San Francisco who may not have much in common with the former two in terms of their shared sexual cultures. However (in)visible these men's sexual subjectivities may be in the context of queerness in the city, Gustavo had no qualms de-emphasizing questions of the closet in his work for HIV prevention. In Proyecto's educational programming, gay and queer visibility for Latinos was as much a part of the equation as was risk reduction. For Felix and Bracho this visibility had everything to do with an ad's target population. Because the ad reflected a segment of Latinos that Cravioto believed never cared about or wanted to identify as anything other than straight, he believed the ad had an important role in reaching out to men who placed themselves and all their sexual partners (including women partners) at risk whenever they did not use condoms.[15]

The Latino MSM ad spoke to the tensions around visibility, identity, and sexual behavior for (gay) Latino men in the Bay Area. While it drew attention to many Latino men's high risk of contracting HIV and spreading it to women, it was also a site for political struggle over identity and visibility. For educators and activists wanting to ensure that gay and queer Latinos had social membership and space through identity, the ad was complicit in not wanting to acknowledge male privilege and heteronormative ideology, while at the same time using it to reach out to MSMs. Others saw the ad as simply an honest and direct reflection of pervasive and risky behavior among men in the community. The gulf between the social and sexual worlds in these interpretations of the ad was not necessarily large. Where *gay-identified* and *straight-identified* begins or ends has always been in flux, whether in a more gay Latino strip (where non-gay-identified Latinos regularly socialize) or in the straight bars and nightclubs of the Mission District (where gays and queers too venture). But in the ad, and importantly in relation to cultural citizenship, one point was clear: the MSM remained a member, a named yet anonymous sexual citizen, a member of the community and of the family, whereas the gay- or bisexually identified Latino did not.

That Felix could walk from her apartment to buy her produce and run into seemingly straight or bisexual Latinos she had seen in the local gay bar just the night before speaks to the varied sexual geography for (queer) Latinos in the city. This intimate geography points out the competing publics and cultures made visible or invisible through seemingly innocuous HIV education ads. Felix's comments about her seeing these men also indicate a dialectic in the realm of cultural citizenship: it is not only where individuals *choose* to go or place themselves that makes them visible; viewers or "witnesses" seeing such individuals, regardless of the former's choice of claiming or occupying a space, invest that visibility with meaning. Queer Latina and Latino cultural citizenship does not always depend on the *literal* sense of visibility (what we see) either. Because neither sexuality nor desire is always a given or publicly seen by all, making Latino bodies queerly visible may require additional knowledge to which not all are privy. Felix identified and interacted with men not wanting to be associated in public with a gay space or community; they had little choice over whether she chose to identify them with a gay public sphere. In a sense, as a health worker and community member Felix took it upon herself (perhaps problematically for some) to invest Latino MSMs with the visibility the ad and its designers worked to deny.

SELLING IDENTITIES: QUEER LATINO BODIES, DIVERSITY, AND THE BUSINESS OF FREEDOM

By the time gay and queer pride came again to San Francisco in June 2000, the Bay Area could count on a handful of weekly and monthly venues catering to a large queer Latino and Latina population. Amid music and dance these social spaces (bars and nightclubs, overwhelmingly but not solely for men) were benefiting from regular, sizable crowds seeking fun and pleasure as lesbians and gays *and* as Latinas and Latinos. The role of identity was key for their success: in order to continue attracting this crowd of consumers the clubs had to produce the visual, textual, and auditory discourses suggesting all things Latino. Multi-colored flyers and phone recordings on club hotlines were the most common means for bringing the crowds in. The spaces themselves and the mood they created were ultimately responsible for keeping those who arrived and ensuring that others would eventually visit. It would not be an exaggeration to declare that, through the business of the club, queer Latino cultural citizenship has been going strong in the Bay Area for at least two decades.[16]

The year 2000, however, was the first time a gay Latin Stage became known far and wide throughout the region via radio broadcasts. While word of mouth and flyers have spread the knowledge of special events targeting the community, advertising a queer Latino event on this scale was something new. And yet, while it was a new local phenomenon on a grander scale, the selling of the Latin Stage fit nicely into a (trans)national circuit of queer consumption predicated on the lofty goals of cultural diversity, of queer multiculturalism. Before discussing this local San Francisco event in relationship to the mass promotion of a cultural space, it is worth considering how the event fit into a larger context of queer cultural citizenship's dependence on the sale and discourse of diversity, on commodity culture in late capitalism.

The year 1999 marked the first time San Francisco had an official magazine for June Pride celebrations. Continuing in 2000 these glossy magazines offered abundant opportunities to address the relationship between commodity culture, queer identity, and visibility. The edition of the magazine in 2000, more than three hundred pages in size and available for free to tens of thousands of residents and tourists, offered several striking points. That year the magazine went nationally homogeneous. As its editor Peter McQuaid explained, *Pride 00* became the "official Gay Pride Magazine for Los Angeles, New York, San Francisco, and Washington D.C." "The whole experience," he continued, "renewed my faith in what we can accomplish together."[17] Regionally, specific content sought to balance the national queer homogeneity of *Pride 00*. While hundreds of ads fixed the main body of all four editions of the magazine, each city's edition also had its own distinct section showcasing local officials, agencies, and events. National gayness, in a sense, could be fixed to a consistent homogeneous corporate look, while local queer flavor could try to make up for the redundancy of the homogeneous queer spine of the magazine.

The most used and abused term in *Pride 00*'s nonadvertising content and the ads themselves was the catchy *diversity*. Amid the pages selling everything from perfumes to antiretroviral medicine, President Bill Clinton set the tone: "Warm greetings to everyone celebrating Gay and Lesbian Pride Month. As Americans, we can be proud of our diversity. Striving together, people of different ethnicities, backgrounds, races, beliefs, and sexual orientation have contributed to the success of our nation, reflecting the profound truth that this rich diversity is one of our greatest strengths. . . . I commend all those who are striving to create a society that celebrates our diversity." Strategically positioned immediately after Clinton's message in this, the year of his failed run for the presidency, Vice President Al Gore's letter similarly observed, "At the beginning of this millennium, I hope that all Americans will join in recognizing that the diversity of our people is the source of our strength."[18]

The circuit of consumer culture and Gay Pride marketed through *Pride* 00 also had a transnational dimension. On several of its pages the magazine observed World Pride in Rome, which replaced that year's Europride. Global celebrations were summarized on one page as "Queer, There and Everywhere. The Millennium Pride Calendar." In a classic colonialist discourse of "othering," this calendar included two columns listing Pride celebrations: the left column, the longer one, was for the United States; the right column was for "Everywhere Else." This exoticizing transnational tourist culture within capitalist consumption was even more present in the ads and articles promising pleasure in "far-away" destinations (Hawaii, Cape Town, Puerto Vallarta). Even when an "exotic" destination did not have the reputation and history of being explicitly accommodating to gay tourism (as Costa Rica did), the magazine spoke to the hope and desire for new lands "to explore."[19]

The Latin Stage was one of the goods sold through *Pride* 00, an exotic translocal destination. The San Francisco Latin Stage for Gay Pride 2000 thus was rather consistent with a trend to commodify queer identities globally through the joint discourses of visibility and diversity. This process was by no means a one-way, top-down co-optation or use of an identity. Queer Latinos answering the call to attend the advertised event experienced forms of collective membership; what they made of this social experience with others is certainly beyond the scope of this analysis, but we can at least surmise that individuals attending the event had the potential to create meanings, projects, and visions of their own.

This link between collective consciousness and the effect of creating and identifying along membership vectors is an important one. Some of the critics of the MSM ad targeting Latino men who do not identify with any queer category understood the potential of queer social membership. For Latinos embracing a gay identity could create opportunities for reflection as racial and sexual beings and for evaluating that identity's potential for developing a consciousness around HIV and AIDS. Cultural and racial identities, of course, can be powerful tools for organizing grassroots community struggles. As Mary Pardo has demonstrated in her work on Mexican American women activists, the social space of ethnic identity can be a powerful, transformative means for engaging the state apparatus.[20] But in advanced capitalism, as *Pride oo* displayed most colorfully, identity can easily turn into a commodity, a good to be sold and consumed in the marketplace. Several recent analyses of the relationship between commodity culture and citizenship have found that commodity citizenship is well equipped to handle and profit from the creation of new identities, racial, sexual, and otherwise.[21]

The predicament of visibility for queer Latinos is particularly vexing in relation to commodity culture's astute utilization of both Latino and queer or gay identities. As more and more companies target and sell products to gays and lesbians typically under the marketing guise of offering access to a chic lifestyle, the economic basis and labor for this culture of visibility is made invisible. While commodity capitalism targets the queer dollar by creating the image (literal and figurative) of community formation through shopping, visibility remains in the realm of marketing. With queer visibility and identity thus fetishized through consumption capitalism, reduced to a lifestyle for sale, only those interested shoppers financially capable of accessing such a community of shoppers remain members of the group.[22]

As members of this community of shoppers queer Latinos too have access to the lifestyle, albeit generally in smaller proportions corresponding to their place in the political economy. Queer Latino men certainly serve as a potential lucrative pool of shoppers for whose attention bus signs, billboards, television programming, and radio ads tactically vie. Once the group of potential shoppers has been identified and targeted the interplay between identity and visibility—two key features of the notion of cultural citizenship—get to work. Through advertising and shopping, a form of (consumer) cultural citizenship is at work.

Consumption for Latinos generally, but for queer Latinos specifically, involves at least two often related facets in the relationship between identity and consumer capitalism. First, Latino bodies act as consumers, that is, as those doing the consumption of queer services and goods: going to the Latin Stage, purchasing subscriptions to queer-themed magazines (mainstream and Latino), viewing gay-themed television comedy series and the commercials sponsoring these, or attending music, theater, and other performances seemingly sexually neutral but clearly with a strong queer following. Like other queers, Latinos also participate actively in these forms of socioeconomic activity, many of them investing a good proportion of their attention and financial resources therein.

Second, the bodies of queer Latinos are themselves consumed in the transnational webs of commodity culture. Others (nonqueer Latinos) consume queer Latino images and identities through the production of advertising materials and the actual selling of products and services. Consumption on these levels, with Latinos as sellers and as objects for sale, makes up a network of cultural and social relations of desire, profit, and visibility. Given the inability to control the circulation and interpretation of materials, events, and services designed for queer Latinos, becoming visible for questions of pride, identity, and community formation can have other (un)intended consequences.

When June 2000 Pride festivities arrived in the Bay Area one of the most popular FM radio stations in the region, Wild 94.9, broadcast to hundreds of thousands of its listeners news about the Latin Stage. Pulling Latina and Latino listeners, their friends, and "their admirers" to the city's famed weekend extravaganza of street and house parties, Wild 94.9's ads went for an essence of identity. Calling for Latinos or latinidad in the larger Gay Pride weekend, the carefully produced, rhythmic mixed-music ads spoke to and for gay Latino presence and fun: simultaneously gay and Latino. Calling for bodies and their disposable income to the stage, such careful marketing of intersecting membership for the promise of fun to thousands of Bay Area residents meant profits for those involved in its production. It was not only the producers of the Latin Stage who profited from this venture; local businesses promoted clothing, magazines, and related queer Latino goods—the stuff of a lifestyle.

The fact that some of the profits made from the Latin Stage went to support Proyecto further complicates this discussion. However meager and largely symbolic this financial gesture of community reciprocity became, that Proyecto received any gain from the sale of the Latin Stage brought it into the interdependent network of consumption, profit, and queer Latino citizenship. We can certainly appreciate these connections between commodification and a cultural apparatus for making identity visible (via Wild 94.9's airwaves, for example) and an intimate relationship between queer Latino cultural citizenship and public health. With the additional presence of a nonprofit queer Latino HIV-prevention agency in this nexus of profit and visibility, capitalist consumption became an ally of local HIV prevention with queer Latinos, simply part of the

1. Gay, male-to-female transgender, and cross-dressing members of Instituto Familiar de la Raza's contingent during the San Francisco LGBT Pride Parade along Market Street in 1995. That year's theme was "A World without Borders." Collection of the author.

2. Staff, volunteers, and attendees at Proyecto ContraSIDA Por Vida's booth during the San Francisco LGBT Pride Festival at Civic Center in 1995. Collection of the author.

larger AIDS economy that includes pharmaceuticals, advertising companies, condom and lubricant manufacturers, and the like.

The dynamics present in the sales pitch for the Latin Stage in June 2000 were not new either for Latinos or for queers. What is different and useful to consider, though, in the selling of an event and space constituted on at least several vectors of identity (racial and ethnic, gender, sexual) is the possibility for successful sales. Although the ads clearly pointed out particular sexual and erotic and racial, ethnic, and cultural markers, there was no checkpoint at the gates of entry to ensure that only those possessing such markers could enjoy the event. Women and men of all sexual, erotic, and cultural persuasions and tastes could enter—and they did—to enjoy the sun-soaked afternoon. They juggled dance, drinks, and dialogue—the consummation of desires in their many possibilities. Not all were queer, not all were Latinas or Latinos, and of course not all were a particular manifestation of the two. This openness is precisely the beauty and the effectiveness of commodity culture: it provides a seemingly equal opportunity to all wanting and *able* to purchase the commodity for sale. For whatever desires they had in mind, those present at San Francisco's 2000 Pride Latin Stage were equal consumers that afternoon. Of course they were not *all* equally consumed in return as commodities in display.

As examples such as the Latin Stage demonstrate, queer Latinos find themselves in the middle of intense commercial battles for their attention and resources. As part of a queer market they are not much different from other queers watching television, reading magazines, and listening to radio ads appealing to their senses linked to discourses of communities of belonging. This evergrowing capitalist commodity culture has its own regional, national, and transnational specificities, but one basic factor remains consistent: the culture exists and thrives to the extent that it reaps profits from its consumers. Identifying the contours of this queer culture of commodification has become more complicated, as the Latin Stage case reveals, given Latinos' closer and closer affiliation with projects claiming queer identities, visibilities, and space as a community, such as Proyecto. This intimacy between cultural citizenship and capitalist consumer culture has entered larger fields of global engagement with civic society through the close relationship between profit, tourism travel, and queer pleasures.

To make queer Latinos an exception in the larger motions of queer visibility and commodification would be an exaggeration. As the clearest example of a broad queer population's attempt to remain visible and make cultural and political claims in San Francisco, the annual June Gay Pride Parade and related events have increasingly sought the financial sponsorship of companies willing to fund the festivities. Since 1999 "the official magazine for San Francisco pride" has been virtually indistinguishable from large department stores' catalogues or high-fashion magazines, complete with sample perfume cards and colorful ads for companies selling queers coveted lifestyle goods: alcohol, cologne, cable programming, antiretroviral drug therapy, clothing, and travel. The growing dependence on corporate sponsorship of Pride events seems to be a given, considering their scope and the costs for producing them. San Francisco's 2000 Pride Festival was no exception. City and County Supervisor Leslie Katz observed, "It would be great if we could [produce Pride events] without corporate sponsorship, but we can't."[23] As with any other annual convention or sporting event, city governments jump on the opportunity to host a large Gay Pride event; queer pride not only sells, but can be quite profitable.

In San Francisco this overreliance on corporate endorsements has shifted the meaning of the congregation of hundreds of thousands marching in the streets to the less politically charged and corporate-friendly parade and festival. As expected, the sale of queer diversity has brought some criticism. The high visibility of "rainbow capitalism" (reducible to the hegemonic rainbow flag) and its overly simplified claims for inclusion have brought conflict to local and national organizing efforts. Not everyone pushing for national anti–gay discrimination legislation, for example, accepts the strong presence of corporations in queer politics. While these critics are also interested in the passage of such national legislation, they are just as, if not more, interested in concentrating their grassroots energies at the local level, and certainly not in having their efforts directed at the production of glossy magazines marketing Pride nationally, even globally. Taking into consideration proportionally higher rates of HIV infection and household displacement through gentrification for Latinos in San Francisco, the marketing of the Latin Stage was a rather odd project for understanding cultural citizenship; while local non-Latino (typically) and Latino entrepreneurs alike want consumers seeking exotic and erotic frolic to believe that indeed "the sweetest things are always Latin," the majority of (queer) Latinos have not been getting the sweetest consumerist deals to ensure their livelihood in the city. Even without access to the financial records of profit for these private ventures selling "the queer Latin," we can surmise they are large enough to support recurring theme parties, increasingly larger in size and expanding beyond the Bay Area region, with long postal and electronic mailing lists and multicolor ads in queer magazines in English and Spanish. Again, just as Proyecto received some funding support from the Latin Stage in

2000, despite these typically non-Latino-owned "Latin" ventures supporting a project or two in the local community, these are but symbolic gestures of limited reciprocity, with communities providing the human, psychic, and financial resources making private gain possible.

The Latino MSM ad campaign from the mid-1990s and the Latin Stage in San Francisco's 2000 Pride Festival engaged questions of identity and visibility for queer Latinos in the city. The ad served as a vehicle to interrogate who became visible in the local queer Latino body. Given the ad's cultural and political position in the context of the AIDS epidemic, the politics of its representations were fertile ground for analysis. While reflective of a segment of Latino men playing with one another with no interest in anything resembling cultural citizenship, the ad simultaneously made Latino queers (bisexual and gay) invisible; this invisibility was an irony for many (but not all) in the 1990s, given more than two decades of community organizing precisely to make queer Latino bodies visible. The Latin Stage, a project that could be considered at the other extreme of the visibility scale, highlighted the growing commodification of queer Latino identity and visibility. In this intensifying profit-through-identity period, more queer Latino subjects than ever entered the visual and sonic cultural field, hardly remaining invisible or inaudible, though for the purposes of individual financial gain. Ultimately, responding to such interests of local cultures of consumption may mean one thing; were the Latin Stage not a financial success in later years we would expect fewer corporate pitches and ads selling "Latin sweetness." In their efforts to keep gay Latinos "sweet and profitable," it is unlikely we will see a clear distinction between private businesses, gay Latino revelers, local health agencies, and city government. The gay Latino bed can indeed be quite an accommodating location.

To return to the original questions of cultural citizenship that Rosaldo proposed, San Francisco is hardly an open, egalitarian cultural space where queer Latinos can enter the house of visibility unscathed. In terms of the politics of representation in public health discourses of HIV prevention, this space has constituted one of the most common fields for representing Latino queerness. The AIDS epidemic of the 1980s and 1990s forced cultural and political dialogues around community membership and belonging, about homophobia and racism, and the queer body and its representations. Less discussed but quite present in these discourses was the question of gender among queer Latinos, and specifically the centrality of patriarchy in the representation of the community. Not working for a common, monolithic project, front-line health workers in particular disagreed about whom to showcase, how to create and strengthen public identities. These too were struggles for queer Latino cultural citizenship: the public space, discourses, and visibility that bus ads can powerfully call upon to invite or detract consumers of the cultural identity in question. The 2000 Latin Stage, on the other hand, hardly encountered any conflicts in representing queer latinidad. The Stage actually *depended* on this identity construct, fetishized primarily through the excessively masculinist Latino figure for the intent of capitalizing on the power of its suggested heteronormativity—ironically. We cannot ignore the fact that such stagings of gay male latinidad are predicated on hegemonic heteronormative constructions of the masculine body, one well consumed by the white and other non-Latino gaze.[24] What became contradictory in this project around the same constructs allowing for cultural citizenship is that while the Stage afforded the opportunity for queer Latinos to come together, they were not in a position to control its parameters, much less its future. Those of us rising to the (Latin) stage of queer excitement during Pride 2000 placed our bodies and desires in a circuit of pleasure and consumption much larger than we could imagine, with much less control.

NOTES

A University of California MEXUS dissertation completion grant in 1999 and a University of California President's Postdoctoral Fellowship in 2001–3 supported part of the research and writing for this discussion. I also acknowledge the feedback from the editors, especially Michael Hames-García for his reading of an earlier draft, and for his patience. A close reading and critical suggestions by David Manuel Hernández helped the narrative and its arguments substantially—gracias, David! As always I thank those I interviewed for allowing me to record parts of their life histories in the San Francisco Bay Area.

1. J. M. Rodríguez, *Queer Latinidad*, 6, my emphasis.

2. Useful analyses centering on people of color in queer history, culture, and politics of the San Francisco Bay Area are Aguirre and Robles, *¡Viva 16!*; Cora, "Nuestras Auto-Definiciones"; Ordona, "Coming Out Together"; J. M. Rodríguez, *Queer Latinidad*; Roque Ramírez, "Communities of Desire"; Rosales, "Papis, Dykes, Daddies"; Mary Guzmán, *Mind If I Call You Sir?*

3. As a legal exception, on 13 November 2007 the San Francisco Board of Supervisors voted 10–1 to issue municipal identification cards to city residents regardless of their legal status in the country.

4. Rosaldo, "Cultural Citizenship," 402, emphasis in original. For further elaborations and case studies on Latino cultural citizenship, see Flores and Benmayor, *Latino Cultural Citizenship*.

5. I focus specifically on *gay Latino* visibility, not directly or inherently that of lesbian Latinas. While the second section of this discussion on Gay Pride festivals offers related implications of visibility and citizenship for queer Latinas, I do not assume that they are the same, much less that they can be understood creatively and critically by an analysis of queer male cultures and politics. For closer examinations of queer *Latina* cultures, politics, and histories in the Bay Area, see Cora, "Nuestras Auto-Definiciones"; Ordona, "Coming Out Together"; J. M. Rodríguez, *Queer Latinidad*; Rosales, "Papis, Dykes, Daddies"; Mary Guzmán, *Mind If I Call You Sir?*

6. This form of denial by gay Latinos was false to the degree that they did have sexual relations with white and other men, a common practice (though culturally taboo to admit for some, especially within the gay nationalist politics of Chicanos and Latinos). Lying made tracking clearly demarcated racial directions of infection difficult, if not impossible. For a candid and critical autobiographical account of gay relations between Chicanos and whites in the context of AIDS, see the late Gil Cuadros's essay "My Aztlán: White Place," among others, in Cuadros, *City of God*, 53–58.

7. The most useful examination of the cultural politics of AIDS in relation to race and sexuality, which includes an assessment of the coining and limitations of the sociobehavioral category "men who have sex with men," is Cohen, *The Boundaries of Blackness*. For an exploration of HIV risk focused on gay Latinos in San Francisco, see R. M. Díaz, *Gay Latino Men*.

8. The multiple Spanish terms describing queer sexualities and subjectivities are historically and geographically specific: *maricón* is the most common and most easily recognized throughout Latin America, and among Latino immigrants' *culero* is specific to Salvadorans; *joto* has a Chicano and Mexican specificity; *queer* is likely the least used given its Anglo-centric coinage. These differences in sexual and gender identities should be acknowledged when considering social membership for addressing sexual behavior.

9. Diane Felix, interview by author, audio tape recording, San Francisco, 19 and 27 April 1995. Unless otherwise noted, all oral history interviews were conducted in English.

10. See Aguirre and Robles, *¡Viva 16!*.

11. Ricardo A. Bracho, interview by author, audio tape recording, San Francisco, 12 April 1995.

12. The most well-known and widely published essay arguing this position is Almaguer, "Chicano Men." While acknowledging queer racial, cultural, gendered, and sexual identities simultaneously is still not an easy feat for many Latinas and Latinos, many have done it for decades. I explore one cultural, social, and political organization born of these struggles among women and men in " 'That's My Place!' " Some of Almaguer's arguments are based on Joseph Carrier's anthropological work on Mexican men in the

1970s and 1980s. An important critique of Carrier and other anthropological studies on Latin American male (homo)sexualities is Bustos-Aguilar, "Mister Don't Touch the Banana."

13. J. M. Rodríguez, *Queer Latinidad*, 79.

14. Martín Gustavo Cravioto, interview by author, audio tape recording, San Francisco, 27 April and 22 May 1995. Translation from Spanish is mine.

15. Cravioto's de-emphasis of the need to claim gay Latino visibility in relation to HIV education does not mean that he does not appreciate gay-identity-based political, health advocacy, and cultural work. I explore some of his own contributions through politicized cultural work in Roque Ramírez, "Claiming Queer Cultural Citizenship."

16. There has been a wide variety of nightclubs, bars, and monthly or occasional queer Latina and Latino social gatherings in the Bay Area, most catering to men but a few to women as well, especially in the 1970s and 1980s. While each one of these has depended on profit typically based on alcohol sales and entrance fees, club owners and managers have varied in the way they give back (or not) to the local community that makes the business possible. I analyze one short-lived multigender queer Latina/o space in San Francisco in the mid-1990s in Roque Ramírez, "'¡Mira, Yo Soy Boricua y Estoy Aquí!'"

17. Profile Pursuit, *Pride oo*, 22.

18. Profile Pursuit, *Pride oo*, 19, 20.

19. Profile Pursuit, *Pride oo*, 101, 211. Analyses of transnational relations between tourist consumption and gay organizing and political identity formation are Cortiñas, "Imperial Desire"; the special issue "Queer Tourism" in GLQ, edited by Jasbir Puar, including Cantú, "*De Ambiente*"; Alexander, "Imperial Desire."

20. Pardo, *Mexican American Women Activists*.

21. Useful studies on the relationship between queer citizenship or gay social membership and commodity culture are Chasin, *Selling Out*; Evans, *Sexual Citizenship*; Gluckman and Reed, *Homo Economics*; Hennessy, *Profit and Pleasure*; Sender, *Business, Not Politics*. For an analysis of the commodification of Latinos as a group and as an ethnic label, see Dávila, *Latinos, Inc.*

22. See the close analysis in Hennessy, "Queer Visibility."

23. Quoted in Jason P. Lorber, "And Now, a Word about Our Sponsors," in Profile Pursuit, *Pride oo*, 91. Lorber is described as "president of Aplomb Consulting, a national, San Francisco–based public relations and marketing firm helping organizations [corporations?] form mutually beneficial relationships with the gay, lesbian, bisexual and transgender communities" (94). According to a summary of costs and revenue generated for the 2000 San Francisco Pride celebration, the event cost $2,080,082 and generated $2,129,898 in revenues. "Corporate contributions" and "donated merchandise/advertising" accounted for 17 percent and 56 percent of total revenues, respectively, for a total of 73 percent. See "Financial Results, SF Pride 2000," in Profile Pursuit, *Pride* 01. Katz's statement in 2000 fits in the economic stage Urvashi Vaid described in the

mid-1990s as "the queer as consumer and its corollary, the selling of gayness" (*Virtual Equality*, 246). Vaid's analysis of this economic stage builds on Jeffrey Escoffier's economic history of lesbian and gay visibility and space in the United States, summarized in four stages and their respective periods: the closet economy, the liberation economy, the territorial economy, and the AIDS economy ("The Political Economy," 123–24). For a sociohistorical analysis of the shift of "lesbian and gay identity from a political to a lifestyle category," see Valocchi, "The Class-Inflected Nature of Gay Identity." For a critique of Vaid's reservations around race- or ethnicity-based queer organizing, see Quiroga, *Tropics of Desire*, 222–24.

24. See bell hooks's useful elaboration in "Eating the Other" on the relationship between seduction and domination in the historical white consumption of the black body.

A Response to "Gay Latino Cultural Citizenship"

Ramón A. Gutiérrez

In "Gay Latino Cultural Citizenship" Horacio Roque Ramírez provocatively asks us to ponder: Is there a visible place for us?

Who precisely the "us" in this essay happens to be is a complicated question. That the invisible be made visible and, as the anthropologist Renato Rosaldo advocates, be given "the right to be different and to belong in a participatory democratic sense" through full membership and individual voice is an even harder imperative in the stratified world of queer and gay Latino identities.[1]

Latino is hardly an unproblematic identity marker. As most Latinas will surely protest, Latino is not a gender-neutral term. It refers to males, pure and simple. Unknown as an identity in the United States much before the 1970s, its etymology, notes the Oxford English Dictionary (1989), is latinoamericano. While this dictionary entry cites a textual reference to Latinos as early as 1946—"Latinos are usually looked on as sinister specimens of an inferior race"—it was in the 1970s, in Black Panther Party publications, that America's racial structure was routinely described as composed of three groups: blacks, Latinos, and whites.

There is a story of recent and undoubtedly apocryphal origin that circulates in popular folklore along the Mexico-U.S. border that gets precisely at the newness and the American genesis of Latino as an identity. The story tells of a miscommunication, born of a mistranslation between a Mexican immigrant traveling north and an officer of the U.S. Border Patrol trying to stem that flow. The immigrant is a woman named Molly standing in line to cross to the American side. After waiting for hours her moment with the U.S. Border Patrol agent finally arrives. In a gruff and raspy voice, or so the tale goes, the officer asks, "Are you Latina?" "No, no, no señor," she replies. "Yo no soy la Tina. Yo soy la Molly. La Tina ya cruzó" (No, no, no sir. I am not Tina. I am Molly. Tina already crossed).

This story of miscommunication vividly illustrates two points. First, ethnic labels operant in one national space do not travel well and often make no sense when transported just a few miles away. Second, ethnic identities are learned relationally, in relationships of opposition between and among ethnic groups that are always in flux; thus the identities are constantly transformed.

What we know about the origins and popularization of *Latino* as an ethnic identity locates its birth in advertising agencies on Madison Avenue and in Miami's Little Havana. Here, seeking to eek out a living and to create a market niche for themselves, advertising agents who were refugees from Castro's Cuba in the years following the 1959 revolution began to covet a share of the advertising budgets of major American corporations. What they invented and what they sold these corporate giants was knowledge of a population. They packaged Latinos as a consumption market that was different and distinct from the American mainstream that General Foods, Sara Lee, Clorox, Coca-Cola, Ford, and Anheuser-Busch already knew. Hailing from Latin America in rapidly rising numbers after the U.S. Immigration and Reform Act of 1965, this new population was putatively white, Spanish-speaking, Catholic, family-centered, law-abiding, and profoundly invested in modernity's conveniences, with a strong work ethic and wallets full of cash. So were created a series of Latin-origin, minority-run and -owned advertising agencies committed to the creation of a pan-ethnic Latino marketing identity that putatively united tastes in South America, and thus in North America as well.[2]

When Horacio Roque Ramírez asks "What is identity for?" What function does it serve? Whose interests does it advance? he is clearly a participant in a conversation describing the corporate sponsorship of a distinctive Latino musical venue and stage at San Francisco's Pride Festival in 2000. "Identity can easily turn into a commodity, a good to be sold and consumed in the marketplace," he notes. Latino identity (read: male) is presented here as fixed, firm, and unambiguous. Corporations lusting for consumers and cash employ a host of sombrero-clad singers and scantily dressed dancers to mesmerize and motivate their Latino audience (read: male) in hopes that during the afternoon's festivities they will sip Cuervo Tequila *margaritas*, drink Miller Lite beer, and later want much more. Armed with their free samples of Wet Lube and Trojans galore the point is driven home, so to speak. What could be better than to ride a new Bronco or Mustang? What ecstasy might an American Airlines vacation to Costa Rica afford? Mission accomplished. The trap worked! From identity to desire to consumption, or so the model has it.

In the 1970s three major pan-ethnic identities emerged in the United States: Asian Americans, Native Americans, and Latinos. Pan-ethnic identities easily became symbolically salient at the level of marketing and consumption. But to become politically potent, to gain the cultural citizenship Ramírez loftily seeks, requires much more than seductive swiveling hips and *maraca*-brandishing performers at a Pride festival. For pan-ethnic identities like Latinos and Latinas to mobilize women and men to collective political action and protest, members of different nationalities must share a common structural relationship to race, class, generation, and geography. If subethnicities have "looked alike" to dominant outsiders and have been the targets of racial discrimination, the chances that such a pan-ethnic political solidarity will develop is high. A shared class position, a high level of residential proximity, and several generations in the United States have led fractionalized ethnic groups to enhance their power through pan-ethnic alliance, hoping thus to more effectively press their claims before the state and its elites. Cultural factors such as a common language, an appreciation for the Latin beat in popular music, and a shared religion are certainly important factors too, but researchers have not yet found them to be determinative in spurring political alliances across Latin-origin national groups in the United States.[3]

Mexicans, Puerto Ricans, Dominicans, Cubans, and Central and South Americans have not yet been able to forge an effective shared Latino identity as political actors with which to claim cultural citizenship because of their extreme racial diversity, their dispersion, and complex stratification by class and immigrant generation. Sixty percent of all Mexicans are geographically concentrated in California and the Southwest. The majority of Puerto Ricans on the mainland live in New York and New Jersey. Cubans reside primarily in Florida. Each of these groups has had very different political priorities. Cubans have focused their political muscle on overthrowing Fidel Castro and "liberating" Cuba. Given the long history of Mexican emigration to the United States under various levels of legality and as guest workers, they too are complexly stratified along nativity, region, generation, and degrees of acculturation and assimilation, as well as by U.S. immigration policies around a guest worker program, border interdiction techniques, and a path to citizenship of illegal immigrants. Some Puerto Ricans want statehood for the island, others independence, and still others have completely forgotten Puerto Rico, except as a remote place associated with the nostalgic yearning of musical chords. Indeed it is this generational distance from the homeland and any direct experiential knowledge of it that makes the commercial marketing of Latino so effective and its political deployment so difficult among more recent immigrants with well-established loyalties to other things.

Ramírez's second San Francisco case study focuses on the dismay among some Latino health care workers in 1995 provoked by the production and placement of a Spanish-language poster on the number 14 and 49 city buses advocating responsible condom use to curtail the spread of HIV infection. The poster targeted Spanish-literate, working-class Latino men who depend on public transport to get to and from work and who also happened to have sex with other men in San Francisco's Mission District, a neighborhood densely populated by recent Mexican and Central American immigrants and shared with a much older Mexican-origin community. Most 49 buses that traverse the Mission District are double length, are usually packed to standing-room capacity at rush hours, and carry no fewer than thirty similar posters in the space above the bus windows, advertising products, services, and personnel in Chinese, Spanish, and English. Leaving aside the issue of how many bus-riding Latino men who have sex with other men would have seen, much less read the ad while exhausted and packed like sardines, at issue was the putative patriarchal privilege the poster endorsed and the pestilential response the campaign generated among Latino HIV-prevention counselors. "In my family no one knows that I have sex with men. That's why I protect them," announces a Latino stud in the contested poster, as he holds up his wrapped condom for spectators to see.

The crux of the controversy was that health officials were pragmatic in targeting unsafe behavior with this ad, not demanding of the poster's viewers a commitment to a specific erotic identity as bisexual or gay. Ramírez asserts that gay activists espoused "notions of open queer sexualities . . . and celebrate[d] queer sex for Latinas and Latinos," but their words and actions clearly reveal quite the opposite, that they imagined erotic identities as fixed, firm, dichotomous, and unambiguous. Ricardo A. Bracho, a worker at the Colegio ContraSIDA, amply demonstrated this when he announced, "I *hate* this whole . . . 'men who sleep with men' shit. . . . Make them gay-identified. That's a *problem.* They should become gay-identified." Diane Felix, a "well-known butch Chicana activist," was equally smug in her certitude that the poster's message would have no effect. She took it upon herself to publicly police erotic behavior between men in the Mission District, moralistically parroting the value of marriage, monogamy, and family to them.

What Ramírez appears to want us to conclude from these two examples about Latino ethnicity, desire, and sexual behavior is not entirely clear. At times he describes a host of sexual identities and erotic possibilities — *maricón, culero, joto,* gay, bisexual, queer — and at other times he reduces them to seemingly inseparable cognates of "gay and queer Latino." Such confabulation clouds the shape and dimension of cultural citizenship he believes is necessary to achieve both full membership and visibility in American society. The gay and lesbian movement at its birth in the 1970s used to announce at its protest marches, "Two, four, six, eight, smash the family, smash the state! Two, four, six, eight, hell no, we won't assimilate!" In 2007 the organized remnants of the move-ment wanted as their principal goal state-sanctioned marriage and the full legal rights of spouses to hold and inherit property, to birth and to adopt, to ac-knowledge such unions as families—in short, to be normalized. Those lesbi-ans and gays who have sought civil unions and marriages in a host of places are pretty visible. Why else the conservative backlash and the cynical exploitation of same-sex marriages as a wedge issue by the Republican Party?

What should become of Latino men who have sex with men? Should they be patrolled and moralistically condemned, as Diana Felix does, or should they be forced to become gay, as Ricardo A. Bracho demands? Should they be granted full citizenship and visibility only as consumers of Coca-Cola, Pepsi and Sprite at Pride, or is more required? Ramírez might want to answer his own questions by providing a thicker description of the sexual geography. Engaging the litera-ture on lesbian identities and behaviors, specifically the work of Adrienne Rich and Barbara Ponce, would be a good place to start. Rich, in her now famous essay, "Compulsory Heterosexuality and Lesbian Existence," noted that there were many ways that women had expressed their love of other women in the past, which a rigid hetero/lesbian dichotomy could not capture. She proposed that a lesbian continuum had long existed, a continuum of women's intimate, romantic, and erotic relationships with other women that went all the way from deep friendship to companionship, romantic partnership, and erotic love.

Barbara Ponce's work likewise considerably complicates our understanding of lesbian identities by proposing four distinct lesbian identities and activi-ties: (1) lesbian identity with lesbian activity; (2) lesbian identity with celibate, heterosexual, or bisexual activity, including political lesbians and lesbians in-volved in heterosexual relations; (3) bisexual identity with lesbian activity; and (4) heterosexual identity with lesbian activity.[4] According to Ponce, the folk wis-dom of American society posits a principle of consistency among sex assign-ment, gender identity, gender roles, sexual object choice, and sexual identity. But in reality each of these varies considerably, by class, ethnicity, and point in the life course.

Such analytic distinctions would begin to provide a much grander and more complex picture of Latino and Latina sexual behaviors and identities. The an-thropologist Matthew Gutmann recently noted that lower-class Mexican boys at young ages were very physical with each other, kissing, pinching, fondling, and holding hands. He reports hearing one group of working-class boys play-fully taunting each other. One boy accused the other of being a maricón, to which the lad replied, "Yeah, well, you're a bisexual."[5] Where twenty years ago boys of that age might not have known much about sexual identities, now they knew that there were gays and bisexuals in their world, as well as the sexual object choices these identities signified.

We might begin the Latino continuum with boys' erotic play just described. When a society places a strong symbolic value on female virginity at marriage and segregates its females, the logical result, as Carlos Monsiváis attests, is that sex between young men ages sixteen to twenty-five is common and tolerated.[6] From Richard Trexler's research we know that in colonial Mexico young boys were introduced to sex by older boys, the young practicing receptive sex, the older boys insertive. As they grew older the sexual object choices became more varied, eventually including both men and women. Most men eventually married and as they aged became more receptive sexually with other men.[7] In adulthood one's sexual object choice could remain exclusively male; Joseph Carrier's and Tomas Almaguer's work certainly document this reality.[8] Or it might lead to that panoply of sexual behaviors and identities that Clark Taylor, Rafael M. Díaz, and Héctor Carrillo have described.[9] From research on male prostitutes, transvestites, and sex workers in Mexico and Latin America we know that the sexual practices of ostensibly married, heterosexual men, at least as described by these sex workers, defies easy classification by any lexical predilections of gay men, such as Ricardo Bracho, quoted above.[10]

Acknowledging such polymorphic realities first requires their naming. If the word *queer* is to mean anything politically, it must not forestall ambiguity and demand fixed erotic identities; it must acknowledge how desire changes over the life course and augurs for the liberation of desire, not its containment and repression.

NOTES

1. Rosaldo, "Cultural Citizenship," 402,

2. Dávila, *Latinos, Inc.*

3. D. López and Espiritu, "Panethnicity in the United States."

4. Ponce, *Identities in the Lesbian World.*

5. Gutmann, *The Meanings of Macho*, 128.

6. Carlos Monsiváis as cited in Gutmann, *The Meanings of Macho*, 126.

7. Trexler, *Sex and Conquest.*

8. Carrier, *De los Otros*; Almaguer, "Chicano Men."

9. Taylor, "El Ambiente"; R. M. Díaz, *Gay Latino Men*; Héctor Carrillo, *The Night Is Young.*

10. Schifter, *Lila's House*; Prieur, *Mema's House*; Aggleton, *Men Who Sell Sex to Other Men.*

Feeling Brown:

Ethnicity and Affect in Ricardo Bracho's

The Sweetest Hangover (and Other STDs)

José Esteban Muñoz

ETHNICITY, AFFECT, AND PERFORMANCE

The theoretical incoherence of the identity demarcation *Latino* is linked to the term's failure to actualize embodied politics which contest the various antagonisms within the social that challenge Latino and Latina citizen-subjects. While important political spectacles have been staged under group identity titles such as *Chicano* and *Nuyorican*, *Latino*, a term meant to enable much-needed coalitions between different national groups, has not developed as an umbrella term that unites cultural and political activists across different national, racial, class, and gender divides. This problem has to do with its incoherence, by which I mean the term's inability to index, with any regularity, the central identity tropes that lead to our understandings of group identities in the United States. *Latino* does not subscribe to a common racial, class, gender, religious, or national category, and if a Latino can be from any country in Latin America, a member of any race, religion, class, or gender or sex orientation, who then is she? What, if any, nodes of commonality do Latinas and Latinos share? How is it possible to know *latinidad*?

Latino/a can be understood as a new social movement. In this sense I want to differentiate between citizen-subjects who subscribe to the category *Latino/a* and those the U.S. census terms *Hispanic*. Rejecting *Hispanic* in and of itself does not constitute a social movement, nor am I suggesting any such thing. But I do want to posit that such a linguistic maneuver is the germ of a self-imaging of Latino as, following the important and path-breaking work of the Chicana feminist Norma Alarcón, an "identity-in-difference." In this schematic an identity-in-difference is one that understands the structuring role of difference as the underlying concept in a group's mapping of collective identity. For Alarcón an identity-in-difference is an optic better suited to consider contemporary mappings of diversity than the now standardized homogenizing logic of multiculturalism.[1] To be cognizant of one's status as an identity-in-difference is to know that one falls off majoritarian maps of the public sphere, that one is exiled from paradigms of communicative reason and a larger culture of consent. This exile is more like a displacement, the origin of which is a historically specific and culturally situated bias that blocks the trajectory of the Latina or Latino citizen-subject to official citizenship-subject political ontology.

This blockage is one that keeps the Latina or Latino citizen-subject from being able to access normativity, playing out as an inability to *perform* racialized normativity. A key component of my thesis is the contention that normativity is accessed in the majoritarian public sphere through the affective performance of ethnic and racial normativity. This performance of whiteness primarily transpires on an affective register. Acting white has everything to do with the performance of a particular affect, the specific performance of which grounds the subject performing white affect in a normative life-world. Latinas and Latinos, and other people of color, are unable to achieve this affective performativity on a regular basis.

In his study *Marxism and Literature* Raymond Williams coined the term "structure of feeling" to discuss the connections and points of solidarity between working-class groups and a social experience that can be described as "in process" yet nonetheless is historically situated.[2] Williams's formulation echoes Alarcón's explication of identity-in-difference as "identity-in-process."[3] I suggest that Williams's approach and a general turn to affect might be a better way to talk about the affiliations and identifications between radicalized and ethnic groups than those available in standard stories of identity politics. What unites and consolidates oppositional groups is not simply the fact of identity but the way they perform affect, especially in relation to an official "national affect" that is aligned with a hegemonic class. Latina/o (and other minoritarian) theater and performance set out to specify and describe ethnic difference and resistance not in terms of simple being, but through the more nuanced route of feeling. More specifically I am interested in plotting the way Latina/o performance theatricalizes a certain mode of "feeling brown" in a world painted white, organized by cultural mandates to "feel white."[4]

Standard models of U.S. citizenship are based on a national affect. English-only legislation initiatives throughout the nation call for English to be declared the official national language. In a similar fashion there is an unofficial, but no less powerfully entrenched, national affect. It is thus critical to analyze the material and historical import of affect as well as emotion to better understand failed and actualized performances of citizenship. May Joseph has brilliantly explicated the ways the performative aspects of citizenship have been undertheorized in previous discourses on citizenship. She reminds readers that within the important discourses on citizenship and participatory democracy, "performance emerges as an implied sphere rather than an actually located project."[5] Following Joseph's lead, I position performance as an actualized sphere, one which needs to be grasped as such to enact an analysis of citizenship. Citizenship is negotiated within a contested national sphere in which performances of affect counter each other in a contest that can be described as official national affect rather than emergent immigrant. The stakes in this contest are nothing less than the very terms of citizenship. It is thus useful to chart and theorize the utility efficacy of different modes of affective struggle. This essay suggests that it is useful to look at contemporary U.S. Latina/o drama and performance as symbolic acts of difference that insist on ethnic affect within a representational sphere dominated by the standard national affect.

I contend that this official national affect, a mode of being in the world primarily associated with white middle-class subjectivity, considers most ethnic affect inappropriate. Whiteness is a cultural logic which can be understood as an affective code that positions itself as the law. The lens of Foucauldian discourse analysis permits us to understand whiteness and the official national affect that represents its interests as a truth game.[6] This game is rigged insofar as it is meant to block access to freedom to those who cannot inhabit or at least mimic certain affective rhythms that have been preordained as acceptable. From the vantage point of this national affect code, Latina/o affect appears over the top and excessive. The media culture, a chief disseminator of official national affect, often attempts to contain Latina/o images as spectacles of spiciness and exoticism.[7] Such mainstream depictions of Latino affect serve to reduce, simplify, and contain ethnic difference. The work of many Latino and Latina playwrights and performers operates in direct opposition to the majoritarian sphere's media representation of Latinos. Much of this performance work functions as political attempts to contest and challenge prefabricated media stereotypes with dense and nuanced accounts of the emotional performances of self that constitute Latina/o difference and survival.

The affect of Latinos and Latinas is often off. One can even argue that it is off-white. The failure of Latino affect in relation to the hegemonic protocols of North American affective comportment revolves around an understanding of the Latina or the Latino as affective excess. I know I risk reproducing some predictable clichés of the Latino being "hot 'n' spicy" or simply "on fire." I answer these concerns by making two points: (1) It is not so much that the Latina/o affective performance is so excessive, but that the affective performance of normative whiteness is minimalist to the point of emotional impoverishment. Whiteness claims affective normativity and neutrality, but for that fantasy to remain in place one must only view it from the vantage point of U.S. cultural and political hegemony. Once we look at whiteness from a racialized perspective, like that of Latinos, it appears to be flat and impoverished. At this moment in history it seems especially important to position whiteness as lack. (2) Rather than trying to run from this stereotype, Latino as excess, it seems much more important to seize it and redirect it in the service of a liberationist politics. Such a maneuver is akin to what I have described elsewhere as a disidentification with toxic characterizations and stereotypes of U.S. Latinos. A disidentification is neither an identification nor a counteridentification; it is a working on, with, and against a form at a simultaneous moment.[8] Thus the "hot 'n' spicy spic" is a subject who cannot be contained within the sparse affective landscape of Anglo North America. This accounts for the ways Latina and Latino citizen-subjects find their way through subgroups that perform the self in affectively extravagant fashions.

Minoritarian identity has much to do with certain subjects' inability to *act* properly within majoritarian scripts and scenarios. Latinos and Latinas are stigmatized as performers of excess: the hot and spicy, over-the-top subjects who simply do not know when to quit. *Spics* is an epithet intrinsically linked to questions of affect and excess affect. Rather than simply reject this toxic language of shame I wish to reinhabit it and suggest that such stigmatizing speech permits us to arrive at an important mapping of the social. Rather than say that Latina/o affect is too much, I want to suggest that the presence of Latina/o affect puts a great deal of pressure on the affective base of whiteness, insofar as it instructs us in a reading of the affect of whiteness as underdeveloped and impoverished.

The inquiry I am undertaking here suggests that we move beyond notions of ethnicity as fixed (something that people are) and instead understand ethnicity as performative (what people do), providing a reinvigorated and nuanced understanding of ethnicity. Performance functions as socially symbolic acts that offer powerful theoretical ways of interpreting and understanding the social sphere. I am interested in crafting a critical apparatus that permits us to read ethnicity as a historical formation uncircumscribed by the boundaries of conventional understandings of identity. In lieu of viewing racial or ethnic difference as solely cultural, I aim to describe how race and ethnicity can be understood as "affective difference," by which I mean the ways various historically coherent groups feel differently and navigate the material world on a different emotional register.

To better understand affective difference a turn to the phenomenological psychology articulated by Jean-Paul Sartre is efficacious. The methodological underpinnings of my approach have included Williams's historicization of feeling and Alarcón's formulations of an identity-in-difference. Sartre's *Sketch for a Theory of Emotions* (1939) first formulated many of the major ideas that would be fully realized in *Being and Nothingness*, the major text of the first half of his career. In that brief book Sartre rejects a Freudian notion of the unconscious and instead insists on a Husserlian description of the "conscious phenomenon" that is emotion. For Sartre consciousness is a conscious activity, the act of knowing that one thinks. Emotion is thus an extension of consciousness, what I would call a performed manifestation of consciousness. According to Sartre, humans comprehend the world as making demands on them. Life in this existentially and phenomenologically oriented description consists in a set of tasks, things we need to do. We encounter routes and obstacles to the actualization of certain goals and make a map for ourselves of the world which includes these pathways and blocks to these goals. But when we are overwhelmed by this map of the world, a map replete with obstacles and barriers to our self-actualization, we enact the "magical" process that Sartre describes as emotions. When facing a seemingly insurmountable object we turn to emotion. Sartre concludes, "The study of emotions has indeed verified this principle: an emotion refers to what it signifies. And what it signifies is indeed, in effect, the totality of human relations of human-reality to the world."[9] I am most interested in this notion of emotion's being the signification of human reality to the world. Such a theory is deeply relational. It refuses the individualistic bent of Freudian psychoanalysis and attempts to describe emotions as emotions, the active negotiations of people within their social and historical matrix.

While these ideas about the relational nature and social contingency of emotion are helpful in the articulation of this writing project, it is equally important to posit that I do not subscribe to Sartre's approach without some deep reservations. Sartre ultimately describes the emotions as regressive, explaining that consciousness can "be-in-the-world" in two different modes. One is what he calls an "organized complex of utilizable things"; the other magical way of being in the world clicks into place when the organized matrix of utensils is no longer perceivable as such and one becomes overwhelmed.[10] Emotions describe for Sartre our relations to a world that has overwhelmed us. In his paradigm the magical realm of emotions is something *we regress into* when under duress. It does not take much critical scrutiny to see that this move betrays a typically misogynist gender logic that positions men as reasonable and better suited to

deploying the world of utensils, whereas women (and men who are overly feminine) are cast as a weaker order who must regress to a magical relation with the
world. Furthermore the discussion of magic and regression resonates with an
understanding of people of color as primitives who forsake reason only to hide
behind jujus.

Yet the actual description of an emotion can nonetheless be useful to a minoritarian theory of affect. Sartre describes emotions as surfacing during moments when one loses one's distance from the world of objects and people. Because stigmatized people are presented with significantly more obstacles and
blockages than privileged citizen-subjects, minoritarian subjects often have difficulty maintaining distance from the very material and felt obstacles that suddenly surface in their own affective mapping of the world. The world is not ideo-
logically neutral. The organization of things has much to do with the way capital
and different cultural logics of normativity that represent capital's interests give
normative citizen-subjects advantageous distance. Sartre's affective sketch is
useful because it can help minoritarian subjects better comprehend the working
of emotion. This mapping can potentially enable a critical distance that represents not a debunking of emotion but an elucidation of emotion's "magical"
nature within a historical web. The phenomenological aspect of Sartre's inquiry
demystifies the magic of emotion, and this in and of itself is an important contribution to a theory of the affective nature of ethnicity.

Unlike Sartre, Walter Benjamin values the realm of affect, which he sees as a
vital human resource under siege by the advent of technology. He believes that
the realm of affect has been compromised within the alienating age of mechani-
cal reproduction. Though some technology (notably cinema) offers the possibility of a utopian return of affect, Benjamin nonetheless longs and searches
for strategies by which affect could work through (not avoiding, ignoring, or
dismissing) the numbing alienation associated with technological moderniza-
tion. Furthermore he pursues aesthetic strategies that, as Miriam Hansen put
it, "reassess, redefine, the conditions of experience, affectivity, memory and the
imagination."[11] Sartre's work, when considered and partially amended in relation to Benjamin, stands as a productive theoretical opening.

Within this field of contested national affect Latina/o drama has the potential to stage theoretical and political interventions. David Román has argued
that the performance of Latino has "been politically efficacious for people from
quite distinct cultural backgrounds and ideological positions to meet and organize under the label of Latina/o and Chicana/o in order to register an oppositional stance to majoritarian institutions."[12] While I have stated that the term

Latino has been politically incoherent, it has nonetheless, as Román has argued, done some important political work.[13] The performance praxis of U.S. Latinas and Latinos assists the minoritarian citizen-subject in the process of denaturalizing the country's universalizing "national affect" fiction as it asserts ontological validity and affective difference. A useful example of this theoretical and political potential is the often misread drama by the Cuban American playwright, Maria Irene Fornes, who eschews identity labels such as Latina. Her refusal or reluctance to embrace an uncritical model of Latina identity is a critical and theoretical act. Only a few of Fornes's plays actually feature Latino and Latina characters: Conduct of Life is staged in a generalized Latin American nation, and Sarita features characters clearly marked as Latina or Latino.[14] Even so I contend that all of her dramatic personages represent Latina/o affective reality. Their ways of being, their modes of negotiating the interpersonal and the social, stand as thick descriptions of ethnic feeling within a hegemonic order. Fornes's oeuvre stands out from the mainstream of American theater partly because one is not easily able to assign motivation to her characters. Traditional narrative arcs of plot development are all but absent in her work, a difference that is often interpreted as the avant-garde nature of her plays. Such a reading is only half right, however. This particular mode of avante-gardism can be characterized as representative of a specifically transcultural avant-garde. Her plays appear mysterious to North American eyes because they represent a specifically Latina/o manera de ser (way of being). This mystery is not accidental or a problem of translation; it is strategic, measured, and interventionist.

THIS BRIDGE CALLED MY CRACK

In the remainder of this essay I focus on a case study that I view as a left theatricalization of the affective overload that is latinidad. Ricardo Bracho's play, The Sweetest Hangover, specifically its 1997 production at Brava Theater in San Francisco, represents a life-world wherein Latina/o affect structures reality. The "excessive" affect that characterizes latinidad (and excess should always be underscored in this context as merely relative) is the fundamental building block of the world imagined in this performance. I suggest that the world of Bracho's production also indexes other antinormative subcultural formations, such as the alternate economies of recreational drug use and homosexual desire.

"This Bridge Called My Crack" is a play on the classic anthology of writing by radical women of color, This Bridge Called My Back, published in 1981. I chose the word crack as part of a playful attempt to highlight the thematics of anal eroticism and recreational drug use; the crack is not crack cocaine but crystal meth, a drug that in certain vernacular orbits is referred to as *crack*. It is important to note that my punning here is meant to serve more than the general cause of irreverence. I am interested in calling attention to the continuation of the radical women of color project by gay men of color. In the foreword to the second edition of *Bridge*, published in 1983, Moraga comments on the shift in cultural climates between the two editions; within a parenthesis she writes: "(I am particularly encouraged by the organizing potential between third world lesbians and gay men in our communities of color)."[15] Granted, I make much of this parenthetical statement; I use it, for instance, to draw a line between the groundbreaking work of the *Bridge* authors and the recent cultural production of gay Latinos like Bracho, Luis Alfaro, Jorge Ignacio Cortiñas, Nilo Cruz, and Jonathan Cineseros. I nonetheless connect the work of such cultural workers because I feel that they do "co-map" Latino life-worlds where Latino affect—manifested in politics, performance, and other passions—is no longer represented as stigmatized excess. The gay male writing tradition that I am attempting to suture to this feminist tradition labors, via affective performance, to enact a powerful utopianism that is most certainly influenced by *Bridge*. Affective performances that reject the protocols of (white) normativity help map out cultural spectacles that represent and are symbolically connected to alternative economies, like the economies of recreational drugs and homoeroticism. Such spectacles and the alternative economies they represent help us, to borrow a phrase from one of Cherríe Moraga's poems, "dream of other planets." The poem itself, titled "Dreaming of Other Planets," works as something of a key to understanding the utopian impulse that reverberates throughout Bracho's play:

my vision is small
fixed
to what can be heard
between the ears

the spot
between the eyes
a well-spring
opening
to el mundo grande

relámpago strikes
between the legs

I open against
my will dreaming

of other planets I am
dreaming
of other ways
of seeing

this life.[16]

This theoretical formulation, "dreaming of other planets," represents the type of utopian planning, scheming, imaging, and performing we must engage in if we are to enact other realities, other ways of being and doing within the world. The play, like the poem, dreams not only of other spaces but of other modes of perceiving reality and feeling the world. While Moraga dreams of other ways of seeing, Bracho's play instructs its audience in other ways of feeling: feeling brown. For Moraga the dream of another time and place is achieved through the auspices of poetry and the act of writing. This notion of dreaming is ultimately descriptive of a critical approach that is intent on critiquing the present by imagining and feeling other temporalities and spaces.

More concretely another planet that is dreamed in the instance of Bracho's play is a nightclub, a place called Aztlantis, a name that signifies both the lost Chicano homeland and the lost city of myth. This other place and time calls us to think about the project of imagining a utopian time and place. It is a scene of what I have referred to elsewhere as "everynight life."[17] Nightlife is a zone where the affective dominance of white normativity is weakened. *The freaks come out at night.* The play's set is wide and spacious, organized by walls of corrugated metal, lit with flashing pinks and blues producing a frenzied nightclub aura. Vinyl shower curtains are deployed to further segment space. The freaks that populate this club include the central protagonist, Octavio Deseo, Chicano club promoter and diva extraordinaire. He runs his nightlife emporium with the help of his ex-lover, the Salvadoran disc jockey djdj. The club's frequent performers are two black women, Plum, a black female student who leaves academia at night and enters the alternative affective register of Aztlantis, and Natasha Kinky, a black woman of transgender origin who dances at the club with Plum. The club regulars are Miss Thing 2 and 1. Thing 2 is a twenty-year-old Filipino gay man, and Thing 1 is a black Puerto Rican gay man, also twenty. The Things, who speak in rhyme and comment on all the play's proceedings, are both Greek chorus and a reference to the Things in Dr. Seuss's *Cat in the Hat*, little monsters who bring the house down. The cast is rounded off by Octavio's love interest, Samson, a thirty-year-old man of mixed Filipino and Chicano ancestry who works as a tattoo artist and a security guard at the club.

Bracho's multiethnic ensemble signals a new moment in minoritarian performance and cultural work in which the strict confines of identitarian politics are superseded by other logics of group identification. The play's cast does not cohere by identity but instead by a politics of affect, an affective belonging. All of these subjects are unable to map themselves onto a white and heterosexually normative narrative of the world. The protocols of theater, literature, and cultural production by people of color in the United States has primarily concentrated on black-white relational chains (which can best be described as colored-white configurations) or ethnic or racial separatist models. The fact that Aztlantis is populated not exclusively by Latinos but by different kinds of people of color of various genders suggests that traditional identitarian logics of group formation and social cohesion are giving way to new models of relationality and interconnectedness. We can understand the ties that bind this utopian nightlife community to be affective ones; shared vibes and structures of feeling assemble utopia in this production.

The play's multiracial and multigender composition is mirrored in the actual audience in attendance on opening night. It seems useful to cite a theater review from the *San Francisco Examiner*, an article whose first two paragraphs focus exclusively on the play's audience and thus stands as a unique document of the play's reception.

> Almost every opening night for a new play has something of the air of a party, given all the friends of the author and cast who turn out to show their support. Saturday at the Brava Theater Center, however, was more like attending a community celebration—perhaps crossed with the peak hour at a popular gay nightclub.
>
> The house was as packed as it possibly could be, short of putting chairs on the stage. The median age was decidedly lower than at most theatrical events and the racial mix considerably broader. The crowd, or a substantial portion of it, greeted the world premiere of Ricardo A. Bracho's "The Sweetest Hangover (& other stds)" as if it were a celebration of a community that rarely gets to see itself depicted in any genre.[18]

The reviewer, Robert Hurwitt, discusses the racial composition of the play, which he describes as "a dramatic treatment of the world of gay people of

color—Hispanic, Asian, African American; male, female and transsexual."
His amazement concerning the play's audience dominates the first three paragraphs of the review. He is especially intrigued by the audience's demographic
relation to the characters on stage. The performative and happening-like nature
of opening night and the play's subsequent extended run are worth considering
since that too is part of the play's intervention. In his influential study of the
Renaissance stage Stephen Orgel explicated the importance of the actual space
of the Swan Theater to the larger culture: "[The] building was the physical embodiment of both an idea of theater and an idea of the society it was created to
entertain."[19] In a similar fashion the space of the Brava Theater and its audience
work in tandem with the play's actual text, representing a certain idea within
the social, one that was first articulated in Bridge. And the literal space of a theater like Brava, a major venue that specializes in feminist, queer, and racialized
performance, is also important to consider. Brava is the literal figuration of an
ideological landscape first laid out in Bridge. The fact that this queer male world
can benefit from and manifest itself in relation to this house, partially built by
racialized feminism, is a legacy from that foundational anthology.[20]

The world of The Sweetest Hangover is a world without white people. During
the play's second act Thing 1 is feeling overwhelmed by the white people at the
nightclub. He complains of what he calls "colonial regression syndrome." He
wears a pith helmet, ascot, and other items of explorer gear and talks about
shooting a film called "Paris Is Gagging—A Study in Whiteness and Other
Forms of Madness." His stalwart yet shady companion, Thing 2, suggests he get
over whiteness by simply blinking his eyes and letting in darkness. This ritual
magically expels whiteness from the play, leaving a brown world of feeling,
organized by the affective belongings between people of color. In this way The
Sweetest Hangover mirrors and reconstructs the composition of This Bridge Called
My Back. The play offers an ensemble of racialized and ethnic characters that,
like Bridge and its contributors, try to reconceptualize the social from a vista that
is not organized around relations to whiteness or the majoritarian sphere. The
play thus offers us a profound way to think through the social that is predicated
on a break from the structuring logic of white normativity.

The play amplifies the message of Bridge by folding in both male homosexuality (and eroticism) and the demimonde of recreational drug use. In the same
way that Bridge argued for modes of female being in the world that white feminism and different modalities of patriarchy rejected, The Sweetest Hangover makes
a case for other ways of being in the world that are deemed outlaw and illicit.
Octavio and most of the other characters are recreational drug users. The pro-

duction resists the moralism that U.S. culture continually rehearses in relation to recreational drug use. In a simpler fashion the play embraces non-couple-oriented, nonmonogamous gay male sexuality—a modality of being queer that is currently being demonized and scapegoated by gay pundits from the right. The "crack" that my subtitle invoked is meant to speak to both demonized identity vectors: recreational drug users and gay men who refuse to compromise their erotic life by conforming to normative and assimilationist modes of comportment.[21] While *Bridge* does not mention the antidrug hysteria that surfaced during Ronald Reagan's so-called war on drugs or the particularities of homophobia directed at men of color, it nonetheless makes a case for antinormative and racialized ways of being in the world.[22]

The major conflict in the play between Octavio and his lover, Samson, is not Octavio's drug problem, but his refusal to conform to a drug-free monogamous ideal that Samson desires. This ideal is a modality of affective normativity. The play enacts reversal in that Samson's desire for this ideal is critiqued with the same critical eye usually reserved for individuals with a drug problem. Octavio's particular relationship to drugs and sex is not moralized against *or* celebrated. Within the logic of the play drugs simply *are*. Such modes of being in the world are folded into the rich affective archive of *latinidad*. Obviously this is not to say that all Latinos participate in the alternative economies of homosexual eroticism or recreational drug use, but to imply that these demonized acts are in part components of some Latino experiences.

Sex and drugs are not the only horizon of Latino affective reality that the play embodies. Sound is as important to the play and the story of Latino feelings as the other nightlife components discussed in this essay. Octavio's ex-lover djdj has taken a "vow of sonics," which entails his refusal to speak through any other vehicle than the records he spins. Octavio asks Samson not to take this refusal to speak to him seriously since djdj broke up with Octavio by playing a song. Djdj's voice is heard in a series of one-scene monologues throughout the play. Since he does not speak, his monologues represent nondiegetic moments in the play, moments when the character speaks directly to the audience.[23] Miss Thing 1 and Miss Thing 2 function as a Greek chorus during these soliloquies, sounding like a catchy pop melody hook chorus. In the first scene of the second act, titled "Djdj Exposes," the master of sonics exposes his affective reality by playing snatches of songs by Latin freestyle pop pioneers of the 1980s, such as Exposé, famous for their hit, "Point of No Return." This melancholic meditation provides a moment of foreshadowing that announces the character's death later in the act. At this point in the drama djdj has literally hit a point of no return.

I met a man last night, and kissing him was hearing Exposé for the first time. *taking me to the point of no return. not the words uh-oh-oh or the tempo uh-oh-oh* just that time of my life. high school keggers in Excelsior, after-parties hanging with the popular girls and all the doggish jocks *and lookout weekend cuz here I cum because weekends were made for fun.* This is the mid 80's high nrg cha-cha *and six minutes, six minutes, six-minutes doug e fresh you're on-uh-uh-on time. Yeah it's like a jungle sometimes getting wasted and I think I'm going under* this numb feeling of lubes and Michelob as I dance with Michelle to Shannon's *Let the Music Play* or is it Lisa Lisa *Lost in Emotion.* Kissing him was a party in some football player's backyard where cops would come, Eddie would start with Lisa, Anita would leave to the backseat of a car, Daisy would fall in love with someone else's boyfriend for the second time that weekend. Straight mating rituals done to *the roof the roof the roof is on fire we don't need no water let the motherfucker burn.* Kissing him in the Mission, coming back from a beer run, Stacey Q singing *We Connect* and we do. But this is Collingwood Jurassic Park. 3 am and I don't know what song is on his radio. I'm kissing him and I feel the jets in my pulse.[24]

The mention of "the jets in [his] pulse" announces the next moment in the play's soundscape, the Jets' "I Got a Crush on You." This monologue is a unique interrogation of a relational chain that connects affect to memory to sonics. Music plays a major role in Bracho's play; its job is to draft an affective schematic particular to the emotional emergence and becoming of a citizen-subject who will not feel American in the way the protocols of official affective citizenship demand. The sappiness of the pop tunes registers as affective excess to majoritarian ears but as something altogether different to the minoritarian listener who uses these songs as part of her affective archive. The sounds of popular culture and the playwright's citational practice tell a story of how the resources of popular culture are deployed to tell an affective story that is different and decidedly dissident in relation to structuring codes of U.S. national affect. Djdj's soliloquy, like the whole of the play, calls on music to conjure a past affective temporality, and that sonic past is important to the utopic reformulated and antiessentialist nationalism of the play.

Djdj's plot line is central to the play's narrative. His death due to AIDS-related complications breaks up the affective community that held the utopic world of the play together. Plum has gone off to law school; Nat, after traveling to Thailand for hormonal injections, has found a man; Samson has fled the urban space, running from a fear of AIDS and urban violence; Octavio goes out in the world of "everynightlife"; Miss Thing 1 and Miss Thing 2 remain as the ruling queens of the bar stool. In the play's final scene the rhyming queens sit at the Endup, an actual gay bar in San Francisco, Thing 1 wearing opera glasses and carrying a butterfly net. These instruments of white gentility are to be deployed for the project of installing a man in his life. The dialogue indicates that even though the world of Aztlantis has crumbled, the affective possibilities it represented are far from diffused. Thing 1 undergoes a brief crisis of consciousness on his bar stool throne, which his co-Thing talks him through.

> Thing 1: Ain't no Aztlantis to go to, no djdj (crosses himself) to sweat to. Ain't no Samson to swoon over, Octavio to gag on. Last I bumped in the girls, Nat had herself a man and Plum was 'bout ready to start law school. What's there for us?
>
> Thing 2: These seats. A new bar. Same old fashions, same old tired faces and tracks. Why, you looking for something else?
>
> Thing 1: I need more, more than kiking with the children, making a world dark and glamorous and giving off vapors to the white girl. Something for us, instead of waiting in line to be put on their lists.
>
> Thing 2: And you got it. Cute fashions, friends in low places that are keeping you high. Major props.
>
> Thing 1: We might have it by the d.j. booth or here in welfare alley at the Endup but turn to the corner and bam! you are punk ass shit. Nothing.
>
> Thing 2: Naw I beg to differ. Being punk ass shit is not nothing. Being a punk is power.
>
> Thing 1: According to whom? Not the fellas on my corner, definitely not my folks. Power don't come in bumps or pumps, girl.
>
> Thing 2: The power of being a punk in the world comes from knowing it's your world and the rest of these sad motherfuckers live in it and to get to your groove. Boypussy Power!
>
> Thing 1: Yeah but how can you hear your beat with the other wall of sound, white noise. . . .
>
> Thing 2: Change the channel and stop listening to college grunge radio.

By advocating for "Boypussy Power!" Miss Thing 2 is riffing on the lessons and important manifestos of biopower made by radical feminists of color. In that instance a line is being drawn between the feminist field of struggle and the struggles that gay men of color face. The work of these radical women of color is instructive and enabling, both for these two characters in the play and for the playwright himself. The most important advice Thing 2 gives Thing 1 is the declaration that being a punk is power once one understands that the world and the groove belong to the punks. Thing 1 worries about the sound of white noise, and Thing 2 makes it clear that he must learn how to tune out such sounds. The sound of white noise is the official national affect, the beat of a majoritarian drum that defies a minoritarian sense of rhythm. Thing 2 (and the playwright) instructs Thing 1 and the audience to believe in one's own affective groove, one's own way of being, dancing, striving, dreaming, loving, fighting, and moving in the world and never to let the affective hum of white normativity overwhelm that very important groove.

This analysis has posited ethnicity as a structure of feeling, as a way of being in the world, a path that does not conform to the conventions of a majoritarian public sphere and the national affect it sponsors. It is my hope that thinking of *latinidad* in this way will help us better analyze the obstacles that must be negotiated within the social for the minoritarian citizen-subject. I have positioned Bracho's work as a continuation of another project begun almost twenty years ago by fierce women of color who also found their way of being in the world labeled wrong, inappropriate, and insane. Many of the contributors to that volume wrote about the way the dominant culture made them feel crazy and wrongminded. Part of *Bridge*'s project was to show that this craziness was a powerful way of being in the world, a mode of being that those in power needed to call crazy because it challenged the very tenets of their existence. Bracho's *The Sweetest Hangover* continues that project, allowing us to continue to dream of other planets and finally to make worlds.

NOTES

I am grateful to David Román for keen and intelligent editorial advice. Conversations with Ricardo Bracho about his work and the world it makes have been useful for the completion of this essay and a source of pleasure and inspiration.

1. See N. Alarcón, "Conjugating Subjects in the Age of Multiculturalism."

2. Williams warns us that it is important to "on the one hand acknowledge (and welcome) the specificity of these elements—specific dealings, specific rhythms—and yet to find their specific kinds of sociality, thus preventing the extraction from social experience which is conceivable only when social experience itself has been reduced." Thus the trick here is to identify specific "dealings" and "rhythms" that might not be recognizable or identifiable in relation to already available grids of classification, while, on the other hand, understanding these specific feelings as part of a larger social matrix and historically situated. See Williams, *Marxism and Literature*, 133.

3. N. Alarcón, "Conjugating Subjects in the Age of Multiculturalism," 136.

4. While this essay is meant to be self-contained and stand on its own, it is also a prolegomenon of sorts to a book-length project on Latino as a structure of feeling, a way of "feeling brown" in the world. That book tentatively shares the same title as this essay.

5. Joseph, *Nomadic Identities*, 14.

6. Foucault discusses truth games (*les jeux de vérité*) throughout his oeuvre. In one particularly useful interview he describes truth games and their relation to the self: "I have tried to find out how the human subject fits into certain games of truth, whether they were to take the form of a science or refer to scientific models, or truth games such as those one may encounter in institutions or practices of control" ("The Ethics of the Concern of the Self as a Practice of Freedom," 281).

7. For more on Latino exoticism, see Aparicio and Chávez-Silverman, *Tropicalizations*.

8. See my book *Disidentifications*, for more on the cultural politics of disidentifications.

9. Sartre, *Sketch for a Theory of Emotions*, 93.

10. Ibid., 93.

11. Hansen, "Benjamin and Cinema," 325. Also see Flatley, *Affective Mapping*.

12. Román, "Latino Performance and Identity," 152.

13. For other crucial interventions that measure the political force of Latino performance, see Sandoval-Sánchez, *José*; Arrizón, *Latina Performance*; Huerta, *Chicano Theatre*.

14. See Fornes, *Plays*.

15. Moraga, "Refugees of a World on Fire," n.p.

16. Moraga, *The Last Generation*, 33.

17. See my coauthored introduction to Delgado and Muñoz, *Everynight Life*.

18. Robert Hurwitt, "Celebrating 'Hangover,'" *San Francisco Examiner*, 14 April 1997.

19. Orgel, *The Illusion of Power*.

20. Here I mean *house* to describe the actual theater and the conceptual and ideological house built by radical women of color.

21. While gay culture generally moves to an assimilationist center, focusing on such debates as gays in the military and gay marriage, Bracho's work and the work of a generation of radical gay men of color insist on resisting the terms of this national debate and instead investing in radicalized and unapologetic forms and practices of gay male difference.

22. The "war on drugs" was understood in certain activist circles as the "war on the poor."

23. I borrow the term *nondiegetic* from the language of cinema studies. Nondiegetic action is part of the actual film text but not part of the plot or narrative.

24. All quotes from *The Sweetest Hangover* are from the unpublished play. My thanks to Ricardo Bracho for granting me permission to quote from his work.

Never Too Much: Queer Performance
between Impossibility and Excess

Ricardo L. Ortiz

José Muñoz's essay "Feeling Brown: Ethnicity and Affect in Ricardo Bracho's *The Sweetest Hangover (and Other STDs)*" describes its own critical project as the configuration and deployment of an "apparatus that permits us to read ethnicity as a historical formation uncircumscribed by the boundaries of conventional understandings of identity," understandings that, Muñoz argues, opt for rational forms of coherence over nonrational, emotion-based forms of affective orientation; these latter forms nevertheless enable "various historically coherent groups [to] feel differently and [to] navigate the material world on a different emotional register." This project has particular value for the intersectional critical engagement of queer and Latino/a cultural expression precisely in its insistence on reading, and situating, both queerness and *latinidad* so explicitly outside the "boundaries of conventional understandings of identity" that they no longer index identity as such, but something closer to the more complex, and internally heterogeneous, construction of what Norma Alarcón (Muñoz tells us) has famously called both "identity-in-difference" and "identity-in-process."

Of the two terms that concern Muñoz in "Feeling Brown," the one that commands the greater part of his attention is *latinidad*, whose "theoretical incoherence" and "failure to actualize embodied politics" the essay opens by lamenting; as Muñoz explains, "*Latino* does not subscribe to a common racial, class, gender, religious or national category, and if a Latino can be from any country in Latin America, a member of any race, religion, class, or gender or sex orientation, who then is she? What, if any, nodes of commonality do Latinas and Latinos share? How is it possible to know *latinidad*?" This last question, introducing as it does the epistemological dimension of the larger critical task occupying Muñoz here, in turn prepares the way for a set of corollary questions, one ontological (given the success of what Muñoz calls the "historically specific and culturally situated bias [in white-majoritarian U.S. culture] that blocks the trajectory of the Latina or Latino citizen-subject to official citizenship-subject political [being]") and the other phenomenological (leading, surprisingly, to

Sartre, from whose *Sketch for a Theory of Emotion* [1939] Muñoz impressively massages a construction of emotion as "an extension . . . [indeed] a performed manifestation of consciousness"). While it is difficult, and not altogether necessary, to separate these dimensions in the practical, rhetorical operations of Muñoz's argument, it is also clear that (as with his greater focus on *latinidad* over queerness), Muñoz here favors the phenomenological approach, as he fashions across the various stages of his essay a theory of affective performance that will allow his readers (and audiences of queer of color performance) to read better precisely how the kind of performance (and performance studies) work that interests him (and us) "theatricalizes a certain mode of 'feeling brown' in a world painted white."

The ambitious engagement that Muñoz manages of so many of the complex and multiple vectors of this brown phenomenology of affect speak directly to the author's formidable resources, certainly as theorist, but just as emphatically as scholar and critic. Indeed one of the key enabling paradoxes of "Feeling Brown" as a simultaneous act of theoretical argumentation and critical, hermeneutical application is precisely the force of its paralogical persuasiveness as it guides readers through its argumentative stages, and the rigor of its strategic and practical, rhetorical paces.

To say that Muñoz in this essay pays greater attention to a "brown" *latinidad* over queerness is not, however, to suggest that he neglects the latter in favor of the former, or that he privileges the latter to the disadvantage of the former; indeed as his queerly brown reading of Ricardo Bracho's *Sweetest Hangover* makes clear, these two categories of what he might call affective registers of collectivity and belonging are conceptually inextricable from one another, unthinkable (given their intimate, constitutive reciprocity) in isolation from one another. In addition queerness and Latina/o brownness bear in Muñoz's thinking congruent, if not equivalent, structural value and force in larger sociosemiotic economies. Affective excess, whether apparently queer or brown, marks both queer *and* brown as excessive refusals of prevailing strictures of normative economies, which are in turn often simultaneously marked as straight and white.

This emphasis on economies of a liberating (brown, queer) abundance over a restricting (white, straight) scarcity (Muñoz at one point calls the affective economy that is "whiteness . . . flat and impoverished," hence bearing the negative value of "lack") also directly corresponds to Muñoz's equally characteristic preference for an open hermeneutical methodology of hope and generosity over one driven by an antispirit of suspicion and refusal. Hence the interested reader should pay generous attention to his equally generous engagement of Bracho's piece. Muñoz's essay, which first appeared in *Theatre Journal* in 2000, is always already engaged in an active, productive relation to a past here marked by the production of *Sweetest Hangover* in 1997, a past that "Feeling Brown" then reanimates to do some valuable, forward-looking work; that the present collection gives "Feeling Brown" itself an afterlife that extends and exceeds that initial appearance, and in turn extends into some indeterminate, open future an active engagement of the performance in 1997, only underscores how potently queer times, and queer knowledges, can operate, and renew themselves, into any variety of possible (queer) futures. Consider, for example, after the careful analytical elaboration which prepares the reader for his introduction of *Sweetest Hangover*, how Muñoz situates it not only in the nurturing intertextual environment of critical and creative work by the radical feminist-of-color editors of *This Bridge Called My Back* (1983) and of Cherríe Moraga's utopian lyric "Dreaming of Other Planets," but even of a contemporary *San Francisco Examiner* review (what Muñoz tells us is "a unique document of the play's reception") to allow any reader, more than a decade after the time of the production in question, to appreciate as fully as possible "the performative and happening-like nature of opening night and the play's subsequent extended run."

This critical, hermeneutical generosity is just as evident in Muñoz's treatment of the more internal properties of Bracho's text and of the production it inspired. Muñoz's reading does authentic justice to the complexity and ingenuity of the play, from the careful delineation of the dramatis personae to the observant perceptions of the play's inspired invocations of, on the one hand, canonical theater history (the Misses Things, we learn, "who speak in rhyme and comment on all the play's proceedings, are both Greek chorus") and, on the other, pop cultural ephemera (they are also "a reference to the Things in Dr. Seuss's *Cat in the Hat*, little monsters who bring the house down"). Muñoz's perhaps more conventionally scholarly erudition concerning the widest range of cultural, citational referentiality in the play certainly extends beyond the borders of what conventionally passes as scholarly knowledge, however, to differently worldly but just as critical, and valuable, forms of worldly knowingness. This latter orientation toward the world (traversing less than official "vernacular orbits" of expression and experience) in turn allows him to more thickly describe the life-world invoked by *Sweetest Hangover*'s setting in an imagined San Francisco nightclub called Aztlantis; the name, Muñoz observes, "signifies both the lost Chicano homeland and the lost city of myth," and in doing so "calls us to think about the project of imagining a utopian time and place." At the same time, as Muñoz signals in the punning use of crack in the title of the piece's second section, Aztlantis the club offers its patrons and frequenters a space of opportunity for the exploration of what he calls "antinormative subcultural formations, such as the alternate economies of recreational drug use and homosexual desire." His observation about Bracho's representation of these "antinormative subcultural forms" leads him later in the discussion to stress their liberatory function; he reads in these representations the play's attempt to make "a case for other ways of being in the world that are deemed outlaw and illicit" primarily for being antinormative and excessive. "Within the logic of the play," Muñoz goes on to conclude, "drugs [and nonmonogamous gay sex] simply are," and as congruent forms of antinormative "modes of being in the world are [in turn] folded into the [play's, and the world's] rich affective archive of latinidad."

That archive is certainly richly inventoried in Muñoz's further descriptions of Sweetest Hangover's most salient properties and most forceful effects. If, as the Examiner review noted, the audience gathered to view the play in 1997 "greeted [it] . . . as if it were a celebration of a community that rarely gets to see itself depicted in any genre," then Muñoz's subsequent commemoration of the play extends that celebration into the indefinite and always hyperpotentialized, hyperpromissory temporality of the after-party. If, for example, Aztlantis is populated with a roster of characters embodying the full variety of shades of queer brownness—from Octavio Deseo, the "Chicano club promoter and diva extraordinaire," to "the Salvadoran disc jockey djdj"; the club's performers, both "black women, Plum, . . . and Natasha Kinky" (the last of "transgender origin"); the aforementioned "Things," one a "Filipino gay man," the other a "black Puerto Rican gay man"; and "Samson, . . . of mixed Filipino and Chicano ancestry"—then it is also home to as rich and varied an inventory of queer brown affective cultural markers. In a passage as brief as the one Muñoz quotes of djdj's "nondiegetic" soliloquy to the audience when the character hits a dramatic "point of no return," we learn of the play's equally wide-ranging and hospitable inclusion of pop-cultural reference points (of rather considerable return): djdj choreographs his emotional dissolution to a playlist as varied as the play's list of characters, from the Miami Cuban Latin girl group Exposé, to African American Shannon's early 1980s Madonna sound-alike track "Let the Music Play," to Nuyorican Lisa Lisa's "Lost in Emotion," to the Pacific Islander American Jets' hit, "Crush on You." The resonant riot of artist names and track titles is at once evocative of the playwright's fertile sowing of cultural memory and as fertile cultural reimagination, but it also speaks to the attentive ear of a critic who has (to quote George Lipsitz) learned (strategically, productively) to listen. Aztlantis, as a hybrid citational reference that stretches back centuries to two incongruous points of cultural and discursive origin, lives on in the echoing conversation between Bracho the playwright and Muñoz the critic, to sing new songs, and make new noise, for readers of the current collection, who can now witness anew how, in Muñoz's words and in Muñoz's hands, expressive work like Bracho's "calls on music to conjure a past affective temporality, . . . [a] sonic past [that] is important to the utopic reformulated and antiessentialist nationalism of the play."

It is one of the more oddly symptomatic features of Muñoz's essay that he never makes mention of the pop-cultural reference in the play's title to Diana Ross's breathy, ecstatic post-Supremes, disco-era hit, "The Sweetest Hangover," which explicitly compares the aftermath to orgasmic overwhelm to a paradoxically pleasurable physical (hence affective) dis-ease of which the singer refuses to be cured. Hearing Miss Ross's Donna Summery expulsions of spent breath punctuate, for example, Miss Thing 2's eloquent expletive concluding her closing dialogue with Thing 1 ("The power of being a punk in the world comes from knowing it's your world and the rest of these sad motherfuckers live in it and to get to your groove. Boypussy Power!") would certainly only underscore Muñoz's own conclusion that this declaration "riff[s directly] on the lessons and important manifestos of biopower made by radical feminists of color," providing a strategic, and felt, frame of reference for the "gay men of color" attentive enough to dance, and act, to their beat.

Future readers of Muñoz's essay should certainly take away from their encounter with it here a clear sense of how "Feeling Brown" also signals historically Muñoz's own evolving intellectual project; appearing as it does a year after *Disidentifications*, the critic's first and profoundly influential study of "queers of color and the performance of politics," the essay anticipates subsequent work by Muñoz on the paired questions of affective excess and the utopian impulse in minoritarian queer and ethnic cultural and intellectual work. In closing these remarks, however, the present writer also urges future readers to attend as well to Muñoz's explicit appreciation of what he calls the "antiessentialist nationalism" of the utopian political vision that Bracho spins in his imagined Aztlantis. Muñoz's queerly committed poststructural critical ethic perhaps most importantly refuses the too easy and fatally conventional dissociation of discursive practices from the things and worlds they render visible, knowable, and always alternatively imaginable; the (im)possible utopia that Bracho imagines as the Aztlantis in his *Sweetest Hangover*, and that Muñoz embraces and celebrates in

"Feeling Brown," even in its being merely imagined (however often performed), is a future, longed-for homeland that promises (to anyone else willing to consider its possibility) a worthy model, and certainly one among very many, of a queer, brown utopia that, in being always only ever to come, remains openly (and hospitably) not only queer, or brown, but also just, and free.

Shifting the Site of Queer Enunciation:
Manuel Muñoz and the Politics of Form

Ernesto Javier Martínez

The urgency for lesbianas Latinas to speak is undeniable. From Carla Trujillo's challenge to Chicana lesbians to "fight for our own voices as women" to Emma Pérez's declaration that "marginalized groups must have separate spaces to inaugurate their own discourses, *nuestra lengua en nuestro sitio*," the call to create our language, to name ourselves, becomes a critical task of survival.

—Yolanda Chávez Leyva, "Listening to the Silences"

I have come to believe over and over again that what is most important to me must be spoken, made verbal and shared, even at the risk of it being bruised or misunderstood. [I have come to believe] that the speaking profits me, beyond any other effect.

—Audre Lorde, "The Transformation of Silence"

To familiarize oneself with the literary production of queer writers of color is, arguably, to witness the importance of crafting a subjective, politicized voice for the abject desiring body. One need only peruse the work of writers as diverse as Audre Lorde and Gloria Anzaldúa, Ricardo Bracho and Essex Hemphill, among others, to see firsthand how resistance and enfranchisement have often been nurtured through narratives where identity and politics are written about *from* the perspective of queers of color. While the importance of this history and practice cannot be overstated, critics of queer ethnic literary production would be remiss if they did not attend to divergences from this tradition, divergences which might not only yield social insights complementary to those produced by first-person narratives, but would also highlight how such insights come to be generated so astutely and provocatively, not only through narrative content, but through narrative form. When and how do queer writers of color differ from this first-person tradition of narration, and what conceptual and critical consequences arise from such departures?[1] If, as the historian Yolanda Chávez Leyva has noted, the urgency to speak is "undeniable," why has such speaking and its "profits" (to borrow language from Audre Lorde) been revisited in some queer ethnic literary production?[2]

I offer some preliminary answers to these questions by turning to the groundbreaking work of the queer Chicano writer Manuel Muñoz and arguing that his debut collection of short stories, Zigzagger, develops a provocative, multifocal narrative approach to queer experience and identity. This approach, which I call *shifting the site of queer enunciation*, astutely decenters queer speaking subjects, doing so in a manner that not only equitably distributes narrative responsibility for queer experience and identity, but that also enables a deeper understanding of the intersubjective and social contexts in which queer subjects come into being. By shifting the anticipated "location" and articulation of queerness—moving it from the queer subject proper to the queer subject's siblings, friends, parents, and neighbors—Muñoz transfers some of the burden of queer representation. More important, he exposes the web of relationships and discourses that constitute queer experience and queer identity in any given context. Such a narrative approach, precisely because it provides what the philosopher María Lugones would term a "peopled sense" of queer experience, produces a fundamental break with logics of domination that refuse marginalized subjects their "social girth," that is, their relationship to various people, places, histories, and socialities.

Shifting the site of queer enunciation, as a narrative practice, provides an opportunity to foreground the following set of observations: (1) that queer experiences are actually *coproduced and shared* by larger collectives, even though these larger collectives often deny their own implicatedness in queer sociality; (2) that in fact it takes studied work to deny such implication, and that such a denial leads to a kind of existential distance that is thoroughly produced rather than natural; (3) that some nonqueer people actually work to resist the logic of social fragmentation mandated by homophobic societies, and that they do so, at times, by bearing "faithful witness" to acts of queer social resistance—even when it is dangerous to do so and even when such acts place them in opposition to homophobic "common sense"; and (4) that queer people define themselves in relation to some of the same webs of cultural meaning that heterosexuals around them draw from, and that, in this sense, queers are engaged participants in the dialogic production of cultural meanings and therefore fundamentally part of the collective experience and imaginary.

Before discussing Muñoz's writing, it is important to briefly acknowledge that narrating queer stories from perspectives other than those of queer subjects can have profound sociopolitical implications. This is particularly so given a political climate in which subaltern resistance is continuously misrepresented through the lens of "individual," "rational" modern agency.[3] María Lugones argues that such a conception of agency is, in reality, a fiction that tends to impede rather than to enable oppressed peoples. She reminds us that the notion of effective individual agency actively hides the institutional setting and backing of commonly understood "individual" potency. It entices people with the apparent power and efficacy of their own individual deliberations and decisions, even as the oppressed have the everyday experiences to understand that their acts of resistance cannot successfully intervene socially unless they are backed up by others.[4] While Lugones acknowledges that it often feels as though agency arises from us alone, she argues that such a feeling actively thwarts a more complex understanding of how one's own intentions arise in social contexts and among people, and that our intentions respond to a nexus of "intentionalities" that are given "up-take" or are diverted and morphed by other constellations of intentions and the institutional backings that support them. With this complex vision of intentionality Lugones argues that the oppressed actualize an "active subjectivity," a mode of responding to oppression that is not the modern conception of agency at all. This is so primarily because "active subjectivity" is a practice that is lacking not only institutional backup but also such institutional backup in a self-aware manner. "Active subjectivity," according to Lugones, is a type of subjectivity that replaces the illusion of individual agency with a horizontal attentiveness to how intentions travel from person to person. "Active subjectivity" in this sense remains attentive and invested in the possibility of actualizing social change, even as it reveals the deeply contextual and attenuated nature of social action and meaning making.[5] From such a complex understanding of active subjectivity and intentionality, the writing of Manuel Muñoz gains importance for its innovative narrative approach. By providing rich descriptions of what it feels like to bear witness to queerness in a complex social context—explicitly elaborating on queer experience as taking shape in contexts of great interaction, ideological influence, and competing intentionality—Muñoz makes explicit and further expands upon the notion of queerness as social, coproduced, and shared.

MANUEL MUÑOZ'S HETERODIEGETIC INTERVENTIONS

Manuel Muñoz's collection of short stories is impressive in regard to the scope and emotional integrity with which it depicts formative experiences in the sociality of queerness. Muñoz's attentiveness to small-town community life—

and the social consequences of that life for how sexuality and intimacy will be played out by those who constitute the community—holds a special place in Chicano letters. Like its literary predecessors (from Rolando Hinojosa's *Estampas del Valle* and Tomas Rivera's *Y no se lo tragó la tierra* to Arturo Islas's *The Rain God* and Ito Romo's *The Bridge*), *Zigzagger* addresses intimate relationships, communal history, and vernacular knowledge. However, quite unlike most of its predecessors, Muñoz's stories are some of the first to make queer experience a tangible, albeit attenuated, presence in the midst of small-town Chicano community life.

I examine three short stories from this collection, stories that convey a sense of queer experience as social and shared precisely because they narrate it from a perspective other than that of the queer subject proper. In the short story "Good as Yesterday," for example, a sister's perspective provides an intimate account of living and learning alongside a queer younger brother. In "The Unimportant Lila Parr" a rural Mexican American community reflects on the murder of a young gay man in their town. In the title story, "Zigzagger," a young man's sexual awakening is narrated in its complex sociality through his parents, who witness its aftermath, and through the son himself, who is fundamentally changed by the experience.

Among the claims I make in this essay, I emphasize that there is an important *heterodiegetic* approach that undergirds these three stories. I claim that crucial information is conveyed about the sociality of queerness when queer experience is narrated, not directly from a character within the story's action (a *homodiegetic* approach), but from a narrative voice outside of the experienced events.[6] Through an omniscient style of narration, for example, these heterodiegetic narratives provide readers a sense of the diversity of people experiencing queerness, giving us access to the many ways queerness is being conceptualized by people situated differently in relation to it.[7] Muñoz's narratives, however, do not strictly speaking convey a plurality of perspectives in any given story, and in fact they often rely on a specific focaliser to consider queerness from a particular perspective (solely from a sister's or solely from a mother's point of view, for example). Still, by writing in a heterodiegetic mode—from a narrative voice outside of the experienced events—Muñoz conveys a subtle but crucial insight about the often *muted sociality* of queerness. His narrative approach, in other words, makes visible the shared quality of queer experience, even if those people sharing in it are not cognizant of it or are not compelled to narrate a story about it. Though focalization helps narratives like those of Muñoz convey an intimate sense of the interiority of characters (e.g., of what they are thinking and feeling), such an interiority is still not at the self-consciously discursive level implied by homodiegetic narratives, where characters have something to say in an explicit way about what they are experiencing.[8]

The three narratives I examine all work within this heterodiegetic logic; however, each is further distinguished by the degree of narrative proximity it employs toward queer ethnic subjects and the insights on muted agency and queer experience that such proximity can convey. In the short story "Good as Yesterday," Vero's intimate perspective on her relationship with her queer younger brother conveys an up-close and embodied understanding of queerness, particularly as it unfolds within the psychological and geographic context of a small Mexican American town in central California. Focalized explicitly through Vero's perspective, the story describes with great detail the emotions and tensions that arise for her in bearing witness to Nicky's struggles as a young gay man. For example, when Nicky is brutally assaulted by neighborhood boys his own age on his sixteenth birthday, Vero is irrevocably affected by it; the incident forms in her mind the moment at which she is compelled (however imperfectly and ambivalently) to love and support Nicky in his complicated sociality:

> She has always wanted to tell him that she loves him because of how he came home on his sixteenth birthday. He had come home running. He had come home bleeding. In one of the alleys in their neighborhood, six boys had dragged and beaten him. All six of them had taken turns, boys he went to school with, boys from another neighborhood, boys he grew up with, boys he had secretly fooled with on back porches. Gaudio, Peter, Alex, Fidel, Israel, and Andy.[9]

Vero's desire to communicate to Nicky that he is loved, as we see in this passage, is a desire to mitigate the emotional, physical, and symbolic damage caused by the violence he is subjected to on his birthday. As we later come to understand, this assault forever changes Nicky; this is so precisely because such an incident represents more than an isolated confrontation. The assault affects Nicky so profoundly because it is carried out communally, by people with whom he has shared intimacies, and because the violence functions for these other boys as their own right of passage, as a symbolic affirmation of their nonabject place within the collective heteronormative order.

Unfortunately Vero's intention to communicate with Nicky that he is loved (in light of such communal and intimate violence) is severely constrained by a peculiar form of speechlessness. That Vero has always "wanted to tell him" that she loves him but never actually has is a significant feature of the type of social stigma they are both facing, *together*, due to Nicky's gender-nonconforming behavior. Although Vero finds it difficult to verbalize what is happening to them—precisely because what is happening (to Nicky and Vero) is something that homophobic communities work hard at erasing from the social—such a difficulty communicating verbally does not trump the cognitive and emotional alignment being established by Vero in regard to her brother. She may not be able to communicate with him all that she knows of his victimization on his birthday, but she has assimilated enough information about the insidiousness of such violence to see herself in the capacity of bearing faithful witness for him.

One dimension of Nicky's victimization that perhaps does not get fully assimilated by Vero is the *sexualized* nature of the violence. There is in fact an undeniable sexual history to Nicky's victimization, being that some of the boys that assault him are also boys he had "fooled with on back porches"—a sexual dimension that once taken into account helps readers to recontextualize the *kind* of physical violence that arises in response to illicit sexual desire. For example, the sentence structure employed in describing such violence makes evident the repetitive abuse to which Nicky is subjected. The two abrupt sentences close to the beginning of the passage—declarative sentences ending in gerunds and contained between longer sentences—narratively produce a contrast (both visual and audible) suggestive of the intimate spatiality and activity of the physical assault. Revisiting such a sentence structure with the knowledge that at least some of the violence is motivated by wanting to *disavow* homosexuality in themselves and *avow* it in Nicky brings forth a sexualized dimension to what might be meant by "all six of them had taken turns."

To read this violence as *sexualized* violence is not to argue that the assault on Nicky is in fact a rape, but more accurately to resist the tendency to desexualize homophobic violence. With this in mind it is important to understand Vero as someone who is assimilating many more things than she is able to fully process or articulate. Although Vero's growing understanding that Nicky needs to be protected (i.e., that what is happening to him must be resisted as opposed to perpetuated) cannot be communicated verbally or directly, it remains a compelling accomplishment given that homophobic violence between men is frequently erased and desexualized as a cultural phenomenon, or, if not erased and desexualized, it is often justified as a necessary right of passage.

Tied to Vero's complex alignment with Nicky is an understanding of the added hostility to which he is subjected precisely because of the lack of publicity he can bring to the specific form of violence he experiences. Closeted with his family about his homosexuality, Nicky is constrained in his ability to make his family respond to his *actual* lived experience. They can respond to the violence inflicted on his body, but they are unable to understand the full import of the homophobic violence to which he has been subjected. Instead they can respond only given their superimposed understandings of who they assume him to be and what relationship they assume he has with other men, with women, and with the world as they know it. This added burden of isolation, which Nicky must deal with on a very personal, emotional level, does not escape Vero's attention. In fact Vero is particularly aware of their mother's absence in this respect. Because the mother cannot attribute queerness to her son, she is unable to understand the violence in its specificity. The failure to read queer identity and experience results in the mother's circumscribed effectiveness in responding to the actual situation in front of her. Given this understanding, Vero's response to Nicky takes on a maternal approach, an approach that reflects not only her own growing sense that she is *responsible for* Nicky as a sister, but that she is responsible for him in the absence of their mother's help:

> And when their mother had tried to calm him down, saying, "Who did this to you? Why did they do this to you? Why?" Vero had known that their mother did not know anything about Nicky and how the cuts and deep bruises spelled out who he really was. . . . Vero had tried to clean him up. She had wanted to tell him that it was okay and that she loved him, but he had his head bent down and cried the way the mothers and grandmothers did at funerals. He had his head down and she had felt like their mother, looking at his beautiful black hair, the cuts on his ears, the scratches on his neck. She wondered why on earth he believed he could act like this with the boys at the high school and not expect this outcome. . . . "Nicky," she had said, but that was all she said.[10]

Their mother's inability to *read* how the cuts and bruises "spelled out who he really was" further emphasizes Vero's attentiveness as a complex (albeit imperfect) act of critical social literacy. She is learning to "read"—in an embodied, culturally specific way—the circumstances affecting Nicky, not only as they pertain to him and his gender-nonconforming behavior, but also as they pertain to the network of cultural expectations to which they are both subject. Vero is in the process of acquiring this skill of reading deeply into the social, but that process is constrained by the very embodied and culturally specific forms of knowing to which she has access. In other words, Vero tries to support her younger brother—assessing correctly that her mother is not sufficiently informed or prepared to provide him with support—and finds recourse in adopting a maternal stance. Unfortunately this maternal stance does not solve, in any easy way, Vero's own doubts about Nicky's behavior, her own doubts that, in some way or another, Nicky is at fault for the violence that is visited upon him.

Vero's attentiveness to her brother is an imperfect attentiveness, perhaps most obviously because, as a member of a community permeated by homophobia, she can receive no social support for the particular disposition she is exhibiting toward her brother. In fact there is no ready-made community of meaning prepared to support her exploration and understanding of what, in all of its complexity, she and her brother are experiencing, separately and together. I say *separately and together* to emphasize that there is a difference in being the person whose body is visited upon by social failure, with psychological and physical violence, and being the one who shares in that experience through, for example, empathy. This difference, however, does not have to be in opposition to the idea of such an experience being shared. Vero comes to understand, at least in part, Nicky's experiences of isolation. She does not know these experiences in their totality, but she knows enough to feel implicated in that produced isolation and knows enough to work against that communal production, even if she finds his effeminate behavior objectionable, and even if she finds herself at a loss for words with which to tell him that he is loved.

The imperfect quality of Vero's attempts at bearing witness to Nicky's pain is crucial to what I am arguing about the effectiveness, not only of this story's thematic focus, but also of its narrative approach. By focalizing the narrative from the perspective of Vero, we are able to see the real difficulty of bearing "faithful witness" to queerness *as* social.[11] It is clear, for example, that Vero and Nicky are constantly being reminded by others that in a homophobic society queerness should not have a social and shared presence; it must always remain demeaned and isolated, stripped of its relational possibilities. Vero's friends, for instance, warn her often of her little brother's gender nonconformity: "*Tell your little brother to stop acting like that. Tell him to stop looking at the guys like that. They don't think it's funny.*"[12] This warning coheres with the logic of social fragmentation that needs to police the boundaries of gender difference in order to continue the "purity" and "naturalness" of the gender dichotomy. By suggesting that Nicky stop acting "like that," Vero's friends are enforcing an understanding of queerness as not having a proper social space, as not even having a proper discursive presence because they won't even speak its name. Of course by having to address "it" as an issue, they are implicitly admitting to "its" existence, but by their tenacity in reminding Vero over and over again that she needs to "mind her brother," these women reaffirm their status as cultural carriers responsible for the status quo; queerness will have no sociality precisely because they will it so and precisely because their will is backed up by a larger ideological and structural framework. The physical assault Nicky is subject to, then, is merely another actualization of this logic of gender purity. Likewise the logic behind the verbal warnings and the physical attack are further buttressed, albeit unintentionally, by the mother's own ignorance of her son's queerness; the mother's silence in this respect produces yet another assurance that queerness cannot have a sociality, for surely, if your own people cannot give you social backup, who can?

Even though Vero is aware of the obstacles that her brother faces, and even though she sometimes succumbs to their professed logic,[13] she consistently tries to back him up. The important part of Vero's complicity with Nicky, the importance of her collaboration with his queerness, is that she often refrains from conveying her culturally ingrained reactions to his overt femininity. And it is through this process of ignoring her misgivings (about his gender nonconformity, about his choice in men, about his choice in friends) that Vero aligns herself with him and his difficult coming-of-age decisions, a tenuous alignment demanding a great deal of intersubjectivity, of worked-at connectedness.

To a certain extent Vero's actions seem selfless in the traditional sense of the word: more preoccupied with the other, willing to sacrifice her needs for others. I resist using the term here, however, for its inaccuracy in reflecting the real sense of self that Vero maintains as she aligns herself with her brother. The narrative in fact suggests that she can collaborate with Nicky only to the extent that she remains present with her sense of self as she extends and aligns herself with her brother. To be sure the narrative encourages us to understand Vero as always having been the type of person to look after her brother. However, the narrative also highlights the emotional and intellectual labor involved in being a faithful witness. In other words the narrative goes to great lengths to suggest that this is both a predisposition of Vero's and that such a witnessing is a great deal of work.

One of the most concrete examples of Vero's worked-at commitment to Nicky has to do with the fact that Nicky actually falls in love with a young man with whom Vero was once sexually intimate, and that these two young men begin a sexual relationship. This unanticipated relationship becomes a source of pain and discomfort for Vero.[14] To say that she overcomes emotions of betrayal and anger is not completely true, for it is clear that she must repeatedly talk herself out of her feelings of jealousy, talk herself out of emotional responses that would leave Nicky further isolated, responses that would not take into account how differently situated they are in relation to the organization of their community.[15] When Nicky's lover, Julián, is jailed for unpaid speeding tickets, Vero is the one who, unbeknown to her parents, secretly drives Nicky for visitation on weekends. There she is often upset by Nicky's overt effeminacies, but is also restrained in how and when she brings this to his attention. Her awareness of his lack of options forces her to remind him only in the most pressured of circumstances. One of these circumstances occurs when they are waiting in line to enter the detention center with the other female visitors:

> Vero walks forward. The voices of her friends keep chiding her. *You do too much for that brother of yours, Vero. Let him be his own.* She stands and waits with him. Her feet hurt. She has a job at the auto parts store in downtown, a family-owned business losing out to the new strip mall, a job where she stands all day at a counter. She is twenty and unmarried in a place where most have either left or married by that age and she knows so many of the men in town from the store. . . . They buy spark plugs and fan belts, handing them over to her with hands just as smooth and young as hers, the wedding bands glimmering. She could have it worse, she knows. She could lose the job if the strip mall takes away too much business. She would have to move to another town for work, she knows, and then what? How long can the Impala run without her father fixing it as he used to? What would happen to her little brother if she were not around?[16]

The experience of waiting in line to enter the detention center serves Vero as a physical and emotional reminder of her own needs, desires, and anxieties. Standing in line with Nicky, *for* Nicky, she is reminded of working all day on her feet. This causes her anxiety, not solely because she is physically tired, but also because she is reminded of her situation as a single woman working in an auto parts store, in contact with married men whom she is often attracted to. This is an important moment in the story because it shows that the moment of reaching out to her brother is also a moment of thinking more critically about her own life. Their lives are surely very distinct, and in fact much of the ideology around gender in the town seems to suggest that they should understand their experiences as utterly different. Yet, as the story suggests, in the resistant act of aligning herself with her brother against the grain of what her family and community are telling her, she explores connections and possible similarities between her brother and herself.

Vero understands, in a profound way, that Nicky needs her in a manner that she does not need him. This becomes apparent in a seemingly inconsequential moment as they proceed in the line to enter the detention facility and must be searched before entering. Since Nicky has brought a series of sealed letters for his boyfriend, sealed and wrapped with orange ribbon, the presiding officer informs him that nothing sealed can be brought into the detention center. This causes Nicky a great deal of frustration that Vero quickly responds to: "Nicky looked pained and when he turns to Vero to begin protest, she gives him a look that says, *Do it*. It is not the way he wanted it to be: these cards are for Julián Orosco, the man he thinks he loves." Because Nicky cannot bring himself to ruin the cards by opening them, and because Vero "can hear the shifting of someone impatient with both the old man's adherence to the rules and Nicky's foolishness in bringing the cards in the first place," she takes the cards away from him and begins unsealing them herself: "She is careful not to rip the envelopes completely and it pains her that she is doing this for her little brother. There are fifteen cards in all and she does the math in her head, the money he has spent for the visit: the cards and the chicken, the cookies and the magazines. She has given him spending money. She has made too much of this possible." That she has perhaps "made too much of this possible" shows that Vero is not unaffected by the homophobic logics of her community, logics that acknowledge the reality of homosexuality precisely in the elaborate forms with which they seek to keep it from manifesting. Muñoz's narrative, however, is interested in the struggle with these logics. The narrative goes on to communicate both the embarrassment and the restraint Vero experiences at seeing her brother so effeminized by his "womanly" devotion to the details of the gifts he brings to his lover: "Vero cannot look at Nicky as he struggles to put the ribbon back in place. Behind them is the rustle of irritation. Nicky cannot get the ribbon to fit again, *but she waits patiently for him to finish because she knows that when he sees Julián, he wants everything to be in order.*"[17] It is precisely in the lovingly, conflicted, but always *corroborating* ways Vero speaks of and acts alongside her brother that we get a sense of queerness as belonging to more people than simply the queer subject proper. I would like to emphasize that it is through the sister's intimate perspective that we also get a deeper sense of the work it actually takes to be a "faithful witness" to queerness as social—to understand, for example, one's deep implicatedness in how queerness will be lived out precisely because one forms part of the sociality in which queerness comes into being as muted or flagrant, as boastful or persecuted. This story, then, gives a rich account of queerness as being intersubjective: as taken in, assessed and manipulated, by those closest to the queer subject. This is conveyed precisely by the way the narrative is focalized through the sister and not Nicky. By "shifting the site of queer enunciation" in this manner, Muñoz renders Nicky's experiences permeable in the sense that they are exposed as constituted relationally. Furthermore the fact that this narrative is heterodiegetic adds an extra sensibility to the mutedness of this intersubjectivity. If Vero had narrated the events herself, in the first person, the sociality conveyed from that perspective would have been of an entirely different order, one that perhaps erroneously implied an *articulate* self-consciousness, erasing through mere narrative structure the experience of intersubjectivity as it was actually lived.

It is from this strategy of narrative proximity that Muñoz moves on to employ a radical distance from queer experience in the short story "The Unimportant Lila Parr." In this story the queer subject is dead, strangled, his body left naked in a roadside motel at the edge of the small town in which he was raised. What this story lacks in leaving unexplored the particulars of his queer subjectivity (or for that matter the intersubjectivity he shared with others) it gains in providing access to the mentality of those *existentially furthest* from him and his experiences. This includes, among other people, his own father (simply referred to in the narrative as "the man"), who epitomizes existential remoteness through his inability to acknowledge his son's homosexuality. The idea of being *existentially* distant, as opposed to literally or physically so, is important to emphasize here, given that the story takes place in a small town characterized by intimacy and closeness. In fact such a contrast raises a question: How does one become estranged from those one is physically and to some extent emotionally closest to? This is an important question to ask, particularly given the hostility queer people encounter primarily from family members who resist being witnesses to their complex experiences. Muñoz's narrative goes a long way to answering this question by suggesting that estrangement, especially estrangement from queer experience, is an unnatural production, a social manifestation that requires labor. This is so because existential distance, particularly as it develops in direct contrast to the town's close social networks, must be worked at in order for it to exist at all. In fact all psychological and emotional separations in the story are conveyed not simply as created separations, but as laborious constructions that, once created, must be self-consciously sustained.

For instance, well before the young man's murder an extreme existential distance is created and sustained by his mother (referred to in the narrative simply as "the wife") in relation to the other townspeople.[18] This existential distance arises in part in the context of an unprecedented inheritance; after an accidental collapse of a barn, which causes the death of their employer, Mr. Parr, the man and his wife inherit from the mourning Mrs. Parr all of their valuable possessions (their home, their car, their farming land and orchards). With this inheritance comes a great deal of attention and a change of lifestyle for the man and his wife. The substantive difference, however, does not arise from the change in economic status, but from the wife's desire to mark the change, both in her daily activities and in the way the town perceives her. This means, for example, that she likes to go into town and "spend more time than she needed to"—a deliberate performance of leisure in order to clearly demarcate her financial status. In particular she enjoys purchasing items that the townspeople will notice. Although she is careful not to spend beyond her means, she deliberately purchases items that do not need to be wrapped or put into paper bags: "About once a month, she walked out of the flower shop with a large basket of daisies. Or she purchased homemade soaps that smell[ed] like oatmeal-honey and lavender, with triple-looped lace as a handle." It is important to note that this behavior arises in response to the type of town in which she lives, a town small enough for residents to monitor behavior and close enough for them to share perceptions and circulate information. It is in response to this social framework that she comes to feel and act with the rigidity and pretentiousness that she does:

> The man's wife drives a fairly new car and she knows that she's been in this town long enough for people to remember how she came into her prosperity. She knows they recognize her car as the Parrs' second-best. She sits rigid against her car seat when she drives, both hands on the steering wheel. Staring ahead, she pretends not to notice people, only bothering to wave at those who greet her first when they step into the crosswalk. She recognizes the change in herself—she doesn't look at people in the eye anymore, only their hands, what they take, and what they give back.[19]

Through her ways of behaving when she is in town—her rigid body comportment, her arrogant self-awareness, her hyperawareness of the townspeople and what they know about her and her hand-me-down prosperity—we come to understand how an existential distance in such an intimate and communal place is always artificial, how it is a separation that once created must be sustained if it is to have longevity.

Where, with whom, and to what effect existential distances of this magnitude are created and maintained in a small town is of particular importance to the queer subplot of this story. One must note in this regard that queer people are often central to the production of certain types of existential distancing.

That is, to the extent that queer people need avenues of privacy through which queer sociality and sexuality can be explored without hostility, they often make use of the existential distance (and often require it) for certain types of homosexual sociality. Queer people cultivate practices of cruising, for example, ways of behaving sexually in public spaces that negotiate and resist the public demand for heteronormativity. In this sense it is important to understand existential distance as a produced "achievement" with complex valences. In other words extreme benefits are reaped from having heterosexuals unaware of homosexuality and its modes of being in the world. Muñoz's short story, however, does not have in mind the most queer-positive valences of this existential distance, or if it does, it wants to remind us through the death of the young gay man that existential distance from homosexuality—from its subjectivity and intersubjectivity—is produced with the logic of fragmentation in mind, with the logic of gender purity and with the logic of homophobia and homohatred. One of this story's greatest achievements is to remind us that queer experience does not take place in some no-place, but in fact negotiates the same geography that other people (with their own illicit practices) negotiate.

It is within this theme of existential distance and its artificiality that the man's estranged relationship to his son's murder and his son's illicit behavior gains significance. From the moment he first hears of his son's murder to the instant when he must identify his son's body at the coroner's office, the father cannot bring himself to acknowledge what the police and coroner's reports suggest, given the evidence: that he was found naked in a motel room, that two needles were found on the nightstand, that a young man his son's age was detained in the next town and was being charged with his son's murder. From the father's narrative perspective none of this information can be assimilated into his conception of himself. He experiences the murder with a great deal of shock, and as the narrative goes on to reveal, it is precisely the insinuation of sexual indiscretions that seems to weigh most heavily on his peace of mind. "He begins to wish," the omniscient narrator tells us, "that it had not been a roadside motel room, but a car accident, a negligent diesel truck, something that would remove the responsibility on his son's part."[20] By focalizing the narrative through the father's perspective, the story conveys the cognitive and emotional dissonance with which queer experience has the semblance of being "recognized" but is always inevitably deferred. From the father's perspective this is all we can know about queer experience: that it leads to dangerous situations and that it causes a great deal of pain for families. From this partial perspective we see only a father's confusion and his mode of coping through denial—a behavior that is further buttressed by the tightly knit community that seems to rally behind his confusion and mode of coping. The people who work for him in the orchards, for example, do not approach him to talk, but work faster and harder in order to leave less work for him to worry about and more time to grieve, alone. Within such a tightly knit context—where neighbors purchase groceries for him and workers demonstrate affection through acts of personal sacrifice—the intimation of homosexuality stands out as an anomaly. Queer sexual experience comes to stand as irrevocably disrupting family and community life.

Yet it is precisely this disposition to understand queer experience as isolatable, as a social phenomenon that one can feel justified in feeling a great deal of estrangement from, that Muñoz's narrative approach helps to circumscribe. It is through the braiding of various perspectives—perspectives that include but are not limited to the father's on the days following the murder—that we get a fuller sense for how estrangement is constituted in this town and how queerness in particular comes to form a part of, as opposed to existing apart from, this shared context. I have already made some comments about the mother producing her own estrangement from others in the town. However, it is precisely the confirmation of this behavior through the focalized perspective of the townspeople that gives us a more accurate understanding of her distance from them as produced. They witness and comment on how she clutches her purse in symbolic performance; they notice that she wants to be seen. This forms an important parallel backdrop for understanding the father's estrangement from his son's queer experience.

By finally focalizing the narrative through someone other than the father, in particular through the motel owner's perspective—the one person in town who knows who frequents his establishment and the many reasons that bring them there—we come to know that the father himself has withheld a very important secret from everyone (perhaps even from himself). As the narrative explains, the father has been having a long-standing affair with his white neighbor, Lila Parr, and the affair has always taken place at the roadside motel where his own son was murdered. This affair is not revealed to us until the very end, when the narrative is focalized through the motel owner's perspective. Looking back on the narrative from the perspective of the motel owner we understand that any lack of acknowledgment on the father's part, any asserted confusion and repulsion regarding his son's sexual indiscretions belie the concrete ways that the father and son have objectively shared similar spaces (the motel) for similar reasons (illicit sex). Queer experience is part of the larger pattern of social secrecy that constitutes the small town's community life. Queer experience exists in time and space and in relationship to the same people, institutions, and ideologies of secrecy that the rest of the town responds to. The motel, in short, enacts a heterotopic quality, in that a heterotopia has the ability to juxtapose in a single real place several emplacements that are incompatible in themselves.[21] The father's and son's sexual indiscretions are inextricably linked in space and time, not simply literally to the motel, but also to the range of social circumstances that make the motel a location of purpose for social subjects in need of covert locations. It is with such information in mind—information that would not be available to us without multiple people accounting for the story—that the father's existential distance regarding his son's homosexuality in particular is understood as having an utterly produced quality. The father can continue to see his son with a great deal of fear as long as he continues to sublimate the reality of his own affair.

One of the major theoretical achievements of Muñoz's writing is its ability to communicate—through form and content—the very real ways that queer experience is a social and shared experience, even as oppressive ideologies work at making it seem less real and shared, and even if the queer subject often seems isolated in the process. As I have tried to point out, queer people come into being and come into a sociality in relationship to others. That queer people often feel isolated is in fact a kind of relationship to the people who surround them. The examples of "Good as Yesterday" and "The Unimportant Lila Parr" prove that estrangement from and proximity to queer experience happens as people with different forms of ideological or institutional backup make them happen. The isolation and violence that queer people are subject to are not by any means natural; they are produced in the very real ways that everyday people live out their lives. When Nicky, for example, starts to adopt a more effeminate and outlandish style (starting to socialize with other flamboyant and effeminate boys in his town), his behavior is not natural per se, but resistant behavior: it is a response to oppressive gender norms and constitutes a resistant sociality. Likewise when the father in "The Unimportant Lila Parr" does not allow his own experiences of sexual indiscretion to inform his relationship to his son's own indiscretions, he is *working* at severing a connection which is undeniably real. The father and son share, if nothing else, a similarly spatialized mode of enacting desire through the heterotopic site of the motel. Together they form part of the town's nexus of relationships that require secrecy and that, whether acknowledged or not, are linked in a shared sociality.

Because I want to emphasize this understanding of queerness as social and shared as one of the consequences of Muñoz's narrative approach, I want to end my discussion by briefly addressing the title story, "Zigzagger." Unlike the other two stories "Zigzagger" uses focalized perspectives from both the queer subject *and* his family and community, shifting narrative perspectives throughout the story. Centering on a young Chicano man's sexual awakening, this story refuses (through content and form) to isolate his agency or his subjectivity as something independent of other people. Muñoz does this precisely through the omniscient narrative style and alternating narrative perspectives with which he provides a collective account of what it means to be a part of, as opposed to *apart from*, the values, experiences, and concerns of a small Mexican and Mexican American community. This is conveyed most explicitly in the undeniable ways subjects in this community are inscribed psychologically and experientially with shared ways of thinking.

The young man's first cathartic homosexual experience stands out in the narrative as mired in religious dogma. Recalling the emotionally charged and titillating experience, he transitions from describing his sexual encounter in realistic terms ("He allowed the man's hands to grab his waist . . . he felt the hot press of the man's belly, the rough texture of hair") to describing the encounter as an incident with a satanic demon:

> The man, his back broad, grunted heavily. . . . The man's sound made him grow, pushing the boy higher and higher, to where the boy could see himself in the arms of the man who glowed in the darkness of the canopy of branches, his skin a dull red, the pants and boots gone. And though he felt he was in air, he saw a flash of the man's feet entrenched fast in the ground—long, hard hooves digging into the soil, the height of horses when they charge—it was then that the boy remembers seeing and feeling at the same time—the hooves, then a piercing in the depth of his belly that made his eyes flash a whole battalion of stars, shooting and brilliant, more and more of them, until he had no choice but to scream out.[22]

Such a fantastic account in a fundamentally realist narrative can provide a perplexing experience for some readers. However, given the manner in which the young man's extraordinary experience is situated within the context of his mother's own religiosity and within the town's circumscribed religiosity, his seemingly implausible recounting gains a great deal of significance as a perceptual consequence of living among others in a shared and complex tradition of negotiating religious doctrines.[23] The young man's mother, as the story makes a point to foreground, understands sexuality through religious dogma in a manner altogether consistent with the way that her son comes to experience his first homosexual encounter. Attempting to cope with what she knows to be her son's sexual indiscretions the morning after he returns home drunk from a night of dancing at the town's local dance hall, the mother speculates:

> She wonders if her husband knows now, if he can tell how the side-to-side swivel of the dancers at the hall and the zigzag of their steps have invited an ancient trouble, if her husband knows the countless stories of midnight goings-on, of women with broken blood vessels streaming underneath their skin from the touch of every man. . . . She wonders now if her husband has ever awakened at night, dreaming of dances where bags of church-blessed rattlesnakes have been opened in the darkness of the place, the mad slithering between feet and the screams, the rightness of that punishment, the snakes that spoke in human voices, the rushed side-to-side movement of the snakes before they coiled underneath tables to strike ankles.[24]

As the example of the mother shows, the son is not the only one whose experience is fundamentally influenced by religious indoctrination. Mother and son in fact share an understanding of sexuality as a problem, one that if not suppressed requires some form of punishment. Indeed the impulse to judge others and oneself by the religious standards of fear and retribution set by church ideology is embodied in the everyday thoughts and actions of the people in the town. This emphasis comes across most poignantly in the way the narrative emphasizes the religious dogma and fears that the entire town is up against as they prepare for the Saturday night dance hall party. In a series of rich details the town is described as entirely focused on this dance, but up against the disapproving eye of the "churchgoers."

> Saturdays in this town are for dancing. The churchgoers think it is a vile day, and when they drive by the fields on their way to morning service, they sometimes claim to see workers swaying their hips as they pick tomatoes or grapes. They say that nothing gets done on Saturday afternoons because the workers go home too early in order to prepare for a long night of dancing. It is not just evenings, but the stretch of day—a whole cycle of temptation.

The churchgoers do not exact their moralizing gaze without critique. Among the community leadership are war veterans who serve as administrators for the use of the Veterans' Hall. These veterans are described as resisting the moralizing tendencies of the majority of churchgoers, some even strategically narrating sexually explicit stories of debauchery during war time, of "Korean girls spreading their legs for soldiers and the relief it brought," in order to scandalize the churchgoers into silence.[25]

By braiding these perspectives into one narrative, Muñoz renders the young man's "fantastic" first sexual experience "of" the community in a substantial way. Even though his homosexual experience can never be directly acknowledged as such, it is through the heterodiegetic narrative approach implemented by Muñoz that the young man's experience can be given a sociality and a rootedness which the rest of the community seems unable or willing to admit to, if only because they have not even conceived of homosexuality so intimately. Through such a narrative approach this young man's cultural education is given proper social reference. By narrating the story from various perspectives Muñoz reminds us of shared and overlapping horizons of possibility.[26]

Shifting the site of queer enunciation, as I have been arguing, is a literary practice that intervenes politically at the level of social literacy, at the level of reading deeply into the social. Such a narrative practice reformulates how queerness is traditionally understood—as belonging, in some shameful and isolatable way, to the queer subject proper—by foregrounding the manner in which (and the people through which) queerness gains consistency or is denied a presence in the social. To suggest, as I have, that some of the most compelling narratives in Manuel Muñoz's collection of short stories exhibit a strong commitment to this resocializing of queerness is to make the case for a narrative tradition for which James Baldwin initially and Manuel Muñoz more recently serve as indispensable benchmarks.[27] As bookends of a sort, they frame the experimental work that developed in the second half of the twentieth century. The acclaimed contemporary African American writer Randall Kenan is perhaps the most obvious example of a writer who fits within the tradition but who has morphed the practice into a trademark writing style. His first novel, *A Visitation of Spirits*, has received attention by critics who see the novel in conversation with Baldwin's writings, particularly the aspect of Baldwin's writings that cast queers as both deeply in conflict with and deeply enmeshed in communities of place. These critics do not all agree on which writings best foreground the literary continuities between Baldwin and Kenan, but they all seem to share an admiration for Kenan's ability to situate queerness within complex historical moments and concrete relationships, and to make such situatedness a moment of reflection about the community at large. Preceding Kenan is the Cuban American writer Miguel Elías Muñoz; his novel *The Greatest Performance*

(1985) is narrated by two childhood friends who bear witness to each other's common history of resistance and gender nonconformity. Because its characters share a horizontal attentiveness (a mutual bearing witness) to each other's predicaments, the novel shares the burden of queer representation in a way that also gestures toward critical reflection on gender, race, and nation. Similarly *Crossing Vines*, the first novel by the award-winning author Rigoberto González layers a variety of narratives into a tapestry of migrant farm worker life. Among these narratives, queer subjects and the people who live, love, and work alongside them form a substantial presence. The pioneering work of Mariana Romo-Carmona should also be understood within this trajectory. In her first-of-its-kind Spanish-language anthology, *Conversaciones: Relatos por padres y madres de hijas lesbianas e hijos gay*, Latino parents are asked to speak about their lives and relationships with their gay and lesbian children. The work of that anthology abides by the logic of shifting the burden of queer representation away from queer subjects. Among the many interesting consequences of such an approach, however, is that at least one of the parents requested to contribute an account comes out in the process, leaving us to ponder the question of where exactly queerness can be said to reside.[28]

Manuel Muñoz's contribution to this tradition of shifting the site of queer enunciation is to stress the tangible but often muted implicatedness of various people in the sociality of queerness. His narratives are powerful interventions, not because they *replace* the urgency of the queer speaking subject, but because they momentarily postpone and reorient that urgency, strategically redeploying what Emma Pérez has called the necessity of *nuestra lengua en nuestro sitio*. The "critical task of survival" becomes modified in this process—not so much the need to find separate spaces in order to inaugurate our own discourses, not so much the need "to create our language, to name ourselves," but the need to find ourselves enmeshed in and constitutive of our communities, to find ourselves implicated in everyday community life (in messy, ambiguous ways, in loving and violent ways, in articulate and never-been-said ways). The critical task of survival becomes, not so much the need for voice, not so much the need to speak one's name, but the need to remind oneself that one has a name in the streets—that someone, somewhere, knows our name—and that there is abundant pleasure and "profit" in finding one's tongue, so to speak, in the mouths of the people one loves.

Thank you to Paula Moya, Michael Hames-García, María Lugones, Yvonne Yarbro-Bejarano, Mary Pat Brady, Carmen San Juan-Pastor, Tania Triana, David Vázquez, Dayo Mitchell, Lynn Fujiwara, and others who commented on drafts of this chapter, including the generous audiences at the Stanford Humanities Center "How Do Identities Matter?" workshop and the Future of Minority Studies Research Project's Mentoring and Multiculturalism Conference at the University of Michigan.

1. The Chicana feminist critic Yvonne Yarbro-Bejarano succinctly describes the impact of this practice when she reflects on the work of Cherríe Moraga that it "enacts an impossible scenario: to give voice and visibility to that which has been erased and silenced" (The Wounded Heart, 3). We should be careful to note, along the lines of what Ramón Saldívar has argued about Chicano narrative, that giving "voice and visibility" is not always a desire to "simply illustrate, represent, or translate a particular exotic reality," but that it can be an intervention of a less essentialist order, working to "shape modes of perception in order to effect new ways of interpreting social reality and to produce in turn a general . . . revaluation of values" (Chicano Narrative, 6–7). Karen Christian echoes and extends Saldívar's and Yarbro-Bejarano's reflections when she writes that gay and lesbian Chicano/a writers intervene culturally and politically by narrating "subject positions that operate as counternarratives to essentialist gender norms" (Show and Tell, 25). Christian argues that this body of work challenges the homophobic and misogynist "unintelligibility" often ascribed to gays and lesbians by actively representing the seemingly unrepresentable, that is, by representing homosexuality in its "multi-faceted and ever-changing character" (27–31).

2. Leyva, "Listening to the Silences in Latina/Chicana Lesbian History."

3. As Paula Moya has noted, examples of this modern concept of agency are evident in the way the minority neocons Shelby Steele, Richard Rodriguez, and Linda Chávez promote "individual" success and "individual" agency against the collective problems faced by minority groups in the United States. For more details of this discussion, see Moya, "Cultural Particularity vs. Universal Humanity."

4. Lugones writes:

All one has to do is try to move with people against oppression, to understand oneself as not able to intend in this sense. What I am proposing is a viable sense of intentionality for moving against the interlocking of oppressions that animates oppressions as intermeshed. As I unveil the collectivity backing up the individual, I am pointing not just to the illusory quality of the individual, but to the need of an alternative sociality for resistant intentionality. Intending may "feel" as arising in a subject, but surely the production of intentions is itself a haphazard and dispersed social production. Subjects participate in intending, but intentions acquire life to the extent that they exist between subjects. (Pilgrimages/Peregrinajes, 216–17)

5. Lugones writes:

The understanding of agency that I propose, which I call "active subjectivity" and which I contrast with the influential understanding of agency of late modernity, is highly attenuated. It does not presuppose the individual subject and it does not presuppose collective intentionality of collectives of the same. It is adumbrated to consciousness by a moving with people, by the difficulties as well as the concrete possibilities of such movings. It is a sense of intentionality that we can reinforce and sense as lively in paying attention to people and to the enormously variegated ways of connection among people without privileging the word or a monological understanding of sense. (Pilgrimages/Peregrinajes, 6)

6. Gerard Genette's distinction in *Narrative Discourse* between heterodiegetic and homodiegetic narratives is useful for the theoretical argument I am developing about the narrative situations in Muñoz's short stories. I do not use the terminology *third-person narration* for the reasons that the narratologist Mieke Bal offers: "By definition, a 'third-person' narrator does not exist: any time there is narrating, there is a narrating subject, one that to all intents and purposes is always in the 'first person.' The 'person' of the narrator . . . can be distinguished only in terms of his presence or absence in the narrative at the level in question" ("The Narrating and the Focalizing," 237).

7. Consider, as a contrasting example, Achy Obejas's novel *Memory Mambo*. Written from the perspective of a Latina lesbian, it conveys an intimate first-person account of queer Latina experience. However, because of this first-person narrative structure, it is restricted in the type of information it can provide, especially as it pertains to foregrounding of queer experience as shared and social.

8. Consider, as just one other example, Achy Obejas's short story, "Above All, a Family Man," which is written from the first-person perspective of a white man living with AIDS, about his relationship with a married, heterosexually identified Latino man. This *homodiegetic* narrative explores queer experience at a highly self-conscious and explicit level. It feels appropriate as a narrative strategy to have the white man speak in the first person, given that the white man speaking has an unproblematized sense of self and a fetishistic relationship with Rogelio's racialized sexuality in the United States. Furthermore by narrating this story in the first person and from the perspective of the white man, his Latino lover remains an enigma (what Rogelio feels and thinks cannot be foregrounded), and hence he becomes reified as the impenetrable Latino man.

9. Muñoz, *Zigzagger*, 126.

10. Ibid. I think this is an important point to emphasize, particularly because the narrative also provides a sense of Vero as someone who has always taken care of her little brother. We see this in scenes where she remembers childhood car trips with her family. She remembers Nicky fearlessly peering out of a moving car window, over a ravine, and she remembers instinctively locking the car door for safety—all of this happening without the parents knowing or sharing any of her anxiety about her brother's safety.

11. "To witness faithfully," María Lugones writes, is to witness "against the grain of power, on the side of resistance. To witness faithfully, one must be able to sense resis-

tance, to interpret behavior as resistant even when it is dangerous, when that interpretation places one psychologically against common sense, or when one is moved to act in collision with common sense, with oppression" (*Pilgrimages/Peregrinajes*, 7).

12. Muñoz, *Zigzagger*, 141.

13. Vero is particularly conflicted about her brother's gender nonconformity. The way that Nicky chooses to inhabit his body, effeminately, bothers her ("She hates to see his hand extended out like that, his exaggerations, his boldness at sixteen"). She often scolds him for acting effeminately in public and is concerned that he has developed friendships with other effeminate boys. At the same time she is very attentive to her younger brother and more frequently than not restrains herself when she thinks she should chastise him. She marks the moment when she started to feel this *ethical* self-restraint as being coterminous with the day her brother was assaulted — the day so much was articulated and so much was left unspoken.

14. "Vero remembers how Julián came on the inside of her thigh: he pushed at her so he could rub himself clean on her skin. . . . Sometimes she can't help thinking about what Julián and her younger brother did at the drive-in. She is ashamed to think of Julián coming on the inside of her younger brother's thigh. She is embarrassed to think of one, then two fingers" (Muñoz, *Zigzagger*, 150).

15. "She tells herself that she is doing the right thing, that she can ignore her own humiliation at having her younger brother carry on like this with someone she had known so intimately. She tells herself that she is stronger, that ultimately she has more options than someone like Nicky will ever have in a place like this" (Muñoz, *Zigzagger*, 144–45).

16. Muñoz, *Zigzagger*, 122–23.

17. Ibid., 123–24, italics added.

18. That the narrative refers to the queer subject's parents as "the man" and "the wife" further emphasizes the patriarchal imaginary that so fundamentally constitutes life in this small town. More important, however, this ascription gestures toward a *generalizability* of this particular story to other contexts. In other words what transpires is being gestured toward as fundamentally relevant to various other situations and circumstances, particularly as married men and women indiscriminately adopt and internalize rigid heteronormative ways of being that truncate their interpretive horizons.

19. Muñoz, *Zigzagger*, 39, 40.

20. Ibid., 41.

21. Foucault, "Of Other Spaces," 181.

22. Muñoz, *Zigzagger*, 17.

23. Arturo Islas's protagonist in *The Rain God*, Miguel Chico, is similarly situated within a community stifled by religious dogma. In such a context his nascent desire to rebel against cultural mores becomes manifest in his interest in hearing stories describing "Satan's pride."

24. Muñoz, *Zigzagger*, 18.

25. Ibid., 6, 7.

26. Through various other narrative perspectives we also come to understand the role that secrecy plays for the young man, as well as for his mother. Unlike the secrecy in "The Unimportant Lila Parr," the secrecy in this story is given a more tangible presence in being acknowledged by the mother as something to self-consciously maintain. Toward the end of the story the mother makes every attempt to keep her son from naming what has transpired, and this need to reproduce silence around taboo subjects is made evident as an extension of her desire to keep quiet about certain aspects of her own life: "The mother sees him, the look in his eye, and she wants to say nothing at all. She believes, as she always has, that talking aloud brings moments to light, and she has refused to speak of her mother's death, of her husband's cheating, of the hatred of her brothers and sisters. She sees her son at the doorway and wants to tell him not to speak" (Muñoz, *Zigzagger*, 18).

27. Two of Baldwin's novels, *Another Country* and *Just Above My Head*, are powerful examples of early experimentations with shifting the site of queer enunciation. These two novels begin in the most provocative of manners, by killing off the queer protagonist and leaving the rest of the characters to make sense of it all.

28. As a way to problematize the generally positive connotation I have been attributing to this tradition, we could also include the controversial short story "Whose Song?" by the Jamaican American writer Thomas Glave. There the shift in queer enunciation occurs as readers inhabit the perspectives of three young men who rape a young black lesbian. The entire perspectival shift is disturbing, but what is gained in the process is an intimately disturbing understanding of how violence against women, and women of color in particular, functions symbolically for some of the young men as their own (dis)avowal of their homosexual and racial fantasies. Here it might prove useful to ask ourselves, if in fact something of political and emotional importance is gained in the process of shifting from the perspective of the young woman to the perspective of the men who rape her, what if anything is lost? What type of violence is redone by inhabiting this perspective? An interesting contrast to Glave's narrative approach would be Junot Díaz's short story "Drown." In that story a young, heterosexually identified man recalls his close friendship with a young queer man. Importantly, the narrative perspective fostered in this story allows readers to see firsthand the negotiations of masculinity and social class that eventually fracture their close bond of friendship and camaraderie. The narrator in Díaz's "Drown," in contrast to the narrative perspectives in Glave's story, bears a certain kind of witness to the homophobia that so permeates relationships between young men. In his own way the narrator takes some responsibility for the ideological investments in class and masculinity that often get in the way of true affection, queer desire, and solidarity between men.

Dancing with the Devil—When the Devil Is Gay

Paula M. L. Moya

Ernesto Martínez's stunningly insightful essay about Manuel Muñoz's collection of short stories, *Zigzagger*, highlights the very real difficulties of representing—speaking for, depicting, or embodying—queer people and their interests through fictional texts. By asking what is at stake in Muñoz's narrative decision to "shift the site of queer enunciation," Martínez's reading of Muñoz's stories helpfully exposes the minute social mechanisms by which queer identity and experience are produced—by queer and straight people alike, in everyday life as in literary works.

According to Martínez, Muñoz takes a "provocative, multifocal narrative approach" to representing gay experience and identity in *Zigzagger*. Rather than always having his gay characters narrate or even focalize those events in their lives that pertain to their nonnormative sexuality, Muñoz spreads the responsibility for representing the lives of his gay characters to other characters in the collection—to Nicky's sister, Vero, in "Good as Yesterday"; to the father of the dead gay man in "The Unimportant Lila Parr"; and to the mother of the boy who has his first sexual experience with the devil in "Zigzagger." Martínez acknowledges that such a narrative approach carries some risks. It can result in talking over or past a population that has too often been silenced and pushed to the margins of society. Moreover, nonqueer characters are prone to representing the identities and interests of queer characters in ways that queer people might not always appreciate. This danger becomes clear when nonqueer characters who have been socialized into heteronormative and homophobic ideologies, *and* who lack the intimate experience of being queer, misrepresent queerness in ways that result in the misunderstanding of, social isolation of, violence against, and even death of, queer characters.

Martínez argues, however, that there are some important political and epistemic advantages to the multifocal narrative approach that Muñoz takes. When Muñoz assigns to nonqueer characters the burden of representing queerness, he exposes the "web of relationships and discourses that constitute queer experience and queer identity in any given context." Martínez argues that Muñoz's stories demonstrate, on both a thematic and a structural level, how deeply *all of us*, queer and nonqueer alike, are implicated in the ongoing production and re-production of queer identity and experience. Moreover because Muñoz's stories take a fictional approach to the constitution of gay subjectivity—because, that is, the stories represent gay characters and their straight family members in ways that make us care about them *as if they were real people*—the stories are able to demonstrate what is at stake when we accept or refuse our own involvement in the lives of the queer people who exist within our own (nonfictional) discursive and relational webs.

Martínez includes in his analysis of Muñoz's stories an astute, but brief, discussion of the title story, "Zigzagger." He notes that the young gay Chicano character whose sexual awakening is at the center of the story has a painfully ambivalent relationship to his community, an ambivalence that is registered at several levels of the story, including at the level of narrative. Martínez further argues that by using an omniscient narrative style while focalizing the narrative perspectives through both the boy and his mother, Muñoz "provides a collective account of what it means [for a gay Chicano] to be a part of, as opposed to *apart from*, the values, experiences, and concerns of a small Mexican and Mexican American community."

In what follows I build on Martínez's insights to illuminate how Muñoz's rewriting of a Mexican American cautionary folk tale, "dancing with the devil," depicts a nonnormative or alternative masculinity. It is a masculinity that does not depend on the denigration of women, but rather has a different relationship to both women and femininity. As such it provides a fictional representation of an alternative way of being in the world that has liberatory potential for men and women of all sexualities.

For those unfamiliar with the "dancing with the devil" folk tale, the basic outline is this: The scene is a Mexican American dance hall in south Texas (or the California central valley, or sometimes even a discotheque in Tijuana, Mexico). At one of the tables is a young Mexican American woman whose conservative and strict parents have expressly forbidden her to be there. In defiance of their authority, and with a girlish desire to have fun, the young woman has snuck out of her house to join her girlfriends at the dance. Once the dance is in full swing and couples are gliding counterclockwise around the dance floor to *conjunto* polka music, in walks a good-looking, strong, tall, and sharply dressed man. He is different from the usual kind of man who comes to these dances; he is expensively dressed, maybe in a suit with expensive boots, and he may even be Anglo. All the single women in the dance hall, especially the young woman, notice him and immediately desire to dance with him. Eventually he asks our rebellious (but still innocent) young woman to dance. She happily agrees to do so and finds him to be everything she has ever dreamed of: charming, suave, a skilled dancer. But then she looks down and sees that his expensive boots have disappeared, and where his feet should be are either chicken feet or hooves. At this point she recognizes that she is dancing with the devil; she screams in terror and falls down in a dead faint. The devil, having failed in his attempt at seduction, then disappears in a puff of smoke.

In his masterful book, *Dancing with the Devil*, the anthropologist and literary critic José Limón notes that this cautionary folk tale is a woman's tale; it is typically narrated by and told to women.[1] Limon interprets the devil's presence in the tale as "a register of the society's initial and shocking encounter with the cultural logic of late capitalism." He suggests that for its narrators it is a "text with a very proximate relationship to the Real of their lived historical experience, though now rewritten symbolically."[2] In other words, the tale of the dancing devil represents women's desire for escape from the choices they face: a life of economic struggle or domestic tedium, or both. The handsome stranger, unlike the lower-class Mexican American men these women normally have to choose among, has both money and cultural (racial) capital that, as their proper provider, he will necessarily share with them. Moreover because the devil is both charming and attentive, he represents the possibility of romance and sexual satisfaction. Importantly, however, the devil disappears before any of these desires can be fulfilled. For Limon, then, the dancing devil represents both women's desire and the limits of that desire—the implacability of the race, class, and gender struggles these women face every day of their lives. According to Limon, the ultimate significance of the tale resides in the fact that it is collectively authored. He argues that the women who participate in its telling and retelling are "active artisans of language" who transform the Real of their existence through a creative and critical reaction to the shared circumstance of their lives. They delight in the making and sharing of the story with one another, thus enhancing their collectivity and nurturing a particularly Mexican American form of solidarity we call *confianza*.

There are of course other meanings we might give to the tale depending on who is telling it and to whom it is being told. In the version recalled by the literary critic Sonia Saldívar-Hull from her own adolescence, perhaps the most significant element of the fable is the fact that the young woman who dances with the devil is at the dance *sin permiso* (without the permission of her parents). Given this emphasis, the young girl's brush with the devil would stand first and foremost as a warning to all other young girls who would consider similar kinds of adolescent misbehavior.

Importantly, Muñoz's rewriting of this woman's tale changes some of its key elements, most notably by making it about *gay* and *male* sexuality. Just as crucial, though, is the fact that Muñoz's version can be fully appreciated only when it is placed in the context of the values, taboos, and symbolism of a larger Mexican American community. Moreover the cautionary aspect of the folk tale that Saldívar-Hull insists upon is crucial to my reading of Muñoz's version. By depicting heterosexual and homosexual relations within the Mexican American community as they are (with all their attendant homophobia and violence), as well as how they might be (with the possibility of more equal and respectful relations between men and women), Muñoz effectively provides a cautionary tale for those who would cling—even to their own emotional detriment—to officially sanctioned and hierarchical heterosexual social roles.

According to the ideology of Mexican American heterosexuality, there are starkly drawn differences in the gender roles of men and women. Men are breadwinners; women are homemakers. Men take care of women; women are taken care of, but are thereby at the mercy of men's immense physicality, both sexually and in terms of physical violence. Unlike the straight male characters that embody the heterosexual norm, the young gay male characters that populate Muñoz's stories have a different relationship to women and to femininity. In "The Unimportant Lila Parr," for example, the relationship between the mother and her gay son is characterized by identification and sharing. The story is focalized by the father, and so we are privy to the father's intensely emotional and private response to the brutal murder of his son in a roadside motel. We find out that the father felt excluded from and threatened by the closeness between the mother and the son: "The father walked into the house one day to see his wife and son sifting through [some] old clothes and laughing."[3] He is disturbed to see his son participating in what he characterizes as a "weakness" signaled by his wife's careful cultivation of mementos from her past. What the father in this story fails to realize, of course, is that his inability to identify with and share in the lives of both his (gay) son and his (female) wife traps them all, as well as Lila Parr, into living lonely and parallel lives in which the possibility of comfort in the face of tragedy is notably absent.

The short story "Zigzagger" opens at dawn on a Sunday morning with a mother and father keeping a vigil at the bedside of their son, who came home violently ill the night before. Through a braided narrative structure that interweaves present time with flashbacks from the day before—and that is narrated from the perspectives of both the mother and son—we learn that the boy had gone out to a dance with a group of his friends, both boys and girls. There he meets a handsome stranger with whom he has his first sexual encounter. After his friends find him sick outside the dance hall they bring him home and leave him raging and cursing like a man possessed, with red welts and deep scratches all over his body. The mother and father tend to their son, communicating with each other as much through silence as with words, until he sleeps peacefully and the welts and scratches disappear. The story ends when the boy's friends come by to check on him and he wakes up psychologically and emotionally transformed. The manner of the story's narration suggests that the story is at least as much about *if* and *how* the community (represented by the mother and father and the boy's friends) will assimilate this disruptive happening into their everyday reality, as it is about the boy's newfound sexual self-acceptance.

Muñoz's gay characters' alternative relationship to femininity is revealed in part by the way women characters mediate the gay male characters' relationships *to* their objects of desire without *being* the objects of desire. In "Zigzagger," for example, two different women facilitate the boy's access to the dancing devil. As in the standard version of the tale, the handsome stranger/devil approaches a young girl, in this case one of the boy's friends. However, in this version of the tale the girl is not impressed. She dismisses the stranger/devil with a flick of her pink-braceleted wrist while the boy watches as if he "were the only one watching." Unlike in the standard tale, where all the women notice the handsome stranger's entrance, in this one "the boy felt as if he had been the only person to notice the man with the plain silver buckle . . . a plain silver buckle that gleamed like a cold eye, open and watching." As the handsome stranger/devil talks to the girl, the boy notices his posture, his hips, his seductive arrogance; he sees "the silver buckle blink at him, as if it watched back, as if it knew where the boy was looking."[4] When the girl subsequently complains to the boy about the man's unwanted attention, she gives the boy the excuse he needs to approach the man who wears the "knowing" silver belt buckle. Later a different woman stands talking to the handsome stranger/devil, thus giving him the pretext he needs to stand around waiting for the boy to approach. Conveniently this woman disappears from the scene (and from the narrative) just as the boy approaches.

The focus on male physicality in Muñoz's stories further figures the male body, as opposed to the female body, as the object of sexual desire. In "Zigzagger," for instance, we learn that the father is a man who makes "the doorways in their house seem narrow and small, his shoulders threatening to brush the jambs."[5] Curiously we get no corresponding description of the mother; we have no idea what her shape and size might be. This is not to say that the mother is not important to the story; she is. She is the character that focalizes the largest part of the narrative. However, it is her *subjectivity* that matters in the story, not her *sexuality or physicality*. Thus the story upends the standard heterosexual structure of power/knowledge: instead of a male subject and a female or feminized sexual object, these stories figure a female or feminized subject and a male sexual object.

At the heart of almost all the stories in the collection, and certainly of this one, is the ambivalent desire for different forms of openness. For the gay male characters this openness is figured both as the bringing of family secrets — many, but not all, involving sexuality — out into the open, and as penetration by the male sexual organ. As strong as these intertwined desires are, however, they are understood by the characters as threatening to the families' physical and spiritual well-being. Noncommunication, accomplished through silence and obfuscation about matters too painful to face, allows the three main characters in "Zigzagger" — father, mother, and son — to coexist in their common solitude. Thus the gay male is represented as being a part of the larger Mexican American community; his actions and behaviors take their meaning from the same set of values, taboos, and symbols that those around him espouse. But his membership in that community is represented as ambivalent and subject to certain conditions.

The noncommunication imposed on the gay son as the price for his membership in the larger Mexican American community is enforced, albeit differently, by the mother, the father, and the friends. On the morning after the dance, when her son awakens and comes out of his bedroom to greet his friends, the mother imagines that if no one, especially her son, talks about what happened, she can refuse its reality: "The mother sees him, the look in his eye, and she wants to say nothing at all. She believes, as she always has, that talking aloud brings moments to light, and she has refused to speak of her mother's death, of her husband's cheating, of the hatred of her brothers and sisters. She sees her son at the doorway and wants to tell him not to speak." For his part the father actively intervenes to prevent the disclosure that is threatening to burst forth. As "they all stand and wait for the boy to talk, the doors and windows open as wide as possible and every last secret of their home ready to make an easy break to the outside," the father moves to prevent the boy's speech. He walks toward the boy and says, "You're awake," before turning to his son's friends and saying, "See? He's fine. Now go home," while motioning them away from the porch. The boy's friends meanwhile "leave without asking [the boy] anything at all."[6] We see dramatized in this scene what Martínez has pointed out as the socially produced and deliberate "estrangement from queer experience" on the part of heteronormative Mexican and Mexican American communities.

This brings us back to the devil motif and how it works in this short story, as well as the collection as a whole. As noted earlier the paradoxical desire for openness in these stories is also expressed as a desire for penetration by the male sexual organ, a desire always accompanied by the fear of being possessed by something dangerous and possibly evil. In "The Third Myth," for example, the gay male protagonist is tormented by the fear that he will be punished for his gay sexual practices. He says, "I . . . worry and fear what I might be made of. What is in me and how it gets out." Similarly the penetration experienced by the boy at the climactic moment (climactic both narratologically and sexually) of "Zigzagger" is simultaneously a moment of transcendent experience and fantastic fear. Into what has been up to this moment a realistic narrative is an irruption of lo real maravilloso:

> And though he felt he was in air, he saw a flash of the man's feet entrenched in the ground—long, hard hooves digging into the soil, the height of the horses when they charge—it was then that the boy remembers seeing and feeling at the same time—the hooves, then a piercing in the depth of his belly that made his eyes flash a whole battalion of stars, shooting and brilliant, more and more of them, until he had no choice but to scream out.[7]

For Muñoz's gay Mexican American characters the act opening oneself up— whether to honest communication about taboo subjects, the possibility of feminine subjectivity, or gay male sexuality—is simultaneously frightening, painful, thrilling, and mind-blowingly beautiful.

The epigraph to Muñoz's short story collection foreshadows the devil motif that is central to the title story and encapsulates the ambivalent rewards offered to a gay Chicano who wants to bring his sexual self out into the open. The epigraph—"The exit is through Satan's mouth"—is a line from the title poem of Satan Says, a book of poetry by Sharon Olds. The poem speaks to a writer's powerful desire to write about, as a way of escaping from, familial bonds woven from memories that are both constraining and painful. At the same time the poem evokes the guilt, shame, and sorrow a writer feels when she betrays her family's dirty secrets by exposing them to the world in the process of achieving her own escape (and creating her art). The lyric "I" in Olds's poem ultimately appears to resist the devil's lure; she accepts her imprisonment even as she warms herself at the fire of the love (presumably for her family) that she discovers at the end of the poem. Muñoz, as a writer, seems to have chosen the scarier, but possibly more rewarding option. For one thing, his epigraph is drawn from the middle of Olds's poem; it does not endorse the conclusion as much as capture the moment at which the "I" in the poem realizes that the only way out of her private hell will necessarily involve a deal with the devil. Muñoz, we come to understand, has made his deal with the devil; he embraces the devil with fear, makes love to the devil with pleasure, and, in the process, exposes the dirty secrets of the Mexican American family (and the larger Mexican American community) to the view of the reader. But this exposure is not without its rewards. By opening up the pathological tangle of lies, silences, and shame that denies the reality of life-affirming sexual and emotional love between men—as well as of satisfying nonsexual love and identification between men and women—Muñoz creates the possibility that men and women of all sexualities might be able to communicate with each other in ways that will relieve their painful isolation and give them alternative modes of being in the world.

Importantly, Muñoz's rewriting of the "dancing with the devil" fable doesn't end with the sighting of the devil's feet. The story continues on through the act of sexual union and ends only after the boy and his mother, father, and friends have gained (an as yet unspoken) knowledge of the boy's homosexuality. In Muñoz's version of the tale, the moral points not to the limits of Mexican American female desire and agency in a race-, class-, and gender-stratified world, but rather to a whole world of transformational possibilities—of alternative forms of Chicano masculinity, of the acceptance of homosexuality in Mexican American communities, of honest, open, and loving communication between family members of all genders and sexualities, and of gay Chicana/o self-love.

As Martínez's cogent analysis of Muñoz's narrative strategies in *Zigzagger* make clear, Muñoz's literary vision does not imply either an individualist or a gays-only social or political project. Rather, it is one that can be accomplished only with the acknowledgment and participation of the Mexican American community as a whole.

1. As one of Limón's informants so charmingly puts it "¡Es puro pedo de viejas!" (Limón, *Dancing with the Devil*, 168).

2. Ibid., 184.

3. Muñoz, *Zigzagger*, 40.

4. Ibid., 13.

5. Ibid., 5.

6. Ibid., 18.

7. Ibid., 30, 17.

Choreographies of Resistance: Latino Queer Dance and the Utopian Performative

Ramón H. Rivera-Servera

Dance vivifies the cultural memory of a common context of struggle that bolsters a cultural identity itself forged through struggle and dance.

—Celeste Fraser Delgado and José Esteban Muñoz, *Everynight Life*

Perhaps part of the desire to attend theatre and performance is to reach for something better, for new ideas about how to be and how to be with each other.

—Jill Dolan, "Performance, Utopia, and the 'Utopian Performative'"

As a migrant to the United States from Puerto Rico in the early 1990s I learned to articulate my sexuality and my political identity at the dance club. Within the erotic realm of clubs like Heaven, Carpe Diem, Club Marcella's, and the Avenue Pub, I embodied my position as a queer Latino.[1] Dancing queerly with my friends—marking my own *latinidad* through rhythmic phrasings that allowed me to feel and to own the music and approaching strangers bodily within the comfort of a shared social space—allowed me to experience communities of pleasure.[2] The club, like the theater, is one of the places where I renew myself, where I am able to witness, in almost religious reverence, the most immediate and affective manifestations of vibrant communities in motion. The club offers me a space to experience what freedom from homophobia, and sometimes from racism, feels like. The club also provides me with spaces where experiences of discrimination can be addressed and exorcised in the company of others who, like me, understand the at times difficult and pleasurable path of being a queer of color. My experience in the club not only allows me to feel desire, love, and community, but gives me the confidence and the knowledge to step proudly into other, more dangerous venues and seek, even demand, similar experiences from the world outside it. The club provides me with strategies of survival, but also with the comfort of knowing that I can return to its realm and experience once more this utopian community of queers.

This essay is my effort to make sense of these experiences in relation to the experiences of other queer Latinas and Latinos who, like me, have come of age within the realm of the club.[3] Through the voices and choreographic approaches of my informants I argue for the formative and utopian potential that dancing in a club engenders. At the heart of this project is an attempt to approach the feelings of community and agency produced in the acts of club dancing. Dance in the club, as an improvisational social practice, is both immediate materiality (getting ready, traveling to the club, interacting with others) and utopian futurity (the emergence of community, the world of possibilities and strategies, the promise of pleasure). Yet the utopian realm of the club (i.e., community and pleasure) must always be negotiated, sometimes even fought for, in its live material context. In the space of the dance floor pleasurable exchanges are complicated by social hierarchies inside and outside the club. In this constantly evolving social environment I identify and look critically at the place of utopia in Latina/o queer club dancing. I suggest that it is in the improvisational bodily articulations of the dancers and in the transactions that unravel from these actions, where utopia, in its connotations, both as liberation from oppression and the constitution of community, resides.

The argument for understanding the gay club as a utopian safe haven is a dominant narrative in gay cultural criticism.[4] Contemporary analysis of club dancing ranges from celebratory approaches to the liberating potential of clubs as sites of uncensored expression, to critical arguments that outline normative forces that dominate social relations in these spaces.[5] In his analysis of gay dances at Sydney's Mardi Gras celebrations Jonathan Bollen discusses how the club is often characterized as "a safe place free from the violence of a homophobic world." He further outlines how this reading offers the dance floor as a "utopian promise that literalizes a metaphor: the dance floor as ecstatic vision and grounded experience of gay and lesbian community."[6] Within a designated "safe place" imaginative self-presentation and communitarian affiliation can occur outside the pressures of a heteronormative society. While the celebration of Mardi Gras offers an event framework that is more publicly sanctioned by outside authoritative structures, in part because of its temporary nature, the gay club offers a similarly carnivalesque environment that allows for the free expression of queer sexuality with its "safe" structure.[7]

However, as the musicologist Walter Hughes argues, the assumptions of *communitas* in the gay dance club may be reframed by understanding the club as a disciplinary social space in itself.[8] Following Hughes's assumption that the beat of the music functions as a dominant sensual mechanism that imposes its rhythmic structure on those who experience it, Bollen adds an equally dramatic layer of disciplinary performance in the mimetic act of dancing with others and its relationship to hierarchies of movement and legitimacy. As Bollen explains, "The beat may register its disciplinary effects not through direct infliction, but through the way in which others dancing to the beat rhythmically textures the choreographic ensemble in which you dance."[9] Dancers in the club negotiate not only the aural stimuli marked on the rhythm but the body and movement ideologies of those surrounding them.

The dance floor is, in this model, always involved in an economy of hierarchies that depend on the binary arrangements of majority-minority relationships in the ownership of queer public spaces.[10] Mainstream gay clubs, for example, are often invested in the construction of normative homosexuality, and in the context of the United States this normativity is generally regarded as white and male.[11] The complex nature of these exchanges is particularly significant when addressing minoritarian subjects who do not fit as easily into the dominant definitions and aspirations that shape the social realm of the club. Latina and Latino queer dancers in the United States enter the "safe place" of the club with a marked difference. Their pursuit of experiences of sexual freedom is often intersected by a similarly intense desire to acknowledge, embody, and act out their latinidad. Dance, as an act of self-presentation and community building, becomes one of the mechanisms through which Latina and Latino queers negotiate their place and membership within and outside the club. Envisioning utopia from the perspective of the dance floor is not as simple as dancing along with others, but the result of serious experiences in multiple communities and their intersections, sometimes in stark contrast to or in conflict with one another. The emergence of utopia for queer Latina/o dancers is both an individual act of survival and a communitarian experience of and yearning for freedom. Addressing utopia in this context requires not only an engagement with the cultures of pleasure that characterize the club, but with cultures of struggle that mark the multiple trajectories and negotiations undertaken by dancers on their way to and as a precondition for the utopian experiences of the dance floor.

Jill Dolan's recent theorization of utopia in performance allows for an engagement with club dancing that retains a material grounding in social exchange while approaching the world-making dynamics of the club.[12] Citing Lyman Tower Sargent's comments regarding utopia's opposition to contemporary conditions, Dolan defines utopia in performance as a phenomenon that "takes place now, in the interstices of present interactions, in glancing moments of possibly better ways to be together as human beings."[13] The utopian performative is deeply rooted in a materialist appraisal of the inadequacies of contemporary experience and addresses them in the moment, through enactments that produce alternative experiences and visions of how things could and should be. This positioning of utopia as critique redirects the analysis of the social relations of the club as interventions in the larger sociopolitical debate over queer sexualities beyond their local geography on the dance floor. That is, the performances in the club are interventions into dominant discourses of sexuality, gender, race, and ethnicity, among others, that construct the very geography of the dance floor as an alternative to structures of oppression and prohibition elsewhere.

Furthermore Dolan locates the utopian performative here and now. This focus on the effects of performance, in present tense, positions practices such as improvised social dance as activities that produce utopia in its affective and most immediate sense. This proposition is central to my understanding of the club, where the improvisational acts of dancers perform alternative modes of being in the extravagant and assertive display of their bodies in motion as well as how to be with each other in their sharing of space, time, and kinesthetic resources with those around them. David Román has recently discussed this notion of performance's utopian construction in the present in his autobiographical essay on dance as liberation. Román comments, "Perhaps the reason that so many accounts of gay club culture read it as utopian has something to do with the idea that dance, as a kinetic experience, enables social configurations of same sex bodies not imaginable elsewhere."[14] The act of dancing in itself constitutes the utopian "doing" of the club by materializing bodily exchanges that articulate, showcase, even flaunt queer sexuality publicly. I argue that for Latina and Latino queers these doings involve the articulation of latinidad and alternatives to it that incorporate queer attitudes to gender and sexuality.

More specifically the practice of dancing in clubs engages bodies in social dance and in the realm of improvisation. These physical exchanges are characterized by dancers constructing their identities as subjects and community members in space, in an environment established for intimate social interaction. These interactions are made possible by the theatricality of the club environment. The visual and aural spectacles of lights, music, and clothing, the mind-altering effects of alcohol and drugs, and the sexually charged interactions between dancers make clubs sites of pleasure. Within this hypersensorial medium improvisation is the central paradigm and possibility of club culture. How dancers react to the sensory stimuli of the club, the body in relation to its surroundings in the moment, constitutes a training of sorts, both in techniques of self-affirmation as dancers attempt to perform themselves in public and in communitarian practice as they share the moment of cultural performance with others. Although structures of power constitute these social spaces and exchanges, the live transactions that take place within them (re)define and at times challenge them through performance. Focusing on the kinesthetic rhetorics of the dancing body and particularly local interventions by individual dancers offers a radically different picture of the club experience. A discourse focused on improvisation allows for the articulation of strategy within the (dis)orderly logic of the dance club. Here perhaps, within the context that showcases spontaneous social relations and the skills developed to thrive within them, lies the utopian potential of club dancing. This is where the presentness of performance, its ability to do something, and the versatility of improvisation, the possibility of transformation and change, become the driving forces of dance club culture.

In her recent and important ethnography of club dancing, Fiona Buckland explores the world-making power of improvised social dance at gay, lesbian, and queer clubs primarily in New York City. She observes that improvised social dancing in the club is

> a playful practice that depends upon the agency of its performers, [which] produces queer club culture, not as a homogenous, transhistorical object, but as a process of counterpoint, contestation, and polyvocality. This more fluid model shifts agency away from culture and its structural forms, including dance, to participants who improvised movement in response to everyday experiences, which, in turn, influenced the experiences and understanding of everyday life.[15]

According to Buckland's argument, dancing serves as a creative forum in which to articulate as well as experience the quotidian. Through dancing, performers navigate the specific social realm of the club. Sexuality, race, gender, and class are negotiated among patrons who travel to these sites in search of both individual pleasure and community. These acts of affirmation and community performed in the club may in turn reshape the attitudes and approaches dancers take to their daily lives.[16] The dramaturgical processes brought into the theater of the dance club are especially significant to queer Latinas and Latinos who require the improvisational skill as a strategy that allows them to inhabit and perform their multiple identities in and out of club environments that differently accommodate the exigencies of their own needs and desires. Improvisation, in the form of code-switching (linguistic and otherwise), enables minority subjects to perform in and out of multiple circumstances and contexts.

I am fully aware of the traps of theorizing improvisation as utopian, as it may lead to a simplistic assertion of improvisation as a fully participatory and democratic alternative to situations that are fully embedded in structures and negotiations of power. I understand improvisation within the club as a practice that is not exclusive of skill, technique, and hierarchical ideologies of proper choreography, fashion, and even body types. However, and here I echo Buckland's focus on contestation and counterpoint, I advocate an approach to improvisation as a survival skill that is at once a participation in the structural realm of the club, including disciplinary performance, and a challenge to it. Positioning improvisation as the driving force of the utopian performative in the club addresses the polyvocality of approaches to the performance of queer latinidad as an emerging identity that is textured by the at times contradictory nature of both of its primary sites of identification.[17]

Latinidad as a marker of identity has for the past decade become a centralizing and strategic label for the mobilization of populations of Latin American descent in the United States. Often substituting for more localized categories such as Cuban American, Chicano, or Nuyorican and marking a difference from institutionally imposed homogenizing labels such as Hispanic, latinidad emerges as a coalitional banner in contemporary U.S. politics and culture that seeks to bridge Latina/o communities across national origin or descent, histories and conditions of arrival or displacement, and racial and ethnic identification. As such latinidad offers a site for identification invested in the articulation of difference from a critical position that addresses the marginality of Latina/o populations relative to U.S. dominant culture. Latinidad constitutes an intersection or home to a diverse community of millions that remains significantly disenfranchised from U.S. material, social, and cultural economies. The assumption of this pan-Latino social imaginary is not exclusively the result of a strategized political affirmation, but is also the emergence of a sensibility, a shared feeling of placeness, and at times placelessness, within the U.S. national imaginary. This sensibility is in part the product of the global circulation of Latina/o popular culture through media networks, but most important it is the result of similar experiences of marginality.

José E. Muñoz's recent writings on Latina/o affect suggest, following Raymond Williams, that there is a "structure of feeling," an identity in becoming, resulting from Latina/o modalities of being that might bridge communities-in-difference. He argues, "What unites and consolidates oppositional groups is not simply the fact of identity but the way in which they perform affect, especially in relation to an official 'national effect' that is aligned with a hegemonic class."[18] Latinidad is presented here less as a programmatic political articulation and more as a performative modality that counteracts the negative marking of Latina/o cultural practice as outside the realm of the nation. For queer Latinas and Latinos, this strategy is further motivated by their search for sexual liberation. Queer Latinas and Latinos not only struggle through exigencies of racial and ethnic marginalization in the United States but encounter, with equal intensity, the homophobia of the multiple communities through which they travel. Queer latinidad brings together multiple migrant and border communities through common cultural traits and affects as well as acknowledgment of similar histories of discrimination and sites of pleasurable investment. And it is within the realm of affect, as Muñoz argues, that I think club dancing manifests most profoundly the nature of the utopian performative.[19]

The dance floor may be one of the most vivid examples of the material conditions from which queer latinidad emerges. Within the club the improvised choreography of the dancers showcases modes of being that are both Latina/o and queer. The world envisioned and embodied in these performances is one that invests strategically in both of these affective registers to produce a utopian third space. The performances of utopia in the club rehearse strategies of survival and interconnectedness that might enable the emergence of queer pan-Latina/o communities beyond it. Dancing in the club produces queer latinidad as a utopian performative that is at once the articulation of something new, an identity in motion that bridges both queerness and latinidad, as well as an intervention in the histories and struggles of these identities.

This possibility for community—enabled in the club by the physical interactions of improvisational dancing—is one of the most salient features of the utopian performative as defined by Dolan. She argues that the experience of performance may produce communitas: "This for me, is the beginning (and perhaps the substance) of the utopic performative: in the performer's grace, in the audience's generosity, in the lucid power of intersubjective understanding, however fleeting. These are the moments when we can believe in utopia. These are the moments theatre and performance make possible."[20] I share Dolan's vision of performance. I similarly propose Latina/o queer dance practices as exercises of "intersubjective understanding" among Latina and Latino communities that differ greatly in their experiences of entry into the United States, but who share similar experiences of racism, cultural marginalization, and homophobia. Dance clubs, I argue, provide sites for dwelling, temporarily limited but spatially vast homes, from which Latina and Latino queers perform the desires often prohibited outside these spaces, to address the structures of dominance that still seep into this "safe haven," and to rehearse strategies by which to survive collectively. These are the queer-world-making strategies Buckland attends to so passionately in her own ethnographic account. And it is precisely in the leap of faith from the experience of everyday life to the imagination of community, even across national, racial, and class borders, where latinidad suggests its most utopian performances.

In my own ethnographic research in gay and lesbian clubs in Texas and New York I have encountered and experienced powerful performances of Latina/o queer utopia. I locate these glimpses into the possibility of Latina/o queer utopia within the choreographic strategies performed by dancers who negotiate the club as both hegemonic discipline and utopian promise. I would like to turn to some examples that illustrate the multilevel sense of negotiation that is required of minoritarian subjects entering the realm of the club.

To begin with it is important to note that for queer Latinas and Latinos the acts performed in social dancing and their location at the gay club bring together a whole series of intersecting identities, experiences, and desires that produce a truly hybrid, at times conflicted notion of place and being in the world. Entering the gay club is an act of affirmation for Latinas and Latinos, many of whom reside in neighborhoods where traditional conceptions of Latina/o heteronormativity and homophobia are prevalent. Dressing up and making the trip to the very public space of the club requires immense courage and strength. Victor is a gay man in his late twenties and a recent migrant from Puerto Rico now living a few blocks from Krash, a Latina/o club in Queens. He explains, "A mi a veces me da un miedo porque mi familia no sabe. Yo salgo a escondidas. Tu sabes, perfumaito y todo . . . pero yo digo que voy a dar la vuelta y ya. Pero dar la vuelta es que camino dos cuadras por ahi pa' bajo y me meto en Krash!"[21] Like Victor, close to a third of the informants interviewed said that they sneak out to the club scene.

Those who were out to their families still commented on the danger of getting to the clubs, especially when these are located in remote sites of the city. In New York City, for example, Nilda, a twenty-two-year-old lesbian of Dominican and Filipino descent, commented that she is often harassed on her three-block walk from Port Authority in Manhattan on her way to Escuelita.[22] "I get off the train and me and my girlfriends are like 'run, run, run!' 'Cause people be coming by, 'Hey baby what's up?' 'Cause there is a lot of hooking around here still," she says. Despite the stress sometimes involved in getting to the club, Latina/o queers venture passionately into this world. This is, after all, one of the few safe places where they can be queer, many of them argue.

In an interview Nestor, a forty-three-year-old Chicano gay man in Rochester, New York, explains, "Dancing in the club is my chance to have space of my own. Even if I am surrounded by a bunch of people, I make sure that my dance floor is my dance floor and nobody better mess with me. I am fierce when I take the stage, honey, and I has got to shine!" For Nestor, who works as a supervisor of seasonal farm workers in Sodus, New York, and shares a small one-bedroom apartment with five other men who labor at the same camp, the club is truly a space of his own. During his weekend outings to Rochester he is able to assume, perform, and live his identity as a gay man, far from the homophobia prevalent in his household. The club offers him an experience of community, a chance to be in the company of those who identify with his interests and desires. This is the utopia of his experience.

However, the gay club is not without its own conflicts, as Nestor explains: "You know, people are generally nice, but you never know. I've seen a lot going on around here, some dude thought I was a *puto* [hustler] the other night! Man, you know, just 'cause I'm Latin and shit. And I'm not about to just fall for the first one that comes around. That's why, you know, you see me in my corner, you know. I like keeping to myself."

"Well, what about relationships? Are you looking for relationships in the club?" I ask.

"Well, I also want to meet someone, you see, I am nice and I flirt and all . . . I just don't want to be messed around with, you know. I got to test people out. You feel me?"

These are the experiences shaping and being shaped by Nestor's performance in the dance club. He sees his time in the club as time for the free expression of his sexuality, but at the same time resents the risks he runs of racism and stereotyping. The mythology of the safe place and unbreakable community is shattered by the possibility of racism often prevalent in these spaces, demonstrating that despite the general free environment, the club's Anglo-dominated power structure remains to be negotiated.

Nestor's choreography on the dance floor engages fully with these contradictions. He takes to the dance floor alone. He is in a small, racially mixed gay club in Rochester. A version of "Rumba," the Latin house track recorded in 1993 by New York City–based Pirates of the Caribbean, plays through the speakers.

In the song a heavy house bass blasts with layers of polyrhythm played out by congas, bongos, timbales, and electronic percussion. He untangles the percussive line with stylized steps in a forward cutting motion across the floor. Nestor's improvised choreography explicitly demarcates space on the dance floor. His movements are characterized by a slight bending of the right knee and a rhythmic pause in which the right shoulder punctuates the beat traveling through his torso onto his hip. This movement is followed by pointing forward his left foot on the step. His movement sequence is adorned with a forward rotation of bent arms performed in Caribbean social dance genres such as salsa.

Nestor further accentuates his assertive use of space by intensely fixing his stare across the room during his cutting forward progression. He ends approximately ten feet of travel with a sudden pause, a coquettish smile, and a slow sway of the hips that ushers in a quick right turn, a sustained pose, a sharp bending of the knees, and a back drop to the floor. An almost immediate recovery to standing impresses onlookers before his return across the floor to the spot where his story began. His travel across the floor synchronizes the performance to the dominant sensory stimuli in the club: the beat. But his on-the-beat motion, matching the intensity of the music, is subverted by the softer feel of his pause-and-pose sequence. These flirtatious instances bookend his movement through space. Slowly shifting his hips to the sides, Nestor tilts his head in synch and smiles both before and after he drops and recovers from the floor. For the next few hours he remains on the dance floor, traveling back and forth on this kinesthetically constructed catwalk, adjusting his strut to the various rhythms of DJ Victor's mix and pausing only to drink water from a bottle strategically placed between the speakers and the go-go boy platform.[23]

Nestor's attract-and-repulse strategy to dance is echoed by Clara, a Puerto Rican lesbian in her midtwenties, who enters the dance floor with her partner at a primarily Anglo gay male club in Austin, Texas. Here a house mix of the Nuyorican actor and singer Jennifer López's "Let's Get Loud" is heard. Clara takes up very little space in her dancing, focusing on a tight kinesphere with her partner. She faces the crowd and positions her back toward her partner, who moves closely from behind with slow, rhythmic weight shifts. These shifts side to side at the knees are initiated with a forward isolation of the shoulder, marking the beat. Clara begins synchronizing her movements with her partner, who also marks the rhythm with her hands on Clara's hips. As the rhythmic line accelerates Clara breaks from her partner's movement and shifts her alignment, teasingly flaunting her behind at the crowd. She makes a quick transition from the slow, cool shift of weight from side to side to isolating the hips in a back-and-forth rocking motion, on the beat. The lyrics in López's song invite the crowd to get loud, to take life on their own terms. Meanwhile Clara's feet remain motionless although she articulates her hips playfully with the rhythm. She pauses counterpointally and then accelerates to a double-time articulation, only to return to the beat again. She repeats this sequence over and over until the song ends. At this point she smiles devilishly at her partner and leaves the floor for a break.

These two examples showcase two different choreographic practices performed by U.S. Latino queers in dance clubs in distinctly different places. Nestor's dance floor is located only forty-five minutes from the northern border of the United States, in a state where the Puerto Rican presence, although no longer demographically dominant, remains the primary referent for *latinidad*. Clara, on the other hand, dances in a city a few hours from the southern U.S. border with Mexico, where *latinidad* is currently defined by historical negation and suspicion of citizens of ethnic Mexican communities. In both examples how the dancer moves and how he or she reacts to other people's movement is both a strategic negotiation of the realm of the gay club and an engagement with larger social issues and discourses. The movements performed by Clara and Nestor are in an immediate sense a matter of pleasure, an engagement with the sensory and sexual realm of the gay club. These actions are also articulate and hopeful performances of desire and agency that enable the possibility of community beyond restrictive notions of national or regional identity.

In the togetherness of dancing along with others, witnessing bodies on display, displaying one's own, and cruising on and off the dance floor, one discovers that a sense of community emerges. Dancers move in relation to each other's movement. Those movements that are witnessed and rehearsed in relation to other dancers become an improvised repertoire of the present moment. The body becomes conditioned to move through those previous but still immediate experiences on the dance floor. As Jonathan Bollen argues:

> Whether the sharing of kinesthetic resources occurs in the present moment—"picking from the crowd"—or whether it is the result of an accumulation or re-performance of past dance floor experiences—"a stock standard type of dancing"—the pleasures of the dance floor are often the pleasures of slotting into a choreographic ensemble, where "moving in a way that fits together" means "connecting" with other dancers.[24]

The exchange of "kinesthetic resources" is one of the many behaviors that dancers negotiate within the realm of the club. Through this exchange dancers also negotiate their identities and desires. Bollen presents a dance floor where dancers learn not only how to move, but how to be in communication with others. What this means for the analysis of dance is that no matter how extemporaneous the interactions between dancers, these interactions carry with them the stamp of prior and future relationships in movement. It is out of this sense of synchronicity and communication that a feeling of community arises.

On the dance floor dancers perform the duality embodied in the club between the individual pursuit of pleasure and safety and the emergence of community out of the collective act of moving together.[25] Nestor's dance, for example, is both an invitation to watch, perhaps engage, and a setting of boundaries. You can look, but be aware that you are not being allowed easy access. The spectator is at once lured and challenged. His cutting across the floor is deliberately about owning the floor for himself, and yet his attitude across the floor is ultimately imbued with irony as he works his upper body in counterpoint to the step progression and eases into the teasing sequences that frame it. His movement is not an emasculated stance; instead it gains its strength from a directed and articulate performance of queer effeminacy. He fiercely combines a repertoire of "queenie attitude," much as in voguing, to accumulate the spectacular sense of groundedness he performs.

Clara, on the other hand, complains about the assumed entitlement of other dancers: "They just think they own the place, especially white boys. They'll just dance around bumping into everyone. That's rude, you know. I keep to myself and to my girlfriend. It's nobody's business how I dance." She continues to describe a series of movements on the dance floor that come close to describing Nestor's choreography in New York. She prefers contained polyrhythmic movements and sees the more open movement choice as intrusive. She explains that she doesn't want to deal with forced contact with other people on the dance floor: "I am tired of it. You grow up going out to straight clubs and all these guys be coming up and trying to get with you. I mean, even the street people are always talking about your ass out loud and shit. That's just wrong!"

Clara's choreography with her girlfriend, although allegedly in total isolation from her surroundings, is also invested in public display and community. While her dancing performs a difference from the crowd that she seemingly ignores, it also becomes a conduit to the communal experience of dance spectatorship in the club. Furthermore her strategy lies in the rhythmical articulation of the body, a strategy that Nestor also prioritizes in his own understanding of his dance choices. She maintains a closed space around her, but by flouting the hip isolation movement facing the audience she commands an attentive spectatorship. On the dance floor she reacts to her spectators on the street by rearticulating the racialized and often racist comments about the size of her glutes through the virtuoso contraction of her rear muscles. Shaking her ass on the dance floor is a way to address her everyday experience, to exorcise the racist fetishism of her onlookers, inside and outside the club. Both performers stress a rhythmic layering of their movement that challenges the more common on-the-beat choreographies characteristic of primarily Anglo clubs. Rhythm, specifically the upbeat sensuous articulation of Latin rhythm, functions as the dominant affect of these performances. Through the articulation of rhythmical proficiency as a shared "kinesthetic resource" and marker of *latinidad*, Clara participates in a community that involves other dancers, like Nestor, despite her keeping to herself. She performs actively as a member of the community, even when critically articulating and resenting the tensions that arise inside and outside the club.

The relationship of identity and rhythm is historical in the case of Latin America, as it is throughout the Caribbean, where rhythm is explicitly connected to an African aesthetic and heritage.[26] Through the circuits of music publishing, promotion, and distribution—including live performance tours, radio, television, and film—Afro-Latin rhythms have become the international marker of *latinidad*. Ana M. López says regarding this transmission of Latino and Latin American musical practices through Hollywood films:

> Rhythm has been—and continues to be—used as a significant marker of national/ethnic difference: the cinema locates and placates Latino/as and Latin Americans rhythmically. But this placing has also served to provide a curiously unfettered space for ethnic and other nationals: a place for performers and a space of multiple identifications. Here we can perhaps begin to think about a different rhythmic cartography, not tied to borders to be crossed or transgressed, but where spaces become lived-in and dancing places in which the body—reclaimed from its subservience to work—can be a locus of resistance and desire and enjoyed on that basis.[27]

López reads the productive process of Latinos forming imagined communities under the influence of global mass media. It requires articulation of local interests through strategic engagement with globalization. In the case of the club, for example, the sexual economies of globalized Latin culture, generally assumed to be heterosexual, are queered at the site of the local, reconfigured under a different cultural economy. A localizing maneuver is preformed at the club, not only bringing a specifically Latino sensibility to a typically urban

American social space, but queering *latinidad* in the process, rearticulating it for the circulation of queer pleasure.

In the club it is generally the DJ who performs the first act of localization by transforming recorded musical tracks into live displays of the local community's taste. As Brian Currid has explained in regard to house music, "This focus on local production and 'ownership' consciously breaks from the slick, universalistic packaging of generalized pop production, reclaiming popular music as local property."[28] The source material for the club's soundscape is formed out of a large pool of recorded tracks. The actual performance of the music is up to the expressive manipulation of the DJ, who will loop, mix, and cut tracks as desired to put out her signature sound. The same popular song will sound completely different depending on the DJ who plays (with) it and thus allows for the characterization of club spaces based on their particular musical styles, even when the source materials are often the same across the board. The music is gathered from the realm of popular music and its global circulation, to be transformed by the DJ into an admittedly local soundscape.

The second move takes place on the body of the dancer who takes upon herself the task of performing through this doubled text, both local and global. A localization of a transnational musical heritage takes place on the dance floor as dancers embody styles of movement. Sarah Thornton has argued for the local nature of club culture: "Although club culture is a global phenomenon, it is at the same time firmly rooted in the local. Dance records and club clothes may be easily imported and exported, but dance crowds tend to be municipal, regional, and national. Dance styles, for example, which need to be *embodied* rather than just bought, are much less transnational than other aspects of culture."[29] As Thornton explains, dance practices in the club are local to the extent that they depend on the improvised interactions of performers to share "kinesthetic resources," and these transactions occur only between bodies. This formulation is based on different scales of access to commodified culture that favors the immediate live interaction at the club but does not deny the role of global systems of transference and their influence in the transmission of choreographic strategies. Primarily through the distribution of film and television, and now most importantly through music video, dancers acquire a kinesthetic repertoire that is inherently global in reach.[30] However, the performance of these media-transmitted knowledges depends on localizing practices very much like the ones the DJ performs in her manipulation of the music in the club. Here dance may be characterized as an intervening agency that translates the global for the pleasurable engagement of local communities. Because live performance cannot guarantee exactitude in transference or execution—whether or not the source material is reached through live or mediatized transmission—the result is always articulated locally. It is the performer, individually and in relation to those around her, who ultimately emerges in the act of localization. And it is precisely in the critical act of rearticulating the dominance of globally distributed media from a Latina/o queer perspective, and the pleasure of doing so in communication with others, where Latina/o queer utopias may be felt.

A similar approach takes place in the choreographies performed by Clara and Nestor, who experience rhythm with an active sense of agency, communicating relationships through the body that go beyond mere synchronization but that display their knowledge and ability to sustain it in their bodies. In the club Nestor and Clara localize music through articulate movement. The showcasing of skill is paramount to these performances. In the display of rhythmical understanding, through flaunting that they get it, arises the assertive embodiment of queer *latinidad*. At this juncture, and through this act of identification with rhythm and the bodily conversation with it, utopia is performed. In this realm of pleasure politics is most pronounced on the body.

Dancing in the club becomes a practice of what I term *choreographies of resistance*, embodied practices through which minoritarian subjects claim their space in social and cultural realms. The Latina/o queer body in motion, the ability to move to the Latin rhythm eloquently, shifts the power dynamics of the dance floor and the club, at least temporarily, to articulate the particularities of queer Latina/o experience. More specifically, although the sensorial stimulations of these safe places are often prepackaged products, even concepts, their architecture is easily overruled by the live actions, performances, executed by the dancers. Similarly club dancing for queer Latinas and Latinos represents an engagement with commodified gay and lesbian popular culture, but one in which the dominant narratives of these cultural products are interpreted and rearticulated. This approach, I argue, exemplifies the performance of queer *latinidad*. In this dynamic the sexual economies of commercially driven Latin culture, generally assumed and marketed as *heterosexual*, are queered at the site of the local, reconfigured under a different cultural economy. Likewise the often unquestioned whiteness of the gay club is challenged by the virtuoso demands of the Latina or Latino dancer. So the maneuvers performed at the clubs not only bring a specifically Latino sensibility to a typically urban American social space, but they queer *latinidad* in the process, rearticulating it for the circulation of queer pleasure.

Moving to or against the rhythmic patterns of Latin music or Latin-beat-layered-house allows the dancer to "own" the club, even if just momentarily. Wilbert, a twenty-one-year-old gay man of Guatemalan descent, showcases this approach in his dancing. I first saw him on the dance floor in 1998 at Krash, a Latina/o gay and lesbian club in Queens.[31] Dancing to a club version of Lou Vega's remix of Perez Prado's "Mambo #5," he assumes the upright position of the body with bent elbow and arms parallel to the floor and palms down characteristic of traditional mambo. He begins a series of short flat-footed forward steps led by a slight bend at the knees directly over the foot, maintaining his weight over his heels. He presses on the floor, left foot first, and straightens his knee, bearing the full weight of his body on the left leg. As he frees his right foot, he performs the forward step with bent right knee and repeats the press down and leg-straightening sequence. He repeats this step fluidly over the 4/4 tempo of the original mambo used as the basic pattern for this musical remix. But this approach to the music does not focus exclusively on the more consistent percussion of the piece; instead Wilbert inserts variations to his upper body movement that initially parallel the rhythmic patterns of his steps as he alternately swings his arms forward, accentuating the motion of the opposite leg, but breaks away into a fast shimmying of his shoulders. During these frenzied instances of polyrhythmic display Wilbert throws his head back in shear enjoyment of the physical experience of dancing. When asked what he felt at these moments, he responds, "Just the rush of shaking like a liquadora. Yo creo que ni escucho la música. Just like an adrenalin rush, that's what they call it right? Se mete la música por dentro."[32] Wilbert mentions that the music comes inside him and simultaneously comments that he doesn't think he listens to it any longer. At this point he is all agency, riding the club's soundscape to experience the ecstatic experience of his dancing.

Wilbert's choreography is equally an articulation of the traditional framework from which the club dance track originates and an individual response to the act of dancing, as he becomes deeply involved in his own actions and the pleasure he derives from them. As such the transaction is at once an identification with the broader category of latinidad, through the recognition of mambo, and an individualized articulation made possible by an engagement with club music in a queer context. Like Nestor, who works both within the rhythmic structure of the music, marking it with his shoulders, and against it, through his commanding use of pose sequences that showcase him in flirtatious acts of self-assertion, Wilbert articulates how the realm of the club opens the possibilities for practices of identity formation and experience. Other dancers in the club, myself included, join this moment of ecstatic display and identify in it the potentiality of our own experiences, the possibility of our own pleasure or utopia. Wilbert's performance allows us to both appreciate the beautiful and skillful performance of queer *latinidad* that he offers us and position ourselves in the intense and pleasurable act of contemplation within a queer community of spectators.

The pleasure derived on the dance floor is also quite simply the pleasure of queering *latinidad*. This aspect of queer Latina/o dancing is equally invested in the circulation of particular affective approaches to dominant cultural practice. In the club this strategy requires a rearticulation of the generally heterosexual nature of Latin music. Popular musical genres such as salsa, often performed at queer Latina/o clubs in San Antonio and New York City, are more often than not about heterosexual courtship or conflict. The cultural critic Frances Aparicio has outlined a genealogy of salsa in Puerto Rico that departs from a patriarchal and heteronormative articulation of gendered relations. She further discusses how these characterizations were equally invested in a racial fetishization of African diasporic cultures.[33] However, Aparicio also discusses postmodern re-articulations of salsa, mostly in literary form, that reassign the orientation of desire within the seemingly heterosexual narrative. This queering may be in part facilitated by the performative excess of salsa. The over-the-top sexuality of the genre allows for the demystification of naturalized gendered or sexual positions through a playful reassignment of gendered categories.

One of the men I interviewed in New York City supports such an assumption. Josué, a young Puerto Rican man in his thirties who frequents primarily Latina/o gay and lesbian clubs, says, "Oh yes, I do listen to the lyrics . . . why not? Sometimes I dance like the man, you know, I sing the song to the other guy on the dance floor like he was the woman. I don't know how to say it . . . tu sabes, it's like you just feel it, lo romántico [the romance], and it's just sexy to dance like that to the music you grew up with."

"Does it matter that the song is about a man and a woman?" I ask.

"Not really. Why, you think it's a problem? I just play along with it. It's how you feel it that's the matter."

Josué outlines a strategy that is inherently playful. His identification is with the feel of the song. He revels in the romance being performed and mimics attitudes rather than narratives. In performing through the heterosexual lyrics of salsa Josué queers it for the distribution of queer pleasure.

Josué's comments are echoed in Clara's opinion about her own dancing: "You just learn to feel it without even caring who is singing to who, you know. The music is the most important thing. . . . I mean if you are at the club, most of the times you don't even listen to the words. It's just rhythm . . . the rest is regular club music. But when you are listening to Spanish music, you also remember the rhythm in the club and groove to it."

Clara's statement enters further into the realm of affect. She admits to not paying attention to the lyrics and opts for "grooving" with the rhythm. She identifies the musical elements that mark latinidad for her and performs her sexuality to it. Talking about the Anglo gay club she frequents in Austin, she says, "You know, in the club we are already all queer . . . so when I dance and the Latin music or just drumming comes on in another song, that's when the puertorriqueña comes out. That's when I get down."

On a recent visit to The Electric Company, a Latino gay bar in San Antonio, I encountered a majestic queering of latinidad that showcases this affective rearticulation of Latino popular music. Lena and Gina, a lesbian couple, both Tejanas in their late twenties, take to the dance floor to Marc Anthony's "La luna sobre nuestro amor." This romantic salsa song is a celebration of love and passionate sexual union between lovers:

> You and me
> caught in a spell
> on the way to paradise
> alone you and me . . .
> lovers without remedy
> you and me
> and desire as always
> betraying reason
> and your eyes begging please
> make love to me.

The couple face each other in traditional Latin social position.[34] Lena places her left hand over Gina's right shoulder and raises her left arm, elbows bent in a right angle to meet Gina's left hand. Gina wraps her right arm around Lena's waist and brings her close to her. As the music plays on the dancers follow the rhythmic structure of the song in unison with short syncopated steps. Gina pushes her partner slightly away from her and almost immediately pulls her back in with a sudden turn under her arm. As this turn is completed the couple reverses the initial position of the arms and Lena assumes the lead. They continue to dance through the song, alternating between leading and following, expertly stepping through the cool insistent rhythm of the song and caressing each other gently as they fully enact the sensual narrative of the lyrics. As the song reaches its end Lena and Gina are locked in a kiss and walk away from the dance floor holding hands.

In this short and simple sequence Lena and Gina articulate their love for one another publicly, through redefinition of the choreographic logic of salsa, which usually requires one partner, gendered male, to lead throughout the full extent of the dance. Lena and Gina refuse the mixed parameters of this convention and share equally in the leading role in this affective exchange. Their public display of affection to the lyrics of a song circulated as an anthem to heterosexual love further queers traditional Latin music for the emergence of queer pleasure. This exchange depends on the safety provided in the club and in the community of equally passionate dancers that surround them as they embrace each other publicly on the dance floor.

Especially for Latinos in the United States, encountering models of gay and lesbian culture offers opportunities for learning and sharing strategies of survival and performing queer *latinidad* as an alternative mode of being. The cultural critic Lisa Sánchez-González has eloquently described this two-level relationship between engagement with utopian aspirations and hopes and the more local quotidian experience as a "p'acá y p'allá" aesthetic, a "here and there" aesthetic. She uses salsa dancing as a metaphor for the social and cultural maneuvers of Puerto Rican as well as other Latino communities in the United States. She explains, "As it glides between p'acá, the whole context of its immediate interaction—the dancing, improvisations, and joy we experience, as well as the racism, exploitation, and sorrow we encounter everyday—the p'allá, a geo-philosophical projection of past, present, and future possibilities, an audaciously hopeful realm that is just beyond reach but so close you can feel it coming."[35]

This dual logic, here and there, is masterfully articulated in Nestor and Clara's choreographies. As Nestor explains, "Anyone can come into the club and walk around, you know. I just think I do something special. I shake my can better. I don't know how to explain it. Like, it's a Latin thing, you know, you just got that rhythm inside you. I just let it loose." This dance between the immediate materiality of the club and the histories embodied, performed, and queered in the act of dancing by Latino queers characterizes identitarian practices on the dance floor. Through these practices dancers assume ownership of and membership in the world of the club and develop strategies that might allow them to assume equally assertive stances outside it.

P'acá y p'allá, here and there, anywhere, when there is one such character assuming her place on the dance floor, flowing majestically with the music, challenging its assumed rhythms and desires, making it pleasurable, grinding the hips in an act of identification, shaking that ass in a gesture of defiance, stepping in a fire of memory and pain, of struggle, of hope — this is where queer *latinidad* dances.

NOTES

I would like to thank Jill Dolan, Ric Knowles, peer reviewers and editorial staff at *Modern Drama* for their comments and encouragement throughout the development of this essay.

1. I frequented these bars between 1991 and 1997. All but the Avenue Pub, a Rochester gay milestone since the 1970s, have closed by the time of this writing.

2. I use the term *Latina/o* to refer to populations of Latin American descent currently residing in the United States. This designation is not based on citizenship status as defined by conventional governmental categories, but by a cultural citizenship model that locates these populations as both active and productive members of the American social and economic realms, as well as through their affirmative identification with their national and ethnic heritage. *Latinidad* is the process of identification and sedimentation of Latina/o identities. *Latinidad* accentuates the process-based nature of identity and seeks to articulate the ways these categories are both social constructs and performative effects of cultural practice. That is, *latinidad* is an identity in process, and it is through serial acts like the performances (theatrical and quotidian) such as those I examine in this essay that it becomes a legible, although fluid identity position.

3. This essay developed out of ethnographic research conducted in eight different dance clubs in Austin, San Antonio, New York City, and Rochester from 1998 to 2003. Three clubs were identified as Latina/o gay clubs; the other five clubs were identified as mainstream gay clubs (often this meant a primarily Anglo clientele). The interviews here cited were conducted by appointment with informants met at these places. A total of twenty-eight initial interviews were conducted, with an additional eleven follow-up interviews conducted with selected informants. Initial interviews ran from fifteen to forty-five minutes. Additional information was gathered from interviewed informants and others not formally interviewed through participant-observation at the clubs. Informants have been assigned substitute names in order to protect their privacy.

4. See Diebold, *Tribal Rites*; Dyer, *Only Entertainment*.

5. See Hughes, "In the Empire of the Beat."

6. Bollen, "Queer Kinesthesia," 287.

7. While carnival has been traditionally accepted as a temporary break from tradition in ways that allow for public displays of sexuality (although not always queer sexuality), gay and lesbian dance clubs have historically developed in relation to aggressive regulatory restrictions against the public display of homosexuality. See Buckland, *Impossible Dance*, on the crackdown of New York City clubs during the 1990s.

8. Hughes, "In the Empire of the Beat," 147–48.

9. Bollen, "Queer Kinesthesia," 297.

10. For a discussion of some of these relationships from the perspective of a recent Puerto Rican migrant in one of the clubs discussed in this essay, see Manuel Guzmán, "Pa' La Escuelita Con Mucho Cuida'o Y Por La Orillita."

11. Gay clubs circulate models of appropriate bodies, ornamentation, and comportment that offer equally hierarchical notions of gay identity that further layer notions of normativity within these locales. See, for example, Fiona Buckland's comparative study of queer clubs in New York City, *Impossible Dance*. She notes significant differences in expectations of body type, dress code, and class performance among the various gay communities she engaged during her four-year ethnography.

12. In referring to the "world-making" power of club dancing I am indebted to Buckland's coining of the term as the critical point of analysis in *Impossible Dance*. In my own work I seek to address some of the same issues from the perspective of queer Latinas and Latinos.

13. Dolan, "Performance, Utopia," 457.

14. Román, "Theatre Journals," n.p.

15. Buckland, *Impossible Dance*, 7.

16. In his discussion of dance and gay liberation, Román observes that in a local bar in Wisconsin "gay men and lesbians were forced to forge alliances for political gain, and . . . met across class, gender, and racial lines to do so" ("Dance Liberation," n.p.).

17. For a recent discussion of queer *latinidad*, see Juan María Rodríguez, *Queer Latinidad*.

18. J. E. Muñoz, "Feeling Brown," 68.

19. Interestingly Muñoz's example of utopian performance focuses on the aesthetic and affective world of Latino club culture as an alternative to white dominance in Ricardo Bracho's *The Sweetest Hangover*.

20. Dolan, "Performance, Utopia, and the 'Utopian Performative,'" 479.

21. "Sometimes I get scared because my family doesn't know. I sneak out. You know, with my perfume and all . . . but I just say that I'm going to go out and that's it. Then I just rush a couple of blocks and get into Krash!" (All translations are my own.)

22. Escuelita is located at 301 West Thirty-ninth Street in Manhattan.

23. Nestor is not a go-go boy and does not stand on the platform during his performance.

24. Bollen, "Queer Kinesthesia," 299.

25. In his essay on dance liberation, David Román also mentions that the emergence of community may also be based on the political radicalization of participants who identified as a group based on their marginalization from society and the urgent need for intervention in relation to this position.

26. See F. Ortiz, *Cuban Counterpoint*.

27. A. M. López, "Of Rhythms and Borders," 340.

28. Currid, "We Are Family," 174.

29. Thornton, *Club Cultures*, 3.

30. Other examples of mediatized transmission of dance practices include television programs such as *Soul Train*; Univision's *Sábado Gigante*, which often presents social dance competitions as part of its four-hour variety show (interestingly this is the world's most-watched television show, based on audience numbers in Latin America and the United States); and MTV's many live dance shows, such as MTV *Beach House*, which showcases MTV groupies dancing to the top-selling tracks of American pop music.

31. The dance steps I describe here were observed in 1998. I did not interview Wilbert until the summer of 2002, after running into him at Escuelita in Manhattan.

32. "Just the rush of shaking like a blender. I think that I don't even hear the music. Just like an adrenalin rush, that's what they call it, right? The music just comes inside me."

33. It is important to note here that the exoticism assigned to forms like salsa is often present in local manifestations. That is, the location of the practice within a Latino context does not eliminate the possibility of racist representation, especially in regard to blackness.

34. The face-to-face position in close proximity characterizes much Latin American social dance. The term has, however, been standardized in formal social dance training both in Anglo and Latin American dance studios.

35. Sánchez-González, *Boricua Literature*, 168.

Response to "Choreographies of Resistance:
Latino Queer Dance and the Utopian Performative"

Daniel Contreras

I read this essay by Ramon H. Rivera-Servera with great interest since I have also thought about utopias quite a bit. I remember feeling a little embarrassed about invoking the word in my own work, wondering whether it contained enough "rigor" to sustain a critique. Did it not instead invoke a sentimentalized schema of politics, something Disneylike and commodified? The concept of utopia received quite a beating in some postmodern conceptions, which argued against totalizing visions. While the press trumpeted the list of failed utopias as I came of age (I will not list them), it did not seem reasonable to expect a utopian suggestion to be taken seriously. But in other ways it was exactly what we were calling postmodernism that opened up my thinking about utopian gestures. Here I am associating cultural studies with the postmodern: a toppling of certainties about what constitutes worthy subjects of study, for example.

For those of us who entered the academy in the 1980s and 1990s cultural studies promised to touch us where we lived. Why not study a dance club for its stylistic codes and its communicative gestures the way someone would study a more literary organism? And for those of us who were not white and not straight, the dizzying possibilities of cultural studies were exhilarating indeed. For me there was a built-in hierarchal disrespect toward elite cultural practices that felt intellectually exciting. By opening up the subjects of study we would also have the ability to make claims about what was most important to us: culture and politics.

George Lipsitz describes cultural politics quite clearly:

> For the Cultural Studies school, culture is neither a direct reflection of societal power relations (as orthodox Marxists generally claim), nor is it a sphere of activity completely isolated from the mundane realities of social life (as bourgeois critics often argue). Instead, Cultural Studies scholarship sees culture as a mediation, a sphere where politics always exists, but almost always in disguise. Cultural Studies scholars bring anthropological and socio-

logical perspectives to cultural practices and texts that have previously been analyzed largely on aesthetic grounds. They open up for sustained analysis the everyday life activities of popular culture consumers, youth subcultures, and ethnic minorities. Most important, they provide sophisticated and convincing arguments about the ways in which the commonplace and ordinary practices of everyday life often *encode* larger social and ideological meaning.[1]

For many of us, I think, it was this attention to the everyday that contained so much utopian potential. It was exciting to imagine uncovering political meanings from pleasures and desires.

These were all-important concepts for me when I undertook my project on gay Latino literature and culture and its connection with the sensation of unrequited love. I was struck by how often in these texts (for example, *Kiss of the Spider Woman* and *Migrant Souls*) unrequited love was a central catalyst for the narrative. (Incidentally it was often, though not always, the love of a queer for a straight man.) I wanted to believe that in the futile quest of unrequited love there was a kernel of a utopian gesture, that believing in the impossible was in fact the basis of any utopian politics.

I think this quest describes Rivera-Servera's project quite well. Here dancing is the arena in which queer Latinas and Latinos are encoding utopian possibilities about the larger world in which they live, the world that makes queer Latino lives as inhabitable, as inhospitable, and as virtually *impossible* as possible. Rivera-Servera uses a version of ethnography to describe various dance places in the United States where queer Latinas and Latinos find entertainment, and records his respondents' narratives about dancing. For example, Nestor is described as a "forty-three-year-old Chicano gay man in Rochester, New York, . . . who works as a supervisor of seasonal farm workers in Sodus, New York, and shares a small one-bedroom apartment with five other men who labor at the same camp." Rivera-Servera then describes the nightclub as offering Nestor an "experience of community, a chance to be in the company of those who identify with his interests and desires. This is the utopia of his experience." Another dancer, Wilbert, who is a "twenty-one-year-old gay man of Guatemalan descent," is described as dancing in such a way as to " 'own' the club." Rivera-Servera provides rich descriptions of these and other dancers and how their choreography can form community and cultural identities. He also describes the uses of ecstatic expression on queer dance floors and how it makes possible feelings of communion and utopia.

Latinidad in this essay is described as a "marker of identity" and a "centralizing and strategic label for the mobilization of populations of Latin American descent in the United States." Drawing on the work of José E. Muñoz, Rivera-Servera positions *latinidad* as a "performative modality," one that exists in the "realm of affect," where "club dancing manifests most profoundly the nature of the utopian performative." The music and dancing then become a crucial component of *latinidad*: "The relationship of identity and rhythm is historical in the case of Latin America, as it is throughout the Caribbean, where rhythm is explicitly connected to an African aesthetic and heritage. Through the circuits of music publishing, promotion, and distribution—including live performance tours, radio, television, and film—Afro-Latin rhythms have become the international marker of *latinidad*."

Dance in these conceptions becomes so constitutive of *latinidad* that in the introduction to their book *Everynight Life: Culture and Dance in Latin/o America*, the editors Celeste F. Delgado and José E. Muñoz write:

> Whether forced into slave labor in the sugarcane fields, migrant labor in the apple groves and vineyards, or undocumented labor in sweatshops and restaurant dish rooms; whether lynched in the newly annexed territory of Texas, sterilized without consent in Puerto Rico or the Dominican Republic, or detained in immigration camps in Haiti and South Florida: Latin/o bodies serve as the site of racial, cultural, and economic conflict. Dance promises the potential reinscription of those bodies with alternate interpretations of that history. Magnificent against the monotonous repetition of everyday oppressions, dance incites rebellions of everynight life.[2]

Whether dance is in fact the nexus of *latinidad* is certainly debatable, but the point is made that what can be seen as "only entertainment" (to borrow Richard Dyer's term) in fact contains important cultural resonances along with strategic utopian resistances.

I would like to briefly discuss a few assumptions in these arguments and speculate on how to continue drawing from the forces of cultural politics. This rich essay leads me to think about various topics, which range from the urgent to the more contemplative. I am drawn to think about how politics "hides" in culture exactly. So much of cultural studies work leads us to untapping this political promise, but I am pragmatically asking how we can make this more visible to the culture at large. Perhaps thinking about dance as utopian is a good example of how this critical process of uncovering utopian gestures takes place. The critic observes dancing taking place in specific environments (Latina/o, queer) and does ethnographic work on what kinds of meanings are circulated therein. I am more than sympathetic to this type of heuristic work since it is exactly what I seek to do in literary and visual texts. I want to see utopian expressions, and so I look for the appropriate texts. But at the same time I wonder about that practice. Which comes first in this exercise, the gesture or its meaning?

I am also speculating whether *latinidad* would benefit from more severe explication on what exactly it consists of, or whether we want to work on giving it an even more amorphous shape. Perhaps *latinidad* as a sensibility may be generating these utopian claims since it functions upon utopian premises. I appreciate the postmodern flexibility of the term and how it encompasses so many varied cultural expressions. The idea of a sensibility feels right to think about in queer terms, and a queer *latinidad* is quite alluring. But I wonder if it is this very dynamic which can prohibit rigorous critical attention. By this I mean that if we identify a queer *latinidad*, could we as critics perhaps begin to ossify what should be dynamic? It seems to me that when we write about culture we begin the process of "authorizing" it, which can have positive and negative consequences. Does thinking about a queer *latinidad* sometimes lead to authorizing stereotypes, for example? I am not convinced that a straight or queer *latinidad* is safe from this process. Here I am thinking too of my own work on Chicano sentimentality and its attraction to representations of heartbreak. Am I contributing to an unwholesome and perhaps outdated, hysterical stereotype?

It makes sense to me to consider dance as utopian. Dance, in its use of movement, is the embodiment of desire. As I watch enviously from the sidelines I can see the various manifestations of identity being choreographed, and I can take for granted that the dance floor is a site of many social and sexual possibilities. Thinking about dance and dance clubs as sites of utopia is a richly interesting idea, and I think we need more of this type of work about queer pleasure. Unfortunately currents seem to be moving toward even more regulation, and at worst, I fear, this type of ethnography and critique might become the only records we have left of these urban utopias.

This essay reminded me in many ways of two important cultural texts: Jennie Livingston's *Paris Is Burning* and José Limón's ethnographic work on Chicano dancehalls.[3] Livingston's work has been accused simultaneously of being sensationalistic and glamorizing, but I think it is time for a more historicizing view not only of the film but also of the climate in which it emerged. The culture wars of the 1980s and 1990s may be in need of historicizing since I think it is from this climate that queers reinvigorated sexuality, pleasure, and ecstasy as utopian forms. I would like to consider how this essay would comment on the sites of display and pleasure in a queer work like *Paris Is Burning* and a straight (and brilliant) work like Limón's.

I want to know more about what we might describe as the ethnography and methodology of "club studies." Arnaldo Cruz-Malavé's recent book, *Queer Latino Testimonio, Keith Haring, and Juanito Xtravaganza: Hard Tails*, offers a superb model of this kind of scholarship. Dance club history is always and already vanishing, and so are the utopias it produces. We should think seriously about how to retrieve these since they are vital forms of Latino history itself.

Clearly I can only begin to draw these points out, but perhaps this process can in turn inform more critique and discussion. I am also raising these questions in the context of my own work and investments since I cannot imagine my ideas outside the realm of queer Chicano cultural studies and work such as Rivera-Servera's. I would also like to add as a disclaimer that since Chicano and Latino cultural studies has made possible a broad range of topics, I am happy to here discuss one that touches me personally very little: dancing. I do not dance, cannot dance, and do not usually frequent places where dance happens. I hope this disclaimer does not make me sound cranky, but instead fills in my perspective.

It can be dramatically satisfying to conclude with pessimism. So I would like to add that my own role as an academic and someone who was trained in cultural studies has caused me some anxiety in the past several years. It seems to me that the turn of the century has brought with it a host of what I call political emergencies, and I fear that working on popular culture has left something out. I wonder if sites of culture remain the best places to look for resistance. I wonder whether we risk privatizing resistance at the expense of more public demonstrations. Perhaps I am arguing that cultural studies requires even more doses of utopia—larger ones, ones that can more spaciously include the public sphere.

NOTES

1. Lipsitz, "Con Safos," 51.
2. Delgado and Muñoz, *Everynight Life*, 10.
3. See Limón, "Dancing with the Devil."

Dance Liberation

David Román

The first time I stepped into a gay bar, a line of people waited in anticipation on a flight of stairs going up to the disco, which was on the second floor of a club called Going My Way? It was the late 1970s in Madison, Wisconsin, and I was a freshman in college. From where I was standing I could not see the space of the dance floor, which threw me for a loop. How many homosexuals were around that corner, I wondered, and would any of them recognize me from French class? Before I knew it people had already positioned themselves behind me on the stairs, and now there was no turning back. This hadn't been my idea. One of the girls from my dorm floor had decided it would be fun to go out dancing at a gay bar, and I, who had no previous interest in disco or dancing, joined her for the adventure. She was a nice Jewish girl from Skokie who wanted to be a stand-up comedian, and I went along for the joke. Years later she would tell me she was bisexual, but that night we were two straight kids out on a dare that had more truth than either one of us could acknowledge at the time.

As we reached the top of the stairs I saw the predominantly male clientele dancing together in what looked to be an activity that had been going on for some time. It both excited and frightened me. I was too scared to have a drink, let alone dance, and insisted we leave right away, which we did. I spouted ugly homophobic comments all the way back to the dorms to deflect my own sense of recognition. I returned to the bar, by myself, shortly afterward and under considerable duress. In fact I was a nervous wreck. The practical concerns were more anxiety producing than the possibility that I might in fact be a homosexual. What if someone saw me on my way to the bar? And once there, would I be recognized? But I had decided that the risks were necessary. I smoked a joint beforehand and prepared for the worst. This time it was a weeknight, and there was no line to get into the club. There was never a cover charge during the week. You simply walked right in. That night I stood on the sidelines and watched as gay men in front of me danced in what seemed to me to be nothing short of a state of joy. Where did they get the nerve?

I can still recall the horror I felt the first time a man asked me to dance. It happened that night. The presumption that I was gay infuriated me nearly as much as the idea that I would want to dance with him of all people. I told him I wasn't interested in dancing, that I wasn't gay, and that I was simply waiting for a friend, a woman, who would be arriving any minute; in fact I should probably go look for her. He said I shouldn't be so afraid of gay people, somehow knowing that what I had just said was a lie. I left danceless and with the bitter sense that gay life, if that's where I was heading, would be full of older lecherous creeps like him. Of course he was a totally nice man in his late twenties studying for a Ph.D., but I didn't know that then. Years later, sometime in the mid-1980s, I helped him cope with his best friend's AIDS diagnosis, a gay man with whom it turned out I had sex a couple of times sometime in between that night at the disco and that day in his hospital room, that is to say between 1978 and 1986, and who turned out to be among the first wave of gay men in Madison to die of AIDS. His friend, someone who worked for the Ford Foundation, was one of a growing number of gay men who had left Madison for one of the coasts and returned very ill. I was his friend's "buddy," part of the small but growing volunteer social services formed in response to AIDS by local gay and lesbian grassroots activism throughout the United States. These services were founded locally in Madison in the mid-1980s by a handful of gay men concerned about AIDS and wanting to do something about it in our community. We, the Madison AIDS Support Network, provided peer-support counseling for people with HIV, practical support for people with AIDS, educational outreach to the various at-risk communities, public speaking and media liaisons for the extended Madison area, hotlines, and ad hoc fundraising to support these activities. Remarkably, in the early years there was only one staff person, who served as our director; the rest of us were volunteers who overlapped in various other roles.

As a buddy I was assigned to administer what was called "emotional support," and that meant anything from accompanying my buddy to doctor's visits, bringing over groceries, or hanging out on his bed sharing stories about our lives. We were also trained to support our buddy's immediate kin; given the stigma of AIDS at the time, more often than not, the client's buddy was the only other person who knew of his HIV status. Confidentiality was the rule. Gay life was always filled with secrets, subcultural codes, insider knowledge, and hidden histories, and AIDS wasn't all that different in that regard. But gay life was also filled with gossip, innuendo, and cruel exposure, and for that reason it was essential that we kept strict confidentiality about the clients we served. Even nearly twenty years later I am reluctant to name these men. In this case my job was to support my buddy and to help his immediate circle of friends navigate the reality of AIDS. But back at the disco that night those years before, my buddy's friend was simply the guy who had the nerve to ask me to dance, and I was simply the questioning youth who didn't have the nerve to take him up on the offer.

While many people subscribed to tired stereotypes of gay men, I cultivated a different impression. Gay people were not merely hairdressers, florists, and psychotherapists; they also danced, together, in public. To be out meant to dance, and to dance meant to be out. It was that simple, or, for me at the time, it was that difficult. And at eighteen I just couldn't do it. Not yet. The next semester I left the dorms and moved in with two older women in their early twenties who were artsy bohemian types. Both were incredibly sexually active, and one, Linda, was especially drawn to dancing. She took dance classes, went to dance workshops, and was an all-around party girl who loved the night-life. One afternoon Linda came home from classes with three new records — Sylvester's *Step II*, Keith Barrow's *Physical Attraction*, and Cheryl Lynn's self-titled solo album featuring the hits "Got to Be Real" and "Star Love" — and brought the disco home. For weeks we would dance around the apartment together to these records, usually free-form, hippie-like motions or whatever recent steps Linda had learned in her jazz improvisation class. My moves were more boy punk rock jumps that surprisingly were as much to the beat of disco as they were to the Talking Heads. Sometimes Linda would choreograph scenes for the two of us in the privacy of our home. These were little performance installations that featured us in various stages of undress. For my nineteenth birthday she made a mock album cover for me of one of these staged vignettes, "David Roman and the Muse." In the image she is the erotic muse and I am the passive subject, although it was supposed to be my dream (figure 1).

Another queer cliché: she knew that I was gay before I did, and she helped bring me out. Our home was a space of both dance rehearsal and sexual exploration. She once even had a three-way with a man and another woman! Linda and her friends were having a lot of sex, and I wasn't. She would tease me about my needing to get laid by a guy and would encourage me to try to pick up men. She even recommended a few of her former lovers who were into sexual experimentation. But for me sexual experimentation meant trying to find ways to get aroused by the cute art student girlfriend I was dating at the time, not hooking up with bisexual men. Once, after more failed heterosexual experimentation than I could handle for one night, I left my girlfriend's apartment at two in the morning to go back home. We lived on opposite sides of The Square, the area surrounding Madison's capitol building. Who knew that this was a major site

1. R.E.M.: *David Roman and the Muse*. Mock album cover. Photograph by Linda Fargo, 1979. Collection of the author.

for gay cruising? Well, apparently and not surprisingly, gay people did, as I was soon to find out. Crossing The Square I met a handsome man who invited me up to L'Etoile, the exclusive French restaurant and bar he managed, to smoke a joint. I told him I was just coming back from my girlfriend's apartment, and he told me about Judy Garland, seahorses, and bisexuality. He was the first gay man I was attracted to with whom I had consensual sex and a lasting conversation. He was twenty-six, and his name was David too.

One night Linda and I went out together to Going My Way? and joined the others on the dance floor. I always loved going out with Linda; she was sexy and outgoing and she commanded attention from whatever crowd she was in, even a roomful of queers. After an hour or so of dancing she remembered that she had a sex date back at our apartment. She left and I stayed. And then it seemed I was out. I started going out dancing nearly every night after studying at the University of Wisconsin's Memorial Library. Sometimes I would meet Linda there, but increasingly I went by myself or would meet David, or some of the gay men I met through him. The bar was only three blocks from my apartment, and while it wasn't the most immediate route from the library, it wasn't really out of the way either.

Mainly I went to dance and to be part of the sense of queer culture that the space enacted. Dance became the entry point to other forms of queer connection: friendship, sex, employment. But it also was a means for me to begin choreographing my own movements through the world as an openly gay man. I loved dancing because it gave me a way to be in my body and to be around other gay people in a way that was very new for me. The best songs of the time literalized the feelings I was experiencing through their titles and lyrics: Patrick Hernandez's "Born to Be Alive," Sylvester's "(You Make Me Feel) Mighty Real," and Cheryl Lynn's "Got to Be Real." "Disco," as Wayne Koestenbaum has written, "was the theme music of gay male sexuality in the late 1970s."[1] I took to this music quickly and readily. Soon enough I became a regular at the bar and within a few months was hired to be the bartender. The lesbian owners of the club liked the energy I brought to the dance floor and thought I'd be a good employee. I became the dancing bartender, a kind of go-go boy serving gimlets. Working there gave me the excuse for being there every night, and if my coming out was going to be happening in bar culture, I figured I might as well get paid for it. I also needed the money.

Shortly after I started bartending I was offered a one-night-a-week spot as a disc jockey. I hosted New Wave and Deep Funk Night. These jobs led me to the other gay-friendly bar in Madison, The Cardinal Bar, which was owned by Ricardo Gonzalez, the only other Latino gay man I had met at the time, and where my friend David was the house disc jockey. Unlike Going My Way?, The Cardinal was a community-gathering place that held benefits for various progressive causes and campaigns and whose clientele was racially and culturally diverse. It wasn't a gay club per se, but all of its employees were gay and gay people were always welcome. I worked the front bar at happy hour three shifts a week and the back bar by the dance floor two nights a week.

My coming out in bar culture enabled me to meet a wide range of queer and queer-friendly people who all helped me figure out how to be gay. Everyone recognized that I was new on the scene, and for the most part people were really cool about it. These jobs initiated me into the often overlapping social networks of Madison's queer, progressive, and multicultural communities. One of the benefits of coming out in smaller cities like Madison in the late 1970s was the nearly immediate access to the relatively modest local lesbian and gay community. Pretty much everyone knew one another. Gay men and lesbians were forced to forge alliances for political gain, and we met across class, gender, and racial lines to do so.

Outside of the annual gay pride parade no other event would symbolize queer community for me more powerfully than the image of us all dancing together, which we did often. I had come out and into a history of gay and lesbian struggle and resistance, in a period in the decade following Stonewall, when gay and lesbian organizing and community building were the mandate of the times. I stepped into an ongoing dance called gay liberation that formed my political and social identity. That meant dancing with butch lesbian cab drivers, who demanded to hear "Mack the Knife," even if the rest of us couldn't dance to it; with recently exiled Cuban Marielito queens, who in their efforts to assimilate into U.S. queer culture sprayed, and subsequently burned, their chests with Nair; with pretty boy model wannabes, who danced carefully so as not to break too much of a sweat; with mixed-race butch-femme couples, who rarely danced free-form and always held each other close; with white boys who went to Chicago once a month for weekends of extreme sex at the baths; with drag queens of all races born in small neighboring towns who moved to Madison to wear wigs and pearls; with guys who had been to San Francisco and came back dancing with tambourines; with graduate students of all genders who were writing term papers on Luce Irigaray, Hélène Cixous, and Monique Wittig; with sexy young gay men who took their shirts off and waved them in the air, and with the occasional baby dyke who did the same; with the town drunks who inevitably brought their drinks — and spilled them, broken glass to deal with now — onto the dance floor because they couldn't dance or be gay otherwise; with charismatic bisexual girls like Linda who knew that this was where it was all happening at the time; and increasingly with men who I would pick up and enjoy for whatever amount of time we both would allow ourselves.

I realize that many accounts of gay culture overly romanticize dance as utopian, as the great democratizing ritual that brings diverse people together and that models a level of sociality that has not yet materialized off the dance floor.[2] (I should add that the same argument has often been made for public sex and the baths.)[3] I understand this impulse to idealize dance, as well as the various caveats that have been introduced to challenge this popular view, including the arguments that drugs and alcohol, so endemic to club culture, are unlikely resources to invest in for political liberation, and that gay clubs have histories of discrimination, which limit who gets to participate in these utopian yearnings. And yet there is something to be said for the image of queer people of all ages, genders, and races dancing together to Chic's "Good Times" in the summer of 1979:

Good times, these are the good times
Leave your cares behind, these are the good times
Good times, these are the good times
Our new state of mind, these are the good times
Happy days are here again
The time is right for makin' friends
Let's get together, how 'bout a quarter to ten
Come tomorrow, let's all do it again.[4]

In the decade after Stonewall and in the years before AIDS, gay liberation had altered queer life in America and those of us coming out in this time were the immediate beneficiaries of years of political resistance and cultural agitation. Something was happening across America in the late 1970s that was drastically shifting life for lesbians and gay men, and it was palpable in dance clubs and in the music that filled these public spaces.

Perhaps the reason that so many accounts of gay club culture read it as utopian has something to do with the idea that dance, as a kinetic experience, enables social configurations of same-sex bodies not imaginable elsewhere. I would go further, however, and say that for me dance was not merely the moment when the future was made manifest. It was also the temporal reality that queer people had made for themselves through prior years of political struggle: "Our new state of mind, these are the good times." This sense of dance's already liberatory enactment refutes the euphoric idea that dance only imagines a future. Dance does not simply forecast a possible world; it puts into motion the material bodies of queers in public spaces that were created out of political and psychological necessity. Dance signaled not the promise of gay liberation but its practice. I knew that the first time I stepped into a gay bar and saw gay people dancing. I just didn't know how I was supposed to step into that dance, and I didn't quite know the necessary moves to get there. But there was no question that these people had figured it out and created something for themselves and for others like me.

Early gay liberationists recognized dance as a fundamental component of the political movement and began to prioritize it as such. Dances were critical to the foundation of early gay organizing, although this history remains to be completely excavated. Harry Hay, one of the pioneers of the gay and lesbian movement and a founder of the Mattachine Society, one of the earliest gay rights groups in the United States, speaks of the importance of dance when recalling the history of the group in an interview from the late 1970s. Hay is reminiscing on the early years of Mattachine in Los Angeles:

> Well, before there was any gay consciousness, before there was any voice speaking for us, we spoke for each other. In 1951, we had our first semi-public dance. People who didn't even know about our discussion groups came to the dance. One guy came up to me in the course of the evening and said, "man, you don't know what it means to be able to hold another man in your arms and dance and all of a sudden walk outside and stand under the stars and breathe." Well, we had a number of dances, with other people who until then maybe knew four or five others within their small circle who danced together. But these dances would draw maybe three hundred guys together. This was something very beautiful and liberating for those who'd never gone through it.[5]

As Hay makes clear, dance was not superfluous to the political mission of the organization but central to it. It was something "very beautiful and liberating" that brought gay people into political consciousness. And yet historical accounts of the lesbian and gay movement generally underplay the importance of dance. Same-sex dance is described as something that was legislated against and that gay people had to carefully choreograph so as to avoid criminal offense. Or it is described as the colorful expressive practice of gays, who strove to entertain themselves in light of the oppressive conditions of day-to-day life, a sign of queer resilience.[6] Sometimes dance is mentioned in historical accounts as an activity to raise money for political organizations; while the dance fundraiser has a long history in gay and lesbian politics, it deserves a fuller account, which has yet to be produced by cultural historians or dance scholars.[7] Apart from the personal memoirs of veteran gay and lesbian people, dance is rarely discussed as a political activity no less critical to the movement than the marches and demonstrations of the pre- and post-Stonewall activists. Consider that in 1970, when the lesbians involved in New York's Gay Liberation Front (GLF) grew tired of the male predominance at GLF's events, they chose dance as the activity to mark lesbian space within the organization and produced the first all-women's dances in the city. The event on 3 April was contentious for the group. Many of the men thought it might prove a waste of resources and a potentially divisive tactic, while some of the women felt it might replicate the worst of lesbian bar culture.[8] But the dance ultimately proved enormously successful. Karla Jay, one of the key activists of GLF, explains:

When we finally held our first dance, it surpassed our expectations. The weather was cold but clear. The place was packed. We even attracted some media stars such as Jill Johnston, a columnist for the *Village Voice*, and noted essayist Susan Sontag. We were thrilled. My straight friends from *Redstockings* and *Rat* sat nervously on the make-out couches and hoped no one would ask them to dance. When no one did, some were insulted. Other straight women unabashedly danced with each other and with us. As one woman wrote in *Rat* afterward: "Dancing with women is something else again. It was one of the most beautiful experiences of my life—a total high. . . . I am learning to love women, and the dance was a first step." A few of the straight women went home together and brought each other out.

The GLF women had a fabulous time as we danced to our favorite music. We danced fast, we did some Greek and Jewish dances in groups and circles, and we even played some slow songs. It was the hip 1970s, and we rarely touched on the dance floor. Free drugs were easier to find than a slow tune. There were times at some GLF dances that I was definitely nostalgic for the bars. Those sexy bar butches, now reclassified as politically incorrect, held me tight when we danced.[9]

Although Jay's account of the early GLF women's dances distinguishes the socializing found among women in bars and women at politically sponsored dances, she nonetheless documents what these dances helped create for women in the early 1970s.[10] It was dance that brought these women together, that brought many of them out of the closet, and that helped organize them politically. For many of these women, "dance," as Jay notes, "was a first step."

Dance was a first step for me too. A few months after I came out I participated in my first gay pride march and rally. While my coming out mainly occurred in bar culture, it was also enabled by the university and a handful of brave lesbian professors who taught me: Evelyn Beck, Elaine Marks, Yvonne Ozzello, and Claudia Card. These professors taught me about feminism and its necessity, about culture and the arts, and about philosophy and the hard work of critical thinking. In their classes I met other young queer undergrads, mainly lesbians, struggling with many of the issues I had been encountering as well. Increasingly my world became more integrated—that's what it means to be out of the closet, I learned—and I socialized with these new friends from the university and my other friends from the bars too.

I spent the day of the march with my friends from The Cardinal and with my friend Trip from Atlanta, whom I had met only a few weeks before. Trip and I

Gays and supporters march for civil rights

By Ron McCrea
Press Connection Writer

Gay Awareness Week got off to a rousing start Sunday as some 400 lesbians, gay men and their supporters paraded down State Street to the Capitol for speeches and songs.

The observance, ordained by the City Council in a resolution, runs through Sept. 16.

The march was the largest demonstration of gay solidarity in Madison since activists began organizing in 1969. The tone of the march ranged from the solemn, with the singing of "We Shall Overcome," to camp, with a Cadillac decked in flowers carrying the legend "Gladiola to be Gay."

At the Capitol, the council's resolution was read by Ald. Iris Walker (Dist. 8), and the four council members who registered votes against it were served notice that gay political clout could be marshalled against them in the next election. The last verse of a song sung by the marchers to the tune of "We Shall Not Be Moved" went:

"Onken and Stewart — they should be removed; Johnson and Holt — they should be removed.

the butter, they should be removed."

The references were to Alds. Warren Onken (Dist. 15), Jean Stewart (Dist. 20), Nancy Johnson (Dist. 13) and James Holt (Dist. 19).

The marchers were also encouraged to join a demonstration in Washington, D.C. on Oct. 14. Information on transportation is available from Michael at 257-1147 and Kathleen at 244-5354.

Later Sunday evening, a board of trustees consisting of prominent gays and community supporters was installed for The United, a non-profit umbrella organization supporting gay civil rights and educational activities in Madison.

Those installed at ceremonies at L'Etoile restaurant were Rita Wlodarczyk, chairwoman of the Dane County Democratic Party; Rep. David Clarenbach (D-Madison); Madison Fire Chief Ed Durkin; Verna Hill, Madison Press Connection General Manager; Elaine Marks, director of the University of Wisconsin Women's Studies Center; Evelyn Beck, also of the Women's Studies Center; Dr. Ruth Bleier, professor of neuroanatomy at

A flowery float lent a touch of camp to Sunday's gay march.

—Press Connection photo by Brent Nicastro

mission members A. Gridley Hall, Bob Greene, and LeAnna Ware; Rev. Tom Woodward, Rev. Vernon Forsberg, D. J. Wipperfurth, Andrea Musher, Karen Ax-

counselor with the Division of Community Services of the State Department of Health and Social Services; Jay Jones, Channel 15 reporter; Jean Pierick of the WSA Pharmacy, and Verena

conferences.

Gay Awareness Week continues today with a benefit for The United at the Cardinal Bar and Cafe, featuring disco with discaire David Martinelli. A $2

2. Local newspaper coverage of the March for Lesbian and Gay Rights on 10 September 1979 in Madison, Wisconsin. Photograph by Brent Nicastro. Collection of the author.

had enjoyed the weekend together uncertain who we were meant to be to each other, which meant we tried a little of everything to see what might work best. Nearly four hundred people paraded up State Street, Madison's main commercial strip, to the capitol, where the street ended. It was the largest march in Madison's history. I rode in the vintage Pontiac convertible which led the parade under the banner "Gladiola to Be Gay" with my friend David, who stood atop the backseat dressed in a white genderfuck outfit as the unofficial queen of the parade (figure 2). The rest of us, who I guess were his court, handed out gladiolas to the crowd. This was the man who had picked me up outside his French restaurant only months before and who helped secure me my summer job at the Cardinal Bar. DJ, the differently sized butch cabdriver, drove the car. The others in the car were coworkers from the bar and the restaurant who had taken me in right away. I was invited into this ever-expanding intergenerational circle without question, the youngest in the group. Granted I slept with a number of the men in the group—not everyone!—but it never felt coercive or weird. But that weekend I was smitten with Trip, and holding his hand at the steps of the state capitol seemed to me to be the point of the rally itself.

Dance Liberation   295

After the rally Trip and I joined the group at Lysistrata, Madison's feminist restaurant and bar collective, and danced together with the others from the rally and the day's parade. The music was selected by David and Chris, the lesbian house disc jockey at Lysistrata, who was also our friend. Throughout the night, DJ, the butch cabdriver, was trying to find the news coverage of the march and spent most of her time standing on a chair, switching channels and hoping for the best. The TV was elevated above the dance floor to allow for videos at night and sports television by day. But that night no one else could get near the TV, and no one else even tried. Everyone knew not to mess with DJ when she was focused on a project. Finally, while the rest of us are dancing, and with DJ standing on a chair with her Scotch and lit cigar, she finds it—the right station at the right moment. There we are on television marching for lesbian and gay rights! Chris and David immediately put on Sister Sledge's "We Are Family," and even DJ jumped down from her chair and joined the dance. Everyone was pleased and proud. And it was there on the dance floor at Lysistrata, in the midst of this queer group of friends, that Trip and I, while making out, decided to go to the first National March on Washington for Lesbian and Gay Rights held the following month.

But a month later Trip couldn't make it to D.C., and I went to the National March with a busload of queer Madisonians. The march, "an end to all social, economic, judicial, and legal oppression of Lesbian and Gay people," was on a Sunday, and we got there on Saturday in time for me to attend Pat Bond's one-woman show as Gertrude Stein, *Gerty, Gerty, Gerty Stein Is Back, Back, Back*, and then go out to the clubs and dance. (While I've never had trouble getting friends to go out dancing, it was more of a challenge getting them to see queer theater.) I joined two Madison friends, Brian and Abe, at D.C.'s popular dance club Lost and Found, which was packed with gay men from all over the country celebrating the March on Washington weekend. Just as the disc jockey put on Thelma Houston's "Don't Leave Me This Way," someone named Tim from Virginia asked me to dance. And this time there was no horror, no hesitation, no alibi, only dancing and kissing and shirts off together. Surrounded and protected by a sea of gay men of all backgrounds and ages and dancing with this cute boy my own age made me feel liberated and alive.

At the end of the four-column mission statement calling for the National March on Washington, and after identifying the multiple reasons for "why we are marching," the organizers wrote, "Most of all, the march will be exhilarating for all of us and give us the boost we need to carry on our work. We will be 'coming out' nationally and greeting our sisters and brothers in a unified demonstration of our pride, our spirit, and our determination to have our rights."[11] The next day's march undoubtedly accomplished that and more for me, but the events the night before at Pat Bond's solo performance and the late-night dancing at Lost and Found added to the exhilaration promised by the march's organizers. Lesbian and gay people had any number of places to go dancing that weekend, and as the lines and crowds made evident, for many of us dancing was a prerequisite to the march itself. Dancing and marching were not antithetical activities, nor were they located at different points on some assumed continuum of political agency.

I imagine that there were many people who went out dancing on the night before the March on Washington who did not participate in the next day's unprecedented political events. (In fact I was out so late dancing and carrying on that I overslept the next morning and missed my transportation to the Mall.) And I imagine that many of those people had no interest in political protests of any kind. But many of us combined the activities because that's what it meant to be out. That was the point. Quite simply, if you were out, you more than likely went out too. You danced and you marched. That's what I was taught by my queer mentors, and that's what I practiced that weekend: dance liberation.

There's an amazing scene in *The Boys in the Band*, Mart Crowley's important and controversial play, when the group of gay friends, who have gathered at the New York apartment of their host, Michael, for their friend Harold's surprise thirtieth birthday party, begin to dance. It's 1968 and the men, who are in their late twenties and early thirties, begin dancing one at a time, each one stepping into the beat and moving to the music. The dance scene comes midway through the first act, at the point in the party when the gay friends have relaxed and allowed themselves a temporary break from the hostilities of the straight world, which will soon interrupt their party as well. But before then, and after loosening up, one guest, Hank, puts on a record and Bernard, the only black man in the group, begins to "move in time to the music."[12] Crowley's stage directions read, "Michael joins in," and then "Michael and Bernard are now dancing freely." After a knock on the door Emory, the resident camp queen, quips, "Oh my God! It's Lily Law! Everybody three feet apart!," a reminder of the high stakes involved in queer dancing and socializing in the years before Stonewall, and a reminder of the routineness of these raids for lesbians and gays at the time. But it's neither "Lily Law" nor Harold, the birthday friend, at the door, but a delivery boy with a cake. Relieved, the group returns to their dancing, a kinesthetic ritual of knowingness that signals the subcultural codes of queer collectivity and belonging.

The party was threatened once already when Michael's old acquaintance Alan (who is married and lives in D.C. but happened to be in New York City that day) called unexpectedly and, in a moment of personal distress, invited himself over. It turned out that Alan and his wife were having trouble, and Alan needed a friend. But by the end of the phone call, Alan decided against stopping by, much to Michael's relief. Michael, who is not out to Alan, is now free to relax into the party's festive and campy antics without the fear of homophobic interruption. He returns to join his dancing friends and, as Crowley writes, "falls in line with them." Here is how Crowley brings the boys in the band back to the dance:

> Larry: Hey Bernard, do you remember that thing we used to do on Fire Island?
> [Larry starts doing a kind of Madison.]
> Bernard: That was "in" so far back I think I've forgotten.
> Emory: I remember.
> [Pops up—starts doing the steps. Larry and Bernard start to follow.]
> Larry: Yeah that's it.
> [Michael enters from the kitchen, falls in line with them.]
> Michael: Well, if it isn't the Geriatric Rockettes!
> [Now they are all doing nearly a precision routine. Donald comes to sit on the arm of a chair, sip his drink, and watch in fascination. Hank goes to the bar to get another beer.
> The door buzzer sounds. No one seems to hear it. It buzzes again. Hank turns toward the door, hesitates. Looks toward Michael, who is now deeply involved in the intricacies of the dance. No one, it seems, has heard the buzzer but Hank, who goes to the door, opens it wide to reveal Alan. He is dressed in black tie.
> The dancers continue, turning and slapping their knees and heels and laughing with abandon. Suddenly Michael looks up, stops dead. Donald sees this and turns to see what Michael has seen. Slowly he stands up.
> Michael goes to the record player, turns it off abruptly. Emory, Larry, and Bernard come to out-of-step halts, look to see what's happened.]
> Michael: I thought you said you weren't coming.
> Alan: I . . . well, I'm sorry . . .
> Michael: [Forced lightly] We were just—acting silly . . . Emory was just showing us this . . . silly dance.[13]

The silly dance, of course, is anything but silly. It was the one activity that the friends were able to do together as a group that demonstrated their affectional connection and provided them a sense of pleasure. The silly dance ruptures the division between public and private as the group integrates the two generally separate spheres of sociality into one where the distinction between them blurs. This moment—of both the closet and its defiance, of both the memory of queer sociality and its enactment—is for me one of the great moments of gay theater. It tells us everything we need to know about queer history, style, and sociality and about the pressures and possibilities of gay life for urban gay men before Stonewall. Dance features prominently in this history, and its importance to the friends in Michael's apartment is made palpable by what is lost with the arrival of the uninvited guest who crashes the party and stops the dance cold. The friends bring the dance home to reenact the liberatory pleasures of the Fire Island retreat in the assumed safety and comfort of domesticity. But Alan's arrival—the classic intruder plot—challenges this achievement and puts it to the test.

In this short scene the friends re-create a moment of queer sociality undertaken through dance in Fire Island and relive it in the moment of the now. This rehearsal of history enables the boys in the band to occupy the present as gay male friends. Emory, the camp queen, is the one who remembers the moves and thus might be said to be the group's historian and preserver of the archive. It is Emory, the most effeminate of them, who can retrieve the body's kinesthetic memory and offer it back to the group so they can continue to dance, "laughing with abandon." And it is Emory who resists the conformity of the regulatory moves of homosexual shame and humiliation that the friends resort to once the music stops. The drama of the play is not whether Alan is gay or straight, or whether he will stay or go—he's the least compelling of the characters—but whether or not the friends can return to that moment of abandon made possible earlier in the evening by the dance. They did it already once before, and the play must be now about figuring out how to do it again.

Most critics read *The Boys in the Band* as a play of gay stereotypes and self-hatred and focus their readings on Michael's gradual decline into hysterical self-loathing. Understandably the scenes where Alan beats on Emory and where Harold admonishes Michael for his behavior become the critical focus. The dance sequence, on the other hand, gets virtually no mention in these assessments of the play.[14] (One critic, however, included, as something of an afterthought, the following remark at the end of his review: "And one more matter—perhaps it's my thing, but I just can't take guys dancing with each other. It only looks like pathetic imitation of men with women.")[15] Though the men are unable to escape the night's demoralizing events, they are not completely defeated at the end. No one leaves alone, and though they are bruised and battered their friendships prevail.[16] Crowley's insertion of the dance scene early on in the play makes a significant representational intervention that showcases the fundamental necessity of gay friendship networks and highlights the moves that might be necessary to keep homophobia and gay shame at bay. Looking at dance also allows for a more complicated and nuanced reading of the play to emerge, one that challenges the reading put forward by critics who mainly interpret the play's text. This scene in *The Boys in the Band* suggests one of the critical roles that dance plays in queer culture and by extension queer history, and it suggests that dance is more central to queer life than scholars have previously acknowledged.

These early dances of gay liberation, each localized and enacted in vulnerable queer space—whether in Los Angeles in 1951 or New York in 1970 or, as in the case of Crowley's play, on an Off-Broadway stage in 1968—predated my own disco excursions of the late 1970s. But they helped form the history that made my participation possible. These earlier events were undertaken in the context of social, political, and cultural struggle, and those dancers, real and imagined, helped move this struggle forward even if many of them had no intention of doing so at the time.

During the intense first decade of the AIDS epidemic many of my Madison friends from the bars, including some of my coworkers from the Cardinal Bar and Going My Way?, would die. Many of these friends, most of whom were in their early twenties, moved from Madison to San Francisco or New York in the early 1980s in order to exchange the intimacy of Madison for the anonymity of the big city, a standard migration for midwestern boys then and now.[17] I made the opposite migration, from the East Coast to the Midwest, and stayed there for nearly ten years and for most of my twenties. In 1987, after nine years in Madison, I moved to Chicago and continued my involvement with community-based AIDS service organizations, including the local chapter of the Names Project, or the AIDS memorial quilt as it is more widely known. During its display at Navy Pier in the summer of 1988, before it would head to Washington, D.C., later that fall and where over eight thousand panels would be displayed on the Ellipse in front of the White House, my partner Doug and I helped with many other volunteers unveil the quilt in Chicago. It was here that I saw the panel for Keith Barrow, the young soulful singer of *Physical Attraction*, one of the albums Linda had brought home those years before. He was never afforded the success of some of the other artists of the disco era, but that might have something to do with the fact that he died at the age of twenty-seven. Stitched on his panel is the simple and urgent message "Find the Cure for AIDS." His mother, an active member of Chicago's African American gospel community, had been invited to read names at the display, and I felt very privileged recognizing her son and his music when she read aloud his name. In his memory, and in the memory of so many others who had died, Doug and I and some of the other volunteers that weekend went out dancing.

A few years later, in 1990, Doug and I moved to Los Angeles. I was teaching at Pomona College on a one-year visiting appointment, my first academic job after securing my Ph.D. While we were both very involved in ACT-UP L.A., we also felt equally at home in AIDS activist groups less devoted to direct action. Too often the history of AIDS activism centers on ACT-UP and less on the community labors that helped local AIDS service organizations do their important work. Many of us who were involved in ACT-UP also volunteered for the agencies that provided direct services to people with HIV/AIDS. Doug got immediately involved in AIDS Project Los Angeles (APLA), helping with various services, including the planning of the annual dance-a-thon (figure 3). Through his involvement in APLA he met our friend Terry, an older gay man in his fifties, who happened to be very close with Christopher Flynn, Madonna's dance teacher and mentor and one of the first to encourage her to be an artist during her formative years in Michigan. Madonna credits Christopher as one of her major life influences: "He was my mentor, my father, my imaginative lover, my brother, everything. He understood me."[18] Christopher, who had been living in Los Angeles, died a few months after we moved there ourselves. In the final months of his battle with AIDS Madonna had bought him a special Posturepedic bed so that he would spend his last weeks in comfort. Christopher had lived in it for only a few weeks before he died. Doug and I inherited this bed after his death. We had been sleeping on a futon for years, and we were more than ready for an upgrade when Terry, who helped manage Christopher's estate after his death, offered the bed to us.

Christopher Flynn has been regularly eulogized by Madonna, and her frequent and consistent work for AIDS is often in his honor. At that year's APLA Dance-a-thon, Madonna, whom I have never met but have always loved, made a surprise appearance (figure 4). She performed a short set and danced in Christopher's honor. That night Doug and I danced with Terry, some of our other friends, and thousands of others who had gathered to raise money for APLA by simply dancing. It was clear that Christopher's spirit would survive in the growing global celebrity of Madonna and in the local intimate exchanges of gay men like us who memorialized him through our dancing and the passing of his material goods (figure 5). I always felt it incredibly poignant that Madonna

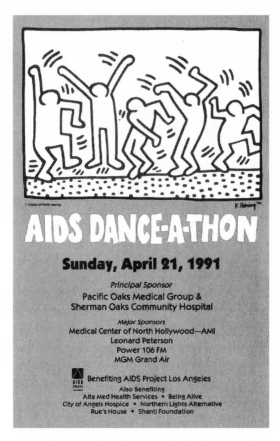

AIDS DANCE-A-THON

Sunday, April 21, 1991

Principal Sponsor
**Pacific Oaks Medical Group &
Sherman Oaks Community Hospital**

Major Sponsors
**Medical Center of North Hollywood—AMI
Leonard Peterson
Power 106 FM
MGM Grand Air**

Benefiting AIDS Project Los Angeles
Also Benefiting
Alta Med Health Services • Being Alive
City of Angels Hospice • Northern Lights Alternative
Rue's House • Shanti Foundation

3. AIDS Dance-a-thon flyer, AIDS Project Los Angeles,
21 April 1991. Courtesy of the estate of Keith Haring and APLA.

comforted her dance teacher and friend in his dying days by buying him a new bed. This man, who taught her how to move and was now immobilized by AIDS, lived his final days under Madonna's care. Christopher's bed, which I slept in for over ten years and is now in my guest room, is a symbol of Madonna's love for him, and subsequently my love for the various men with whom I've come to share it.

A year later, in the fall of 1991, Doug and I—and Christopher's bed—headed up to Seattle. Once again we got involved in the local ACT-UP chapter and the various AIDS community-based projects there. Doug volunteered at the Chicken Soup Brigade, Seattle's meals-on-wheels program, and I volunteered

MADONNA *dancing*
with participants
at the
first APLA
AIDS Dance-a-thon . . .

JUST IMAGINE
this year's event at
its new, larger location . . .
the L.A. Sports Arena.

4. Flyer for AIDS Project Los Angeles featuring Madonna for the APLA Dance-a-thon, 1991. Collection of the author.

Christopher Flynn
April 29, 1931-October 27, 1990

Do not go gentle into that good night.
Rage, rage against the dying of the light.

—Dylan Thomas

5. Memorial card for
Christopher Flynn, 1931–90.
Collection of the author.

at the Bailey-Boushay House, a round-the-clock skilled nursing care facility for people living and dying with HIV. Most of the residents moved into the house during their final stages of HIV and would die there within days or weeks. Few people moved out of the the Bailey-Boushay House during the time I volunteered there. It was an incredibly sad place, but it was also a place of deep care, queer intimacy, and real love. I volunteered there on Wednesday afternoons and on Saturdays. Whenever someone died—either in the House, among my circle of friends, or in the extended AIDS community of which I was part—I would go out dancing as a way to memorialize him. Sometimes I wondered if I just used this as an excuse to go out and forget about AIDS—dance as hedonism and escape—and perhaps that was a part of it as well. But mainly it felt like the right thing to do, a ritual to celebrate a life now lost.

Often I would go with my friend John, perhaps the angriest AIDS activist I ever met and undoubtedly one of the most astute. John, who was an instrumental force in ACT-UP L.A., had moved with his lover, Larry, to Seattle a few years back. I met both of them through my involvement in ACT-UP Seattle. John and I would go out to local Seattle bars and pound the floor, sometimes with our partners but not always, and we would not stop dancing until the lights came up. There was nothing lyrical about our dancing, just endless physical motion that kept us grounded in our bodies. At the Bailey-Boushay House I visited with men whose bodies were afflicted with neuropathy, a disease of the nervous system that numbs the limbs, especially the feet; men who were confined to wheelchairs and beds, whose mobility was completely compromised by HIV and who could barely move without the help of others; and men who were in states of semiconsciousness and whose relationship to their body was one of extreme distress or morphine-induced calm. I would visit with these men and sometimes wheel them out to the smoking room, where, with their IV-drip, they would sit for an afternoon smoke or two. Or we would go for a stroll up and down the halls, simply to "get some air," as one man would request. Or I would sit quietly with them and gently rub their back or hold their frail hands so that they might have some nonclinical touch. Some of these men were alone and, except for the staff and volunteers, had no one in their immediate life. Some had already lost lovers and close friends and were themselves the last of their friendship circle to die. Of course the staff and volunteers established close relations with many of the residents, not as surrogates of love necessarily, but as the real deal.

The simple choreography of getting in and out of bed for many was, well, not so simple. To be among these gay men and to have shared with them their final days was for me one of the most profound and heartbreaking experiences of my life. I cannot tell these stories without being overwhelmed with feelings and memories that to this day I do not quite know how to manage. At the time I dealt with this confusion through dance. Dancing was a way to return to my own body and to differentiate it from theirs, a reminder that despite the prevalence of HIV in my life I was not infected. I could go out and dance, and so I did. It meant I didn't have to talk about it, even though I couldn't anyway, given the rules of confidentiality. Dancing also connected me with a history of queer resilience, a kind of reenergizing necessary to get through the week. But mainly, and especially when I went out with John, dance was a way to express my anger and feelings of despair brought on by the relentless death toll I was witnessing.

Perhaps the reason I found *Movin' Out*, Twyla Tharp's current Broadway dance musical based on the songs and music of Billy Joel, so unexpectedly powerful and emotionally effective has to do with the way it brought me back to the complicated feelings I've carried about AIDS over time. How strange that we never really know which performances will speak to us. Sometimes—out of nowhere, really—a chord is struck, a memory triggered, an emotion invoked that opens up a production that held no promise of connection. To be open to these moments is the challenge of our theatergoing.

Movin' Out tells the story of a group of youthful heterosexual friends who are torn apart by the Vietnam War. Each of the main characters undergoes a transformative experience brought upon by the death of friends and the terrible effects of war. Those who survive are forced to rebuild their lives with a sense of this history, because, as Joel sings, "the memory stays."[19] The production, set on Long Island in the 1960s, chronicles the group's emotional journey through this volatile period of time. Tharp tells their story exclusively through dance, which is performed by members of her company and from the world of ballet, and through Billy Joel's songs, which are performed by a singer and a nine-piece band who are set apart on an elevated stage above the dramatic action. *Movin' Out* is neither a musical revue nor a dance recital, but a hybrid of dance and theater that troubles easy categorizations. It can be seen as part of the larger trend of returning dance to the American musical and to the Broadway stage, a movement led by choreographers such as Susan Stroman, Jerry Mitchell, and others that started in the late 1990s.

In one brilliant moment early on in the second act Tharp, who conceived, directed, and choreographed the production, has Eddie, the main protagonist, expertly danced by John Selya in one of the 2002–3 Broadway season's most beautiful performances, rage against his war experiences. In a sequence of vigorous dance moves that has Selya and other men from the ensemble leaping across the stage to the song "Angry Young Man," Tharp and her dancers hit the emotional registers of rage and resentment. While the dancing is fast and aggressive, it nonetheless conveys the vulnerability that comes with loss and that fuels deep-rooted anger. It spoke to the pain of a generation of young men broken by war, and while this was neither my generation nor my life experience, it felt intimately familiar to me.

I did not anticipate my own response to this particular scene, let alone the entire production that framed it. Although I recognize and respect Billy Joel's talent, I have never been a fan and I own none of his recordings. His music does not inform my life, so my response was not already weighted with nostalgia or recognition. In fact I had little interest in seeing *Movin' Out* precisely for these reasons. I went because my partner, Richard, was curious about it and recommended we give it a try. More often than not, given that I am the theater scholar, I end up researching and recommending the performances we attend. Every once in a while Richard will suggest something that is not on my list. That's how we first ended up at *Movin' Out*, but it is the strength of the production and its talented cast that have brought me back to the Richard Rodgers Theatre to see it again and again on my own.

Movin' Out pays tribute to a particular historical experience of generational loss that may or may not be the lived reality of all of its audiences. It succeeds by allowing for intergenerational identifications that do not rely on the music of Billy Joel but on the movements of the dancers themselves. I did not anticipate having my experiences with AIDS summoned by this production, but scenes such as "Angry Young Men," and others later in the production that addressed the hope of communal regeneration, triggered them. "The thing that makes dance powerful," Tharp explains in the liner notes to the original Broadway cast soundtrack, "is that the audience can project its own story up there. . . . Not Billy Joel's, not mine, but yours."[20]

Shortly after *Movin' Out*'s opening, one of the cast's principal dancers was killed when the motorcycle he was driving struck a taxi in midtown Manhattan. William Marrié, who performed the role of Eddie at the Wednesday and Saturday matinees, was on his way to the theater. He was thirty-three and, according to Tharp, "he was a wonderful dancer and a huge heart. He was passionate as a human being, very smart, and there was nothing phony about him," a tribute that could easily describe the production in which he was cast.[21] Near the end of *Movin' Out*, in a scene titled "Eddie Attains Grace" and composed of three songs—"River of Dreams," "Keeping the Faith," and "Only the Good Die Young"—the ensemble, led by the dancer performing the role of Eddie, performs an exuberant ritual of renewal. Tharp releases her dancers to showcase their individual moves while keeping the idea of the ensemble, which is to say the community, alive. It's a well-earned moment for both the dancers and the audience. I would have liked to see William Marrié perform in this ensemble and notice the intricacies of his movements, and how he would have engaged with the other members of the *Movin' Out* company. But I trust that those moves are now embedded in this remarkable company's performances.

I had hoped that a similar type of memorial and celebration would mark the much anticipated musical *Radiant Baby*, which was based on the life and work of Keith Haring, the charismatic and multitalented gay artist whose graffiti-inspired artwork took the New York art world by storm in the 1980s. Haring's influence was worldwide, and the momentum behind him was cut short only by his AIDS-related death at thirty-one in 1990. *Radiant Baby* was directed by George C. Wolfe and was premiering at the Public Theatre, and the combination of Wolfe, Haring, and the Public made this a must-see event for me. Unlike *Movin' Out*, *Radiant Baby* chronicles a world I know well and parallels my own life experience. Haring was only a year older than I, and we frequented many of the same New York clubs throughout the 1980s. Beyond that I am a huge fan of his work, which effortlessly unites the political with the whimsical and is full of color and life. I went to *Radiant Baby* with Raphy, one of my oldest friends from Madison; my ex-lover Doug; and my friend Tim, who knew Keith Haring from his East Village years. We had bought advanced tickets and coordinated schedules from Los Angeles, Wisconsin, and New York to be there.

Radiant Baby did not do well with critics or audiences; its run at the Public was not extended, and a hoped-for transfer did not happen. My friends and I weren't all that drawn to the musical either. Despite our efforts, investments, and projected identifications, we were disappointed in the production's one-dimensional portrait of the East Village art scene; the overly cartoonish parodies of figures such as Madonna and Andy Warhol, who, while easy targets for satire, deserve a more nuanced representation in this context; and the annoying insistence on having children serve as the production's narrative frame.

One scene, however, saved the production for me and made the effort to see it worthwhile. In a musical sequence that pays tribute to the legendary talents of Sylvester and that perfectly captures the exuberance of gay liberation in the post-Stonewall years, the young actor playing Keith Haring discovers the subaltern world of Manhattan's downtown queer club scene. Beautifully choreographed by Fatima Robinson and joyfully and sexily danced by the young company, the scene showcases dance's centrality to queer life and culture. Young Keith finds himself at Paradise Garage, and in the midst of an infectious dance rhythm that he finds irresistible, locates the community that will shape his future. He learns the moves—or, more aptly, recognizes that the moves are already his—and joins the dance. He peels off his shirt to reveal his lanky white body and integrates himself into this racially diverse world, as so many young gay men have done before him and so many continue to do to this day, into the ongoing dance. This scene, "Paradise/Instant Gratification," is the one moment in *Radiant Baby* that, well, radiates. It was thrilling theater. Not only did it capture the energy and vitality that fueled Haring's work, but it also captured the liberatory and erotic nature of dance. The scene reminded me of my own disco excursions of the period and the reasons I was drawn to coming out. And yet there was more than mere nostalgia at the heart of this scene. It presented an archival embodiment of a queer history that was mainly experienced through dance.[22] This history of dance is one that has not been fully archived by scholars despite its constitutive role in pre- and post-Stonewall queer life.

I've been out now for over two decades, and while I still listen compulsively to dance music I rarely go out dancing. When I do it is to celebrate an occasion—the turn of the millennium, a friend's birthday, gay pride—that seems worth marking with what was once routine. Every once in a while Richard, my partner, and I will go out dancing when we are on vacation. In Provincetown one recent summer we danced together at the A-House, one of the resort's larger and more popular nightclubs. On weekends the place is always packed with wall-to-wall dancers, gay people from everywhere, it seems, who all end up in Provincetown for the same reason we do: queer ubiquity.

We find a spot on the dance floor and try to step into the rhythm of the dance that's already at work. I find this period of adjustment, those tentative moves of the body—a small step, a turn of the hip, a nodding head—a familiar rehearsal of the ambivalence I once felt about queer life and queer public space when I was first coming out. Soon enough I find my step and begin to dance. I turn to look at Richard; he too has found his rhythm, and we are now dancing with hundreds of others. I draw him near me, bringing his sweaty body closer to mine. Here, on the dance floor, I experience the incredible intimacy of sustained touch, an erotics that so often seems permissible only on the dance floors of queer clubs. In these moments I feel very much in love with him and indebted to the queers who have come before us so that he and I can dance in this sweet embrace.

NOTES

1. Koestenbaum, The Queen's Throat, 18.

2. This is a standard reading of queer dance clubs. Diebold's Tribal Rites remains the classic text. The best work on disco is still Dyer's "In Defense of Disco" and Hughes's "Feeling Mighty Real." But see also more recent arguments for dance and queer culture, including Bollen, "Queer Kinesthesia"; Buckland, Impossible Dance.

3. See, for example, Delany's important account and analysis in Times Square Red/Times Square Blue.

4. Edwards and Rogers, "Good Times."

5. "Harry and John," in Adair and Adair, Word Is Out, 242.

6. Chauncey's Gay New York is the best resource for these accounts, but see also Siegel, "A Right to Boogie Queerly."

7. Duberman documents some of the earliest gay dance fundraisers in Stonewall, and I describe early AIDS dance fundraisers in my book Acts of Intervention.

8. For a fascinating critique of dancing from the perspective of lesbian feminists of the 1970s, see Newman, "Why I'm Not Dancing." See also in the same volume, Dobson, "Dance Liberation," who argues for the radical possibilities of dance outside of gay bar culture.

9. Jay, *Tales of the Lavender Menace*, 129. See also Kissack's "Freaking Fag Revolutionaries" for a discussion of these early GLF dances.

10. And yet, as Jay suggests, with these political gains something was also lost. In this case, it was the touch dancing of butch-femme choreography.

11. "Why We Are Marching," unsigned political pamphlet, National March on Washington for Lesbian and Gay Rights, 14 October 1979.

12. Crowley, *The Boys in the Band*, 54.

13. Ibid., 56–57.

14. See, for example, Clum, *Still Acting Gay*; Sinfield, *Out on Stage*. But see also Kaiser, *The Gay Metropolis 1940–1996*, for the historical backdrop to the play's reception at the time.

15. Martin Gottfried, review of *The Boys in the Band* in *Women's Wear Daily*, 15 April 1968.

16. Vito Russo offers an alternative reading to *The Boys in the Band* when discussing the 1970 film adaptation of the play in his classic, *The Celluloid Closet*. Russo addresses the standard critiques of the play but allows for a representational breakthrough through the characters of the homosexual couple Hank and Larry. "The possibility that there could be non-stereotypical homosexuals who are also staunch advocates of a working gay relationship is presented by the two lovers throughout the film," he writes. But he also adds, "They are the two characters most often ignored by critics and analysts of the film" (175).

17. On this topic see Fellows, *Farm Boys*.

18. Madonna, quoted in A. Morton, *Madonna*, 56.

19. Billy Joel, "Keeping the Faith," from *Movin' Out*, 17.

20. Twyla Tharp, quoted in Emily King's liner notes to *Movin' Out*, 9.

21. Twyla Tharp, quoted in Anna Kisselgoff, "Obituary: William Marrié," *New York Times*, 18 November 2002.

22. Here I would like to call attention to the ongoing research of Ricardo Montez, an advanced graduate student in performance studies at New York University whose projected dissertation is on Keith Haring.

Dance with Me

Frances Negrón-Muntaner

"Dance signaled not the promise of gay liberation but its practice," wrote the scholar David Román in his classic essay "Dance Liberation." In other words, dance is never just dancing; it is a medium for identity and a fulcrum for political mobilization. As I found this to be a provocative idea begging for many a response, when the volume editors Michael Hames-García and Ernesto Javier Martínez asked me to offer one, I immediately agreed. Not only because Román's work, as good music, has always moved my thinking, but also because accepting felt very similar to joining an outstretched hand, saying "Dance with me."

On reading "Dance Liberation" my first impulse was to remember. It was 1985 and I was a nineteen-year-old senior at the University of Puerto Rico. A friend of mine named Bea, who swore she was bisexual although I always thought that she was straight, decided that it was time to do it. So one Friday night she took me to my first lesbian bar, along with some friends of hers, a goth butch-femme couple that spoke little and smoked much. The bar had a name that exercised your lips and roused the imagination: Boccaccio. The Italian alias notwithstanding, this bar was in a dead-end street in the financial district of Hato Rey and was owned by two Cuban lesbians who kept an over-sized figure of Santa Barbara-Changó as half-man and half-woman right at the entrance.

True to the bar's volatile protector Changó, this was a rough place, one known for its woman-to-woman dancing as much as for its woman-on-woman brawls. To prevent any trouble Bea instructed me to pay close attention to whether any woman that I may be interested in was accompanied or alone, and to avoid bumping into people, since fights were often started when patrons ran into each other while dancing fast tracks such as salsa or merengue. Needless to say I did not dance at all that night. Instead I longingly looked at the dancers sweating their workday away on the floor.

Yet it was not long before I figured out the necessary moves to find my way through this dark and terrifying place. In what seemed like an instant the original fear gave way to a narcotic sensation of freedom. A freedom that had the feel of carnival, or in the theorist Mikhail Bakhtin's words, "the world upside down." For this was a space so queer that not only could women dance with women (a common and otherwise acceptable practice in Puerto Rico, if the ladies are presumed to be straight) but men could dance with men, a completely prohibited activity in public. My understanding of the queer club as carnivalesque probably explains why the song I most associate with this period of my life is a merengue sung by Fernando Villalona titled "Carnaval," whose lines—

baile en la calle de noche	dance in the streets at sunset
baile en la calle de día dance	in the streets at sunrise
para que juntemos nuestras	so we bring together all of our
alegrías	joys

—echoed inside my head day in and day out.[1]

At the same time the minute that I walked into Boccaccio I understood that this dancing floor was not entirely removed from the world beyond its doors. Perhaps because dance is so central to the constitution of Latino/a American national identities and so clearly embodies normative gender roles and other social attributes, dancing is always assumed to be implicated in what the sociologist Pierre Bourdieu called "the structures of the world."[2] In this sense dancing in the queer club taught you more than the steps needed to become a gay man or lesbian, to use Román's eloquent if universalizing terms. It also taught you whether you were comfortable leading or being led, identified as butch or femme, trigueña or white, suburbia or caserío, among other possibilities. It taught you, in essence, not only that you were a lesbian but also what kind of lesbian you were.

The ways that the broader social context is indispensable to understanding when, where, how, and for whom dance can be linked to gay liberation may become even more evident when people take their dancing shoes far away from home, which is precisely what I did only a year later. Like other middle-class Puerto Ricans, I left San Juan after I graduated college and migrated first to Amherst, Massachusetts, and then to Philadelphia, where I lived until 1997. In Puerto Rico that I had to dance on the margins of "decent" society was a sign of my exclusion from the national community; in the United States dancing became more complicated, in both familiar and foreign ways.

A conspicuous complication dodged by many scholars, including Román, revolves around the assumed class, ethnic, and racial neutrality of queer space in the United States. Decades before Latin rhythms like reggaetón became a staple of some queer clubs and the Latino population surged across the country, going clubbing was at times harder than just calling up your friends. In highly segregated cities like Philadelphia dancegoers had to make tough choices that tended to split them along various ethnoracial and sexual fault lines. Do you opt, for example, to dance Latin music with your fellow (and presumably heterosexual) ethnics, or do you go to the majority-white queer bars and dance theirs instead?[3] The answer to this question often depended as much on one's class and racial identifications as one's sexual orientation. For those Puerto Rican middle-class gays that the sociologist Manuel Guzmán once ironically called "bourgeois sexiles," the discos catering to affluent white gay men may have been a "safer" and better-heeled alternative than the working-class Latino straight clubs.[4] But for those wishing to enjoy themselves in a particular "Latin" way, this well-exercised option could leave you wanting. Although dancing to another's beat can be pleasurable or distressing depending on the context, to the extent that the white clubs also offered lessons in how to step into a specifically "American" gay dance, they constituted what the historian Juliet McMains called "a model for assimilation" that a good number of Latinos had no interest in.[5]

It is thus not surprising that for Latino queers finding a hospitable place to dance has frequently been a top priority in the United States. In fact one of the first items on the agenda for Fuego Latino, a Philadelphia gay and lesbian group that I joined in the summer of 1992, was precisely pressuring the local club owners for "Latin nights."[6] The desire for a different dancing space stemmed from a sense that Latino queers in Philadelphia were homeless, for convergent if not identical reasons. Members who had lived or worked in the city for years had reached the frustrating conclusion that there was, literally, no place for them either in the downtown clubs or in the barrio, particularly after the closing of Bravo's, the only Latino gay club in the city's history. And for those who, like myself, had recently arrived directly from Latin America or the Caribbean and were used to a vibrant club scene, there was an acute need for a home outside home.

This yearning, fueled by histories of mass migration and discrimination as well as the common experience of expulsion from the familial home, is not, however, specific to Philadelphia. With telling consistency it is recounted in almost all available Latino queer narratives. In Guzmán's text, for instance, he explains that none of the many unsavory elements of the New York Latin queer club La Escuelita, including "ill-mannered waiters . . . less than civil bartenders . . . [and] brutish heterosexual bouncers," was successful in keeping him away. The reason why bargoers like Guzmán were willing to accept such conditions is playfully articulated in a near mathematical proposition: "[If] New York might be the urban center with the largest concentration of gay and 'differently homosexualed' Latino men and La Escuelita the gay Latino club in the City, then La Escuelita might be considered the house of gay Latino men in the city of New York."[7]

Likewise, commenting on Pan Dulce, a queer Latino nightclub owned by the Puerto Rican promoter Rafael Negrón in San Francisco, the scholar Horacio N. Roque Ramírez conveys the excitement that patrons felt when this "new nonwhite queer space" opened its doors in the mid 1990s: "[We] Latinas and Latinos . . . got on the bus, walked, drove, rode our bike, or went on a quick taxi ride to the corner of 11th and Folsom streets for the promise of pleasures Pan Dulce signified. When you know you don't have a permanent social space, when you realize that you don't have musical and dancing choices every night of the week, or even once a week, as queer Latinas have experienced as far back as queer Latino anything in San Francisco goes, being in the house of dance matters."[8]

Yet a longing for home in the most primal way was not the only motivating factor, especially for the dance organizers. To the extent that gay clubs are at the center of queer culture in many cities, that Latinos were not seen dancing downtown created the impression that there were no Latino gays or lesbians at all or, if they existed, were closeted and hence impossible to mobilize or serve. While these assumptions raise vexing questions about the workings of identity politics, they had clear consequences for Latino queer activists trying to hold gay-led organizations and city officials accountable in their delivery of services, particularly around AIDS treatment and prevention.

The perceived absence of Latino bodies from the clubs also raised doubts as to the value of this group as consumers, begging the question of whether it was worth it for white gay and lesbian businesses to let them in. "The easiest way to get cooperation from the owners," recalls David Acosta, a fellow member of Fuego Latino and the founder of the Gay and Lesbian AIDS Education Initiative, "was to say that the dance was about AIDS prevention. If you said it was about the need of Latino queers getting together, no one really cared about that. They didn't see us as valuable community members."[9] Which is why the next issue on the table was as fraught as the first: deciding whether Latin nights could take place during the most desirable dancing days of Friday, Saturday, or Sunday. These battles, never won despite the financial success of the dances, exemplified how owners persisted in associating Latinos with poverty, low cultural capital, and other markers of outsider status.

The activists' near epic struggle to obtain the best days—finally settling on a

Thursday at the lesbian bar Hepburn's—was then not only about affirming identity or wanting to be recognized as members of the mainstream queer community. It was also about critiquing the segregation and racism endured by Latinos in the city on a daily basis. Since for many dancegoers stepping out to Center City for a queer dance was one of the few times they left their neighborhoods, these events allowed patrons to dance away segregation and take a certain distance from poverty, even if within the confines of another kind of ghetto. As Marguerite de la Cuesta, a frequent Fuego Latino dancegoer and AIDS activist, put it, "The Latina lesbians really looked forward to it because at the dances there were other Latinas, they played Latin music. It was like bringing the barrio downtown."[10] In this regard dancing in the city as a Latin queer was also a practice of Latinization, a process that, as the sociologist Agustín Lao-Montes has written, constitutes "a mode of production and appropriation of urban space."[11]

But what did this queer Latinization look like? Given that altering the club's decor was impractical and otherwise prohibited, the main step to Latinize the queer (white) club was to change the music. During the 1990s this meant bringing in DJs who were aware of the latest in Latin music, playing songs in Spanish, and only spinning those English tracks that by affinity or *filin* had become Latino favorites, such as Boy George's "Karma Chameleon" or Gloria Gaynor's "I Will Survive." The importance of the DJ to the Latinization of space speaks volumes to the ways that music provides a sense of place, concrete and imagined, and invites a feeling of belonging or exclusion. The fact that "American" or "white" clubs never played Latin music at the time was in itself a loud reminder of the group's marginalized status within the city.

Notably, though as Acosta recalls, "the main idea of the Fuego Latino dances was to bring Latinos together," some non-Latinos, mostly whites and African Americans, also attended. Many of these dancegoers were active in city politics and had positions of power in queer and service-oriented organizations. In this context the very familiar practice of couple dancing, which at home (whether in our countries of origin or in the barrio) so strongly accentuated local gender, class, and racial power dynamics, now took on new layers of signification. Prioritizing on Latin (couple) dancing over (uncoupled) American "free" styles, for instance, had the potential to unsettle citywide ethnoracial hierarchies that rendered Latinos invisible by minimizing the distance between people and enabling the formation of previously nonexistent connections. Even the simple act of walking through the Latinized dance floor created unprecedented possibilities of interaction. As the scholar Jonathan Bollen reminds us, "Moving through the dance floor entails moving through networks of ongoing social relations. Finding somewhere to dance entails inserting one's self into these networks."[12]

At another level, since the Latinized queer club attracted both men and women, Latin dancing underscored that a powerful political community required all of its members in motion—men dancing with men, men dancing with women, women with women, of all and any sexual orientation, ethnicity, or race—to overcome common obstacles. In great contrast to white queer clubs, which are generally conceived as the opposite of a familial space, more than a few gay and lesbian dancegoers brought their straight relatives with their spouses to the dances. "Latin Nights," recalls a dancegoer who did not want her name used, "was actually the only space where the entire family could enjoy themselves."[13] Moreover Latin dance styles implied that to turn movement into political muscle, queers not only needed to engage with various partners but to move as much forward as sideways, backward, and in spirals, as is typical when dancing salsa, merengue, or guajira. It suggested further that the linear empowerment narrative of mostly white urban gay men in the United States was not as universally attractive as some would like to think, that other bodies danced to different beats and notions of liberation.

The reversibility of Latin dance, that one can lead and be led, ultimately embodied a desire for a different way of interrelating. In this regard the Fuego Latino dances were not an attempt to bring various disparate groups together in a multicultural universal queer identity. Rather they provided a space to try out different community configurations and dynamics of power. Inside the Latinized club the muscled white gay man may follow the Latin butch, and a Latin femme may lead a black gay man in drag. Being able to dance together in this way materialized the idea that people with dissimilar ways of understanding sexuality and freedom may at times be able to work together. This is why for Latinos teaching a non-Latino partner how to dance was a political experience. Within this context it signaled the new partner's willingness to incorporate Latino practices and produced an alternative relationship to power and knowledge, however ephemeral.[14] Opening space at the white clubs was then also an invitation to "dance with us," addressed to non-Latinos.

Not surprisingly, dancing downtown eventually led to other things. As the clubs became less hostile Fuego Latino members and allies started using them as an organizing resource. Among the events that Fuego Latino supported were fundraisers for HIV-positive women of color to attend AIDS-prevention conferences and benefit dances for Latino queer filmmakers. The idea to create Philadelphia's popular "alternative prom," where queer kids of all kinds, including gay, lesbian, transvestite, transgender, goth, and geeks, could feel comfortable was born on the Fuego Latino dance floor as well. But perhaps the most overtly political of the activities following on Fuego Latino's dance steps was the resolution to march in the Puerto Rican Day Parade in 1994. This was a historic decision: in the nearly thirty years of the parade's existence it had never been done. On the surface this outcome could be read as confirmation of the equation between dance and queer liberation. Yet the process instead stressed the instability of this relationship.

Despite the group's apparent cohesion on the dance floor, nearly half of Fuego Latino's members did not support the decision to march. This vote underscored that at the heart of Fuego Latino there had always been a split, between those who wanted to dance for its various pleasures and those who saw dance as a means to organize. This divide made itself acutely felt before the big day as the handful of members who decided to march, including myself, sensed the need to recruit outside supporters. As part of the first-ever queer contingent to participate in the parade, we were truly afraid of the crowd's reactions. Our fear was compounded by the fact that the event organizers located our party at the tail of the parade and refused a request to place our group in a more visible part of the route. In the end our marching contingent had little resemblance to the Fuego Latino dance floor. Over half of the group was composed of veteran New York ACT-UP Latino Caucus members, black and white queer allies, and not a few straight friends with their toddlers.

Although our experience at the parade pleasantly surprised us—the largely uptown Puerto Ricans lining the streets were more stunned or impressed than angry or violent—the decision to march began a process of internal combustion for Fuego Latino. Not long after the momentous occasion the organization disbanded and the dances came to a halt. The activist members felt abandoned; the committed dancers, pushed in a direction that they had no interest in going. This outcome led Acosta to conclude, "Those of us who braved it would have marched if we had not danced together. Dancing was the glue as far as affirming our identities as Latino queers. But it offered no guarantee for political empowerment."

Looking back I have no doubt that my one year of dancing in Puerto Rico's queer clubs helped me build the courage to take that overly long walk. Still it is clear that dancing cannot always be choreographed to the beat of gay liberation or be primarily meaningful in that context, even if it is done by queers. Arguably Fuego Latino's greatest accomplishment was not to dance in the white queer clubs nor march in the Puerto Rican Pride Parade but to embrace the idea that Latino queers could dance *wherever* they pleased, in excess of their designated identities. This was another possible notion of dance liberation, one that laid claim to greater social space without the need to march or embrace an exclusive sexual or ethnic identity. As Guzmán ironically notes about his first visit to La Escuelita, the freedom offered by the queer movement often felt spatially restricted: "It had been years since my first gay club. Hence, I had already had ample opportunity to understand how gay liberation had liberated me to go in pursuit of my homosexual desires down into the darkness of basements without the view of the outside world." [15]

Which leads me to this concluding thought: The last time I danced was just one week before I sat down to write this response. Bored at a friend's wedding, I went to the DJ and pleaded with him to get the party going. After my partner opted out due to a bad case of uncomfortable heels, I was lucky that one of her coworkers brought along her daughter, Michelle, a young Cuban American with a deep passion for dance. For some reason, in the way that Latin girls sometimes decide, she picked me as her partner for the night, and we just danced, sharing classic moves and the latest variations. Michelle's choice was perhaps too much for the (many) straight Latin boys who perhaps were also bored. So they did what straight Latin boys frequently do: they constantly cut in. But when we chose to coolly carry on with our flow, the boys perhaps made their best move yet: one by one, they each opted to dance beside us, in what could also be thought of as another kind of dance liberation.

NOTES

1. Translation mine, with some poetic license.

2. Bourdieu, *Outline of a Theory of Practice*, 87.

3. Certainly other ethnic clubs, particularly African American, would have constituted additional alternatives. Yet although by the 1990s Philadelphia's overall population was nearly half African American and many Latinos identified themselves as of color or black, the absence of black queer clubs during this period bolstered the sense of a white/other binary when it came to queer public space.

4. Manuel Guzmán, " 'Pa' La Escuelita con Mucho Cuida'o y por la Orillita,' " 210.

5. McMains, "Brownface," 67.

6. This was not the first time that such an effort was attempted; beginning in 1989 David Acosta, an AIDS activist, organized a series of smaller gatherings in various bars across the city aimed at Latino men in an attempt to "access the community and impart prevention messages" around HIV.

7. Guzmán, "'Pa' La Escuelita con Mucho Cuida'o y por la Orillita,'" 211–12, 215.

8. Roque Ramírez, "'¡Mira, Yo Soy Boricua y Estoy Aquí!,'" 276.

9. Telephone interview with David Acosta, 6 April 2007.

10. Personal interview with Marguerite de la Cuesta, 28 March 2007.

11. Laó-Montes, "Mambo Montage," 17.

12. Bollen, "Queer Kinesthesia," 292.

13. Phone interview, 25 March 2007.

14. For further theorization on the notion of incorporation, see Bollen, "Queer Kinesthesia," 297.

15. Guzmán, "'Pa' La Escuelita con Mucho Cuida'o y por la Orillita,'" 210.

bibliography

Abelove, Henry, Michèle Aina Barale, and David M. Halperin, eds. *The Lesbian and Gay Studies Reader*. New York: Routledge, 1993.

Abu-Lughod, Lila. "Writing against Culture." *Recapturing Anthropology: Working in the Present*, edited by Richard Gabriel Fox, 137–62. Santa Fe: School of American Research Press/University of Washington Press, 1991.

Adair, Nancy, and Casey Adair, eds. *Word Is Out: Stories of Some of Our Lives*. San Francisco: New Glide, 1978.

Aggleton, Peter. *Men Who Sell Sex to Other Men: International Perspectives on Male Prostitution and HIV/AIDS*. Philadelphia: Temple University Press, 1999.

Aguilar, Laura. *Three Eagles Flying*. 1990.

Aguirre, Valentín, and Augie Robles, producers and directors. *¡Viva 16!*. Video. 21st Century Aztlán, 1994.

Aiavao, Tunumafono Apelu. "Who's Playing Naked Now? Religion and Samoan Culture." *Pacific Perspective* 12, no. 2 (1983), 8–10.

Alarcón, Francisco X. *De amor oscuro/Of Dark Love: Poems*. Translated by Francisco Aragón. Santa Cruz, Calif.: Moving Parts, 1992.

———. "Dialectics of Love." *Ya Vas, Carnal*, by Rodrigo Reyes, Francisco X. Alarcón, and Juan Pablo Gutiérrez, 48. San Francisco: Humanizarte, 1985.

———. *From the Other Side of Night/Del otro lado de la noche: New and Selected Poems*. Tucson: University of Arizona Press, 2002.

Alarcón, Norma. "Conjugating Subjects in the Age of Multiculturalism." *Mapping Multiculturalism*, edited by Avery Gordon and Christopher Newfield, 127–48. Minneapolis: University of Minnesota Press, 1996.

Alcoff, Linda Martín. *Visible Identities: Race, Gender, and the Self*. New York: Oxford University Press, 2006.

Alcoff, Linda Martín, Michael Hames-García, Satya P. Mohanty, and Paula M. L. Moya, eds. *Identity Politics Reconsidered*. New York: Palgrave Macmillan, 2006.

Alexander, M. Jacqui. "Imperial Desire/Sexual Utopias: White Gay Capital and Transnational Tourism." *Pedagogies of Crossing: Meditations on Feminism, Sexual Politics, Memory, and the Sacred*, 66–88. Durham: Duke University Press, 2005.

———. *Pedagogies of Crossing: Mediations on Feminism, Sexual Politics, Memory, and the Sacred*. Durham: Duke University Press, 2005.

———. "Remembering *This Bridge*, Remembering Ourselves: Yearning, Memory, and

Desire." In *This Bridge We Call Home*, edited by Gloria Anzaldúa and Analouise Keating, 81–103. New York: Routledge, 2002.

Alfaro, Luis. "Cuerpo Politizado." *Uncontrollable Bodies: Testimonies of Art and Culture*, edited by Rodney Sappington and Tyler Stallings, 216–41. Seattle: Bay Press, 1994.

———. *Down Town*. Recording. New Alliance Records, 1993.

———. "Downtown." *O Solo Homo: The New Queer Performance*, edited by Holly Hughes and David Román, 313–48. New York: Grove Press, 1998.

———. "Pico-Union." *Men on Men 4: Best New Gay Fiction*, edited by George Stambolian, 268–83. New York: Plume, 1992.

———. "Straight as a Line." *Out of the Fringe: Contemporary Latina/Latino Theatre and Performance*, edited by Caridad Svich and María Teresa Marrero, 1–42. New York: Theatre Communications Group, 2000.

Alfaro, Luis, Beto Araiza, and Monica Palacios. "Deep in the Crotch of My Latino Psyche." Performance at the *Out on the Edge Festival 2*, Theatre Offensive, Boston, MA, 1993.

Algarín, Miguel. *Love Is Hard Work: Memorias de Loisaida*. New York: Simon and Schuster, 1997.

Algarín, Miguel, and Miguel Piñero, eds. *Nuyorican Poetry: An Anthology of Puerto Rican Words and Feelings*. New York: Morrow, 1975.

Almaguer, Tomás. "Chicano Men: A Cartography of Homosexual Identity and Behavior." *differences: A Journal of Feminist Cultural Studies* 3, no. 2 (1991), 75–100. Reprinted in *The Lesbian and Gay Studies Reader*, edited by Henry Abelove, Michèle Aina Barale, and David M. Halperin, 255–73. New York: Routledge, 1993.

———. *Racial Fault Lines: The Historical Origins of White Supremacy in California*. Berkeley: University of California Press, 1994.

Alonso, Ana María, and María Teresa Koreck. "Silences: 'Hispanics,' AIDS, and Sexual Practices." *The Lesbian and Gay Studies Reader*, edited by Henry Abelove, Michèle Aina Barale, and David M. Halperin, 110–26. New York: Routledge, 1993.

Alurista. *Floricanto en Aztlán*. Los Angeles: UCLA Chicano Studies Research Center, 1971.

Álvarez, Julia. "Freeing La Musa: Luz María Umpierre's *The Margarita Poems*." *The Margarita Poems*, by Luz María Umpierre-Herrera, 4–7. Bloomington, Ind.: Third Woman Press, 1987.

Anderson, Benedict R. *Imagined Communities: Reflections on the Origin and Spread of Nationalism*. Revised and extended edition. London: Verso, 1991.

Anthony, Marc. "La luna sobre nuestro amor." *Contra la corriente*. Recording. RMM Records, 1997.

Anzaldúa, Gloria. *Borderlands/La Frontera: The New Mestiza*. 1987. 2nd ed. San Francisco: Aunt Lute Books, 1999.

Aparicio, Frances R. *Listening to Salsa: Gender, Latin Popular Music, and Puerto Rican Cultures.* Hanover, N.H.: University Press of New England, 1998.

Aparicio, Frances R., and Susana Chávez-Silverman, eds. *Tropicalizations: Transcultural Representations of Latinidad.* Hanover, N.H.: University Press of New England/Dartmouth College, 1997.

Aponte-Parés, Luis. "Outside/In: Crossing Queer and Latino Boundaries." *Mambo Montage: The Latinization of New York,* edited by Agustín Laó-Montes and Arlene Dávila, 363–85. New York: Columbia University Press, 2001.

Aponte-Parés, Luis, and Jorge B. Merced. "Páginas Omitidas: The Gay and Lesbian Presence." *The Puerto Rican Movement: Voices from the Diaspora,* edited by Andrés Torres and José E. Velázquez, 296–315. Philadelphia: Temple University Press, 1998.

Armas, José. *La Familia de la Raza.* Self-published, 1972.

———. "Machismo." *De Colores: Journal of Emerging Raza Philosophies* 2, no. 2 (1975), 52–64.

Armas, José, and Bernice Zamora, eds. *Flor y Canto IV and V: An Anthology of Chicano Literature.* N.p.: Pajarito/Flor y Canto Committee, 1980.

Arrizón, Alicia. *Latina Performance: Traversing the Stage.* Bloomington: Indiana University Press, 1999.

Ayala, George. "Foreward." *Corpus Magazine: AIDS Project Los Angeles* 1, no. 1 (2003), v–ix.

Baca Zinn, Maxine. "Chicano Men and Masculinity." *The Sociology of Gender: A Text-Reader,* edited by Laura Kramer, 221–32. New York: St. Martin's Press, 1991.

Badinter, Elizabeth. *XY: On Masculine Identity.* New York: Columbia University Press, 1995.

Bal, Mieke. "The Narrating and the Focalizing: A Theory of the Agents in Narrative." Translated by Jane E. Lewin. *Style* 17 (1983), 234–69.

Baldwin, James. *Another Country.* New York: Vintage, 1962.

———. *Just above My Head.* New York: Dial Press, 1979.

Barber, Stephen M., and David L. Clark. "Queer Moments: The Performative Temporalities of Eve Kosofsky Sedgwick." *Regarding Sedgwick: Essays on Queer Culture and Critical Theory,* edited by Stephen M. Barber and David L. Clark, 1–53. New York: Routledge, 2002.

Barber, Stephen M., and David L. Clark, eds. *Regarding Sedgwick: Essays on Queer Culture and Critical Theory.* New York: Routledge, 2002.

Barber, Stephen M., David L. Clark, and Eve Kosofsky Sedgwick. "This Piercing Bouquet: An Interview with Eve Kosofsky Sedgwick." *Regarding Sedgwick: Essays on Queer Culture and Critical Theory,* edited by Stephen M. Barber and David L. Clark, 243–62. New York: Routledge, 2002.

Barbosa, Peter, and Garrett Lenoir, directors. *De Colores.* Motion picture. Eyebite Productions, 2001.

Barrera, Frankie. *The Diary of Baby Chulo.* Sacramento: Popol Vuh Press, 1999.

Beam, Joseph, ed. *In the Life: A Black Gay Anthology*. New York: Alyson, 1986.

Benavidez, Max. *Gronk*. Minneapolis: University of Minnesota Press, 2007.

Berlant, Lauren, and Michael Warner. "What Does Queer Theory Teach Us about X?" PMLA: *Publications of the Modern Language Association* 110, no. 3 (1995), 343–49.

Bergmann Emilie L., and Paul Julian Smith, eds. *¿Entiendes? Queer Readings, Hispanic Writings*. Durham: Duke University Press, 1995.

Bersani, Leo. "Is the Rectum a Grave?" October 43 (winter 1987), 197–222. Reprinted in AIDS: *Cultural Analysis, Cultural Activism*, edited by Douglas Crimp, 197–222. Cambridge: MIT Press, 1988.

Bhabha, Homi. *The Location of Culture*. New York: Routledge, 1994.

Bollen, Jonathan. "Queer Kinesthesia: Performativity on the Dance Floor." *Dancing Desires: Choreographing Sexualities on and off the Stage*, edited by Jane Desmond, 285–314. Madison: University of Wisconsin Press, 2001.

Bourdieu, Pierre. *Distinction: A Social Critique of the Judgment of Taste*. Cambridge: Harvard University Press, 1994.

———. *Outline of a Theory of Practice*. Translated by Richard Nice. Cambridge: Cambridge University Press, 1977.

Bracho, Ricardo, Jorge Ignacio Cortiñas, and José Esteban Muñoz. "Towards Translocalism: Latino Theatre in the New United States." *Trans-Global Readings: Crossing Theatrical Boundaries*, edited by Caridad Svich, 66–70. Manchester, England: Manchester University Press, 2003.

Bright, Brenda Jo. "Mexican American Low Riders: An Anthropological Approach to Popular Culture." Ph.D. diss., Rice University, 1994.

———. "Remappings: Los Angeles Low Riders." *Looking High and Low: Art and Cultural Identity*, edited by Brenda Jo Bright and Liza Bakewell, 89–123. Tucson: University of Arizona Press, 1995.

Brouwer, Daniel C. "Counterpublicity and Corporeality in HIV/AIDS 'Zines." *Critical Studies in Mass Communication* 22, no. 5 (2005), 351–71.

Brown, Wendy. *States of Injury: Power and Freedom in Late Modernity*. Princeton: Princeton University Press, 1995.

Bruce-Novoa, Juan. "Homosexuality and the Chicano Novel." *Confluencia* 2, no. 1 (1986), 69–77.

Buckland, Fiona. *Impossible Dance: Club Culture and Queer World-Making*. Middletown, Conn.: Wesleyan University Press, 2002.

Bustos-Aguilar, Pedro. "Mister Don't Touch the Banana: Notes on the Popularity of the Ethnosexed Body South of the Border." *Critique of Anthropology* 15, no. 2 (1995), 149–70.

Butler, Judith. *Bodies That Matter: On the Discursive Limits of "Sex."* New York: Routledge, 1993.

———. "Critically Queer." GLQ: *A Journal of Lesbian and Gay Studies* 1, no. 1 (1993),

17–32. Reprinted in Judith Butler, *Bodies That Matter: On the Discursive Limits of "Sex."* 223–42. New York: Routledge, 1993.

———. *Gender Trouble: Feminism and the Subversion of Identity.* New York: Routledge, 1990.

———. *The Psychic Life of Power: Theories in Subjection.* Stanford: Stanford University Press, 1997.

Campo, Rafael. *Diva.* Durham: Duke University Press, 1999.

———. *The Other Man Was Me: A Voyage to the New World.* Austin: Arte Público Press, 1994.

———. *What the Body Told.* Durham: Duke University Press, 1996.

Candelaria, Cordelia. *Chicano Poetry: A Critical Introduction.* Westport, Conn.: Greenwood Press, 1986.

Cantú, Lionel, Jr. "*De Ambiente*: Queer Tourism and the Shifting Boundaries of Mexican Male Sexualities." *GLQ: A Journal of Lesbian and Gay Studies* 8, nos. 1–2 (2002), 139–66.

———. "Entre Hombres/Between Men: Latino Masculinities and Homosexualities." *Gay Masculinities*, edited by Peter Nardi, 224–46. Thousand Oaks, Calif.: Sage, 2000.

———. "Latino Poverty and Immigration in California and Orange County: An Analysis of Household Income in the 1990 Census." Working Paper No. 1. Center for Latinos in a Global Society, University of California, 1997.

———. "A Place Called Home: A Queer Political Economy of Mexican Immigrant Men's Family Experiences." *Queer Families, Queer Politics: Challenging Culture and the State*, edited by Mary Bernstein and Renate Reimann, 112–36. New York: Columbia University Press, 2001.

———. *The Sexuality of Migration: Border Crossings and Mexican Immigrant Men.* Edited by Nancy A. Naples and Salvador Vidal-Ortiz. New York: New York University Press, 2009.

Carrier, Joseph. *De los Otros: Intimacy and Homosexuality among Mexican Men.* New York: Columbia University Press, 1995.

Carrigan, Tim, Bob Connell, and John Lee. "Toward a New Sociology of Masculinity." *The Making of Masculinities: The New Men's Studies*, edited by Harry Brod, 63–100. Boston: Allen and Unwin, 1987.

Carrillo, H. G. *Loosing My Espanish.* New York: Random House, 2005.

Carrillo, Héctor. *The Night Is Young: Sexuality in Mexico in the Time of AIDS.* Chicago: University of Chicago Press, 2002.

Case, Sue-Ellen. "Toward a Butch-Feminist Retro Future." *Cross-Purposes: Lesbians, Feminists, and the Limits of Alliance*, edited by Dana Heller, 205–20. Bloomington: Indiana University Press, 1997.

Chappell, Ben. "'Take a Little Trip with Me': Lowriding and the Poetics of Scale." *Technicolor: Race, Technology, and Everyday Life*, edited by Alondra Nelson and Thuy

Linh N. Tu, with Alicia Headlam Hines, 100–120. New York: New York University Press, 2001.

Chasin, Alexandra. *Selling Out: The Gay and Lesbian Movement Goes to Market*. New York: Palgrave, 2000.

Chauncey, George. *Gay New York: Gender, Urban Culture, and the Making of the Gay Male World, 1890–1940*. New York: Basic Books, 1994.

Chavez, Leo R. "The Power of the Imagined Community: The Settlement of Undocumented Mexicans and Central Americans in the United States." *American Anthropologist* 96, no. 1 (1994), 52–73.

Chavoya, C. Ondine. "Internal Exiles: The Interventionist Public and Performance Art of Asco." *Space, Site, and Intervention: Situating Installation Art*, edited by Erika Suderburg, 189–208. Minneapolis: University of Minnesota Press, 2000.

———. "Pseudographic Cinema: Asco's No-Movies." *Performance Research* 3, no. 1 (1998), 1–14.

Chay, Deborah G. "Rereading Barbara Smith: Black Feminist Criticism and the Category of Experience." *New Literary History* 24, no. 3 (1993), 635–52.

Christian, Barbara. "The Race for Theory." *Feminist Studies* 14, no. 1 (1988), 67–79.

Christian, Karen. *Show and Tell: Identity as Performance in U.S. Latina/o Fiction*. Albuquerque: University of New Mexico Press, 1997.

Clifford, James. *The Predicament of Culture: Twentieth-Century Ethnography, Literature, and Art*. Cambridge: Harvard University Press, 1988.

Clum, John. *Still Acting Gay: Male Homosexuality in Modern Drama*. New York: St. Martin's Press, 2000.

Cohen, Cathy J. *The Boundaries of Blackness: AIDS and the Breakdown of Black Politics*. Chicago: University of Chicago Press, 1999.

Colón, Jesús. *A Puerto Rican in New York and Other Sketches*. New York: Mainstream, 1961.

Coltrane, Scott. *Theorizing Masculinities in Contemporary Social Science*. Thousand Oaks, Calif.: Sage, 1994.

Combahee River Collective. "A Black Feminist Statement." *Capitalist Patriarchy and the Case for Socialist Feminism*, edited by Zillah R. Eisenstein, 362–72. New York: Monthly Review Press, 1979.

Comenas, Gary. *Warholstars 2002*. Web site of Warholstars. (accessed 12 October 2003).

Contreras, Daniel T. *Unrequited Love and Gay Latino Culture: What Have You Done to My Heart?* New York: Palgrave Macmillan, 2005.

Cora, María. "Nuestras Auto-Definiciones/Our Self-Definitions: Management of Stigma and Identity by Puerto Rican Lesbians." Master's field study report, San Francisco State University, 2000.

Coronado, Raúl. "Bringing It Back Home: Desire, Jotos, Men, and the Sexual/Gender Politics of Chicana and Chicano Studies." *The Chicana/o Cultural Studies Reader*, edited by Angie Chabram-Dernersesian, 233–40. New York: Routledge, 2006.

Cortez, Jaime, ed. *Virgins, Guerrillas, and Locas: Gay Latinos Writing about Love*. San Francisco: Cleis Press, 1999.

Cortiñas, Jorge Ignacio. "Imperial Desire: The Not So New Gay Multinationalism." Typescript and paper presented at the Crossing National and Sexual Borders: Queer Sexualities in Latin/o America conference, New York, 4 October 1996.

Crenshaw, Kimberlé Williams. "Beyond Racism and Misogyny: Black Feminism and 2 Live Crew." *Words That Wound: Critical Race Theory, Assaultive Speech, and the First Amendment*, edited by Mari J. Matsuda, Charles R. Lawrence III, Richard Delgado, and Kimberlé Williams Crenshaw, 111–32. Boulder: Westview Press, 1993.

———. "Mapping the Margins: Intersectionality, Identity Politics, and Violence against Women of Color." *Critical Race Theory: The Key Writings That Formed the Movement*, edited by Kimberlé Williams Crenshaw, Neil Gotanda, Gary Peller, and Kendall Thomas, 35–83. New York: New Press, 1995.

Crimp, Douglas. "Mario Montez, for Shame!" *Regarding Sedgwick: Essays on Queer Culture and Critical Theory*, edited by Stephen M. Barber and David L. Clark, 57–70. New York: Routledge, 2002.

Crowley, Mart. *The Boys in the Band*. New York, Noonday Press, 1968.

Cruz-Malavé, Arnaldo. "Para virar al macho: La autobiografía como subversión en la cuentística de Manuel Ramos Otero." *Revista Iberoamericana* 59 (1993), 239–63.

———. *Queer Latino Testimonio, Keith Haring, and Juanito Xtravaganza: Hard Tails*. New York: Palgrave Macmillan, 2007.

———. "Toward an Art of Transvestism: Colonialism and Homosexuality in Puerto Rican Literature." *¿Entiendes? Queer Readings, Hispanic Writings*. edited by Emilie L. Bergmann and Paul Julian Smith, 137–67. Durham: Duke University Press, 1995.

———. "What a Tangled Web! Masculinity, Abjection, and the Foundations of Puerto Rican Literature in the United States." *differences* 8, no. 1 (1996), 132–51.

Cruz-Malavé, Arnaldo, and Martin F. Manalansan IV, eds. *Queer Globalizations: Citizenship and the Afterlife of Colonialism*. New York: New York University Press, 2002.

Cuadros, Gil. *City of God*. San Francisco: City Lights, 1994.

Cunningham, John. " 'Hey, Mr. Liberace, Will You Vote for Zeta?' Looking for the Joto in Chicano Men's Autobiographical Writing." *Race-ing Masculinity: Identity in Contemporary U.S. Men's Writing*, 69–94. New York: Routledge, 2002.

Currid, Brian. "We Are Family: House Music and Queer Performativity." *Cruising the Performative: Interventions into the Representation of Ethnicity, Nationality, and Sexuality*, edited by Sue-Ellen Case, Philip Brett, and Susan Leigh Foster, 165–96. Bloomington: Indiana University Press, 1995.

Dávila, Arlene. *Latinos, Inc.: The Marketing and Making of a People*. Berkeley: University of California Press, 2001.

DeCurtis, Anthony. "Eminem's Hate Rhymes." *Rolling Stone*, 3 August 2000, 17–18, 21.

de la Garza, Luis Alberto, and Horacio N. Roque Ramírez. "Queer Community History and the Evidence of Desire: The Archivo Rodrigo Reyes, a Gay and Lesbian Latino Archive." *The Power of Language: Selected Papers from the Second* REFORMA *National Conference*, edited by Lillian Castillo-Speed and the REFORMA National Conference Publications Committee, 181–98. Englewood, Colo.: Libraries Unlimited, 2000.

de la Mora, Sergio. *Cinemachismo: Masculinities and Sexuality in Mexican Film*. Austin: University of Texas Press, 2006.

Delaney, Samuel. *Times Square Red/Times Square Blue*. New York: New York University Press, 1999.

de la tierra, tatiana. "Activist Latina Lesbian Publishing: *Esto no tiene nombre* and *Conmoción*." Aztlán 27, no. 1 (2002), 139–78.

———. *For the Hard Ones: A Lesbian Phenomenology/Para las duras: Una fenomenología lesbiana*. Buffalo: Chibcha Press, 2002.

———. "Las Sinvergüenzas." Unpublished manuscript, 3 July 1998, El Paso, Texas.

———. "Maybe I Should Be Ashamed but I'm Not: Autobiography of una Sinvergüenza." Unpublished manuscript, 5 May 1998, El Paso, Texas.

———. *Píntame una mujer peligrosa*. Buffalo: Chibcha Press, 2005.

———. *Porcupine Love and Other Tales from My Papaya*. Buffalo: Chibcha Press, 2003.

de Lauretis, Teresa. "Queer Theory: Lesbian and Gay Sexualities: An Introduction." *differences* 3, no. 2 (1991), iii–xviii.

Delgado, Celeste Fraser, and José Esteban Muñoz. *Everynight Life: Culture and Dance in Latin/o America*. Durham: Duke University Press, 1997.

Delhi Center. *Encuentro Entre Hombres IV*. Brochure. Santa Ana, Calif., 1998.

D'Emilio, John. "Capitalism and Gay Identity." *The Lesbian and Gay Studies Reader*, edited by Henry Abelove, Michèle Aina Barale, and David M. Halperin, 467–76. New York: Routledge, 1993.

de Souza Santos, Boaventura. "A Critique of Lazy Reason: Against the Waste of Experience." *The Modern World-System in the Longue Durée*, edited by Immanuel Wallerstein, 157–98. Boulder: Paradigm, 2004.

Díaz, Junot. "Drown." *Drown*. New York: Riverhead Books, 1997.

Díaz, Rafael M. *Gay Latino Men and* HIV: *Culture, Sexuality, and Risk Behavior*. New York: Routledge, 1998.

Díaz Barriga, Miguel. "*Vergüenza* and Changing Chicana and Chicano Narratives." *Men and Masculinities* 3, no. 3 (2001), 278–98.

Diebold, David. *Tribal Rites: San Francisco's Dance Music Phenomenon*. Northridge, Calif.: Time Warp, 1986.

Dobson, Rob. "Dance Liberation." *Lavender Culture*, edited by Karla Jay and Allen Young, 171–81. New York: New York University Press, 1978.

Dolan, Jill. "Performance, Utopia, and the 'Utopian Performative.'" *Theatre Journal* 53, no. 3 (2001), 455–79.

Doty, Alexander. *Flaming Classics: Queering the Film Canon*. New York: Routledge, 2000.

Duberman, Martin. *Stonewall*. New York: Dutton, 1993.

Duggan, Lisa. "The New Homonormativity: The Sexual Politics of Neoliberalism." *Materializing Democracy: Toward a Revitalized Cultural Politics*, edited by Russ Castronovo and Dana D. Nelson, 175–94. Durham: Duke University Press, 2002.

Dyer, Richard. "In Defense of Disco." *On Record: Rock, Pop, and the Written Word*, edited by Simon Firth and Andrew Goodwin, 410–18. New York: Pantheon, 1990.

———. *Only Entertainment*. New York: Routledge, 1992.

Edelman, Lee. *Homographesis: Essays in Gay Literary and Cultural Theory*. New York: Routledge, 1994.

———. *No Future: Queer Theory and the Death Drive*. Durham: Duke University Press, 2004.

Edwards, Bernard, and Nile Rogers, music and lyrics. "Good Times." *Risqué*. Recording. WEA/Atlantic Records, 1979.

Eng, David L. *Racial Castration: Managing Masculinity in Asian America*. Durham: Duke University Press, 2001.

Eng, David L., with Judith Halberstam and José Esteban Muñoz. "Introduction: What's Queer about Queer Studies Now?" *Social Text* 84–85/23, nos. 3–4 (2005), 1–17.

Eng, David L., Judith Halberstam, and José Esteban Muñoz, eds. "What's Queer about Queer Studies Now?" Special issue of *Social Text* 84–85/23, nos. 3–4 (2005).

Eng, David L., and Alice Y. Hom, eds. Q & A: *Queer in Asian America*. Philadelphia: Temple University Press, 1998.

Escoffier, Jeffrey. "The Political Economy of the Closet: Notes toward an Economic History of Gay and Lesbian Life before Stonewall." *Homo Economics: Capitalism, Community, and Lesbian and Gay Life*, edited by Amy Gluckman and Betsy Reed, 123–34. New York: Routledge, 1997.

Espinoza, Dionne. *Revolutionary Sisters: Chicana Activism and the Cultural Politics of Chicano Power*. Austin: University of Texas Press, forthcoming.

Esquibel, Catriona Rueda. *With Her Machete in Her Hand: Reading Chicana Lesbians*. Austin: University of Texas Press, 2006.

Evans, David T. *Sexual Citizenship: The Material Construction of Sexualities*. New York: Routledge, 1993.

Fanon, Frantz. *Black Skin/White Masks*. New York: Grove Press, 1967.

Fellows, Will, ed. *Farm Boys: Lives of Gay Men from the Rural Midwest*. Madison: University of Wisconsin Press, 1996.

Ferguson, Roderick A. *Aberrations in Black: Toward a Queer of Color Critique*. Minneapolis: University of Minnesota Press, 2004.

———. "Of Our Normative Strivings: African American Studies and the Histories of Sexuality." *Social Text* 84–85/23, nos. 3–4 (2005), 85–100.

Firestone, Shulamith. *The Dialectic of Sex: The Case for Feminist Revolution*. New York: Morrow, 1970.

Flatley, Jonathan. *Affective Mapping: Melancholia and the Politics of Modernism*. Cambridge: Harvard University Press, 2008.

Flores, William V., and Rina Benmayor, eds. *Latino Cultural Citizenship: Claiming Identity, Space, and Rights*. Boston: Beacon Press, 1997.

Fornes, María Irene. *Plays*. New York: PAJ, 2001.

Foster, David William. *Chicano/Latino Homoerotic Identities*. New York: Routledge, 1999.

———. *El Ambiente Nuestro: Chicano/Latino Homoerotic Writing*. Tempe: Bilingual Press/ Editorial Bilingüe, 2006.

Foucault, Michel. "The Ethics of the Concern of the Self as a Practice of Freedom." *Ethics: Subjectivity and Truth*, edited by Paul Rabinow, 281–301. New York: New Press, 1997.

———. *The History of Sexuality: An Introduction*. Translated by Robert Hurley. 1978. New York: Vintage Books, 1990.

———. "Of Other Spaces." Translated by Jay Miskowiec. Foucault.info web site. 13 September 2004.

———. *La volonté de savoir: Histoire de la sexualité 1*. Paris: Gallimard, 1976.

Frye, Marilyn. *The Politics of Reality: Essays in Feminist Theory*. Freedom, Calif.: Crossing Press, 1983.

Fusco, Coco. "Who's Doing the Twist? Notes toward a Politics of Appropriation." *English Is Broken Here: Notes on Cultural Fusion in the Americas*, 65–77. New York: New Press, 1995.

Fuss, Diana. *Essentially Speaking: Feminism, Nature, and Difference*. New York: Routledge, 1989.

Fuss, Diana, ed. *Inside/Out: Lesbian Theories, Gay Theories*. New York: Routledge, 1991.

Gabel, Chantal. "English Professor Hiram Perez Denied Tenure after Dean's Review." *The Montclarion* (Montclair State University, N.J.), 17 November 2005.

Gagnon, John H., and William Simon. *Sexual Conduct: The Social Sources of Human Sexuality*. 2nd ed. New Brunswick, N.J.: AldineTransaction, 2005.

Gallop, Jane. *Anecdotal Theory*. Durham: Duke University Press, 2002.

———. *Feminist Accused of Sexual Harassment*. Durham: Duke University Press, 1997.

Garber, Linda. *Identity Poetics: Race, Class, and the Lesbian-Feminist Roots of Queer Theory*. New York: Columbia University Press, 2001.

García, Alma M., ed. *Chicana Feminist Thought: The Basic Historical Writings*. New York: Routledge, 1997.

García, Bernardo. *The Development of a Latino Gay Identity*. New York: Garland, 1998.

García, Ramón. "Against *Rasquache*: Chicano Identity and the Politics of Popular Culture in Los Angeles." *Crítica* 3 (spring 1998), 1–26.

Gaspar de Alba, Alicia, ed. *Velvet Barrios: Popular Culture and Chicana/o Sexualities*. New York: Palgrave Macmillan, 2002.

Gay Shame San Francisco. "Gay Shame: A Celebration of Resistance." Web site of Gay Shame (accessed 25 August 2005).

———. "Gay Shame: A Virus in the System." Web site of Gay Shame (accessed 25 August 2005).

Genette, Gerard. *Narrative Discourse: An Essay in Method*. Translated by Jane E. Lewin. Ithaca: Cornell University Press, 1972.

Gil, Carlos. *El orden del tiempo: Ensayos sobre el robo del presente en la utopía puertorriqueña*. San Juan, Puerto Rico: Editorial Postdata, 1999.

Gilroy, Paul. "Cultural Studies and Ethnic Absolution." *Cultural Studies*, edited by Lawrence Grossberg, Cary Nelson, and Paula A. Treichler, 187–98. New York: Routledge, 1992.

Gluckman, Amy, and Betsy Reed, eds. *Homo Economics: Capitalism, Community, and Lesbian and Gay Life*. New York: Routledge, 1997.

Goldberg, Jonathan. *Sodometries: Renaissance Texts, Modern Sexualities*. Palo Alto: Stanford University Press, 1992.

———. "Sodomy in the New World: Anthropologies Old and New." *Fear of a Queer Planet: Queer Politics and Social Theory*, edited by Michael Warner, 3–18. Minneapolis: University of Minnesota Press, 1993.

González, Deena. "Malinche as Lesbian: A Reconfiguration of 500 Years of Resistance." *California Sociologist* 14 (1991), 90–97.

González, Gilbert, and Raul Fernández. "Chicano History: Transcending Cultural Models." *The Latino Studies Reader: Culture, Economy, and Society*, edited by Antonia Darder and Rodolfo D. Torres, 83–100. Malden, Mass.: Blackwell, 1998.

González, Rigoberto. *Butterfly Boy: Memories of a Chicano Mariposa*. Madison: University of Wisconsin Press, 2006.

———. *Crossing Vines*. Norman: University of Oklahoma Press, 2003.

———. *The Mariposa Club*. New York: Alyson, 2009.

———. *Men without Bliss*. Norman: University of Oklahoma Press, 2008.

———. *Other Fugitives and Other Strangers*. Dorset, Vt.: Tupelo Press, 2006.

Gopinath, Gayatri. *Impossible Desires: Queer Diasporas and South Asian Public Cultures*. Durham: Duke University Press, 2005.

Guerra, Erasmo. *Between Dances*. New York: Painted Leaf, 2000.

Gutiérrez, Eric-Steven. "Latino Issues: Gay and Lesbian Latinos Claiming La Raza." *Positively Gay: New Approaches to Gay and Lesbian Life*, edited by Betty Berzon, 240–46. Berkeley: Celestial Arts, 1992.

Gutiérrez, José Angel. "Ondas y Rollos (Wavelengths and Raps): The Ideology of Contemporary Chicano Rhetoric." *A War of Words: Chicano Protest in the 1960s and 1970s*, edited by John C. Hammerback, Richard J. Jensen, and José Angel Gutiérrez, 121–62. Westport, Conn.: Greenwood Press, 1985.

Gutiérrez, Ramón. "Community, Patriarchy and Individualism: The Politics of Chicano History and the Dream of Equality." *American Quarterly* 45, no. 1 (1993), 44–72.

———. "The Erotic Zone: Sexual Transgression on the U.S.-Mexican Border." *Mapping Multiculturalism*, edited by Avery Gordon and Chris Newfield, 253–63. Minneapolis: University of Minnesota Press, 1996.

Gutiérrez-Jones, Carl. *Rethinking the Borderlands: Between Chicano Culture and Legal Discourse*. Berkeley: University of California Press, 1995.

Gutmann, Matthew C. *The Meanings of Macho: Being a Man in Mexico City*. Berkeley: University of California Press, 1996.

Guzmán, Manolo. *Gay Hegemony/Latino Homosexualities*. New York: Routledge, 2006.

Guzmán, Manuel. "'Pa' La Escuelita Con Mucho Cuida'o y por La Orillita': A Journey through the Contested Terrains of the Nation and Sexual Orientation." *Puerto Rican Jam: Rethinking Colonialism and Nationalism*, edited by Frances Negrón-Muntaner and Ramón Grosfoguel, 209–28. Minneapolis: University of Minnesota Press, 1997.

Guzmán, Mary, director. *Mind If I Call You Sir? A Discussion between Latina Butches and Female-to-Male Transgendered Latinos*. Video. Produced by Karla E. Rosales. 2004.

Halberstam, Judith. "The Real Shame: White Gay Men!" Unpublished manuscript, 2003.

———. "Shame and White Gay Masculinity." *Social Text* 84–85/23, nos. 3–4 (2005): 219–33.

Hall, Donald, Jean Walton, and Garry Leonard, eds. "Queer Utilities: Textual Studies, Theory, Pedagogy, Praxis." Special issue of *College Literature* 24, no. 1 (1997).

Halperin, David M., and Valerie Traub, eds. *Gay Shame*. Chicago: University of Chicago Press, 2009.

Hames-García, Michael. "Between Repression and Liberation: Sexuality and Socialist Theory." *Toward a New Socialism*, edited by Richard Schmitt and Anatole Anton, 247–65. New York: Lexington Books, 2007.

———. "Can Queer Theory Be Critical Theory?" *New Critical Theory: Essays on Liberation*, edited by Jeffrey Paris and William Wilkerson, 201–22. New York: Rowman and Littlefield, 2001.

———. *Fugitive Thought: Prison Movements, Race, and the Meaning of Justice*. Minneapolis: University of Minnesota Press, 2004.

———. "How Real Is Race?" *Material Feminisms*, edited by Stacy Alaimo and Susan Hekman, 308–39. Bloomington: Indiana University Press, 2008.

———. *Identity Complex: Gender, Race, and Sexuality from Oz to Abu Ghraib*. Minneapolis: University of Minnesota Press, forthcoming.

———. "What's at Stake in 'Gay' Identities?" *Identity Politics Reconsidered*, edited by Linda Martín Alcoff, Michael Hames-García, Satya P. Mohanty, and Paula M. L. Moya, 78–95. New York: Palgrave Macmillan, 2006.

———. "Who Are Our Own People? Challenges for a Theory of Social Identity."

Reclaiming Identity: Realist Theory and the Predicament of Postmodernism, edited by Paula M. L. Moya and Michael Hames-García, 102–29. Berkeley: University of California Press, 2000.

Hammonds, Evelynn M. "Black (W)holes and the Geometry of Black Female Sexuality." *Feminism Meets Queer Theory*, edited by Elizabeth Weed and Naomi Schor, 136–56. Bloomington: Indiana University Press, 1997. Reprinted in *Feminism and Race*, edited by Kum-Kum Bhavnani, 379–93. New York: Oxford University Press, 2001.

Hansen, Miriam Bratu. "Benjamin and Cinema: Not a One-Way Street." *Critical Inquiry* 25, no. 2 (1999), 306–43.

Hawley, John C. *Postcolonial, Queer: Theoretical Intersections*. Albany: State University of New York Press, 2001.

Hearn, David, and David L. Collinson. "Theorizing Unities and Differences between Men and between Masculinities." *Theorizing Masculinities*, edited by Harry Brod and Michael Kaufman, 97–118. Thousand Oaks, Calif.: Sage, 1994.

Hennessy, Rosemary. *Profit and Pleasure: Sexual Identities in Late Capitalism*. New York: Routledge, 2000.

———. "Queer Visibility in Commodity Culture." *Social Postmodernism: Beyond Identity Politics*, edited by Linda Nicholson and Steven Seidman, 142–83. Cambridge: Cambridge University Press, 1995.

Hernández, Benjamin Francisco. "Note from the Publisher." *Firme* 1, no. 2 (1981), 7.

———. "Note from the Publisher." *Firme* 1, no. 5 (1981), 5.

Hernández, Carlos. "A Gay Life Style (Only If *La Familia* Approves)." *Firme* 1, no. 5 (1981), 18–19.

Hernández, Robb. *The Fire of Life: The Robert Legorreta-Cyclona Collection, 1962–2002*. Los Angeles: UCLA Chicano Studies Research Center Press, 2008.

Hinojosa, Rolando. *Estampas del valle*. Berkeley: Quinto Sol, 1973.

Hocquenghem, Guy. *Homosexual Desire*. Translated by Daniella Dangoor. Durham: Duke University Press, 1993.

Holland, Sharon P. "Foreword: 'Home' Is a Four-Letter Word." *Black Queer Studies: A Critical Anthology*, edited by E. Patrick Johnson and Mae G. Henderson, ix–xiii. Durham: Duke University Press, 2005.

Hondagneu-Sotelo, Pierrette, and Michael A. Messner. "Gender Displays and Men's Power: The 'New Man' and the Mexican Immigrant Man." *Theorizing Masculinities*, edited by Harry Brod and Michael Kaufman, 200–18. Thousand Oaks, Calif.: Sage, 1994.

hooks, bell. "Eating the Other: Desire and Resistance." *Media and Cultural Studies: Key Works*, edited by Meenakshi Gigi Durham and Douglas M. Kellner, 424–38. New York: Blackwell, 2001.

———. "Is Paris Burning?" *Black Looks: Race and Representation*, 145–56. Boston: South End, 1992.

Hope, Dale, and Gregory Tozian. *The Aloha Shirt: Spirit of the Islands.* Hillsboro, Ore.: Beyond Words, 2000.

Huerta, Jorge. *Chicano Theatre: Themes and Forms.* Ypsilanti: Bilingual Press, 1982.

Hughes, Walter. "Feeling Mighty Real: Disco and Discourse and Discipline." *The Village Voice: Rock and Roll Quarterly,* 1993, 7–11+.

———. "In the Empire of the Beat: Discipline and Disco." *Microphone Fiends: Youth Music and Youth Culture,* edited by Andrew Ross and Tricia Rose, 147–57. New York: Routledge, 1994.

Hull, Gloria T., Patricia Bell Scott, and Barbara Smith, eds. *All the Women Are White, All the Blacks Are Men, But Some of Us Are Brave: Black Women's Studies.* New York: Feminist Press/City University of New York Graduate Center, 1982.

Humphreys, Laud. *Tearoom Trade: Impersonal Sex in Public Places.* Chicago: Aldine, 1970.

Islas, Arturo. *La Mollie and the King of Tears.* Albuquerque: University of New Mexico Press, 1996.

———. *Migrant Souls.* New York: Morrow, 1990.

———. *The Rain God: A Desert Tale.* 1984. New York: Avon Books, 1991.

Jaffe, Sara. "Gay Shame—A Challenge to Gay Pride." *Pacific News Service,* 25 June 2002, online. (accessed 31 August 2003).

Jagose, Annamarie. *Queer Theory: An Introduction.* New York: New York University Press, 1996.

Jaschik, Scott. "Tricks of the Trade." *Inside Higher Ed,* 2 January 2009, online (accessed 25 February 2009).

Jay, Karla. *Tales of the Lavender Menace: A Memoir of Liberation.* New York: Basic Books, 1999.

Johnson, E. Patrick. " 'Quare' Studies, or (Almost) Everything I Know about Queer Studies I Learned from My Grandmother." *Text and Performance Quarterly* 21 (2001), 1–25. Reprinted in *Black Queer Studies: A Critical Anthology,* edited by Johnson and Henderson, 124–57. Durham: Duke University Press, 2005.

———. "SNAP! Culture: A Different Kind of 'Reading.' " *Text and Performance Quarterly* 3 (1995), 121–42.

———. "Strange Fruit: A Performance about Identity Politics." TDR 47, no. 2 (2003), 88–116.

Johnson, E. Patrick, and Mae G. Henderson, eds. *Black Queer Studies: A Critical Anthology.* Durham: Duke University Press, 2005.

Joseph, May. *Nomadic Identities: The Performance of Citizenship.* Minneapolis: University of Minnesota Press, 1999.

Julien, Isaac, director. *Frantz Fanon: Black Skin, White Mask.* Motion picture. California Newsreel, 1995.

———. *Looking for Langston.* Motion picture. Waterbearer Films, 1992.

Kaiser, Charles. *The Gay Metropolis 1940–1996.* Boston: Houghton Mifflin, 1997.

Karr, W. Wayne, and Cory Roberts-Auli, eds. *Infected Faggot Perspective*, nos. 1–14 (1991–93).

Kimmel, Michael S., and Michael A. Messner, eds. *Men's Lives*. Boston: Allyn and Bacon, 1995.

Kinsey, Alfred C., Wardell Baxter Pomeroy, and Clyde E. Martin. *Sexual Behavior in the Human Male*. Philadelphia: W. B. Saunders, 1948.

Kissack, Terrance. "Freaking Fag Revolutionaries: New York's Gay Liberation Front, 1969–1971." *Radical History Review* 62 (1995), 104–34.

Kleinberg, Seymour. "The New Masculinity of Gay Men, and Beyond." *Men's Lives*, edited by Michael S. Kimmel and Michael A. Messner, 45–57. Boston: Allyn and Bacon, 1995.

Koestenbaum, Wayne. *The Queen's Throat: Opera, Homosexuality, and the Mystery of Desire*. New York: Poseidon Press, 1993.

La Fountain-Stokes, Lawrence. "Culture, Representation, and the Puerto Rican Queer Diaspora." Ph.D. diss., Columbia University, 1999.

———. "Cultures of the Puerto Rican Queer Diaspora." *Passing Lines: Sexuality and Immigration*, edited by Bradley Epps, Keja Valens, and Bill Johnson González, 275–309. Cambridge: Harvard University Press, 2005.

———. "Dancing La Vida Loca: The Queer Nuyorican Performances of Arthur Avilés and Elizabeth Marrero." *Queer Globalizations: Citizenship and the Afterlife of Colonialism*, edited by Arnaldo Cruz-Malavé and Martin F. Manalansan IV, 162–75. New York: New York University Press, 2002.

———. "1898 and the History of a Queer Puerto Rican Century: Gay Lives, Island Debates, and Diasporic Experience." *Centro Journal* 11, no. 1 (1999), 91–110.

———. "Entre boleros, travestismos y migraciones translocales: Manuel Ramos Otero, Jorge Merced, y *El bolero fue mi ruina* del Teatro Pregones del Bronx." *Revista Iberoamericana* 212 (2005), 887–907.

———. "La mierda." *Uñas pintadas de azul/Blue Fingernails*, 130–49. Tempe: Bilingual Review Press/Editorial Bilingüe, 2009.

———. *Queer Ricans: Cultures and Sexualities in the Diaspora*. Minneapolis: University of Minnesota Press, 2009.

Lamos, Colleen. "The Ethics of Queer Theory." *Critical Ethics: Text, Theory, and Responsibility*, edited by Dominic Rainsford and Tim Woods, 141–51. New York: St. Martin's Press, 1999.

Lancaster, Roger N. *Life Is Hard: Machismo, Danger, and the Intimacy of Power in Nicaragua*. Berkeley: University of California Press, 1992.

Laó-Montes, Agustín. "Mambo Montage: The Latinization of New York City." *Mambo Montage: The Latinization of New York*, edited by Agustín Laó-Montes and Arlene Dávila, 1–52. New York: Columbia University Press, 2001.

Lee, Wenshu. "*Kuaering* Queer Theory: My Autocritography and a Race-Conscious,

Womanist, Transnational Turn." *Queer Theory and Communication: From Disciplining Queers to Queering the Discipline(s)*, edited by Gust A. Yep, Karen E. Lovaas, and John P. Elia, 147–70. Binghamton, N.Y.: Harrington Park/Haworth, 2003.

Leo, John. "The Familialism of 'Man' in American Television Melodrama." *Displacing Homophobia: Gay Male Perspectives in Literature and Culture*, edited by Ronald R. Butters, John M. Clum, and Michael Moon, 31–51. Durham: Duke University Press, 1989.

León-Portilla, Miguel. *Aztec Thought and Culture: A Study of the Ancient Nahuatl Mind*. Translated by Jack Emory Davis. Norman: University of Oklahoma Press, 1963.

Lewis, Oscar. *Five Families: Mexican Case Studies in the Culture of Poverty*. New York: Basic Books, 1959.

Leyva, Yolanda Chávez. "Listening to the Silences in Latina/Chicana Lesbian History." *Living Chicana Theory*, edited by Carla Trujillo, 429–34. Berkeley: Third Woman Press, 1998.

Limón, José E. *Dancing with the Devil: Society and Cultural Poetics in Mexican-American South Texas*. Madison: University of Wisconsin Press, 1994.

———. "Dancing with the Devil: Society, Gender, and the Political Unconscious in Mexican American South Texas." *Criticism in the Borderlands: Studies in Chicano Literature, Culture, and Ideology*, edited by Hector Calderón and José David Saldívar, 221–36. Durham: Duke University Press, 1991.

Lipsitz, George. "Con Safos: Can Cultural Studies Read the Writing on the Wall?" *The Chicana/o Cultural Studies Reader*, edited by Angie Chabram-Dernersesian, 47–60. New York: Routledge, 2006.

Livingston, Jennie, director. *Paris Is Burning*. Video. Academy Entertainment, 1992.

"Lola Montez." Web site of Zpub. (accessed 25 February 2009).

López, Ana M. "Of Rhythms and Borders." *Everynight Life: Culture and Dance in Latin/o America*, edited by Celeste Fraser Delgado and José Esteban Muñoz, 310–44. Durham: Duke University Press, 1997.

López, David, and Yen Le Espiritu. "Panethnicity in the United States: A Theoretical Framework." *Ethnic and Racial Studies* 13, no. 2 (1990), 198–224.

López, Erika. *Flaming Iguanas: An Illustrated All-Girl Road Novel Thing*. New York: Simon and Schuster, 1997.

Lorde, Audre. "Man Child: A Black Lesbian Feminist's Response." *Sister Outsider*, 72–80. Berkeley: Crossing Press, 1984.

———. "The Master's Tools Will Never Dismantle the Master's House." *Sister Outsider*, 110–13. Berkeley: Crossing Press, 1984.

———. *Sister Outsider*. Berkeley: Crossing Press, 1984.

———. "The Transformation of Silence." *Sister Outsider*, 40–44. Berkeley: Crossing Press, 1984.

———. "The Uses of Anger: Women Responding to Racism." *Sister Outsider*, 124–33. Berkeley: Crossing Press, 1984.

———. *Uses of the Erotic: The Erotic as Power*. Berkeley: Crossing Press, 1978. Reprinted in *Sister Outsider*, 53–69. Berkeley: Crossing Press, 1984.

———. *Zami: A New Spelling of My Name*. Berkeley: Crossing Press, 1982.

Love, Heather. "Gay Shame Redux." Paper presented at the annual meeting of the American Studies Association. Web site of All Academic.

Lozada, Angel. *La patografía: Novela*. Mexico City: Paneta, 1998.

Lugones, María. "Heterosexualism and the Colonial/Modern Gender System." *Hypatia* 22, no. 1 (2007), 186–209.

———. *Pilgrimages/Peregrinajes: Theorizing Coalition against Multiple Oppressions*. New York: Rowman and Littlefield, 2003.

Luibhéid, Eithne, and Lionel Cantú, eds. *Queer Migrations: Sexuality, U.S. Citizenship, and Border Crossings*. Minneapolis: University of Minnesota Press, 2005.

Maciel, David R., Isidro D. Ortiz, and María Herrera-Sobek, eds. *Chicano Renaissance: Contemporary Cultural Trends*. Tucson: University of Arizona Press, 2000.

Manalansan, Martin F., IV. *Global Divas: Filipino Gay Men in the Diaspora*. Durham: Duke University Press, 2003.

Manrique, Jaime, ed. *Bésame Mucho: An Anthology of Gay Latino Fiction*. New York: Painted Leaf Press, 1999.

———. *Eminent Maricones: Arenas, Lorca, Puig, and Me*. Madison: University of Wisconsin Press, 1999.

———. *Latin Moon in Manhattan: A Novel*. New York: St. Martin's Press, 1992.

———. *Twilight at the Equator*. Boston: Faber and Faber, 1997.

Marcos, Sylvia. *Taken from the Lips: Gender and Eros in Mesoamerican Religions*. Leiden, Netherlands: Brill, 2006.

Marcuse, Herbert. *An Essay on Liberation*. Boston: Beacon Press, 1969.

Martin, Biddy. *Femininity Played Straight: The Significance of Being Lesbian*. New York: Routledge, 1996.

Martin, Biddy, and Judith Butler, eds. "Critical Crossings." Special issue of *diacritics*, 24, nos. 2–3 (1994).

Martínez, Ernesto Javier. "Dying to Know: Identity and Self-Knowledge in Baldwin's *Another Country*." PMLA: *Publications of the Modern Language Association* 124, no. 3 (2009), 782–97.

———. "On Butler on Morrison on Language." *Signs: A Journal of Women in Culture and Society* 35, no. 4 (2010), 821–42.

Martínez-San Miguel, Yolanda. "Más allá de la homonormatividad: Intimidades alternativas en el Caribe hispano." "Los estudios lésbico-gays y 'queer' latinoamericanos," edited by Luciano Martínez. Special issue of *Revista Iberoamericana* 74, no. 225 (2008), 1039–57.

Massad, Joseph A. *Desiring Arabs*. Chicago: University of Chicago Press, 2007.

Mattilda [Matt Bernstein Sycamore]. "Gay Shame: From Queer Autonomous Space to Direct Action Extravaganza." *That's Revolting! Queer Strategies for Resisting Assimilation.* 237–62. New York: Soft Skull, 2005.

McBride, Dwight A. *Why I Hate Abercrombie and Fitch: Essays on Race and Sexuality.* New York: New York University Press, 2005.

McClintock, Anne. *Imperial Leather: Race, Gender, and Sexuality in the Colonial Contest.* New York: Routledge, 1995.

McMains, Juliet. "Brownface: Representations of Latin-ness in Dancesport." *Dance Research Journal* 33, no. 2 (2001), 54–71.

Mignolo, Walter D. *Local Histories/Global Designs: Coloniality, Subaltern Knowledges, and Border Thinking.* Princeton: Princeton University Press, 2000.

Mirandé, Alfredo. *Hombres y Machos: Masculinity and Latino Culture.* Boulder: Westview Press, 1997.

Mohanty, Chandra Talpade, Ann Russo, and Lourdes Torres, eds. *Third World Women and the Politics of Feminism.* Bloomington: Indiana University Press, 1991.

Mohanty, Satya P. *Literary Theory and the Claims of History: Postmodernism, Objectivity, Multicultural Politics.* Ithaca: Cornell University Press, 1997.

Moliner, María. *Diccionario de uso del español.* Madrid: Editorial Gredos, 1992.

Móntez, Ricardo. "Trade Marks: LA2, Keith Haring, and a Queer Economy of Collaboration." *GLQ: A Journal of Lesbian and Gay Studies* 12, no. 3 (2006), 425–40.

Moraga, Cherríe. *Heroes and Saints and Other Plays.* Albuquerque: West End Press, 1994.

———. *The Last Generation.* Boston: South End Press, 1993.

———. *Loving in the War Years: Lo que nunca pasó por sus labios.* Boston: South End Press, 1983.

———. "Queer Aztlán: The Reformation of Chicano Tribe." *The Last Generation,* 145–74. Boston: South End Press, 1993.

———. "Refugees of a World on Fire: Foreword to the Second Edition." *This Bridge Called My Back: Writings by Radical Women of Color,* edited by Cherríe Moraga and Gloria Anzaldúa. New York: Kitchen Table/Women of Color Press, 1983.

Moraga, Cherríe, Dorothy Allison, Tomás Almaguer, and Jackie Goldsby. "Writing Is the Measure of My Life . . . : An Interview with Cherríe Moraga." *Out/Look* 4 (winter 1989), 53–57.

Moraga, Cherríe, and Gloria Anzaldúa, eds. *This Bridge Called My Back: Writings by Radical Women of Color.* 1981. 2nd ed. New York: Kitchen Table/Women of Color Press, 1983.

Moraga, Cherríe, and Amber Hollibaugh. "What We're Rollin' Around in Bed With: Sexual Silences in Feminism." *Heresies* 12 (1981), 58–62. Reprinted in *Powers of Desire: The Politics of Sexuality,* edited by Ann Snitow, Christine Stansell, and Sharon Thompson, 440–59. New York: Monthly Review Press, 1983.

Morton, Andrew. *Madonna.* New York: St. Martin's Press, 2001.

Morton, Donald. "Birth of the Cyberqueer." PMLA: *Publications of the Modern Language Association* 110, no. 3 (1995), 169–81.

Movin' Out. Original Broadway cast recording. Sony Classical, SK 87877, 2002.

Moya, Paula M. L. "Cultural Particularity vs. Universal Humanity: The Value of Being Asimilao." *Learning from Experience: Minority Identities, Multicultural Struggles*. Berkeley: University of California Press, 2002.

———. *Learning from Experience: Minority Identities, Multicultural Struggles*. Berkeley: University of California Press, 2002.

Moya, Paula M. L., and Michael Hames-García, eds. *Reclaiming Identity: Realist Theory and the Predicament of Postmodernism*. Berkeley: University of California Press, 2000.

Muñoz, José Esteban. *Disidentifications: Queers of Color and the Performance of Politics*. Minneapolis: University of Minnesota Press, 1999.

———. "Feeling Brown: Ethnicity and Affect in Ricardo Bracho's *The Sweetest Hangover (and Other STDs)*." *Theatre Journal* 52, no. 1 (2000), 67–79.

Muñoz, Manuel. *The Faith Healer of Olive Avenue*. Chapel Hill: Algonquin Books, 2007.

———. *Zigzagger*. Evanston: Northwestern University Press, 2003.

Muñoz, Miguel Elías. *The Greatest Performance*. Houston: Arte Público Press, 1991.

Murray, Stephen O. *Latin American Male Homosexualities*. Albuquerque: University of New Mexico Press, 1995.

Najmabadi, Afsaneh. *Women with Mustaches and Men without Beards: Gender and Sexual Anxieties of Iranian Modernity*. Berkeley: University of California Press, 2005.

Nava, Michael. *The Burning Plain*. New York: Putnam, 1997.

———. *Goldenboy*. Boston: Alyson, 1988.

———. *The Hidden Law*. New York: Harper Collins, 1992.

———. *How Town*. New York: Ballantine, 1991.

———. *The Little Death*. Los Angeles: Alyson, 1986.

Negrón-Muntaner, Frances. *Boricua Pop: Puerto Ricans and the Latinization of American Culture*. New York: New York University Press, 2004.

Negrón-Muntaner, Frances, and Rita González. "Boricua Gazing: An Interview with Frances Negrón-Muntaner." *Signs: A Journal of Women in Culture and Society* 30, no. 1 (2004), 1345–60.

Newman, Felice. "Why I'm Not Dancing." *Lavender Culture*, edited by Karla Jay and Allen Young, 140–45. New York: New York University Press, 1978.

Newton, Esther. *Mother Camp: Female Impersonators in America*. 1972. Chicago: University of Chicago Press, 1979.

Newton, Huey P. "The Women's Liberation and Gay Liberation Movements." *To Die for the People*, edited by Toni Morrison, 152–55. New York: Writers and Readers, 1995.

Obejas, Achy. "Above All, a Family Man." *We Came All the Way from Cuba So You Could Dress Like This? Stories*. San Francisco: Cleis Press, 1994.

————. *Memory Mambo*. San Francisco: Cleis Press, 1996.

Olds, Sharon. *Satan Says*. Pittsburgh: University of Pittsburgh Press, 1980.

Olvera, Joe. "Gay Ghetto District." *Flor y Canto IV and V: An Anthology of Chicano Litera-ture*, edited by José Armas and Bernice Zamora, 111. N.p.: Pajarito/Flor y Canto Committee, 1980.

Ongiri, Amy Abugo. "We Are Family: Black Nationalism, Black Masculinity, and the Black Gay Cultural Imagination." *College Literature* 24, no. 1 (1997), 280–94.

Ordona, Trinity A. "Coming Out Together: An Ethnohistory of the Asian and Pacific Is-lander Queer Women's and Transgendered People's Movement of San Francisco." Ph.D. diss., University of California, Santa Cruz, 2000.

Orgel, Stephen. *The Illusion of Power: Political Theater in the English Renaissance*. Berkeley: University of California Press, 1975.

Ortiz, Christopher. "Hot and Spicy: Representation of Chicano/Latino Men in Gay Pornography." *Jump Cut*, no. 39 (June 1994), 83–90.

Ortiz, Fernando. *Cuban Counterpoint: Tobacco and Sugar*. Translated by Harriet De Onís. New York: Knopf, 1955.

Ortiz, Ricardo L. *Cultural Erotics in Cuban America*. Minneapolis: University of Minne-sota Press, 2007.

————. "Sexuality Degree Zero: Pleasure and Power in the Novels of John Rechy, Arturo Islas, and Michael Nava." *Journal of Homosexuality* 26, nos. 2–3 (1993), 111–26.

Pardo, Mary S. *Mexican American Women Activists: Identity and Resistance in Two Los Angeles Communities*. Philadelphia: Temple University Press, 1998.

Paredes, Américo. *Folklore and Culture on the Texas-Mexican Border*. Edited by Richard Bau-man. Austin: University of Texas/CMAS, 1993.

Parker, Pat. *Movement in Black*. 1978. Berkeley: Crossing Press, 1983.

Partnoy, Alicia. "The Art of Poetry." *Volando Bajito*. Translated by Gail Wronsky. Los Angeles: Red Hen Press, 2005.

"Patronímicos." Web site of Culturitalia (accessed 27 August 2005).

Patton, Cindy, and Benigno Sánchez Eppler, eds. *Queer Diasporas*. Durham: Duke Uni-versity Press, 2000.

Peña, Manuel. "Class, Gender, and Machismo: The 'Treacherous-Woman' Folklore of Mexican Male Workers." *Men's Lives*, edited by Michael S. Kimmel and Michael A. Messner, 176–87. Boston: Allyn and Bacon, 1995.

Pérez, Daniel Enrique. *Rethinking Chicana/o and Latina/o Popular Culture*. New York: Pal-grave Macmillan, 2009.

Pérez, Emma. "Irigaray's Female Symbolic in the Making of Chicana Lesbian Sitios y Lenguas (Sites and Discourses)." *Living Chicana Theory*, edited by Carla Trujillo, 87–101. Berkeley: Third Woman Press, 1998.

————. "Sexuality and Discourse: Notes from a Chicana Survivor." *Chicana Lesbians:*

The Girls Our Mothers Warned Us About, edited by Carla Trujillo, 159–84. Berkeley: Third Woman Press, 1991.

Pérez, Hiram. "You Can Have My Brown Body and Eat It, Too!" Social Text 84–85/23, nos. 3–4 (2005), 171–91.

Pérez, Vivian, and Luisa Peguero. "María Montez: A Dominican Star." Web site of Geocities (accessed 25 February 2009).

Piedra, José. "Nationalizing Sissies." In ¿Entiendes? Queer Readings, Hispanic Writings, edited by Emilie L. Bergmann and Paul Julian Smith, 371–409. Durham: Duke University Press, 1995.

Piñero, Miguel. Short Eyes. New York: Farrar, Straus and Giroux, 1975.

Plascencia, Luis F. B. "Low Riding in the Southwest: Cultural Symbols in the Mexican Community." History, Culture and Society: Chicano Studies in the 1980s, edited by Mario T. Garcia, Bert N. Corona, and the National Association for Chicano Studies, 141–75. Ypsilanti: Bilingual Press/Editorial Bilingüe, 1983.

Ponce, Barbara. Identities in the Lesbian World: The Social Construction of Self. Westport, Conn.: Greenwood Press, 1978.

Povinelli, Elizabeth A. "Sexual Savages/Sexual Sovereignty: Australian Colonial Texts and the Postcolonial Politics of Nationalism." Diacritics 24, nos. 2–3 (1994), 122–50.

Powers, Lloyd D. "Chicano Rhetoric: Some Basic Concepts." Southern Speech Communication Journal 3 (summer 1973), 340–46.

Prieur, Annick. Mema's House, Mexico City: On Transvestites, Queens, and Machos. Chicago: University of Chicago Press, 1998.

Profile Pursuit, Inc. Pride 99: The Official Magazine for San Francisco Pride 99. San Francisco: Profile Pursuit, Inc., 1999.

———. Pride 00: The Official Magazine for San Francisco Pride 00. San Francisco: Profile Pursuit, Inc., 2000.

———. Pride 01: The Official Magazine for San Francisco Pride 01. San Francisco: Profile Pursuit, Inc., 2001.

Pronger, Brian. "Gay Jocks: A Phenomenology of Gay Men in Athletics." Men's Lives, edited by Michael S. Kimmel and Michael A. Messner, 115–24. Boston: Allyn and Bacon, 1995.

Puar, Jasbir, ed. "Queer Tourism." Special issue of GLQ: A Journal of Lesbian and Gay Studies 8, nos. 1–2 (2002).

Quiroga, José. Tropics of Desire: Interventions from Queer Latin America. New York: New York University Press, 2000.

Ramírez, John. "The Chicano Homosocial Film: Mapping the Discourses of Sex and Gender in American Me." PRE/TEXT: A Journal of Rhetorical Theory 16, nos. 3–4 (1995), 260–74.

Ramos Otero, Manuel. "La otra isla de Puerto Rico." Página en blanco y stacatto, 9–23. Madrid: Playor, 1987.

———. *Página en blanco y staccato*. Madrid: Playor, 1987.

Rattazzi, Erin. "Gay Latino/as Receive Support at Conference." *Daily Bruin* (UCLA), 22 November 1999, online (accessed 31 August 2003).

Rechy, John. *City of Night*. New York: Grove, 1963.

———. *The Miraculous Day of Amalia Gomez*. New York: Arcade, 1991.

———. *The Sexual Outlaw: A Documentary*. New York: Grove, 1977.

Reid-Pharr, Robert F. *Black Gay Man: Essays*. New York: New York University Press, 2001.

Reiss, Albert J., Jr. "The Social Integration of Queers and Peers." *Sociology of Homosexuality*, edited by Wayne R. Dynes and Stephen Donaldson, 296–314. New York: Garland, 1992.

Reyes, Israel. "Conference Sex." Talk presented at the Modern Language Association annual convention, San Francisco, 30 December 2008.

Reyes, Rodrigo, "Carnal Knowledge." *Ya Vas, Carnal*, by Rodrigo Reyes, Francisco X. Alarcón, and Juan Pablo Gutiérrez, 8–9. San Francisco: Humanizarte, 1985.

———. "Latino Gays: Coming Out and Coming Home." *Nuestro* 5, no. 3 (1981), 42–45, 64.

Reyes, Rodrigo, Francisco X. Alarcón, and Juan Pablo Gutiérrez. *Ya Vas, Carnal*. San Francisco: Humanizarte, 1985.

Rich, "Compulsory Heterosexuality and Lesbian Existence." *Signs* 5, no. 4 (1980), 631–60. Reprinted in *The Lesbian and Gay Studies Reader*, edited by Henry Abelove, Michèle Aina Barale, and David M. Halperin, 227–54. New York: Routledge, 1993.

Ríos Ávila, Rubén. "The End of Gay Culture?" Talk presented at the University of Michigan, Ann Arbor, 10 March 2006.

———. *La raza cómica: Del sujeto en Puerto Rico*. San Juan, Puerto Rico: Editorial Callejón, 2002.

Rivera, Tomás. . . . *y no se lo tragó la tierra/And the Earth Did Not Devour Him*. Translated by Evangelina Vigil-Piñón. Houston: Arte Público Press, 1992.

Rivera-Servera, Ramón. "Choreographies of Resistance: Latina/o Queer Dance and the Utopian Performative." *Modern Drama* 47, no. 2 (2004), 269–89.

Robles, Augie. *Cholo Joto*. Video. 1993.

Rodríguez, Juana María. *Queer Latinidad: Identity Practices, Discursive Spaces*. New York: New York University Press, 2003.

Rodriguez, Richard. *Hunger of Memory*. New York: Bantam, 1982.

Rodríguez, Richard T. "Imagine a Brown Queer: Inscribing Sexuality in Chicano/a-Latino/a Literary and Cultural Studies." *American Quarterly* 59, no. 2 (2007), 493–501.

———. *Next of Kin: The Family in Chicano/a Cultural Politics*. Durham: Duke University Press, 2009.

———. "Queering the Homeboy Aesthetic." *Aztlán: A Journal of Chicano Studies* 31, no. 2 (2006), 127–37.

Román, David. *Acts of Intervention: Performance, Gay Culture, and* AIDS. Bloomington: Indiana University Press, 1998.

———. "Latino Performance and Identity." *Aztlan: A Journal of Chicano Studies* 22, no. 2 (1997), 151–68.

———. "Theatre Journals: Dance Liberation." *Theatre Journal* 55, no. 3 (2003), n.p.

Romo, Ito. *The Bridge*. Albuquerque: University of New Mexico Press, 2000.

Romo-Carmona, Mariana. *Conversaciones: Relatos por padres y madres de hijas lesbianas y hijos gay*. New York: Cleis Press, 2001.

Roque Ramírez, Horacio N. "Claiming Queer Cultural Citizenship: Gay Latino (Im)Migrant Acts in San Francisco." *Queer Migrations: Sexuality, U.S. Citizenship, and Border Crossings*, edited by Eithne Luibhéid and Lionel Cantú, Jr., 161–88. Minneapolis: University of Minnesota Press, 2005.

———. "Communities of Desire: Queer Latina/Latino History and Memory, San Francisco Bay Area, 1960s–1990s." Ph.D. diss., University of California, Berkeley, 2001.

———. "'¡Mira, Yo Soy Boricua y Estoy Aquí!': Rafa Negrón's *Pan Dulce* and the Queer Sonic *Latinaje* of San Francisco." CENTRO: *Journal for the Center of Puerto Rican Studies* 19, no. 1 (2007), 274–313.

———. "Rodrigo Reyes." LGBT: *Lesbian, Gay, Bisexual, and Transgender History in America*, edited by Marc Stein, 3, nos. 33–34. New York: Charles Scribner's Sons/Thomson Gale, 2004.

———. "'That's My Place': Negotiating Racial, Sexual, and Gender Politics in San Francisco's Gay Latino Alliance, 1975–1983." *Journal of the History of Sexuality* 12, no. 2 (2003), 224–58.

Rosaldo, Renato. "Cultural Citizenship and Educational Democracy." *Cultural Anthropology* 9, no. 3 (1994), 402–11.

Rosales, Karla. "Papis, Dykes, Daddies: A Study of Chicana and Latina Self-Identified Butch Lesbians." Master's thesis, San Francisco State University, 2001.

Rubin, Gayle S. "Thinking Sex: Notes for a Radical Theory of the Politics of Sexuality." *Pleasure and Danger: Exploring Female Sexuality*, edited by Carole S. Vance, 267–319. Boston: Routledge and Kegan Paul, 1984. Reprinted in *The Lesbian and Gay Studies Reader*, edited by Henry Abelove, Michèle Aina Barale, and David M. Halperin, 3–44. New York: Routledge, 1993.

———. *The Traffic in Women: Notes on the "Political Economy of Sex*. New York: Monthly Review Press, 1975.

Russo, Vito. *The Celluloid Closet: Homosexuality in the Movies*. Revised edition. New York: Harper and Row, 1987.

Said, Edward. *Orientalism*. New York: Pantheon Books, 1978.

Saldívar, Ramón. *Chicano Narrative: The Dialectics of Difference*. Madison: University of Wisconsin Press, 1990.

Sánchez-González, Lisa. *Boricua Literature: A Literary History of the Puerto Rican Diaspora*. New York: New York University Press, 2001.

Sandoval, Chela. *Methodology of the Oppressed*. Minneapolis: University of Minnesota Press, 2000.

Sandoval, Denise Michelle. "Cruising through Low Rider Culture: Chicana/o Identity in the Marketing of *Low Rider Magazine*." *Velvet Barrios: Popular Culture and Chicana/o Sexualities*, edited by Alicia Gaspar de Alba, 179–96. New York: Palgrave Macmillan, 2002.

Sandoval-Sánchez, Alberto. *José, Can You See? Latinos on and off Broadway*. Madison: University of Wisconsin Press, 1999.

Sartre, Jean-Paul. *Sketch for a Theory of the Emotions*. London: Methuen, 1962.

Schifter, Jacobo. *Lila's House: Male Prostitution in Latin America*. New York: Harrington Park Press, 1998.

Scott, Joan W. "The Evidence of Experience." *Critical Inquiry* 17 (1991), 773–97.

Sedgwick, Eve Kosofsky. *Between Men: English Literature and Male Homosocial Desire*. New York: Columbia University Press, 1985.

———. *Epistemology of the Closet*. Berkeley: University of California Press, 1990.

———. "Queer Performativity: Henry James's *The Art of the Novel*." *GLQ: A Journal of Lesbian and Gay Studies* 1, no. 1 (1993), 1–16.

———. *Tendencies*. Durham: Duke University Press, 1993.

Seidman, Steven. "Identity and Politics in a 'Postmodern' Gay Culture: Some Historical and Conceptual Notes." *Fear of a Queer Planet: Queer Politics and Social Theory*, edited by Michael Warner, 105–42. Minneapolis: University of Minnesota Press, 1993.

Sender, Katherine. *Business, Not Politics: The Making of the Gay Market*. New York: Columbia University Press, 2004.

Seymour, Bruce. *Lola Montez: A Life*. New Haven: Yale University Press, 1998.

Shearer, Michael, Beowulf Thorne, Tom Ace, and Michael Botkin, eds. *Diseased Pariah News*, nos. 1–11 (1990–99).

Siebers, Tobin. *Disability Theory*. Ann Arbor: University of Michigan Press, 2008.

Siegel, Paul. "A Right to Boogie Queerly: The First Amendment on the Dance Floor." *Dancing Desires: Choreographing Sexualities on and off the Stage*, edited by Jane Desmond, 267–84. Madison: University of Wisconsin Press, 2001.

Sigal, Pete, ed. *Infamous Desire: Male Homosexuality in Colonial Latin America*. Chicago: University of Chicago Press, 2003.

Sigal, Pete, and John F. Chuchiak IV, eds. "Sexual Encounters/Sexual Collisions: Alternative Sexualities in Colonial Mesoamerica." Special issue of *Journal of the American Society for Ethnohistory* 54, no. 1 (2007).

Simpson, Mark. *Anti-Gay*. London: Freedom Edition, 1996.

Sinfield, Alan. *Out on Stage: Lesbian and Gay Theatre in the Twentieth Century*. New Haven: Yale University Press, 2000.

Smith, Andrea. *Conquest: Sexual Violence and American Indian Genocide.* Cambridge, Mass.: South End Press, 2005.

———. "Heteropatriarchy and the Three Pillars of White Supremacy: Rethinking Women of Color Organizing." *The Color of Violence: The Incite! Anthology,* ed. Incite! Women of Color against Violence, 66–73. Cambridge, Mass.: South End Press, 2006.

Smith, Barbara, ed. *Home Girls: A Black Feminist Anthology.* 1983. New Brunswick, N.J.: Rutgers University Press, 2000.

———. "Toward a Black Feminist Criticism." 1977. *All the Women Are White, All the Blacks Are Men, but Some of Us Are Brave: Black Women's Studies,* edited by Gloria T. Hull, Patricia Bell Scott, and Barbara Smith, 157–75. New York: Feminist Press/City University of New York Graduate Center, 1982.

Smith, Dorothy E. *The Everyday World as Problematic: A Feminist Sociology.* Boston: Northeastern University Press, 1987.

Smith, Valerie. "Black Feminist Theory and the Representation of the Other." *Changing Our Own Words: Essays on Criticism, Theory, and Writing by Black Women,* edited by Cheryl A. Wall, 38–57. New Brunswick, N.J.: Rutgers University Press, 1989.

Snitow, Ann, Christine Stansell, and Sharon Thompson, eds. *The Powers of Desire: The Politics of Sexuality.* New York: Monthly Review, 1983.

Solomon, Melissa. "Flaming Iguanas, Dalai Pandas, and Other Lesbian Bardos (A Few Perimeter Points)." *Regarding Sedgwick: Essays on Queer Culture and Critical Theory,* edited by Stephen M. Barber and David L. Clark, 201–16. New York: Routledge, 2002.

Sontag, Susan. "Notes on 'Camp.'" *Against Interpretation,* 275–92. New York: Farrar, Straus and Giroux, 1966.

Soto, Sandra K. "Cherríe Moraga's Going Brown: 'Reading Like a Queer.'" *GLQ: A Journal of Lesbian and Gay Studies* 11, no. 2 (2005), 237–63.

Stavans, Ilán. "The Latin Phallus." *Muy Macho: Latino Men Confront Their Manhood,* edited by Ray González, 143–64. New York: Doubleday, 1996.

Steele, H. Thomas. *The Hawaiian Shirt: Its Art and History.* New York: Abbeville Press, 1984.

Stoler, Ann Laura. *Carnal Knowledge and Imperial Power: Race and the Intimate in Colonial Rule.* Berkeley: University of California Press, 2002.

Stone, Michael Cutler. "'Bajito y Suavecito': Low Riding and the 'Class' of Class." *Studies in Latin American Popular Culture* 9 (1990), 85–126.

Stongman, Roberto. "Syncretic Religion and Dissident Sexualities." *Queer Globalizations: Citizenship and the Afterlife of Colonialism,* edited by Arnaldo Cruz-Malavé and Martin F. Manalansan IV, 176–92. New York: New York University Press, 2002.

Suárez, Juan A. "The Puerto Rican Lower East Side and the Queer Underground." *Grey Room* 32 (summer 2008), 6–37.

Sullivan, Edward J., Agustín Arteaga, and Cristina Pacheco. *Nahum Zenil: Witness to the Self*. San Francisco: Mexican Museum, 1996.

Sycamore, Matt Bernstein, ed. *That's Revolting! Queer Strategies for Resisting Assimilation*. New York: Soft Skull, 2005.

Taylor, Clark. "El Ambiente: Male Homosexual Social Life in Mexico City." Ph.D. diss., University of California, Berkeley, 1978.

Teaiwa, Teresia K. "Bikinis and Other S/Pacific N/Oceans." *Contemporary Pacific* 6, no. 1 (1994), 87–109.

Teuton, Sean Kicummah. *Red Land, Red Power: Grounding Knowledge in the American Indian Novel*. Durham: Duke University Press, 2008.

Thornton, Sarah. *Club Cultures: Music, Media, and Subcultural Capital*. Hanover, N.H.: University Press of New England, 1996.

Tinsley, Omise'eke Natasha. "Black Atlantic, Queer Atlantic: Queer Imaginings of the Middle Passage." *GLQ: A Journal of Lesbian and Gay Studies* 14, nos. 2–3 (2008), 191–215.

Torres, Lourdes, and Inmaculada Pertusa, eds. *Torilleras: Hispanic and U.S. Latina Lesbian Expression*. Philadelphia: Temple University Press, 2003.

Trask, Haunani-Kay. *From a Native Daughter: Colonialism and Sovereignty in Hawai'i*. Revised edition. Honolulu: University of Hawai'i Press, 1999.

Trexler, Richard. *Sex and Conquest: Gendered Violence, Political Order, and the European Conquest of the Americas*. Ithaca: Cornell University Press, 1995.

Trillin, Calvin, and Ed Koren. "Low and Slow, Mean and Clean." *The New Yorker*, 10 July 1978, 70–74.

Trujillo, Carla, ed. *Chicana Lesbians: The Girls Our Mothers Warned Us About*. Berkeley: Third Woman Press, 1991.

———. *Living Chicana Theory*. Berkeley: Third Woman Press, 1998.

Vaid, Urvashi. *Virtual Equality: The Mainstreaming of Gay and Lesbian Liberation*. New York: Anchor Books/Doubleday, 1995.

Valocchi, Steve. "The Class-Inflected Nature of Gay Identity." *Social Problems* 46, no. 2 (1999), 207–24.

Vance, Carole S., ed. *Pleasure and Danger: Exploring Female Sexuality*. 1984. New York: Harper Collins, 1993.

Vega, Bernardo. *Memoirs of Bernardo Vega*. Edited by César Andreu Iglesias. Translated by Juan Flores. New York: Monthly Review Press, 1984.

Viego, Antonio. "The Place of Gay Male Chicano Literature in Queer Chicana/o Cultural Work." *Discourse* 21, no. 3 (1999), 111–31.

Vigil, James Diego. "Car Charros: Cruising and Lowriding in the Barrios of East Los Angeles." *Latino Studies Journal* 2, no. 2 (1991), 71–79.

Warner, Michael, ed. *Fear of a Queer Planet: Queer Politics and Social Theory*. Minneapolis: University of Minnesota Press, 1993.

———. *The Trouble with Normal: Sex, Politics, and the Ethics of Queer Life*. Cambridge: Harvard University Press, 2000.

Weed, Elizabeth, and Naomi Schor, eds. *Feminism Meets Queer Theory*. Bloomington: Indiana University Press, 1997.

Weston, Kath. *Families We Choose: Lesbians, Gays, Kinship*. New York: Columbia University Press, 1991.

Williams, Raymond. *Marxism and Literature*. Oxford: Oxford University Press, 1977.

Wilson, Carter. *Hidden in the Blood: A Personal Investigation of AIDS in the Yucatán*. New York: Columbia University Press, 1995.

Xavier, Emanuel. *Americano*. Cleveland: Suspect Thoughts Press, 2002.

———. *Christ-Like*. New York: Painted Leaf Press, 1999.

———. *Pier Queen*. New York: Pier Queen Productions, 1997.

Yarbro-Bejarano, Yvonne. "Laying It Bare: The Queer/Colored Body in Photography by Laura Aguilar." *Living Chicana Theory*, edited by Carla Trujillo, 277–305. Berkeley: Third Woman Press, 1998.

———. *The Wounded Heart: Writing on Cherríe Moraga*. Austin: University of Texas Press, 2000.

Zentella, Ana Celia. *Growing Up Bilingual: Puerto Rican Children in New York*. Malden, Mass.: Blackwell, 1997.

contributors

Tomás Almaguer is a professor of ethnic studies at San Francisco State University. He is the author of *Racial Fault Lines: The Historical Origins of White Supremacy in California*.

Luz Calvo is an associate professor of ethnic studies at California State University, East Bay. She is author of essays on Chicana feminism and visual culture in journals and collections, including *Meridians* and *Beyond the Frame: Women of Color and Visual Representation*.

Lionel Cantú (1965–2002) was an assistant professor of sociology at the University of California, Santa Cruz. Posthumous publications include *The Sexuality of Migration: Border Crossings and Mexican Immigrant Men*, edited by Nancy Naples and Salvador Vidal-Ortiz, and a collection edited with Eithne Luibheid, *Queer Migrations: Sexuality, U.S. Citizenship, and Border Crossings*.

Daniel Contreras is an assistant professor of English at Fordham University. He is the author of *Unrequited Love and Gay Latino Culture: What Have You Done to My Heart?*

Catriona Rueda Esquibel is an associate professor of race and resistance studies at San Francisco State University. She is the author of *With Her Machete in Her Hand: Reading Chicana Lesbians*.

Ramón García is an associate professor of Chicana and Chicano studies at California State University, Northridge. He has published essays on literary, visual, and cultural studies in collections such as *The Chicana/o Cultural Studies Reader* and poetry and fiction in journals, including *Story* and *Los Angeles Review*.

Ramón A. Gutiérrez is the Preston and Sterling Morton Distinguished Service Professor in United States History at the University of Chicago. He is the author of *When Jesus Came the Corn Mothers Went Away: Marriage, Sexuality, and Power in New Mexico, 1500–1846* and the editor of *Mexican Home Altars*. He is the co-editor of several books, including *Contested Eden: California before the Gold Rush, Festivals and Celebrations in American Ethnic Communities*, and *Recovering the U.S. Hispanic Literary Heritage*.

Michael Hames-García is a professor of ethnic studies at the University of Oregon. He is the author of *Fugitive Thought: Prison Movements, Race, and the Meaning of Justice* and *Identity Complex: Making the Case for Multiplicity* and coeditor of *Reclaiming Identity: Realist Theory and the Predicament of Postmodernism* and *Identity Politics Reconsidered*.

Lawrence La Fountain-Stokes is an associate professor of American culture and of Romance languages and literatures as the University of Michigan, Ann Arbor. He is the author of *Queer Ricans: Cultures and Sexualities in the Diaspora* and *Uñas pintadas de azul/Blue Fingernails*.

María Lugones is an associate professor of comparative literature and of philosophy, interpretation, and culture at Binghamton University of the State University of New York. She is the author of *Pilgrimages/Peregrinajes: Theorizing Coalition against Multiple Oppressions* and the translator of Martin Kusch's *Indigenous and Popular Thinking in América*.

Ernesto Javier Martínez is an assistant professor of women's and gender studies and of ethnic studies at the University of Oregon. He has published essays on race and sexuality in *Signs: Journal of Women in Culture and Society* and PMLA: *Publications of the Modern Language Association*. He is currently working on a book manuscript titled *Queer Race Narratives* and a coedited collection titled *Engaging Our Faculties: New Dialogues on Diversity in Higher Education*.

Paula M. L. Moya is an associate professor of English at Stanford University. She is the author of *Learning from Experience: Minority Identities, Multicultural Struggles* and coeditor of *Doing Race: 21 Essays for the 21st Century*, *Reclaiming Identity: Realist Theory and the Predicament of Postmodernism*, and *Identity Politics Reconsidered*.

José Esteban Muñoz is an associate professor of performance studies at New York University. He is the author of *Disidentifications: Queers of Color and the Performance of Politics* and *Cruising Utopia: The Politics and Performance of Queer Futurity* and coeditor of *Pop Out: Queer Warhol* and *Everynight Life: Culture and Dance in Latin/o America*.

Frances Negrón-Muntaner is an associate professor of English and comparative literature and of the study of ethnicity and race at Columbia University. She is a prolific filmmaker and the author of *Boricua Pop: Puerto Ricans and the Latinization of American Culture* and *Anatomía de una sonrisa*. She is the editor of *None of the Above: Puerto Ricans in the Global Era* and coeditor of *Puerto Rican Jam: Rethinking Colonialism and Nationalism*.

Ricardo L. Ortiz is an associate professor of English at Georgetown University. He is the author of *Cultural Erotics in Cuban America*.

Daniel Enrique Pérez is an associate professor of Chicana/o and Latina/o studies at the University of Nevada, Reno. He is the author of *Rethinking Chicana/o and Latina/o Popular Culture*.

Ramón H. Rivera-Servera is an assistant professor of performance studies at Northwestern University. He has published essays on Latina/o performance in *Text and Performance Quarterly*, *Modern Drama*, *Theatre Journal*, TDR: *The Journal of Performance Studies*, and other journals.

Richard T. Rodríguez is an associate professor of English and Latina/Latino studies at the University of Illinois, Urbana-Champaign. He is the author of *Next of Kin: The Family in Chicano/a Cultural Politics* and coeditor of *Chicanos, Latinos, and Cultural Diversity: An Anthology.*

David Román is a professor of English and American studies and ethnicity at the University of Southern California. He is the author of *Performance in America: Contemporary U.S. Culture and the Performing Arts* and *Acts of Intervention: Performance, Gay Culture, and AIDS* and coeditor of *O Solo Homo: The New Queer Performance.*

Horacio N. Roque Ramírez is an associate professor of Chicana and Chicano studies at the University of California, Santa Barbara. He has published essays in CENTRO: *Journal for the Center for Puerto Rican Studies, Oral History Review,* and *Queer Migrations: Sexuality, U.S. Citizenship, and Border Crossings,* among other journals and collections.

Antonio Viego is an associate professor of literature and Romance studies at Duke University. He is the author of *Dead Subjects: Toward a Politics of Loss in Latino Studies.*

index

Cantú, Lionel, 3, 6, 137n20

capitalism, 41–42, 170–72, 177; commodity consumption and, 188–91, 199

Card, Claudia, 294

Carrier, Joseph, 151, 195n12, 203

Carrillo, H. G., 3

Chauncey, George, 152, 171, 309n6

Chávez, César, 135n2

Chavez, Leo R., 166n31

Chavoya, Ondine, 3, 18n20, 66

Chic, 292

Chicana lesbians. *See* Latina lesbians

Chicanas. *See* Latinas

Chicanismo: 1980s and 1990s and, 123–24; familia and, 118, 121–23, 130–31, 137n18, 139n35, 142; *Firme* and, 125–26; homosexuality and, 113–21, 127–35; masculinity and, 117–18, 139n40. *See also* Chicano movement

Chicano gay men. *See* gay Latino men

Chicano movement, 113–14, 117–23. *See also* Chicanismo

Christian, Barbara, 56–57

Christian, Karen, 246n1

Christianity, 128–29, 242–44

Clifford, James, 150

Clinton, Bill, 187

coalition, 1–2, 4

Collinson, David L., 163

colonialism, 40–42, 62–63, 143–44

Coltrane, Scott, 154

Combahee River Collective, 26

Contreras, Daniel, 3, 16

Coronado, Raúl, 3

Corpus Magazine, 3

Cortez, Jaime, 3

Cravioto, Gustavo Martín, 183–84, 196n15

Crenshaw, Kimberlé, 51

Crimp, Douglas, 63–70, 71, 80n51

Crowly, Mart, 297–300

Cruz-Malavé, Arnaldo, 3, 65, 285

Cuadros, Gil, 3

cultural citizenship, 176–77, 185, 189; capitalism and, 185–93, 194, 196n21, 199

cultural studies, 281–82, 285

culture: explanations of identity, behavior, and, 6, 147–52, 164, 168, 172–74; gender roles and, 150, 151–52, 165n15, 166n20, 169–70; homophobia and, 157; politics and, 283–84

Cunningham, John, 116, 137n23

Currid, Brian, 272

dance, 14–16; AIDS and, 301, 304–5; class and, 313; community and, 259–60, 263, 265–67, 273–78, 290–93, 296–97, 299, 308, 312–18; discrimination and, 259–60, 267, 270–71, 300, 312–14; emotional response to, 306–7; gay and lesbian clubs and, 259–61, 266, 278n7, 279n11, 286–87, 289–90, 309n2, 311, 313–18; identity and, 259, 261, 263–66, 267, 270–71, 273–78, 288, 290–93, 296–97, 311, 312, 318n3; improvisation and, 263–64, 269; music and, 271–72, 275, 315; pleasure and, 259, 265, 269, 275, 317; politics and, 292–93, 310n10, 311, 316–17; queer Latinas and Latinos and, 260–63, 266–69, 270–71, 273–78, 282, 312–18; television and, 280n30; utopianism and, 259–61, 265–66, 284, 291–92. *See also* disco; performance; salsa

Decena, Carlos Ulises, 3

de la Mora, Sergio, 3

Delany, Samuel, 309n3

de la tierra, tatiana, 73, 74

Michael Hames-García is a professor of ethnic studies
at the University of Oregon. He is the author of *Fugitive
Thought: Prison Movements, Race, and the Meaning of Justice*
(2004) and *Identity Complex: Making the Case for Multiplicity*
(2011). He edited (with Linda Martín Alcoff, Satya P.
Mohanty, and Paula M. L. Moya) *Identity Politics Reconsidered* (2006) and (with Paula M. L. Moya) *Reclaiming Identity: Realist Theory and the Predicament of Postmodernism*
(2000).

Ernesto Javier Martínez is an assistant professor of
women's and gender studies and of ethnic studies at
the University of Oregon. He is completing a book
manuscript titled *Queer Race Narratives: On the Practice and
Politics of Intelligibility*, and an edited collection (with
Stephanie Fryberg) titled *Engaging Our Faculties: New Dialogues on Diversity in Higher Education*.

Library of Congress Cataloging-in-Publication Data
Gay Latino studies : a critical reader / edited by Michael
Hames-García and Ernesto Javier Martínez.
p. cm.
Includes bibliographical references and index.
ISBN 978-0-8223-4937-2 (cloth : alk. paper)
ISBN 978-0-8223-4955-6 (pbk. : alk. paper)
1. Hispanic American gays — Social conditions
2. Minority gays — United States — Social conditions.
3. Gays — United States — Identity.   I. Hames-García,
Michael Roy.   II. Martínez, Ernesto Javier.
HQ76.3.U5G384 2011
306.76′6208968073 — dc22   2010044958